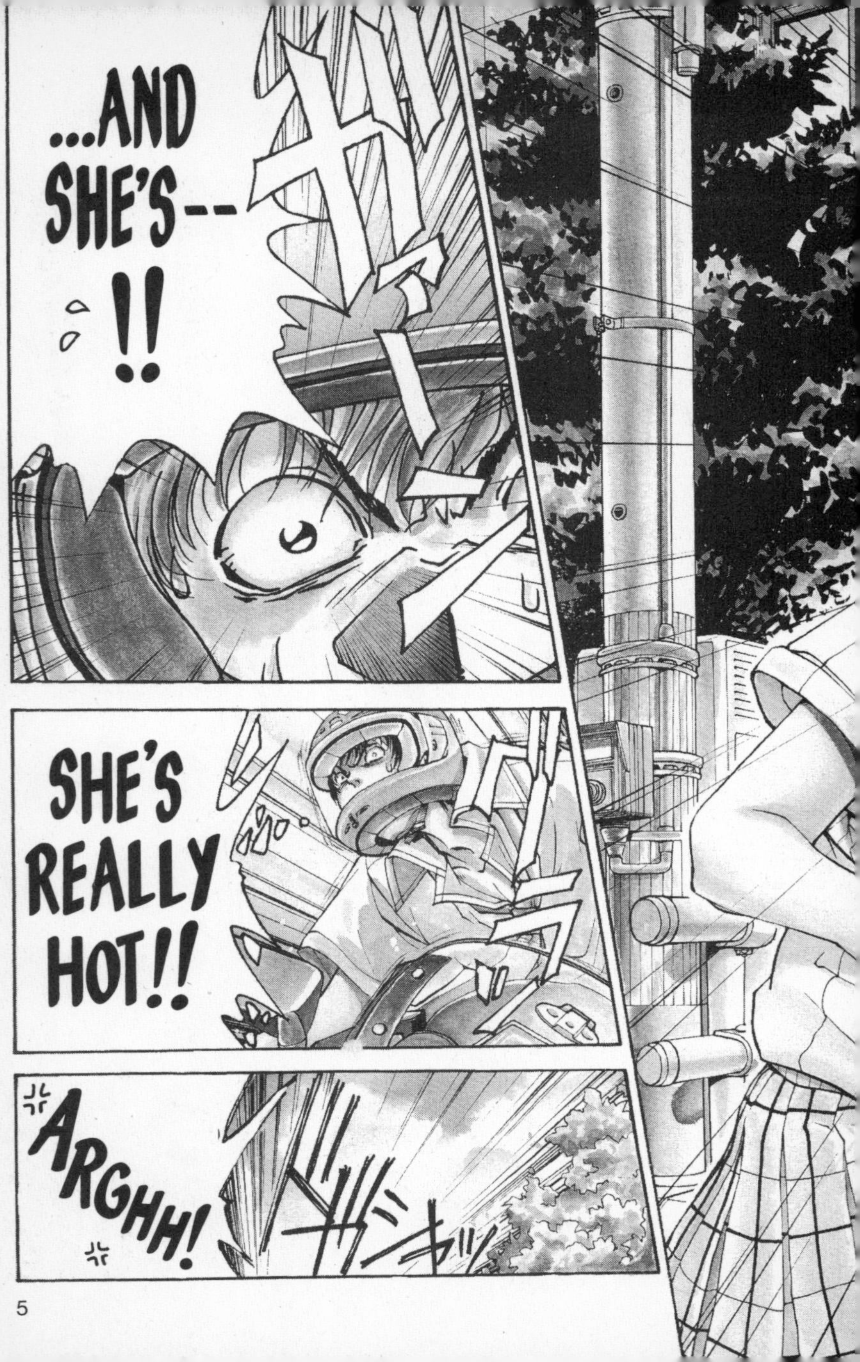
...AND SHE'S--
!!
SHE'S REALLY HOT!!
ARGHH!

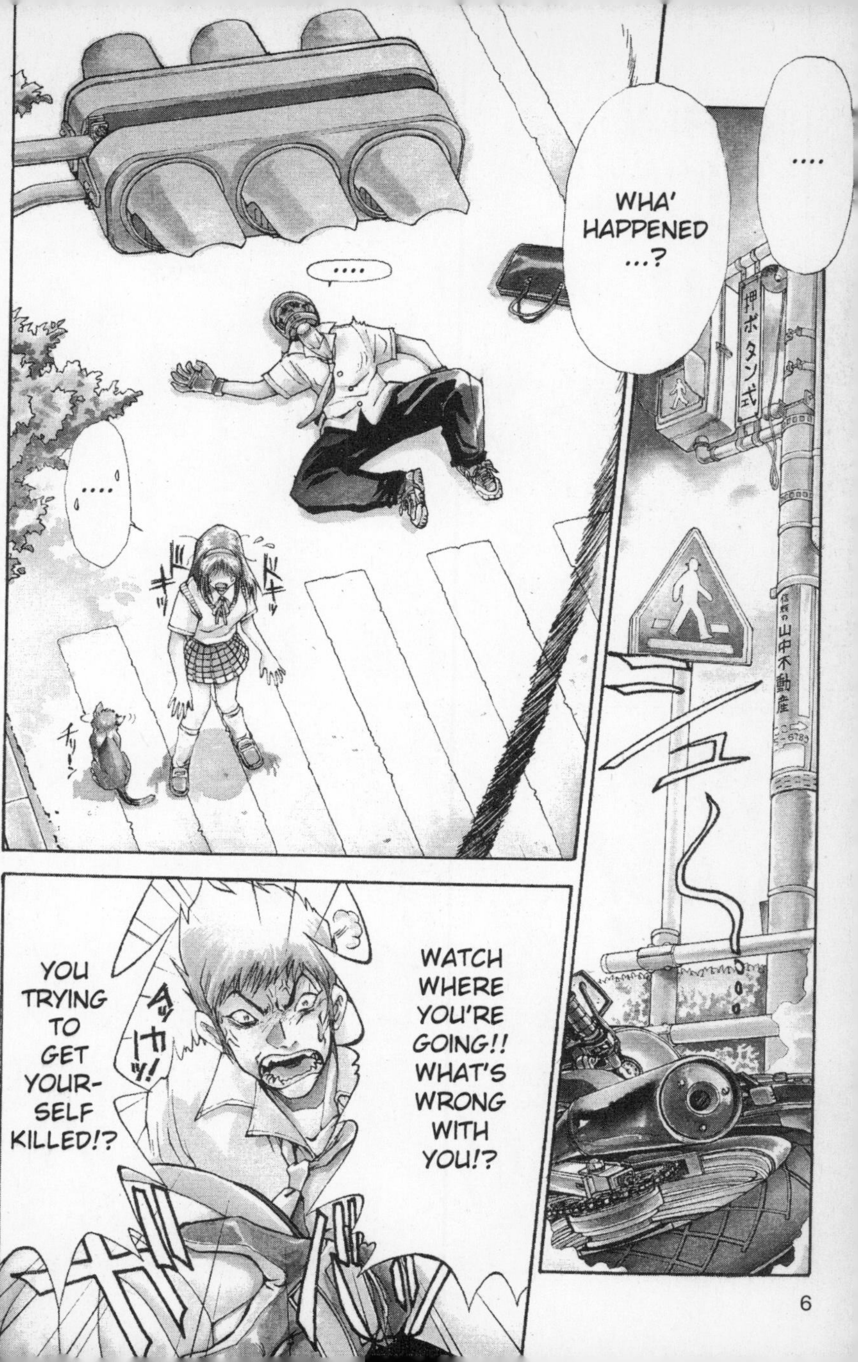
....
WHA' HAPPENED ...?
押ボタン式
山中不動産
....
....
WATCH WHERE YOU'RE GOING!! WHAT'S WRONG WITH YOU!?
YOU TRYING TO GET YOUR-SELF KILLED!?

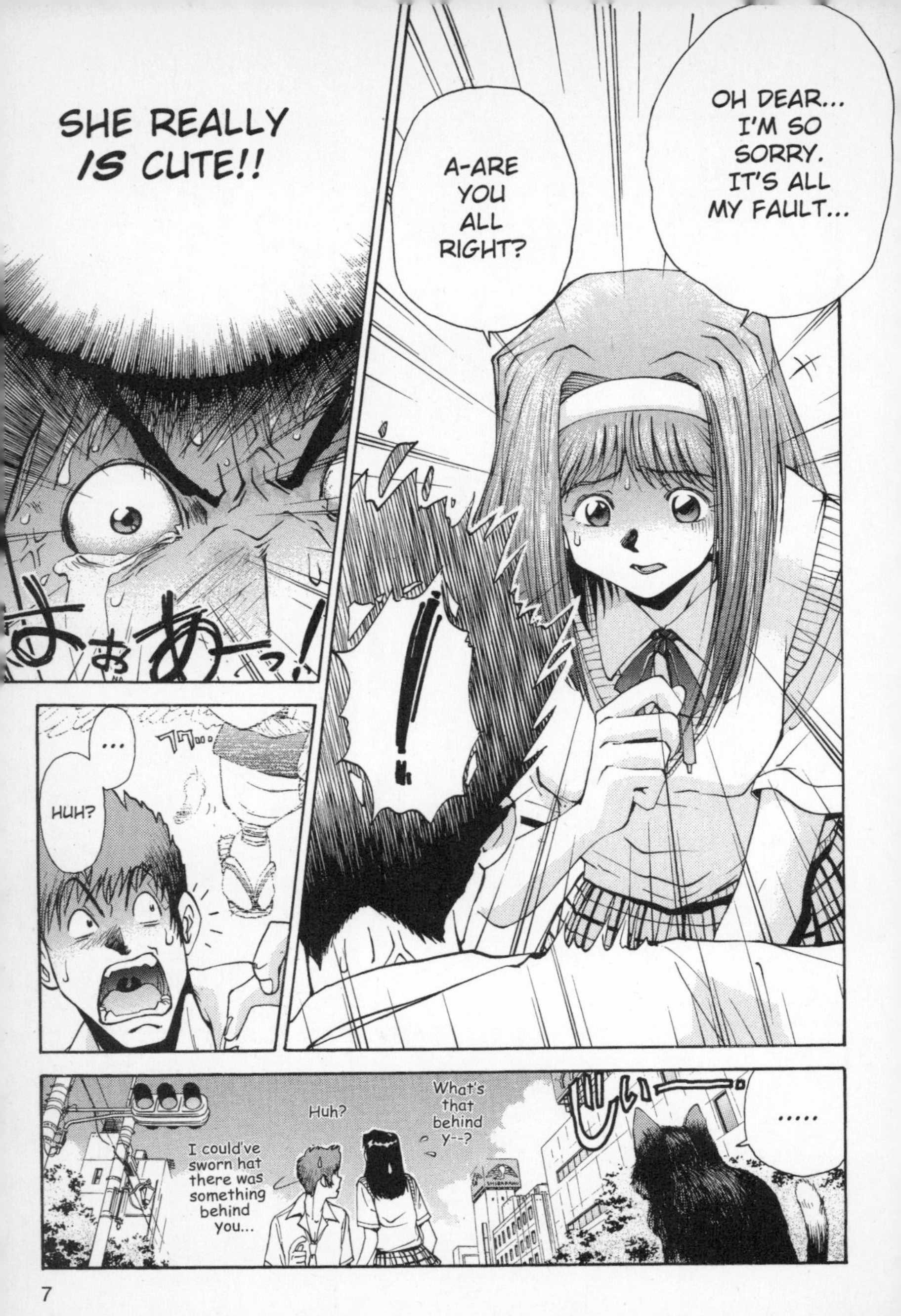
OH DEAR... I'M SO SORRY. IT'S ALL MY FAULT...
A-ARE YOU ALL RIGHT?
SHE REALLY *IS* CUTE!!
...
HUH?
.....
What's that behind y--?
Huh?
I could've sworn hat there was something behind you...

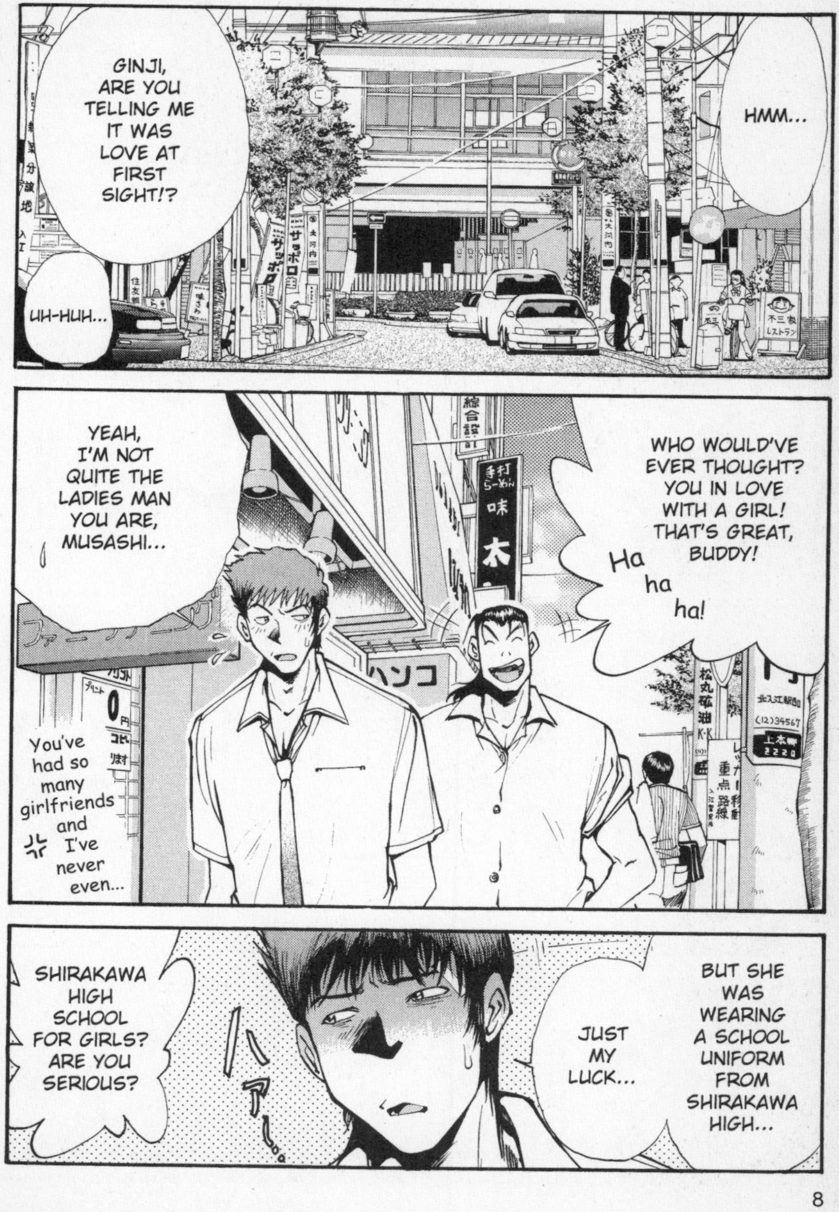
HMM...
GINJI, ARE YOU TELLING ME IT WAS LOVE AT FIRST SIGHT!?
UH-HUH...
WHO WOULD'VE EVER THOUGHT? YOU IN LOVE WITH A GIRL! THAT'S GREAT, BUDDY!
Ha ha ha!
YEAH, I'M NOT QUITE THE LADIES MAN YOU ARE, MUSASHI...
You've had so many girlfriends and I've never even...
BUT SHE WAS WEARING A SCHOOL UNIFORM FROM SHIRAKAWA HIGH...
JUST MY LUCK...
SHIRAKAWA HIGH SCHOOL FOR GIRLS? ARE YOU SERIOUS?

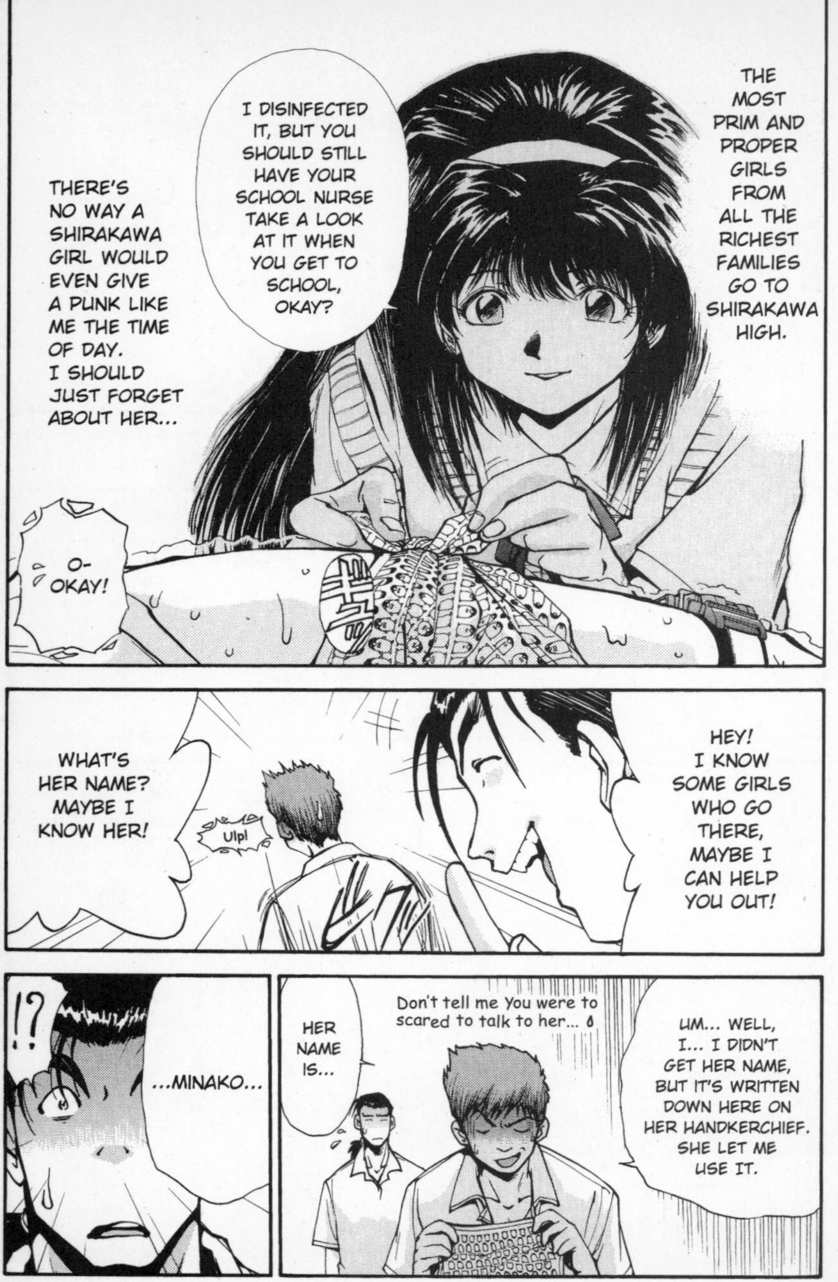
THE MOST PRIM AND PROPER GIRLS FROM ALL THE RICHEST FAMILIES GO TO SHIRAKAWA HIGH.
I DISINFECTED IT, BUT YOU SHOULD STILL HAVE YOUR SCHOOL NURSE TAKE A LOOK AT IT WHEN YOU GET TO SCHOOL, OKAY?
THERE'S NO WAY A SHIRAKAWA GIRL WOULD EVEN GIVE A PUNK LIKE ME THE TIME OF DAY. I SHOULD JUST FORGET ABOUT HER...
O- OKAY!
HEY! I KNOW SOME GIRLS WHO GO THERE, MAYBE I CAN HELP YOU OUT!
Ulp!
WHAT'S HER NAME? MAYBE I KNOW HER!
UM... WELL, I... I DIDN'T GET HER NAME, BUT IT'S WRITTEN DOWN HERE ON HER HANDKERCHIEF. SHE LET ME USE IT.
Don't tell me you were to scared to talk to her...
HER NAME IS...
!?
...MINAKO...

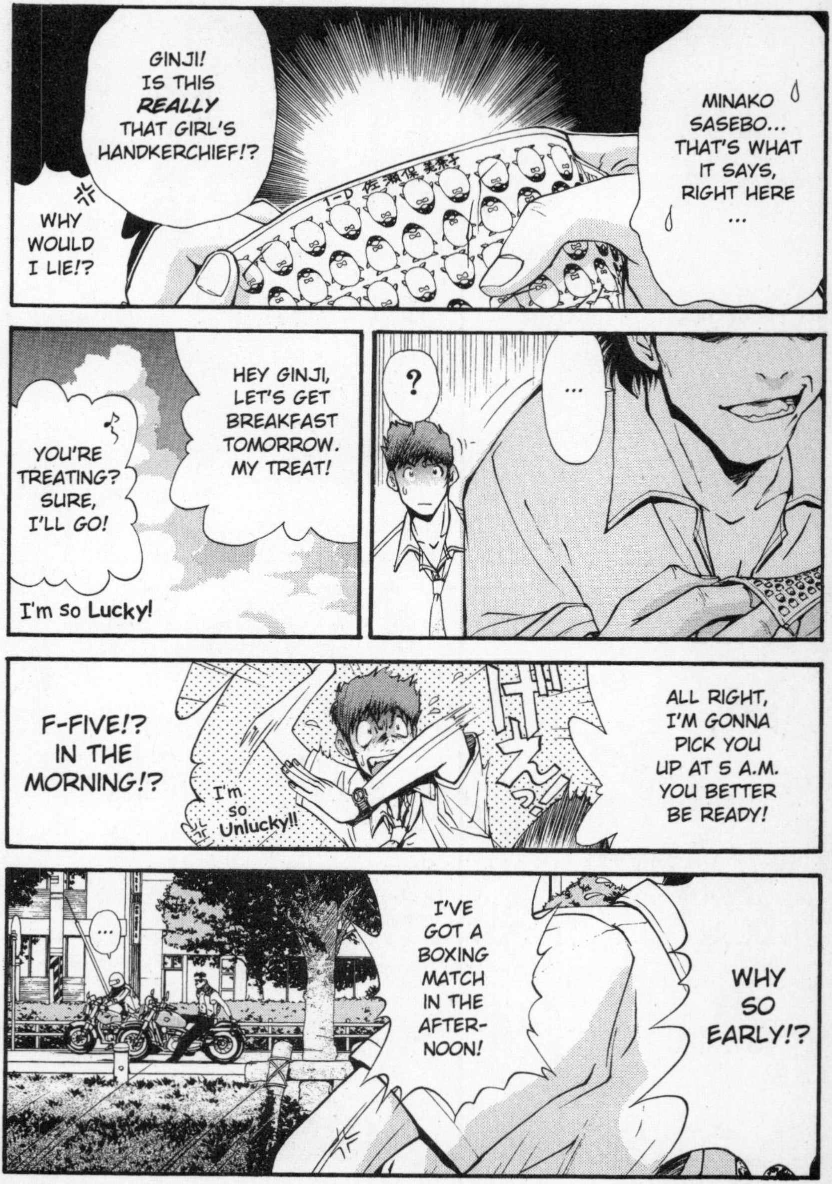
GINJI! IS THIS ***REALLY*** THAT GIRL'S HANDKERCHIEF!?
WHY WOULD I LIE!?
MINAKO SASEBO... THAT'S WHAT IT SAYS, RIGHT HERE ...
...
?
HEY GINJI, LET'S GET BREAKFAST TOMORROW. MY TREAT!
YOU'RE TREATING? SURE, I'LL GO!
I'm so Lucky!
ALL RIGHT, I'M GONNA PICK YOU UP AT 5 A.M. YOU BETTER BE READY!
F-FIVE!? IN THE MORNING!?
I'm so Unlucky!!
WHY SO EARLY!?
I'VE GOT A BOXING MATCH IN THE AFTER-NOON!
...

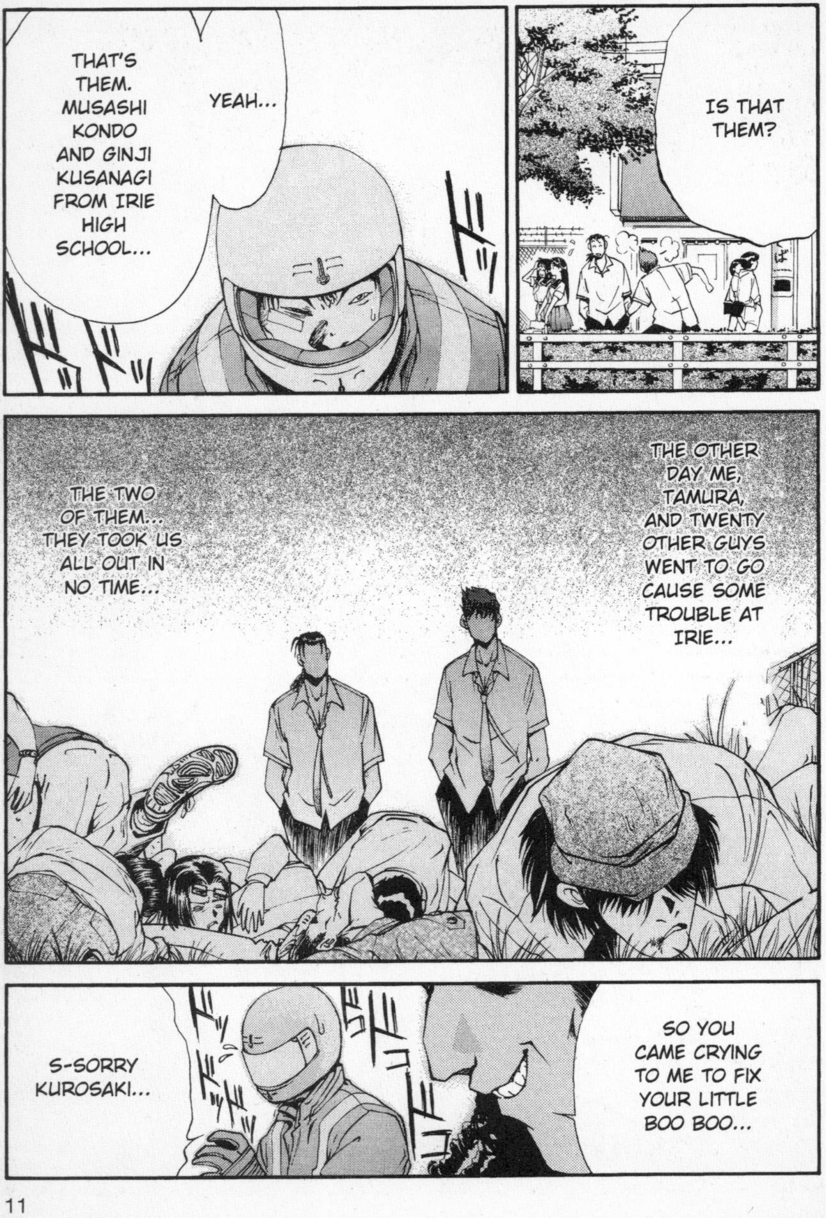
IS THAT THEM?
YEAH...
THAT'S THEM. MUSASHI KONDO AND GINJI KUSANAGI FROM IRIE HIGH SCHOOL...
THE OTHER DAY ME, TAMURA, AND TWENTY OTHER GUYS WENT TO GO CAUSE SOME TROUBLE AT IRIE...
THE TWO OF THEM... THEY TOOK US ALL OUT IN NO TIME...
SO YOU CAME CRYING TO ME TO FIX YOUR LITTLE BOO BOO...
S-SORRY KUROSAKI...

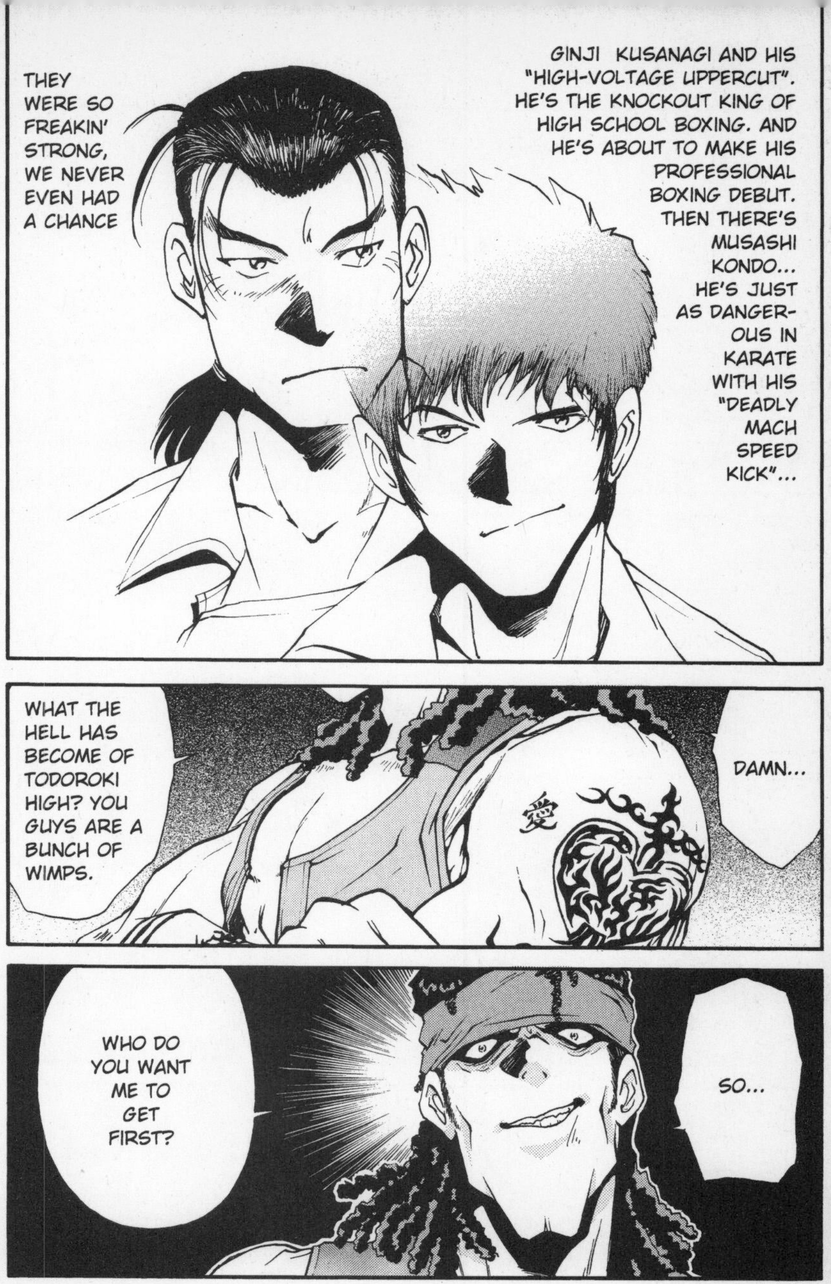
GINJI KUSANAGI AND HIS "HIGH-VOLTAGE UPPERCUT". HE'S THE KNOCKOUT KING OF HIGH SCHOOL BOXING. AND HE'S ABOUT TO MAKE HIS PROFESSIONAL BOXING DEBUT. THEN THERE'S MUSASHI KONDO... HE'S JUST AS DANGER-OUS IN KARATE WITH HIS "DEADLY MACH SPEED KICK"...
THEY WERE SO FREAKIN' STRONG, WE NEVER EVEN HAD A CHANCE
DAMN...
WHAT THE HELL HAS BECOME OF TODOROKI HIGH? YOU GUYS ARE A BUNCH OF WIMPS.
SO...
WHO DO YOU WANT ME TO GET FIRST?

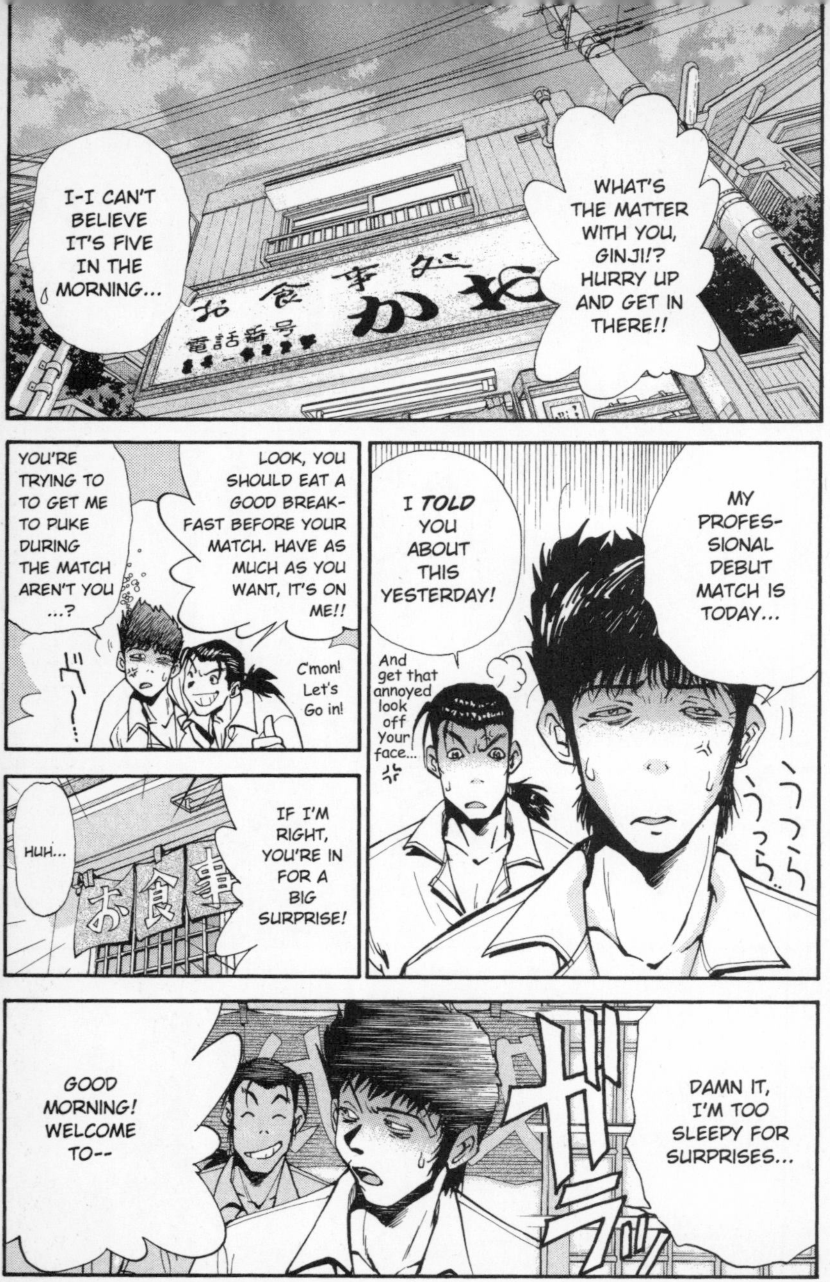
WHAT'S THE MATTER WITH YOU, GINJI!? HURRY UP AND GET IN THERE!!
I-I CAN'T BELIEVE IT'S FIVE IN THE MORNING...
MY PROFES-SIONAL DEBUT MATCH IS TODAY...
I TOLD YOU ABOUT THIS YESTERDAY!
And get that annoyed look off Your face...
LOOK, YOU SHOULD EAT A GOOD BREAK-FAST BEFORE YOUR MATCH. HAVE AS MUCH AS YOU WANT, IT'S ON ME!!
YOU'RE TRYING TO TO GET ME TO PUKE DURING THE MATCH AREN'T YOU ...?
C'mon! Let's Go in!
IF I'M RIGHT, YOU'RE IN FOR A BIG SURPRISE!
HUH...
DAMN IT, I'M TOO SLEEPY FOR SURPRISES...
GOOD MORNING! WELCOME TO--

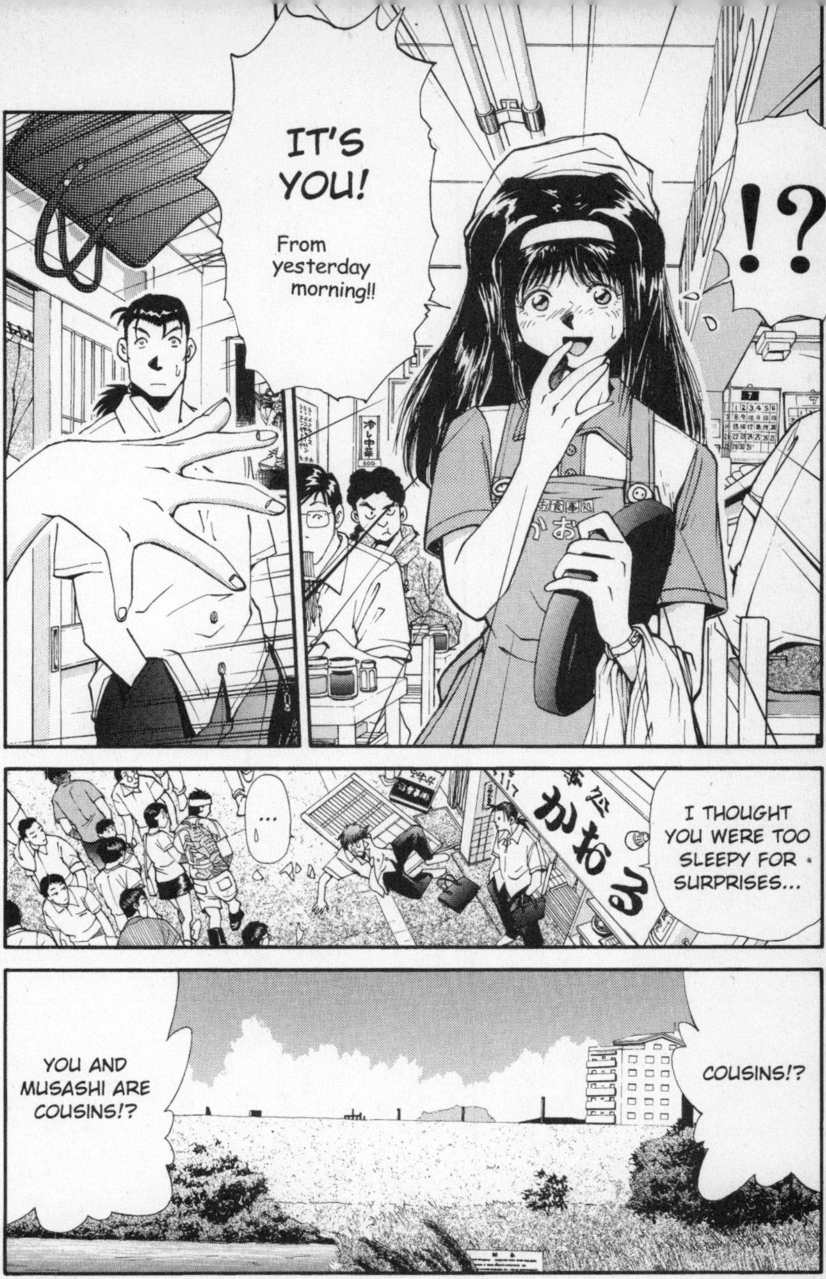
IT'S YOU!
From yesterday morning!!
!?
I THOUGHT YOU WERE TOO SLEEPY FOR SURPRISES...
かおる
...
COUSINS!?
YOU AND MUSASHI ARE COUSINS!?

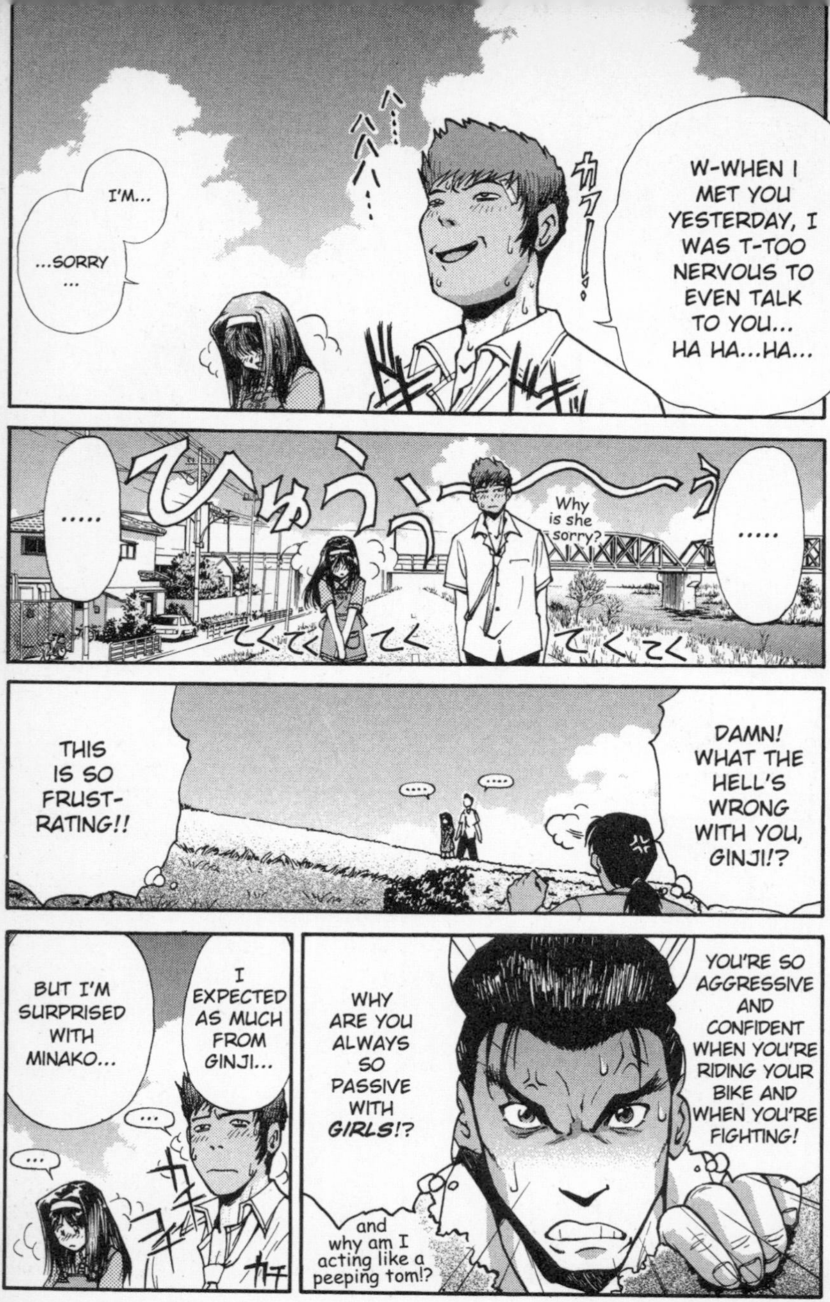
W-WHEN I MET YOU YESTERDAY, I WAS T-TOO NERVOUS TO EVEN TALK TO YOU... HA HA...HA...
ハ…ハハハ…
I'M...
...SORRY ...
.....
Why is she sorry?
.....
DAMN! WHAT THE HELL'S WRONG WITH YOU, GINJI!?
....
....
THIS IS SO FRUST-RATING!!
YOU'RE SO AGGRESSIVE AND CONFIDENT WHEN YOU'RE RIDING YOUR BIKE AND WHEN YOU'RE FIGHTING!
WHY ARE YOU ALWAYS SO PASSIVE WITH GIRLS!?
and why am I acting like a peeping tom!?
I EXPECTED AS MUCH FROM GINJI...
BUT I'M SURPRISED WITH MINAKO...
...
...

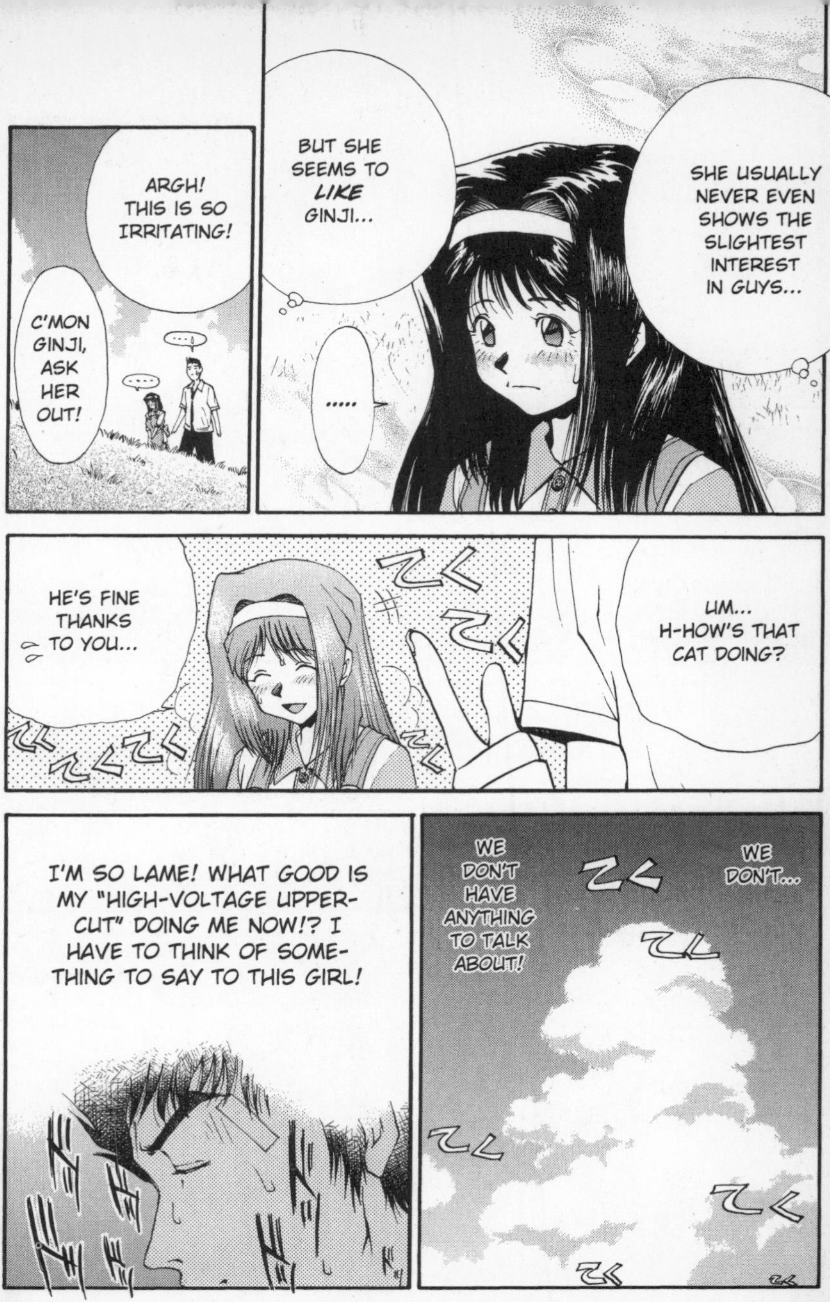
SHE USUALLY NEVER EVEN SHOWS THE SLIGHTEST INTEREST IN GUYS...
BUT SHE SEEMS TO LIKE GINJI...
.....
ARGH! THIS IS SO IRRITATING!
C'MON GINJI, ASK HER OUT!
UM... H-HOW'S THAT CAT DOING?
HE'S FINE THANKS TO YOU...
WE DON'T...
WE DON'T HAVE ANYTHING TO TALK ABOUT!
I'M SO LAME! WHAT GOOD IS MY "HIGH-VOLTAGE UPPER-CUT" DOING ME NOW!? I HAVE TO THINK OF SOME-THING TO SAY TO THIS GIRL!

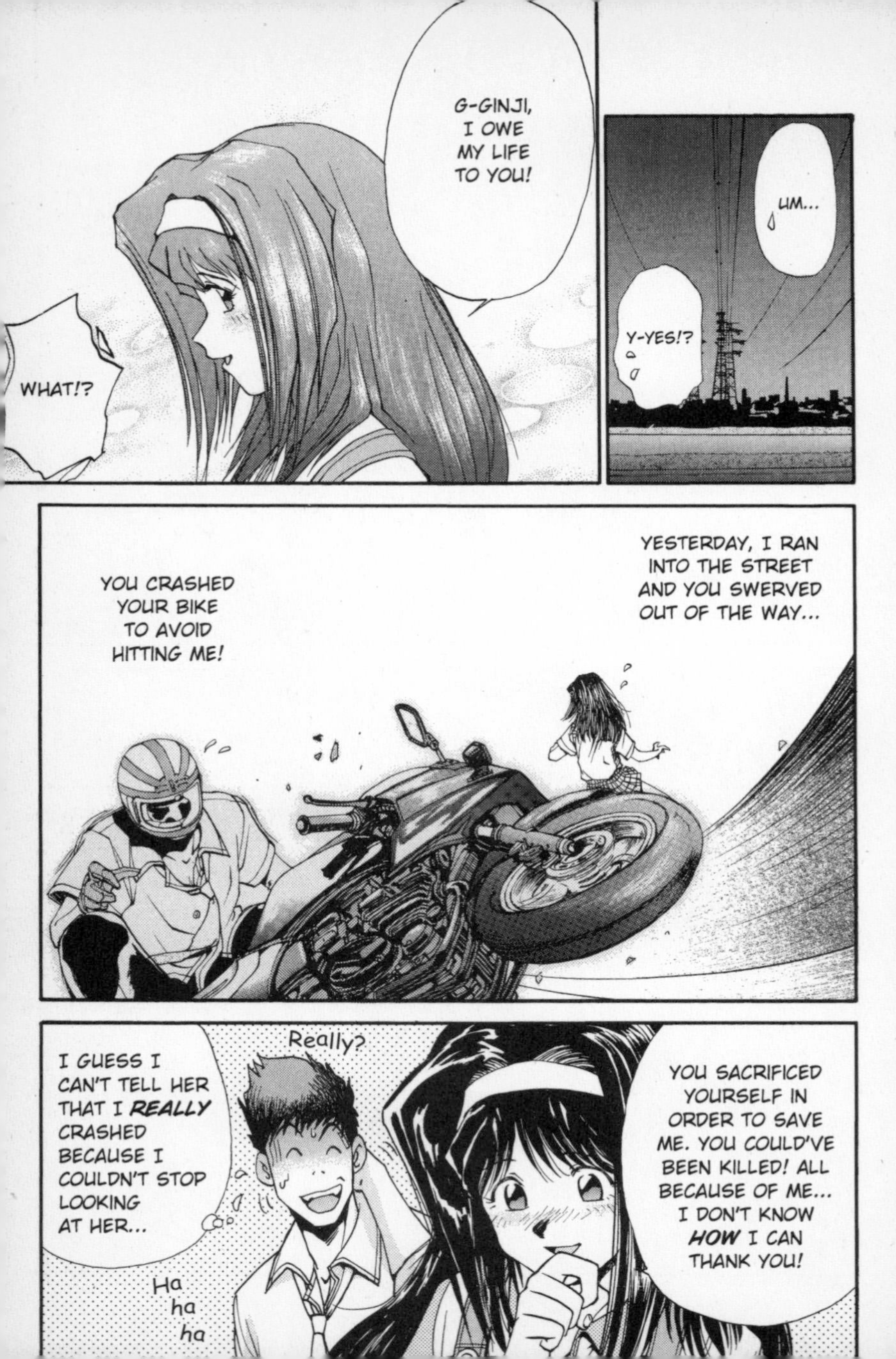
UM...
Y-YES!?
G-GINJI, I OWE MY LIFE TO YOU!
WHAT!?
YESTERDAY, I RAN INTO THE STREET AND YOU SWERVED OUT OF THE WAY...
YOU CRASHED YOUR BIKE TO AVOID HITTING ME!
YOU SACRIFICED YOURSELF IN ORDER TO SAVE ME. YOU COULD'VE BEEN KILLED! ALL BECAUSE OF ME... I DON'T KNOW ***HOW*** I CAN THANK YOU!
Really?
I GUESS I CAN'T TELL HER THAT I ***REALLY*** CRASHED BECAUSE I COULDN'T STOP LOOKING AT HER...
Ha ha ha

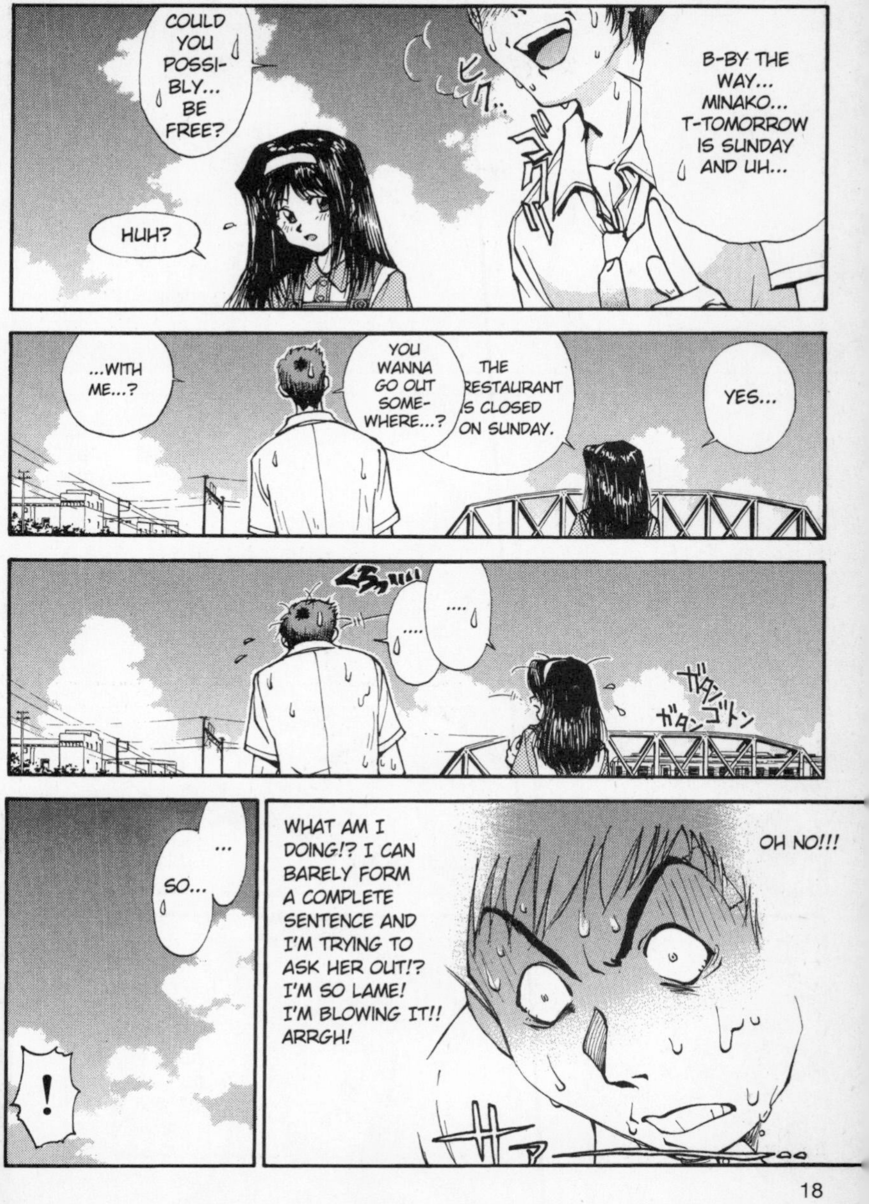
B-BY THE WAY... MINAKO... T-TOMORROW IS SUNDAY AND UH...
COULD YOU POSSIBLY... BE FREE?
HUH?
YES...
THE RESTAURANT IS CLOSED ON SUNDAY.
YOU WANNA GO OUT SOMEWHERE...?
...WITH ME...?
ガタンゴトン
ガタンゴトン
....
....
OH NO!!!
WHAT AM I DOING!? I CAN BARELY FORM A COMPLETE SENTENCE AND I'M TRYING TO ASK HER OUT!? I'M SO LAME! I'M BLOWING IT!! ARRGH!
... SO...
!

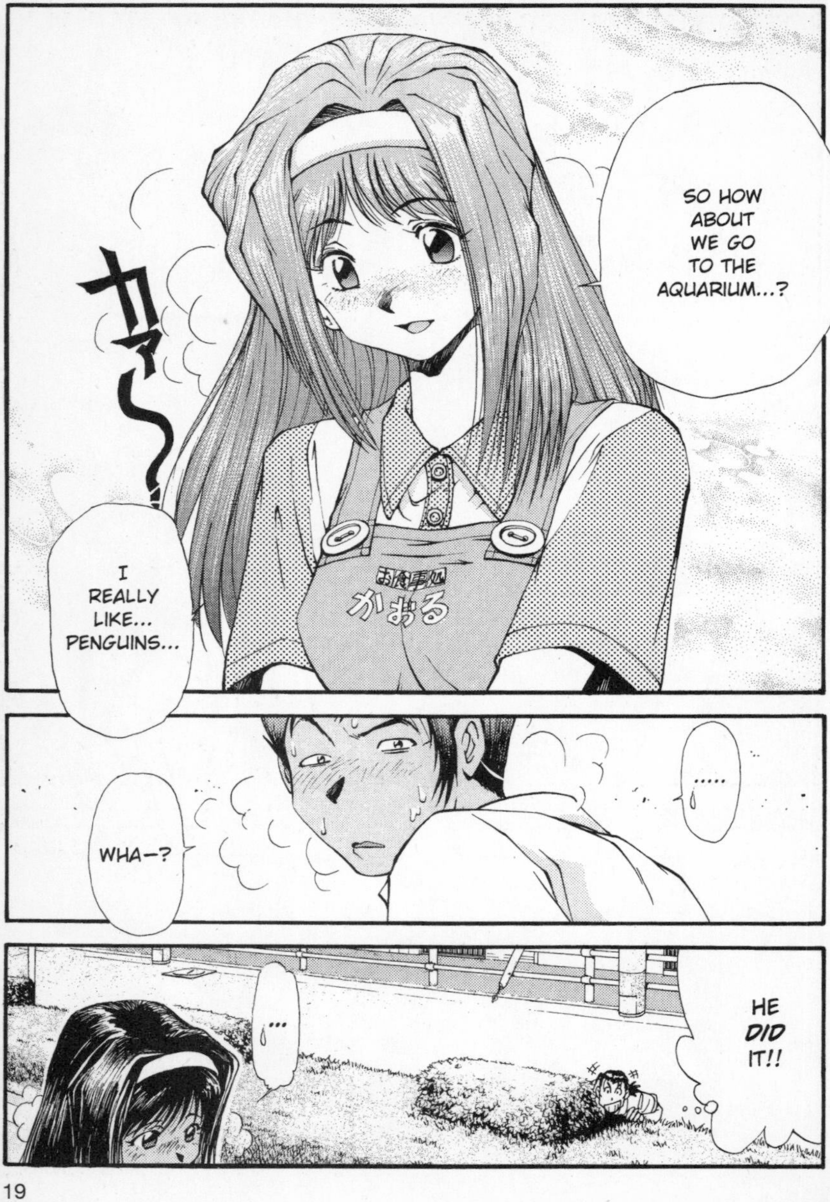
SO HOW ABOUT WE GO TO THE AQUARIUM...?
カァ〜
お食事処
かおる
I REALLY LIKE... PENGUINS...
.....
WHA–?
HE DID IT!!
...

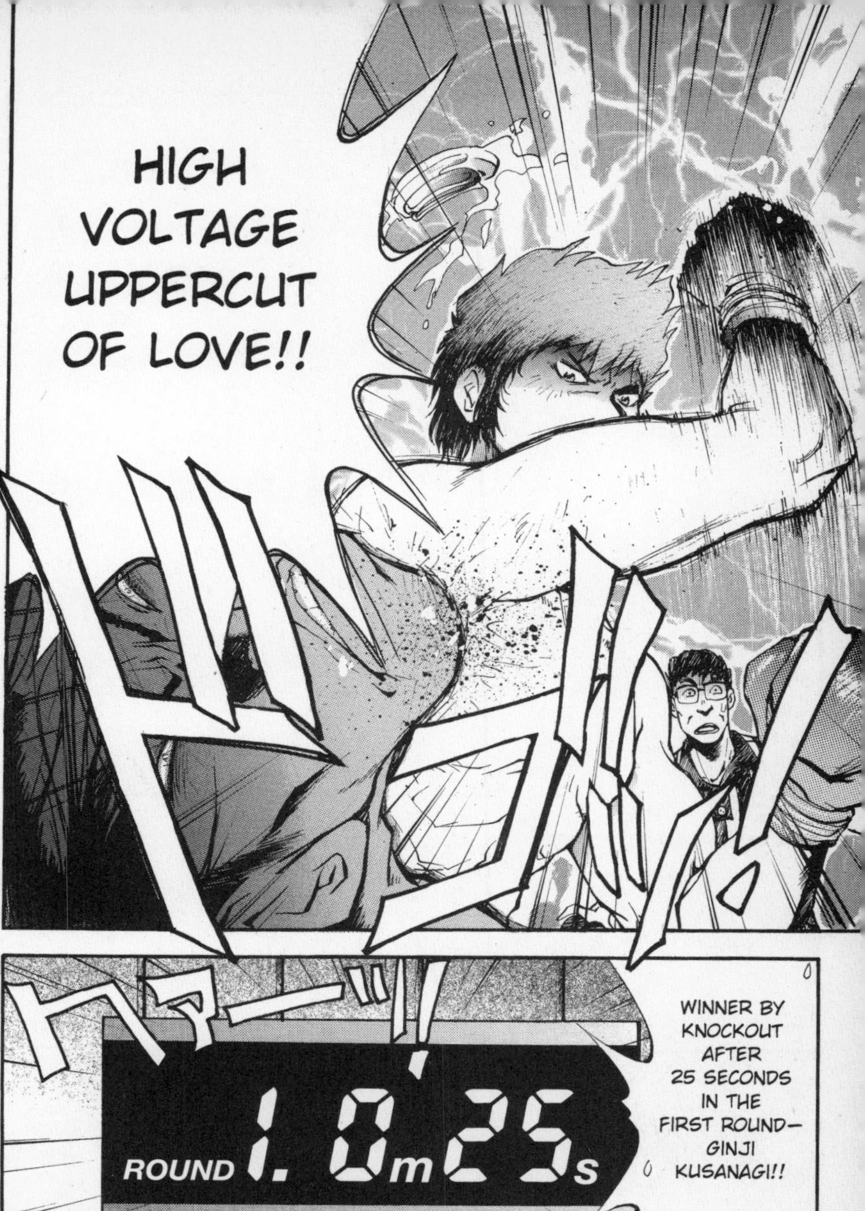
HIGH VOLTAGE UPPERCUT OF LOVE!!
WINNER BY KNOCKOUT AFTER 25 SECONDS IN THE FIRST ROUND— GINJI KUSANAGI!!
ROUND 1. 0m 25s

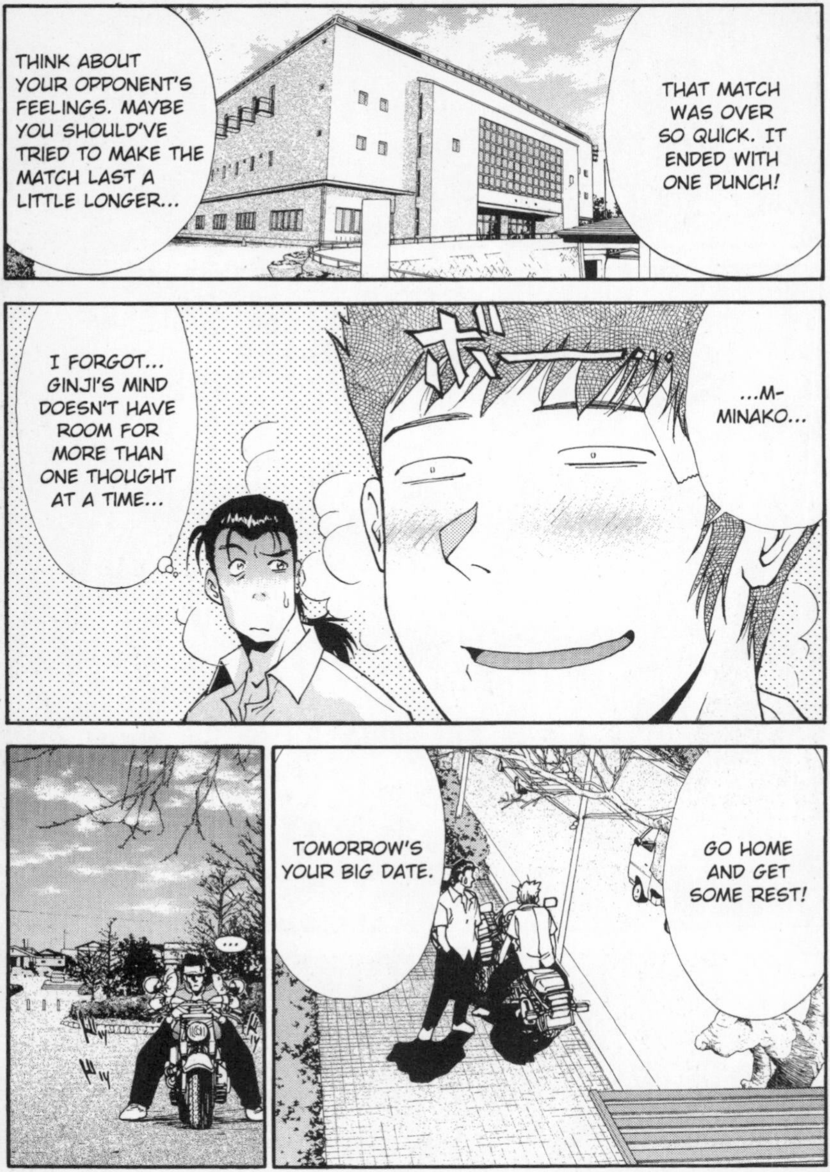
THAT MATCH WAS OVER SO QUICK. IT ENDED WITH ONE PUNCH!
THINK ABOUT YOUR OPPONENT'S FEELINGS. MAYBE YOU SHOULD'VE TRIED TO MAKE THE MATCH LAST A LITTLE LONGER...
...M- MINAKO...
ボー
I FORGOT... GINJI'S MIND DOESN'T HAVE ROOM FOR MORE THAN ONE THOUGHT AT A TIME...
GO HOME AND GET SOME REST!
TOMORROW'S YOUR BIG DATE.
...

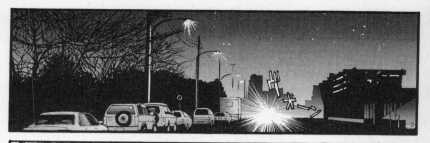

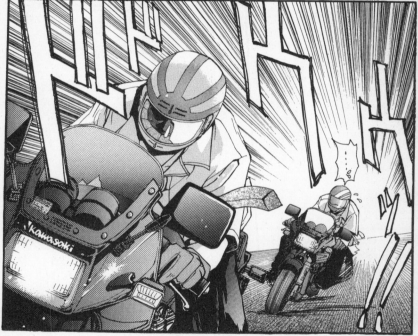

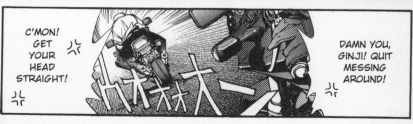

DAMN YOU, GINJI! QUIT MESSING AROUND!
C'MON! GET YOUR HEAD STRAIGHT!

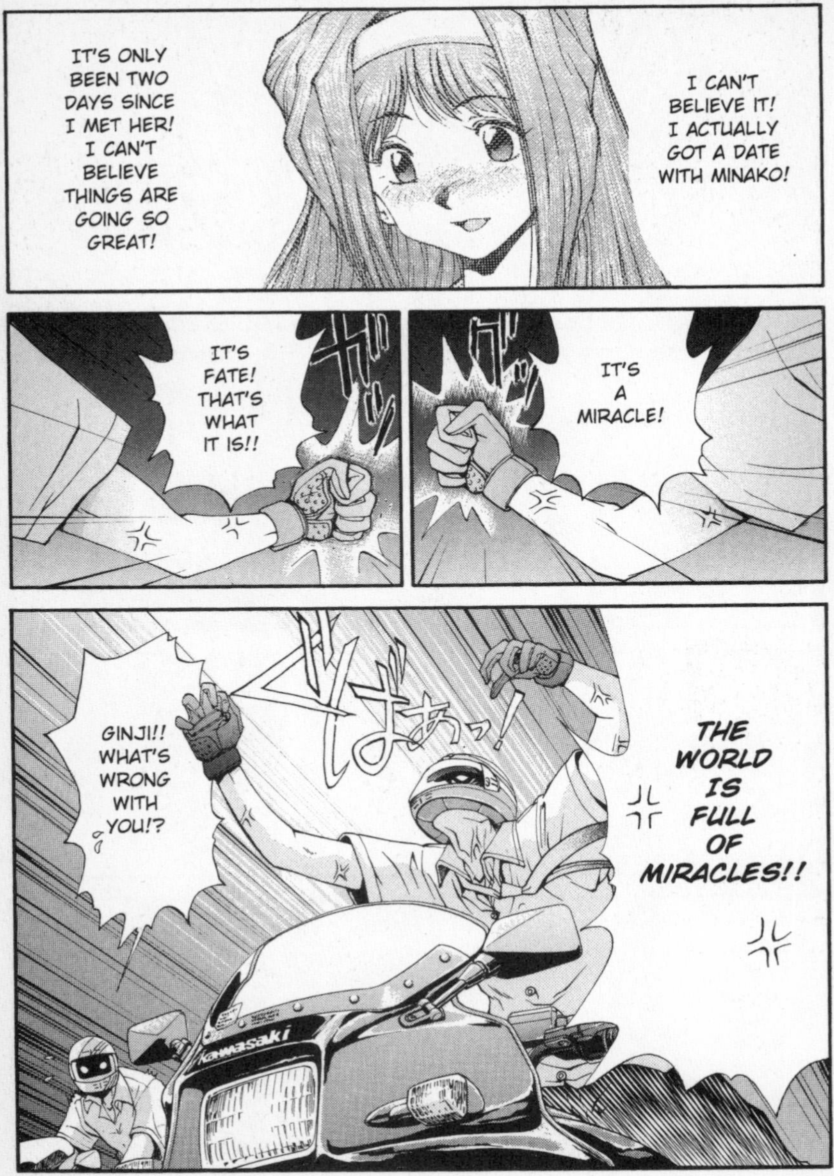
I CAN'T BELIEVE IT! I ACTUALLY GOT A DATE WITH MINAKO!
IT'S ONLY BEEN TWO DAYS SINCE I MET HER! I CAN'T BELIEVE THINGS ARE GOING SO GREAT!
IT'S A MIRACLE!
IT'S FATE! THAT'S WHAT IT IS!!
THE WORLD IS FULL OF MIRACLES!!
GINJI!! WHAT'S WRONG WITH YOU!?
Kawasaki

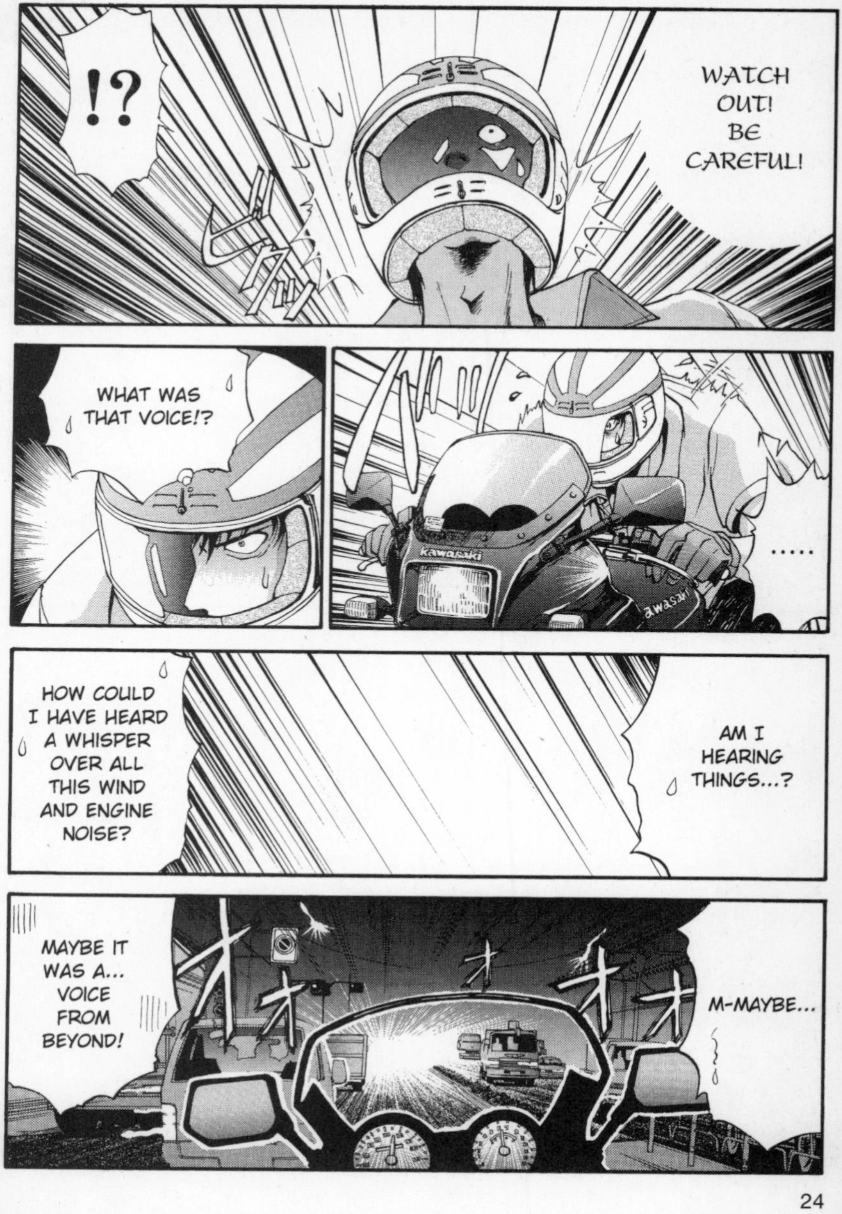
WATCH OUT! BE CAREFUL!
!?
.....
WHAT WAS THAT VOICE!?
AM I HEARING THINGS...?
HOW COULD I HAVE HEARD A WHISPER OVER ALL THIS WIND AND ENGINE NOISE?
M-MAYBE...
MAYBE IT WAS A... VOICE FROM BEYOND!

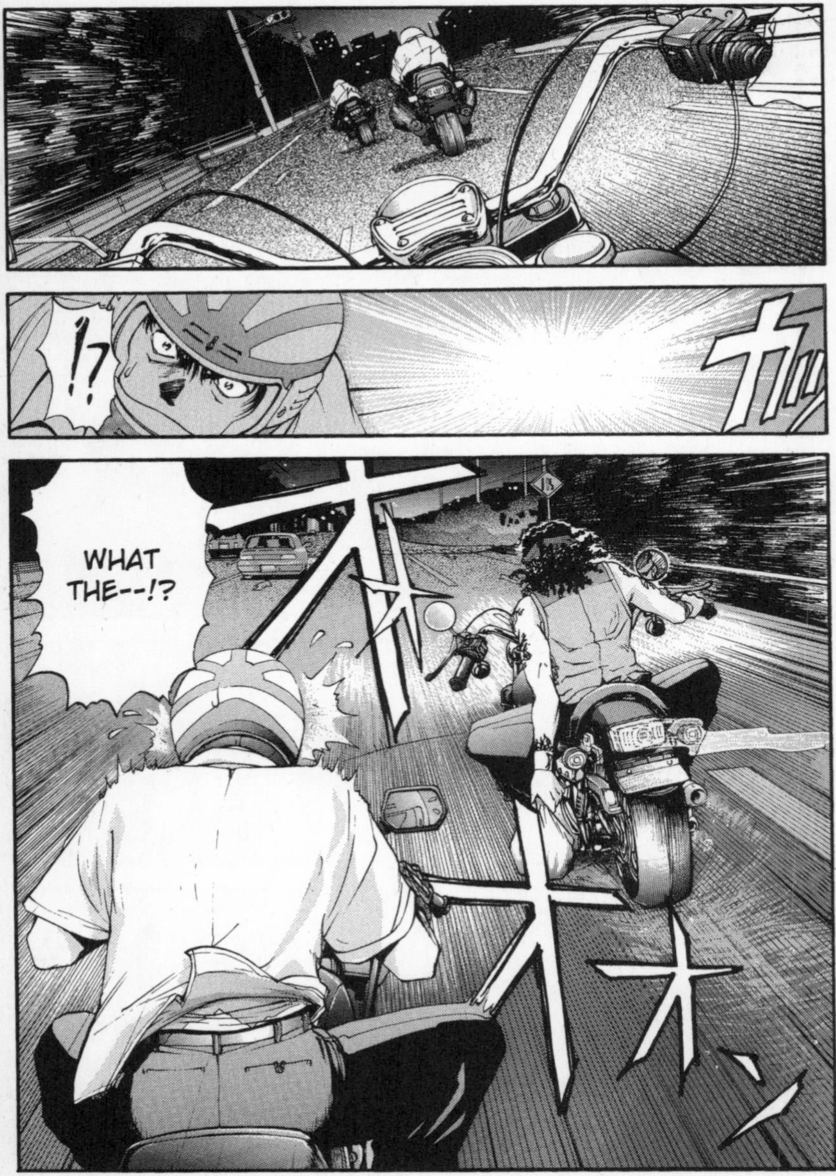
!?
カッ
WHAT THE--!?

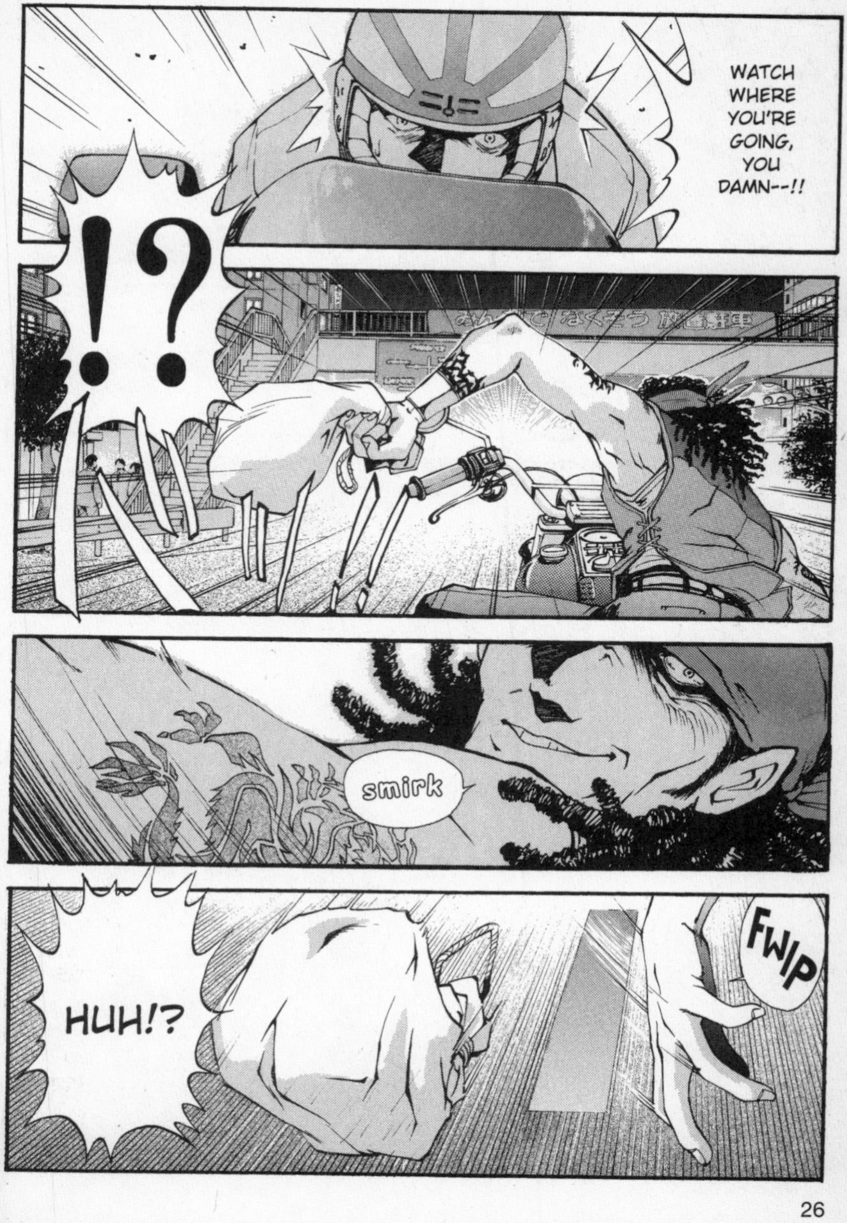
WATCH WHERE YOU'RE GOING, YOU DAMN--!!
!?
smirk
FWIP
HUH!?

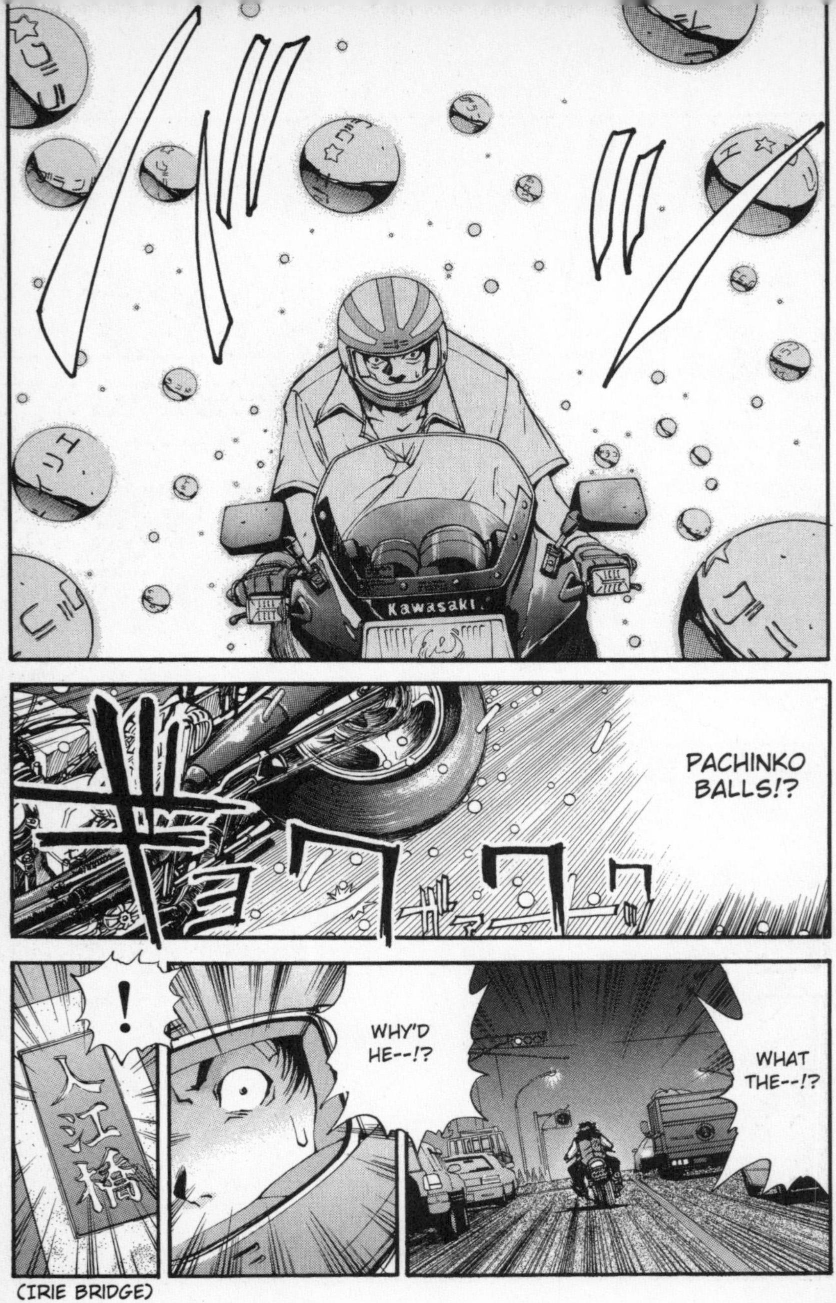
PACHINKO BALLS!?
WHAT THE--!?
WHY'D HE--!?
!
入江橋
(IRIE BRIDGE)

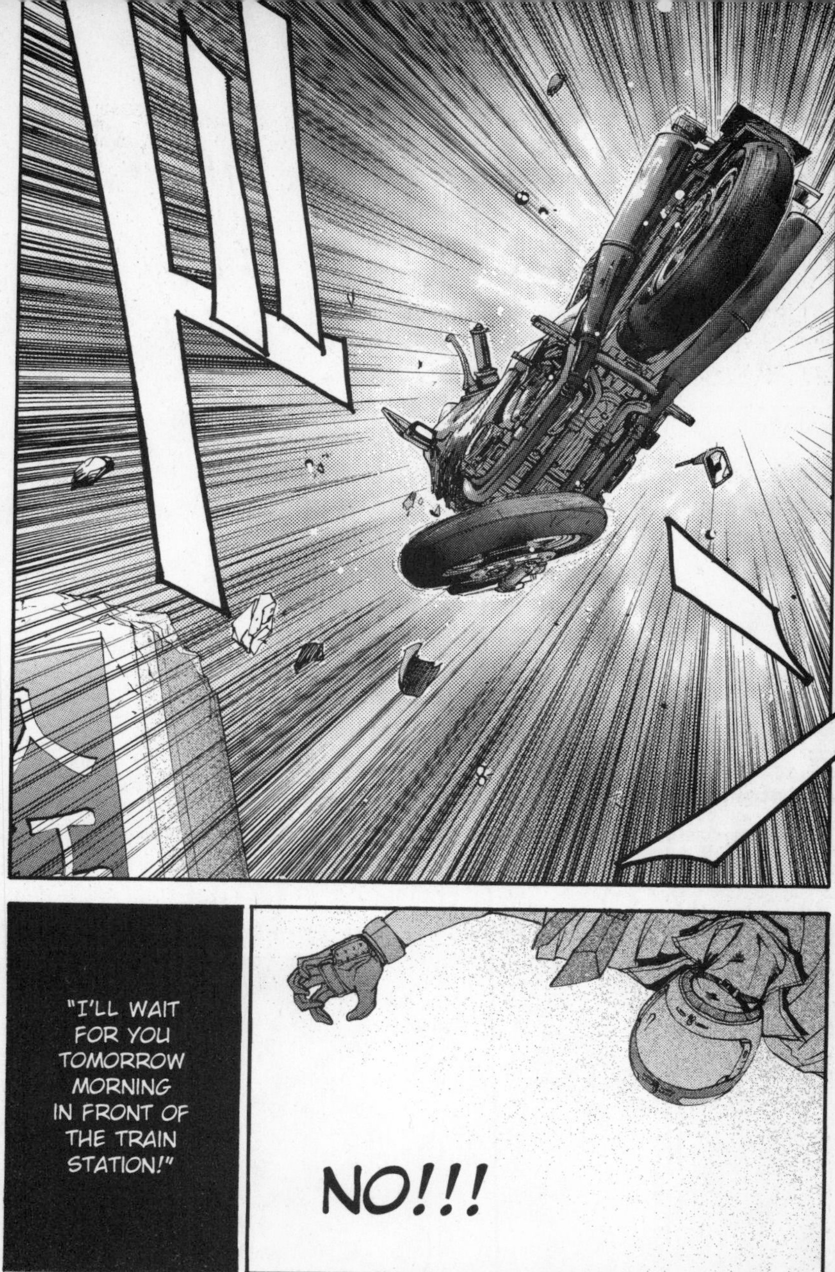
NO!!!
"I'LL WAIT FOR YOU TOMORROW MORNING IN FRONT OF THE TRAIN STATION!"

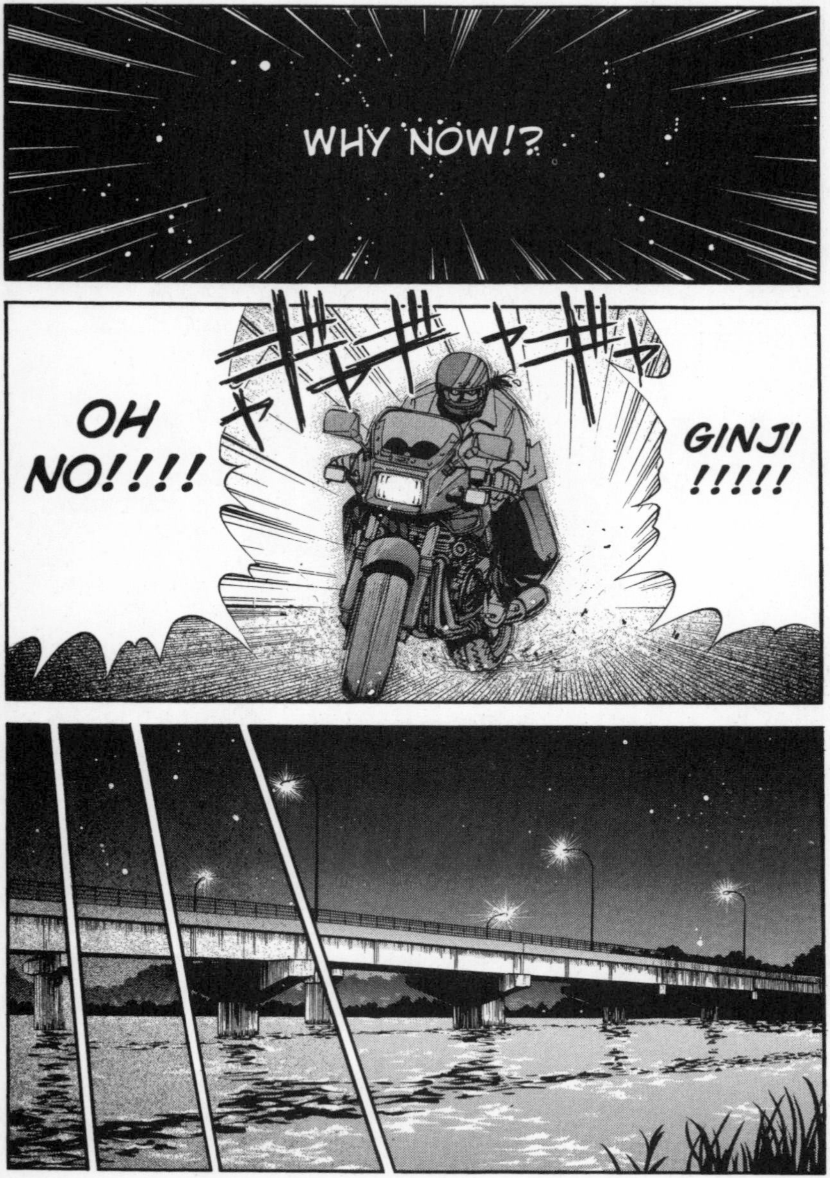
WHY NOW!?
GINJI !!!!!
OH NO!!!!

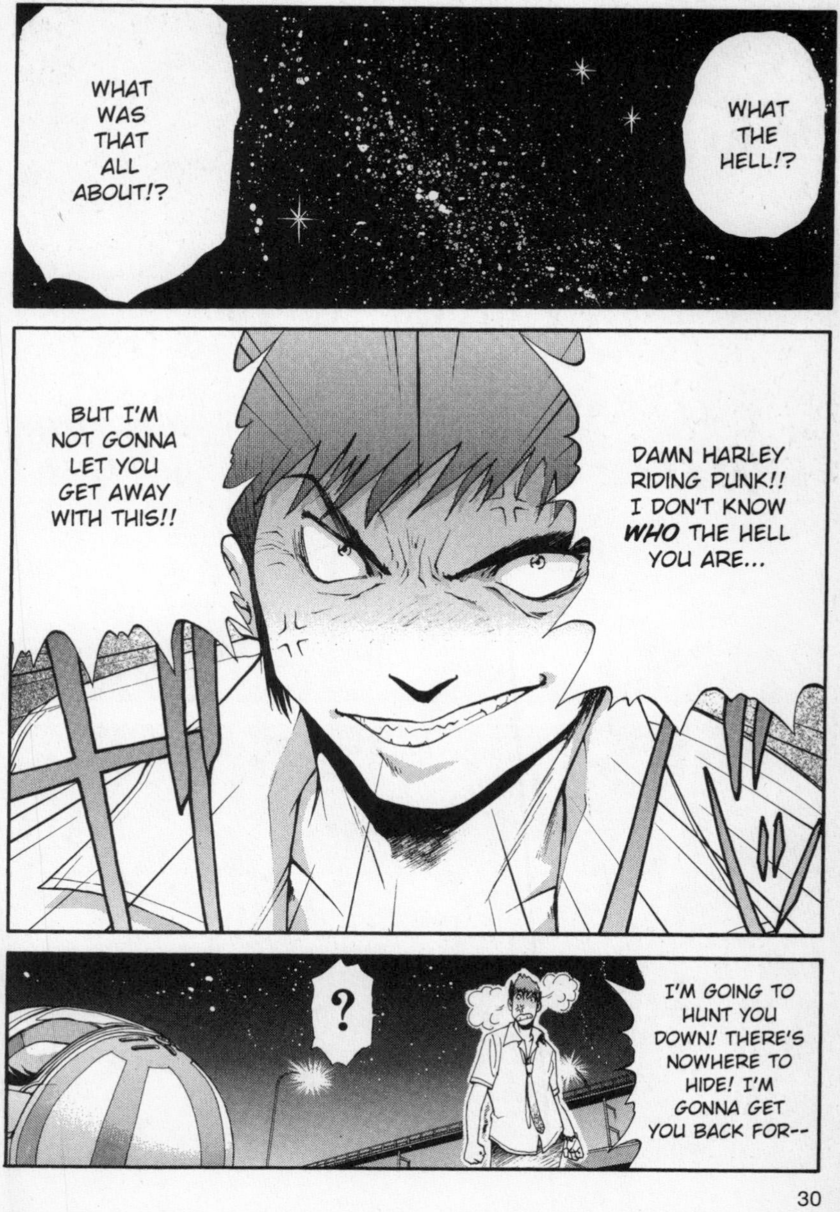
WHAT THE HELL!?
WHAT WAS THAT ALL ABOUT!?
DAMN HARLEY RIDING PUNK!! I DON'T KNOW ***WHO*** THE HELL YOU ARE...
BUT I'M NOT GONNA LET YOU GET AWAY WITH THIS!!
I'M GOING TO HUNT YOU DOWN! THERE'S NOWHERE TO HIDE! I'M GONNA GET YOU BACK FOR--
?

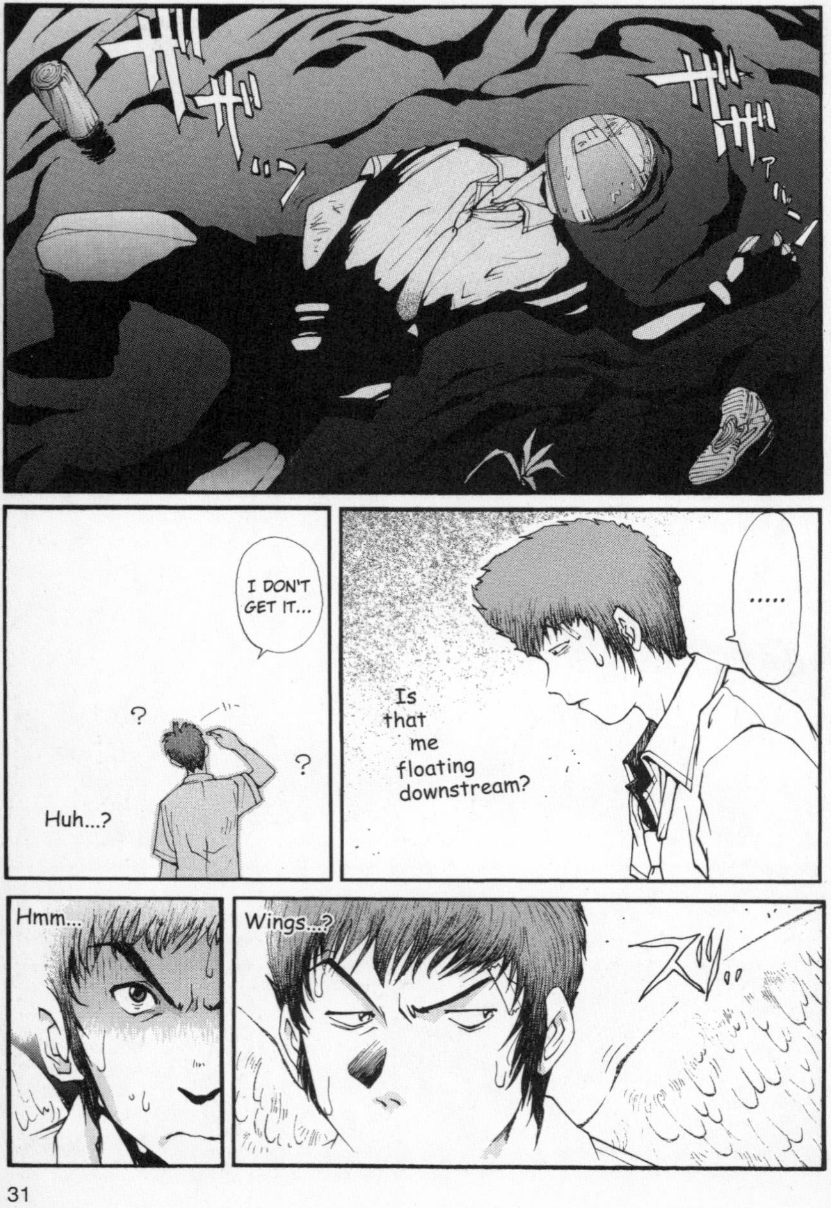
.....
Is that me floating downstream?
I DON'T GET IT...
?
?
Huh...?
Wings...?
Hmm...

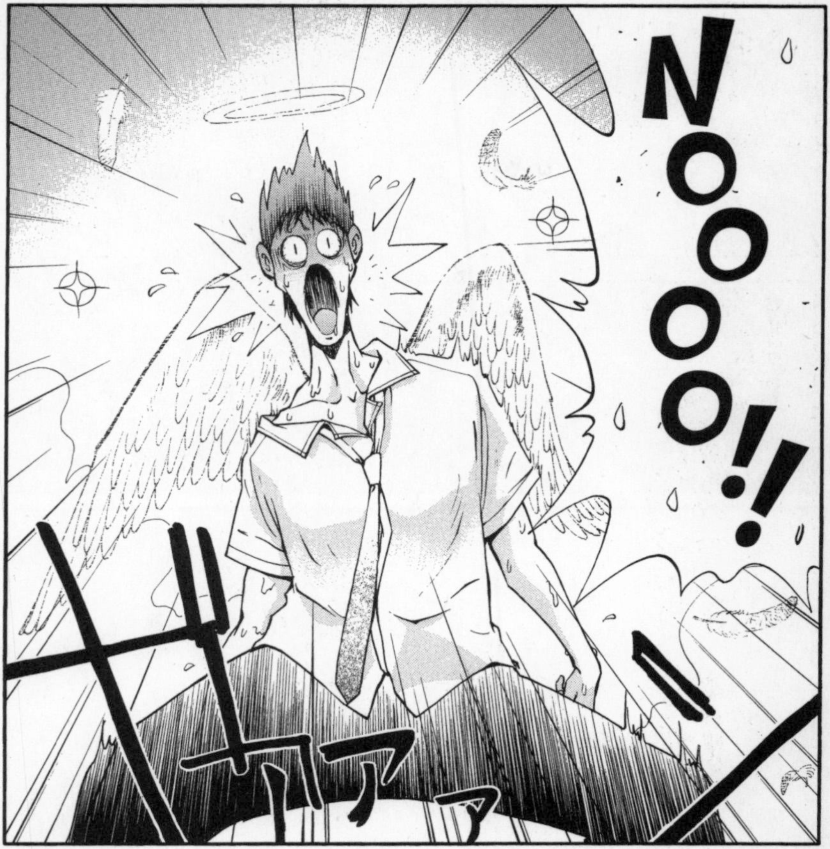
NOOOO!!

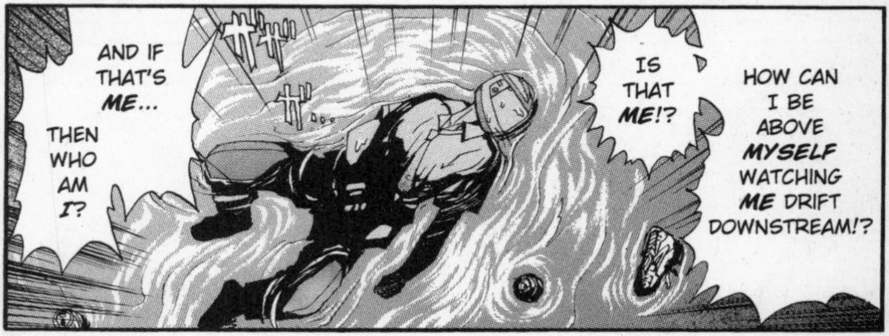
HOW CAN I BE ABOVE ***MYSELF*** WATCHING ***ME*** DRIFT DOWNSTREAM!?
IS THAT ***ME***!?
AND IF THAT'S ***ME***...
THEN WHO AM ***I***?

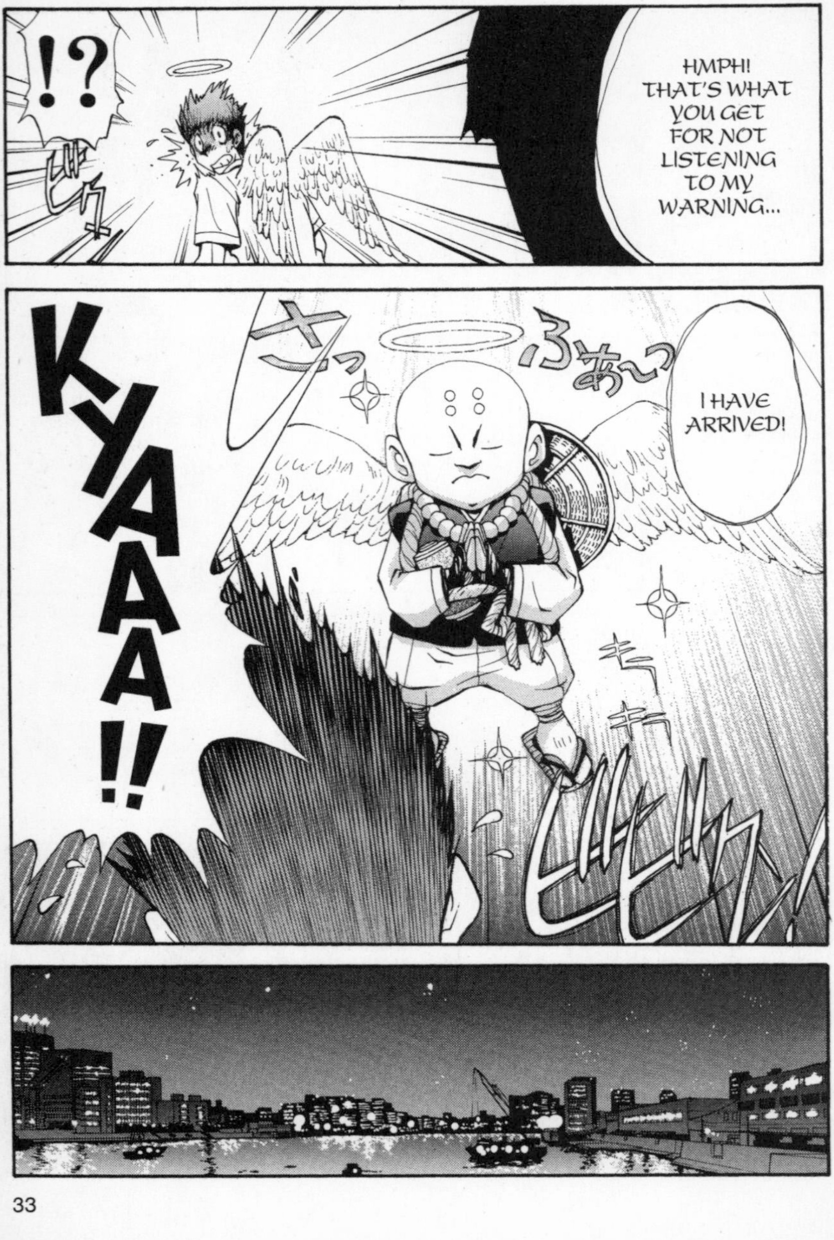
HMPH! THAT'S WHAT YOU GET FOR NOT LISTENING TO MY WARNING...
!?
I HAVE ARRIVED!
KYAAA!!

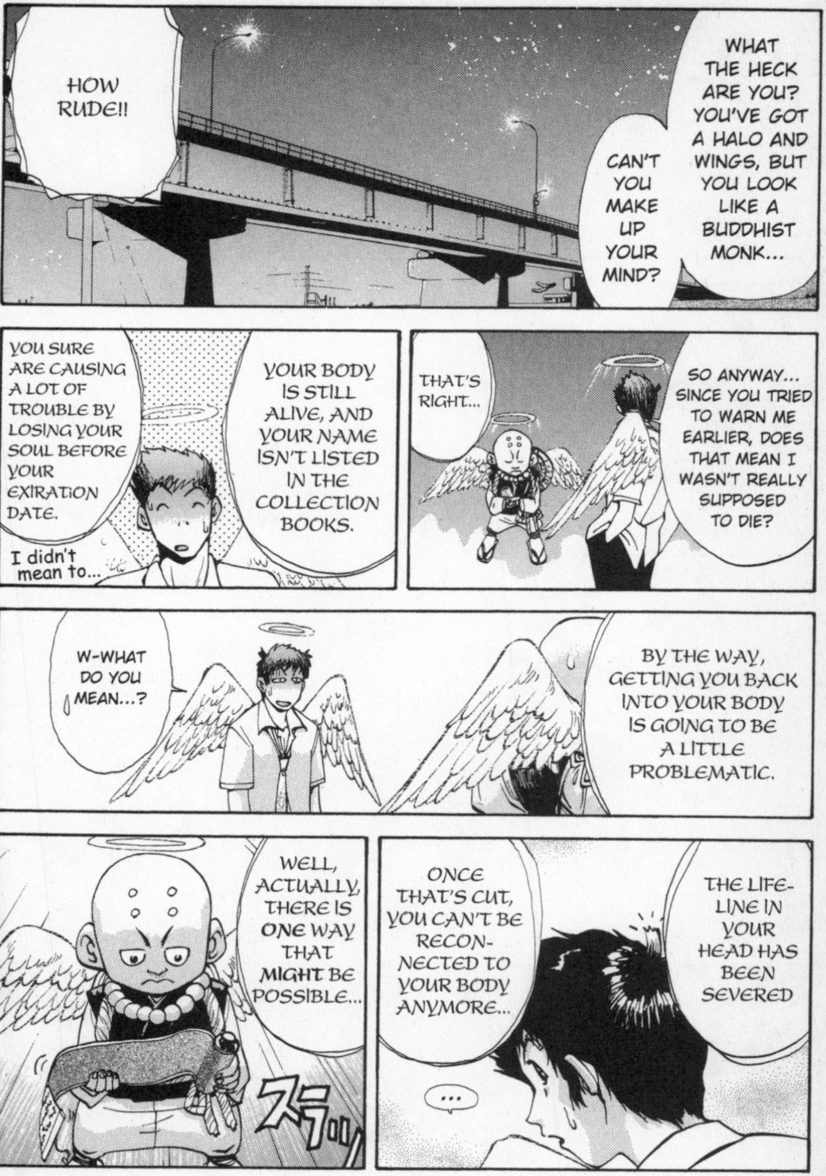
WHAT THE HECK ARE YOU? YOU'VE GOT A HALO AND WINGS, BUT YOU LOOK LIKE A BUDDHIST MONK...
CAN'T YOU MAKE UP YOUR MIND?
HOW RUDE!!
SO ANYWAY... SINCE YOU TRIED TO WARN ME EARLIER, DOES THAT MEAN I WASN'T REALLY SUPPOSED TO DIE?
THAT'S RIGHT...
YOUR BODY IS STILL ALIVE, AND YOUR NAME ISN'T LISTED IN THE COLLECTION BOOKS.
YOU SURE ARE CAUSING A LOT OF TROUBLE BY LOSING YOUR SOUL BEFORE YOUR EXIRATION DATE.
I didn't mean to...
BY THE WAY, GETTING YOU BACK INTO YOUR BODY IS GOING TO BE A LITTLE PROBLEMATIC.
W-WHAT DO YOU MEAN...?
THE LIFE-LINE IN YOUR HEAD HAS BEEN SEVERED
ONCE THAT'S CUT, YOU CAN'T BE RECON-NECTED TO YOUR BODY ANYMORE...
...
WELL, ACTUALLY, THERE IS ONE WAY THAT MIGHT BE POSSIBLE...

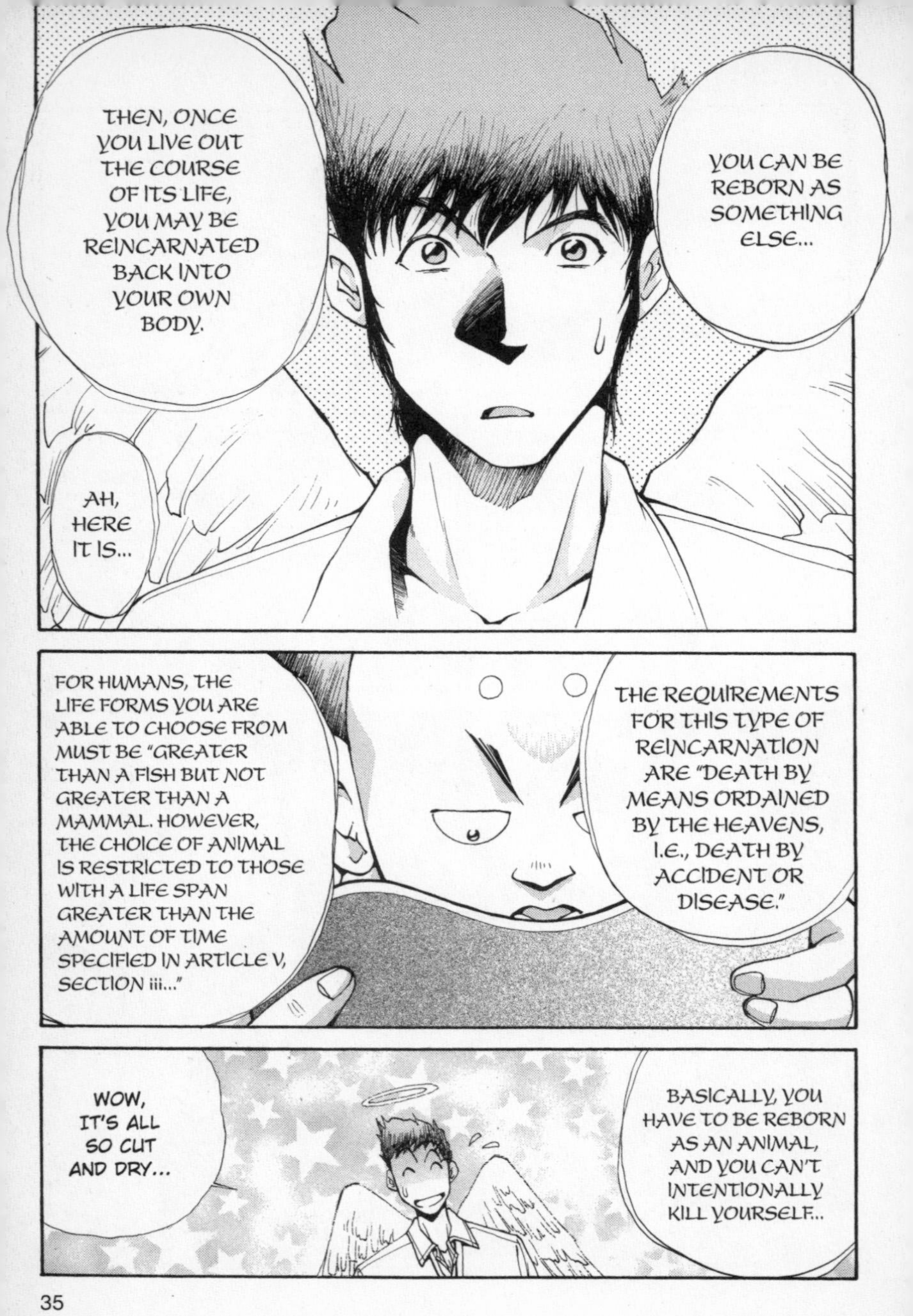
YOU CAN BE REBORN AS SOMETHING ELSE...
THEN, ONCE YOU LIVE OUT THE COURSE OF ITS LIFE, YOU MAY BE REINCARNATED BACK INTO YOUR OWN BODY.
AH, HERE IT IS...
THE REQUIREMENTS FOR THIS TYPE OF REINCARNATION ARE "DEATH BY MEANS ORDAINED BY THE HEAVENS, I.E., DEATH BY ACCIDENT OR DISEASE."
FOR HUMANS, THE LIFE FORMS YOU ARE ABLE TO CHOOSE FROM MUST BE "GREATER THAN A FISH BUT NOT GREATER THAN A MAMMAL. HOWEVER, THE CHOICE OF ANIMAL IS RESTRICTED TO THOSE WITH A LIFE SPAN GREATER THAN THE AMOUNT OF TIME SPECIFIED IN ARTICLE V, SECTION iii..."
BASICALLY, YOU HAVE TO BE REBORN AS AN ANIMAL, AND YOU CAN'T INTENTIONALLY KILL YOURSELF...
WOW, IT'S ALL SO CUT AND DRY...

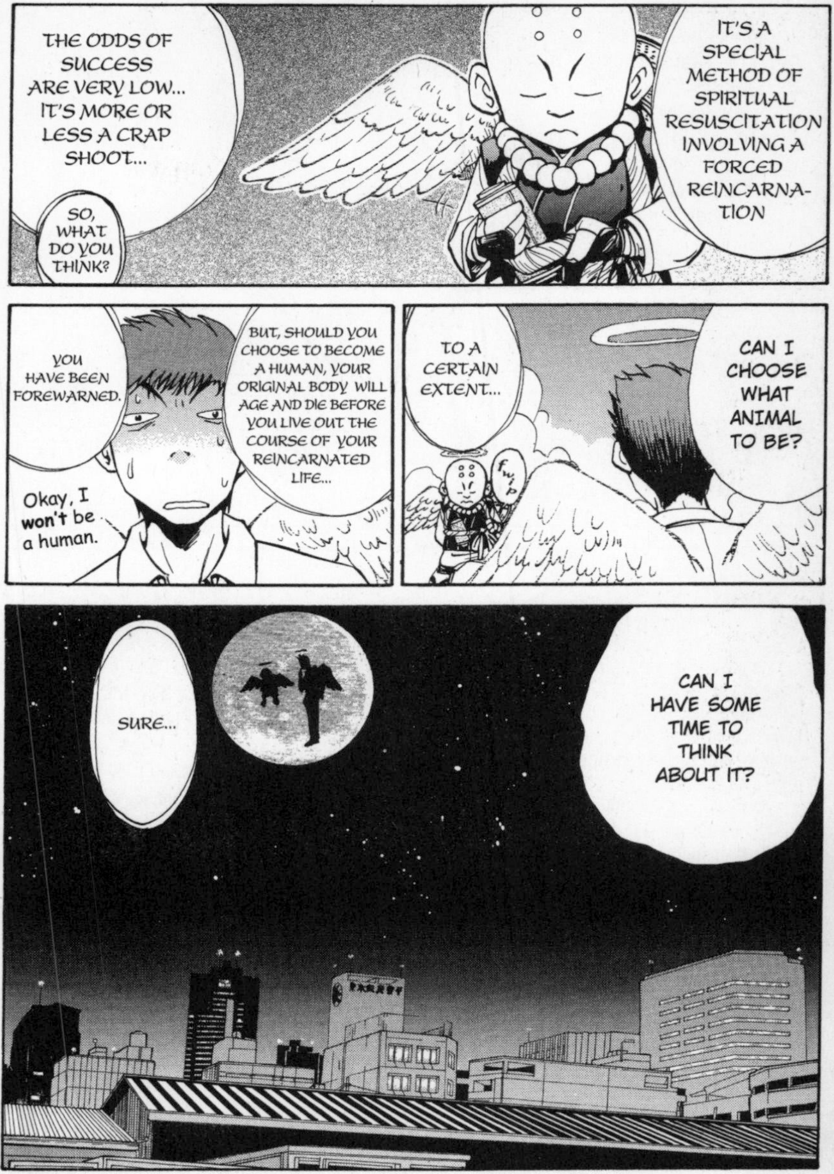
IT'S A SPECIAL METHOD OF SPIRITUAL RESUSCITATION INVOLVING A FORCED REINCARNATION
THE ODDS OF SUCCESS ARE VERY LOW... IT'S MORE OR LESS A CRAP SHOOT...
SO, WHAT DO YOU THINK?
CAN I CHOOSE WHAT ANIMAL TO BE?
TO A CERTAIN EXTENT...
fwip
BUT, SHOULD YOU CHOOSE TO BECOME A HUMAN, YOUR ORIGINAL BODY WILL AGE AND DIE BEFORE YOU LIVE OUT THE COURSE OF YOUR REINCARNATED LIFE...
YOU HAVE BEEN FOREWARNED.
Okay, I won't be a human.
CAN I HAVE SOME TIME TO THINK ABOUT IT?
SURE...

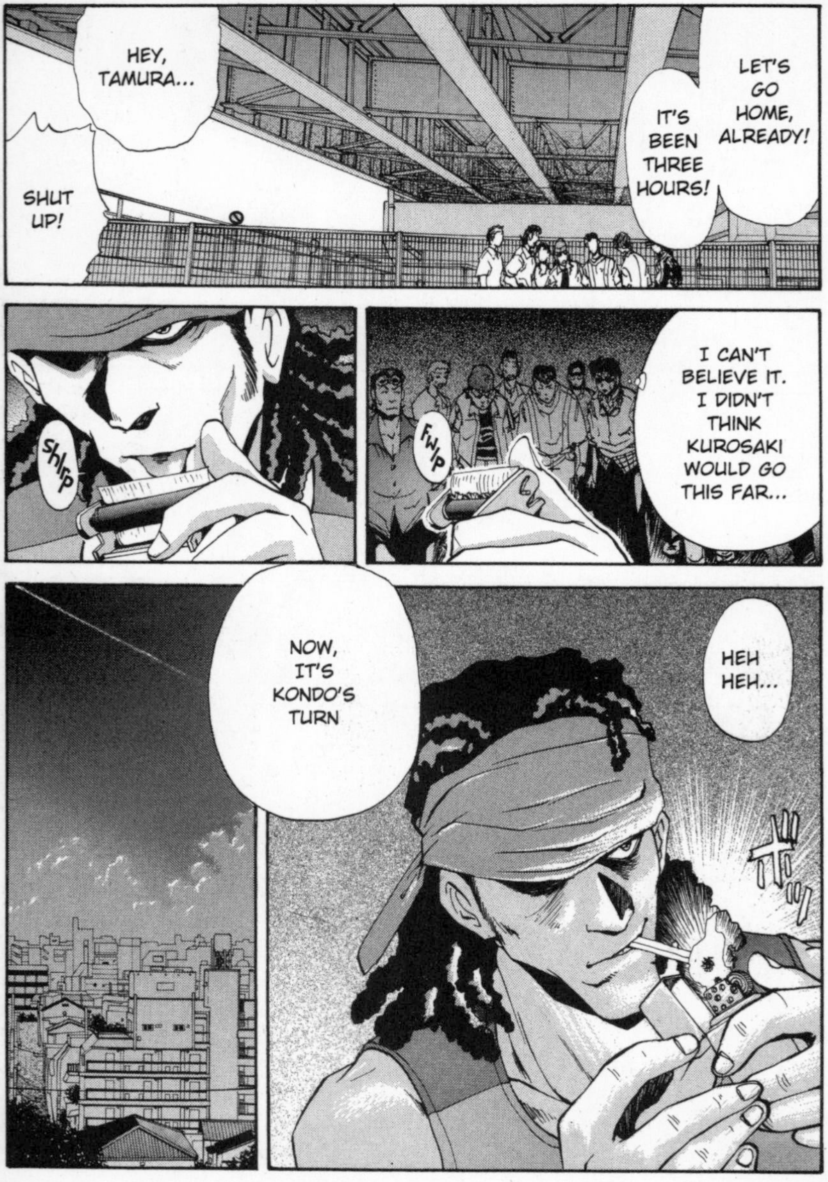
LET'S GO HOME, ALREADY!
IT'S BEEN THREE HOURS!
HEY, TAMURA...
SHUT UP!
I CAN'T BELIEVE IT. I DIDN'T THINK KUROSAKI WOULD GO THIS FAR...
FWIP
Shlrp
HEH HEH...
NOW, IT'S KONDO'S TURN

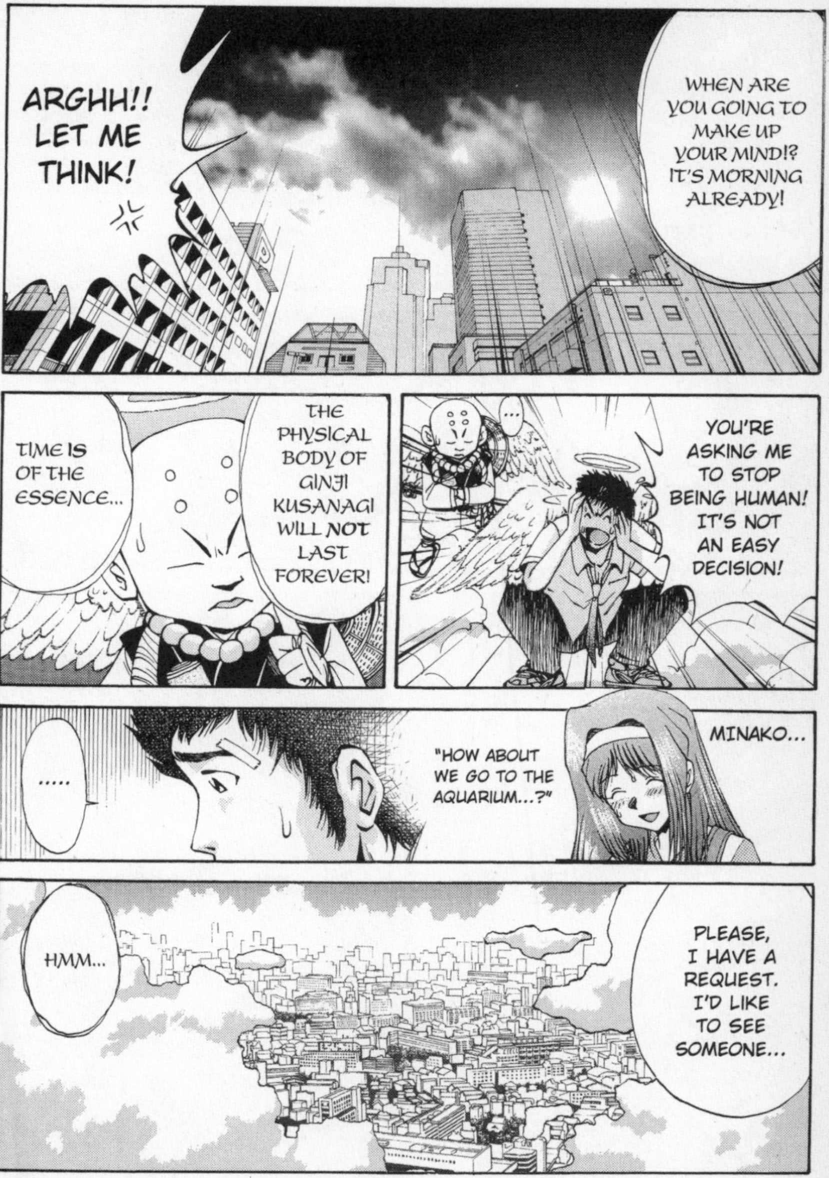
WHEN ARE YOU GOING TO MAKE UP YOUR MIND!? IT'S MORNING ALREADY!
ARGHH!! LET ME THINK!
YOU'RE ASKING ME TO STOP BEING HUMAN! IT'S NOT AN EASY DECISION!
...
THE PHYSICAL BODY OF GINJI KUSANAGI WILL NOT LAST FOREVER!
TIME IS OF THE ESSENCE...
MINAKO...
"HOW ABOUT WE GO TO THE AQUARIUM...?"
.....
PLEASE, I HAVE A REQUEST. I'D LIKE TO SEE SOMEONE...
HMM...

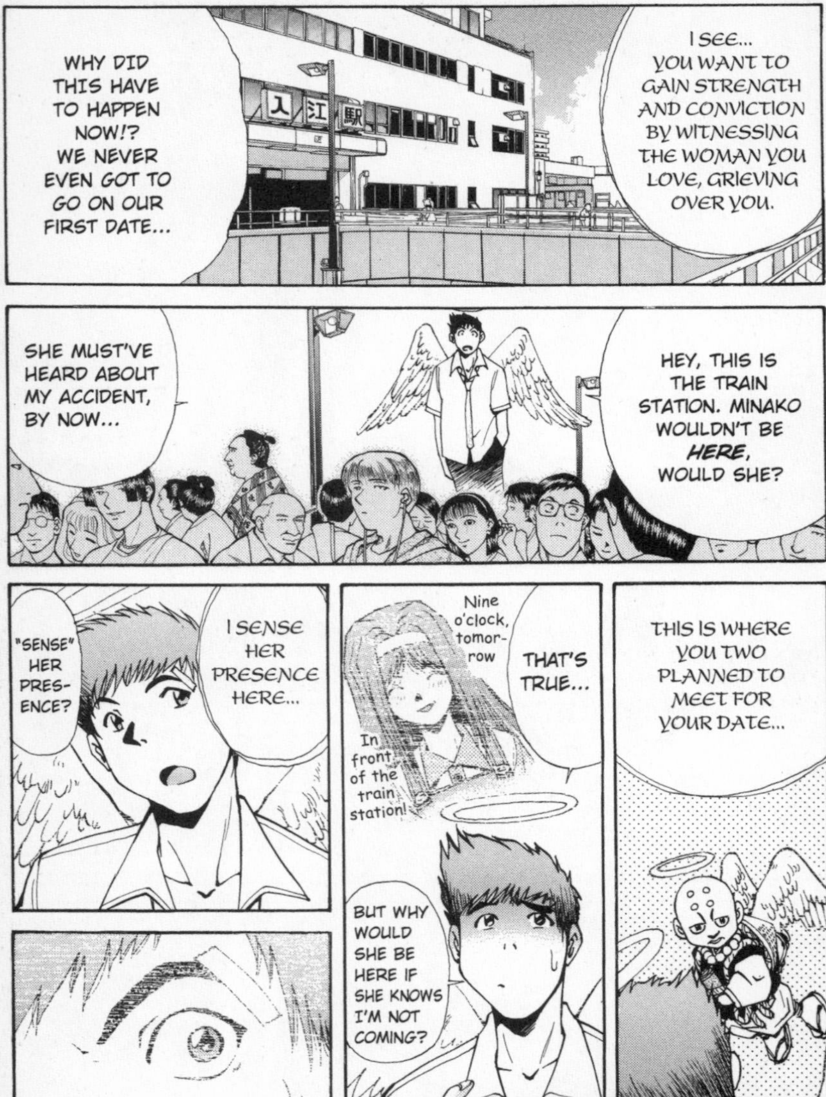
I SEE... YOU WANT TO GAIN STRENGTH AND CONVICTION BY WITNESSING THE WOMAN YOU LOVE, GRIEVING OVER YOU.
入江駅
WHY DID THIS HAVE TO HAPPEN NOW!? WE NEVER EVEN GOT TO GO ON OUR FIRST DATE...
HEY, THIS IS THE TRAIN STATION. MINAKO WOULDN'T BE *HERE*, WOULD SHE?
SHE MUST'VE HEARD ABOUT MY ACCIDENT, BY NOW...
THIS IS WHERE YOU TWO PLANNED TO MEET FOR YOUR DATE...
THAT'S TRUE...
Nine o'clock, tomorrow
In front of the train station!
BUT WHY WOULD SHE BE HERE IF SHE KNOWS I'M NOT COMING?
I SENSE HER PRESENCE HERE...
"SENSE" HER PRESENCE?

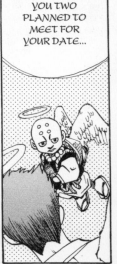

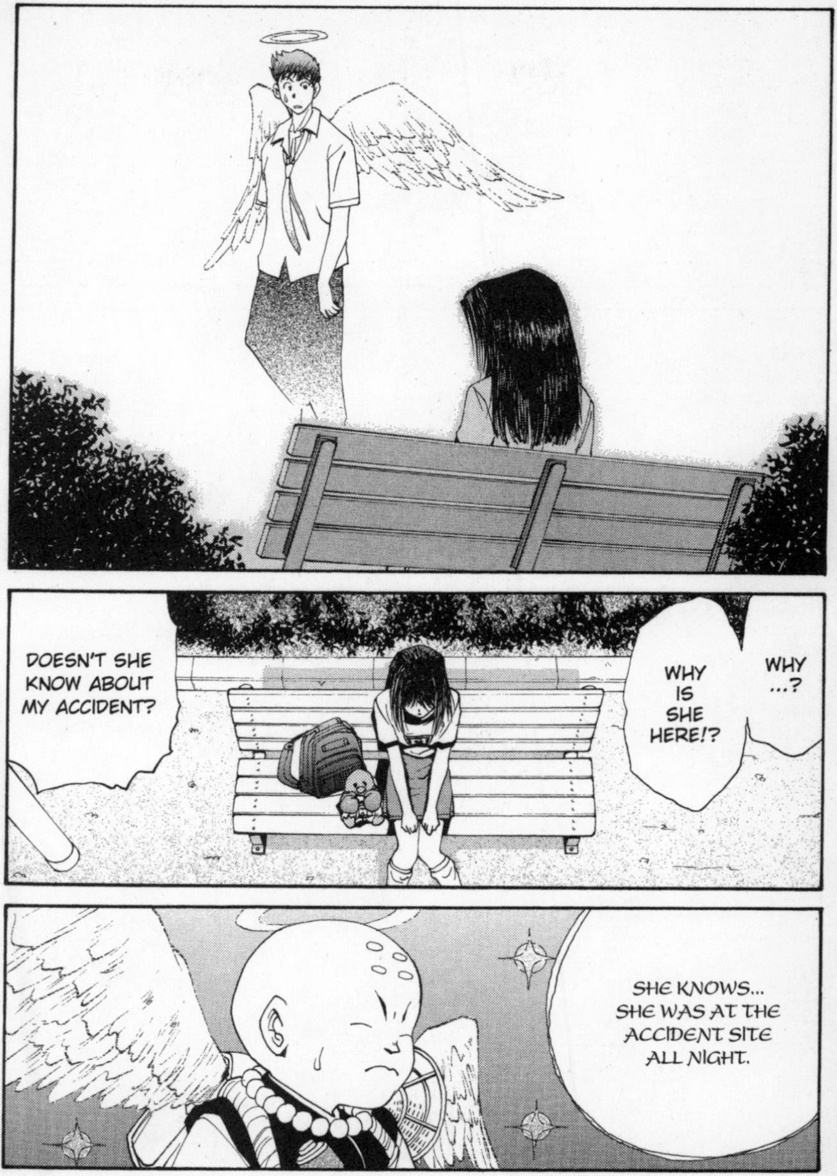
WHY ...?
WHY IS SHE HERE!?
DOESN'T SHE KNOW ABOUT MY ACCIDENT?
SHE KNOWS... SHE WAS AT THE ACCIDENT SITE ALL NIGHT.

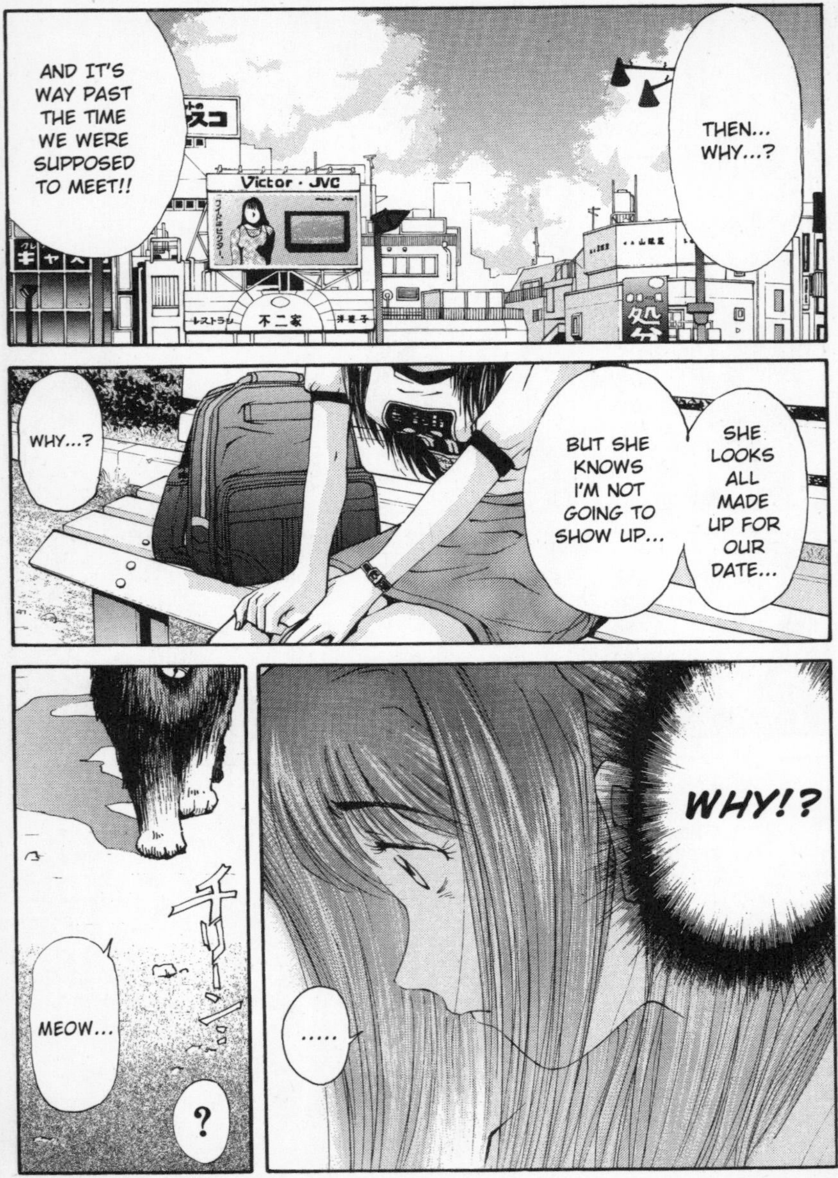
THEN... WHY...?
AND IT'S WAY PAST THE TIME WE WERE SUPPOSED TO MEET!!
Victor · JVC
不二家
SHE LOOKS ALL MADE UP FOR OUR DATE...
BUT SHE KNOWS I'M NOT GOING TO SHOW UP...
WHY...?
WHY!?
.....
MEOW...
?

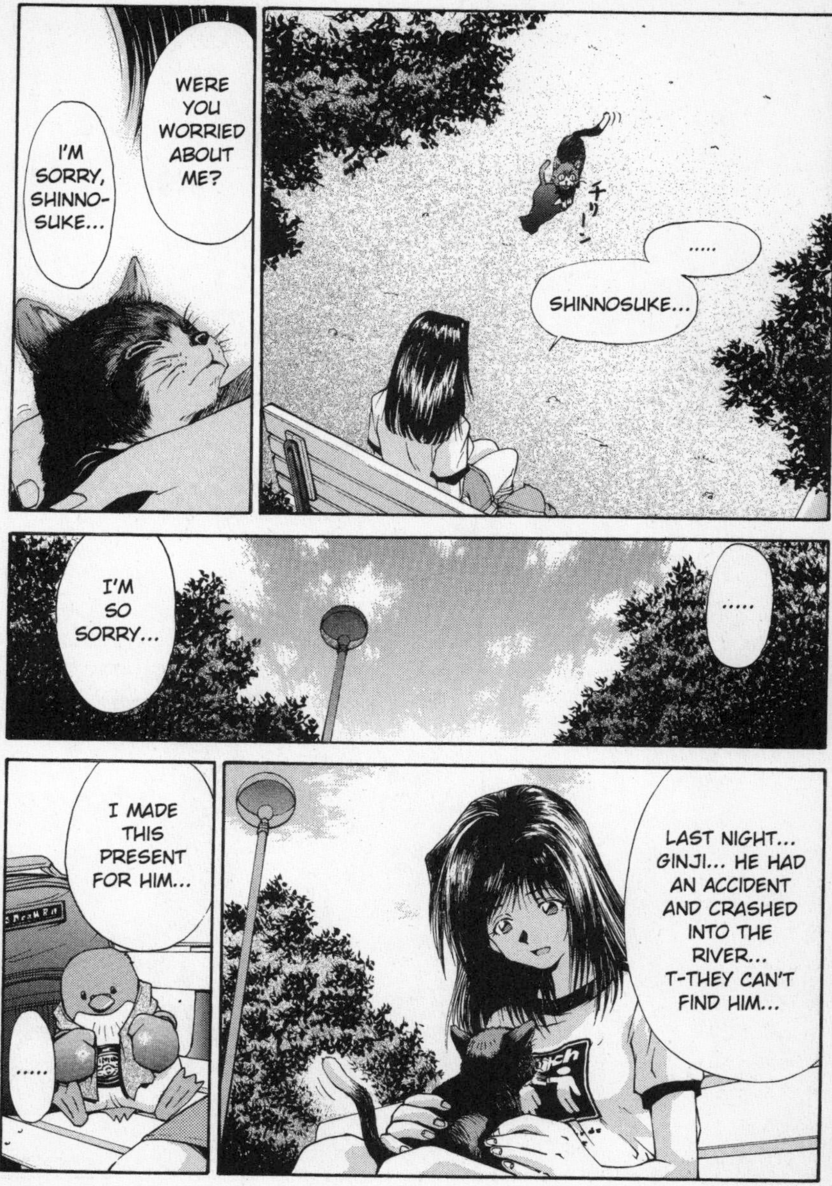
.....
SHINNOSUKE...
チリーン
WERE YOU WORRIED ABOUT ME?
I'M SORRY, SHINNO-SUKE...
.....
I'M SO SORRY...
LAST NIGHT... GINJI... HE HAD AN ACCIDENT AND CRASHED INTO THE RIVER... T-THEY CAN'T FIND HIM...
I MADE THIS PRESENT FOR HIM...
.....

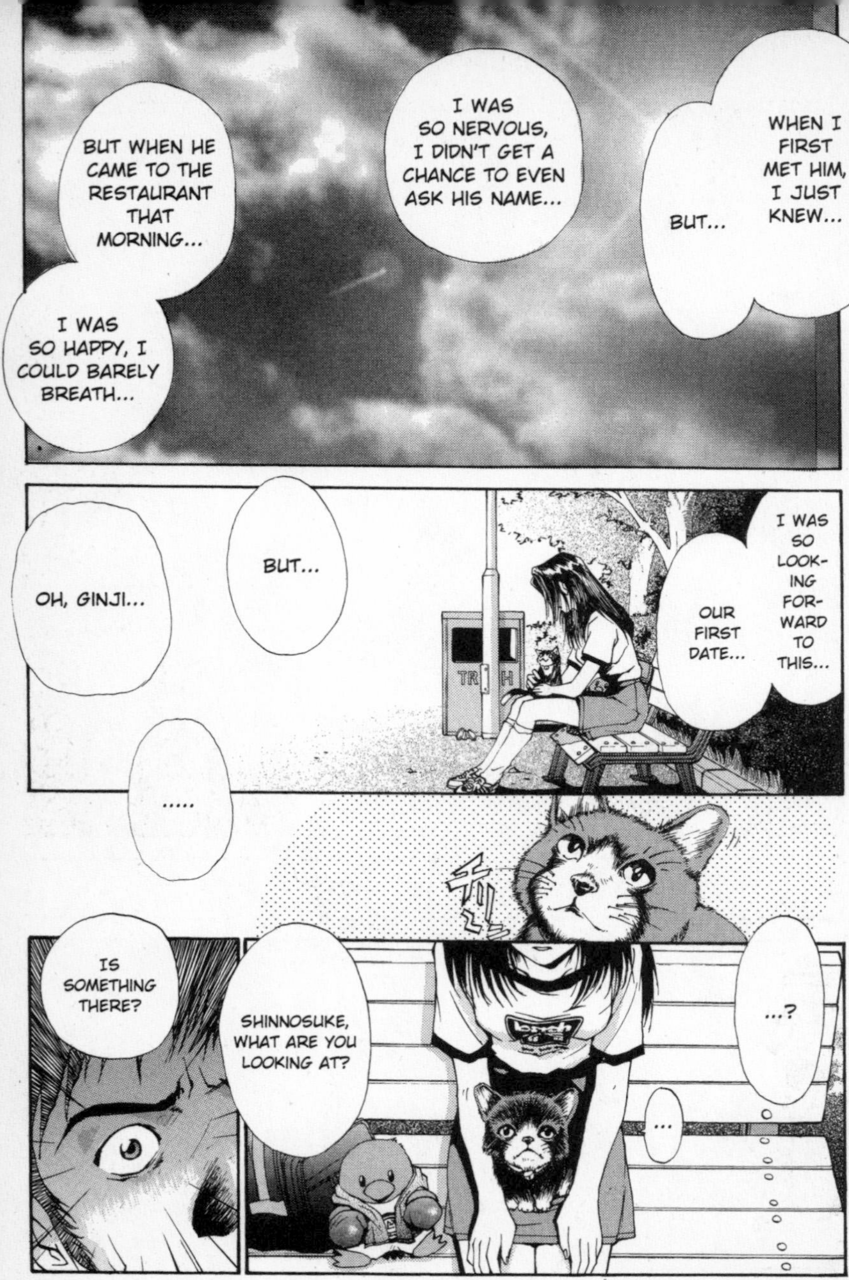
WHEN I FIRST MET HIM, I JUST KNEW...
BUT...
I WAS SO NERVOUS, I DIDN'T GET A CHANCE TO EVEN ASK HIS NAME...
BUT WHEN HE CAME TO THE RESTAURANT THAT MORNING...
I WAS SO HAPPY, I COULD BARELY BREATH...
I WAS SO LOOKING FORWARD TO THIS...
OUR FIRST DATE...
BUT...
OH, GINJI...
.....
...?
...
SHINNOSUKE, WHAT ARE YOU LOOKING AT?
IS SOMETHING THERE?

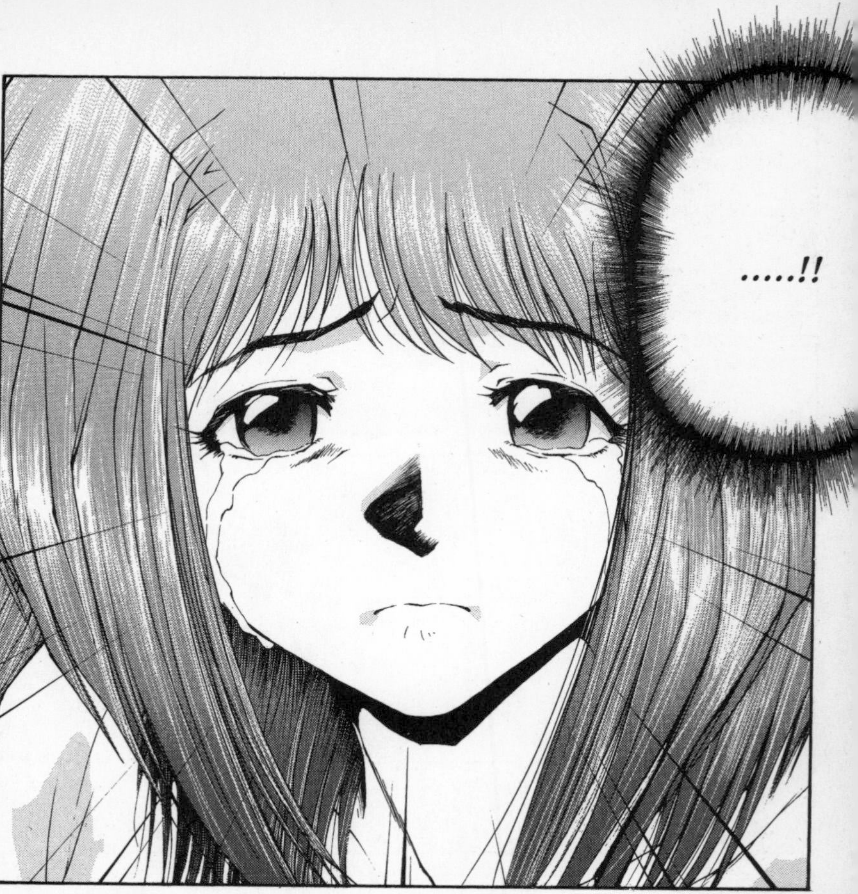
.....!!

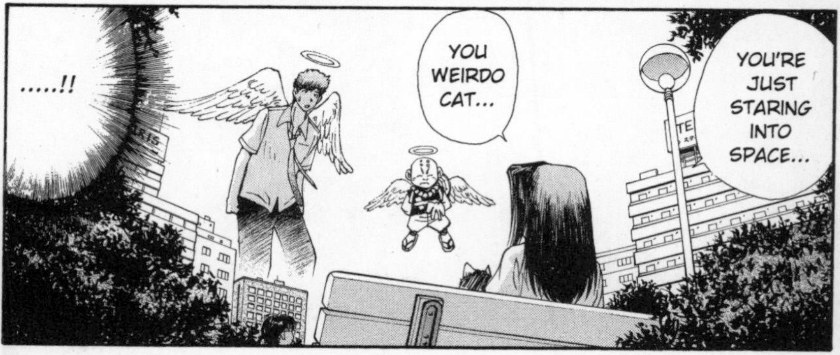
YOU'RE JUST STARING INTO SPACE...
YOU WEIRDO CAT...
.....!!

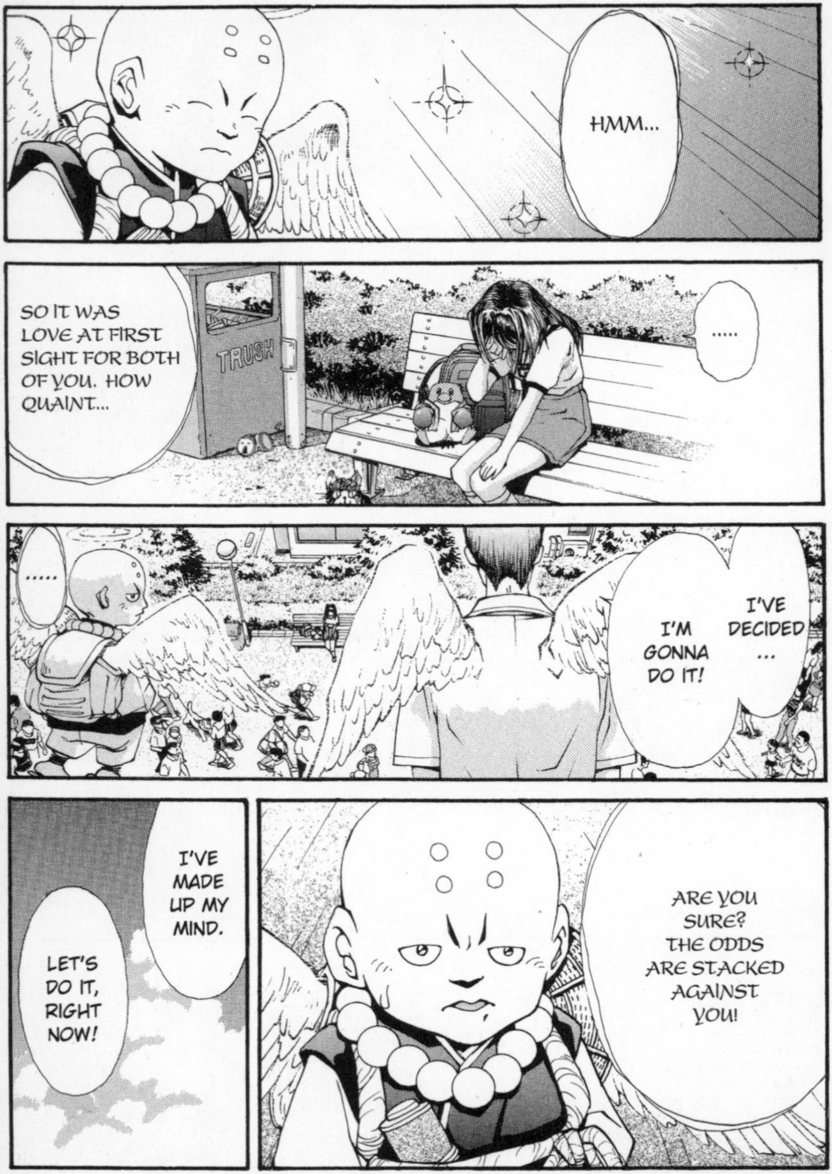

HMM...
.....
SO IT WAS LOVE AT FIRST SIGHT FOR BOTH OF YOU. HOW QUAINT...
TRUSH
I'VE DECIDED ...
I'M GONNA DO IT!
.....
ARE YOU SURE? THE ODDS ARE STACKED AGAINST YOU!
I'VE MADE UP MY MIND.
LET'S DO IT, RIGHT NOW!

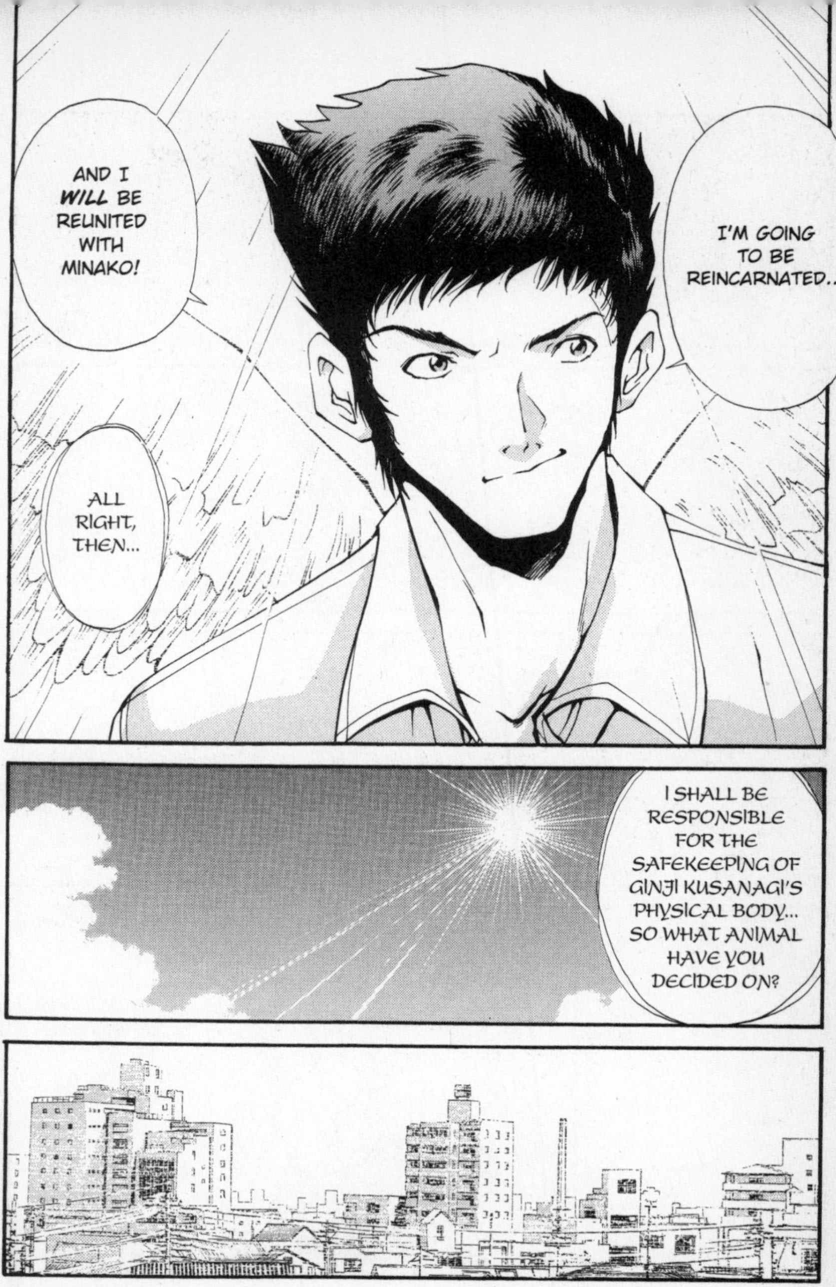
I'M GOING TO BE REINCARNATED...
AND I *WILL* BE REUNITED WITH MINAKO!
ALL RIGHT, THEN...
I SHALL BE RESPONSIBLE FOR THE SAFEKEEPING OF GINJI KUSANAGI'S PHYSICAL BODY... SO WHAT ANIMAL HAVE YOU DECIDED ON?

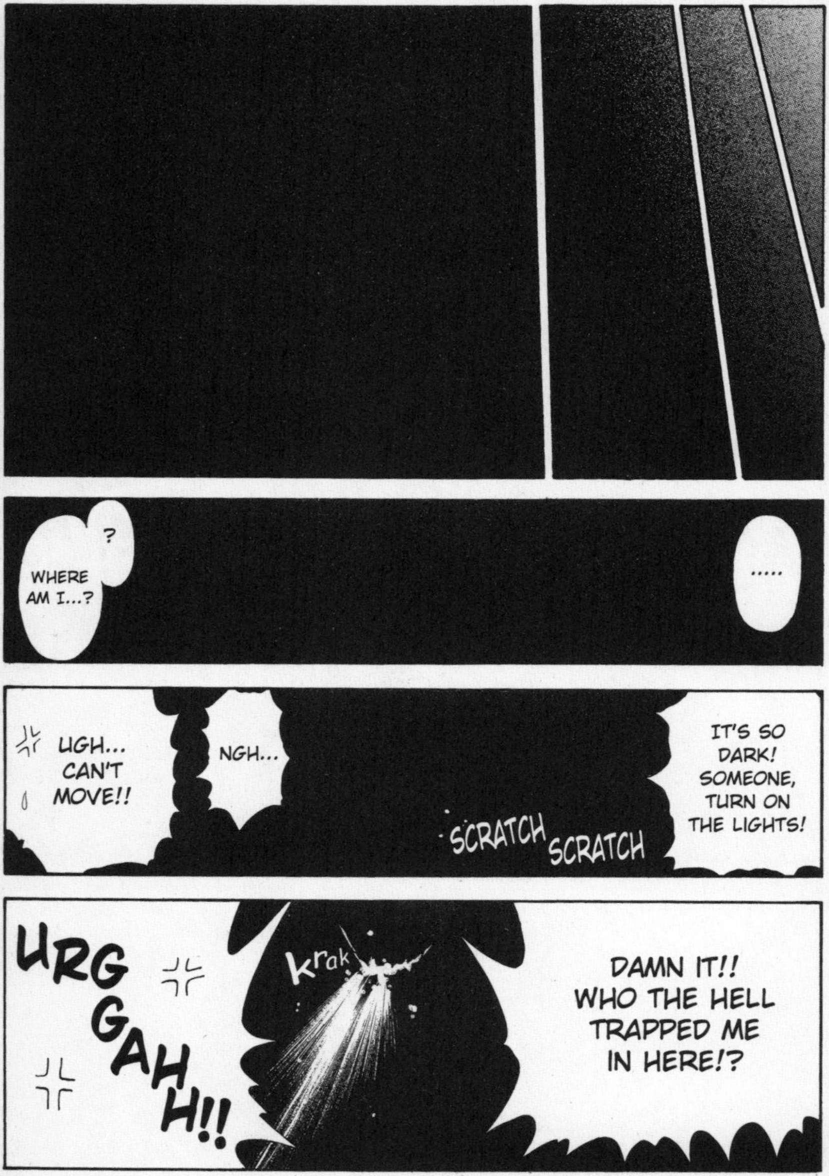
.....
?
WHERE AM I...?
IT'S SO DARK! SOMEONE, TURN ON THE LIGHTS!
SCRATCH SCRATCH
NGH...
UGH... CAN'T MOVE!!
DAMN IT!! WHO THE HELL TRAPPED ME IN HERE!?
krak
URG GAHH!!

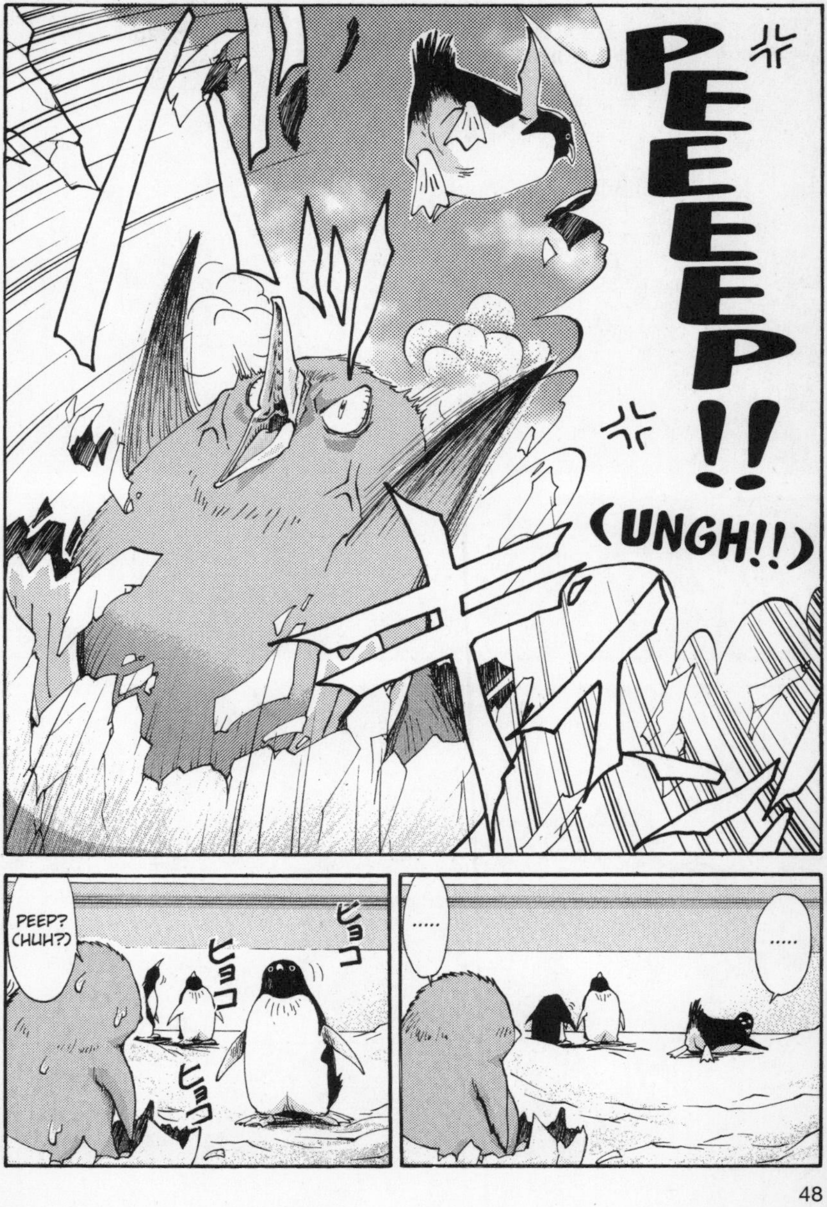
PEEEEP!!
(UNGH!!)
.....
.....
PEEP? (HUH?)
ヒョコ
ヒョコ
ヒョコ

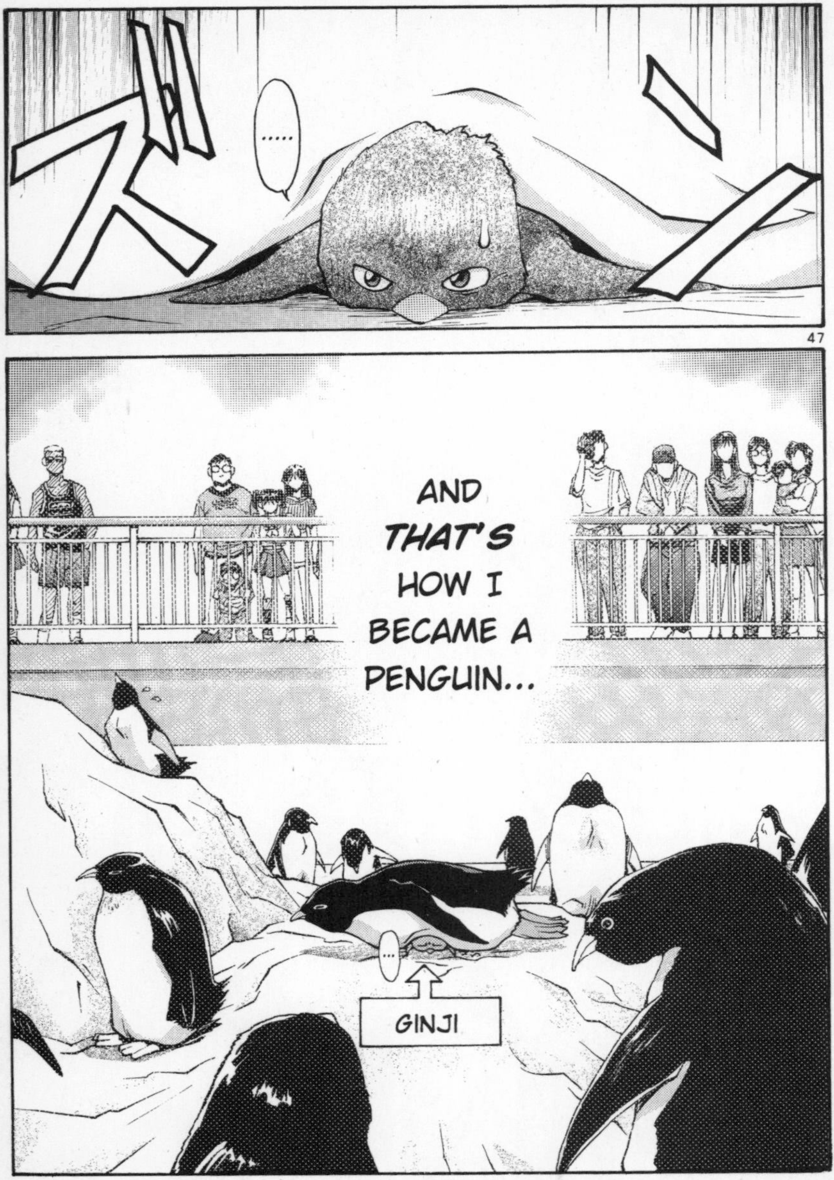
......
47
AND *THAT'S* HOW I BECAME A PENGUIN...
...
GINJI

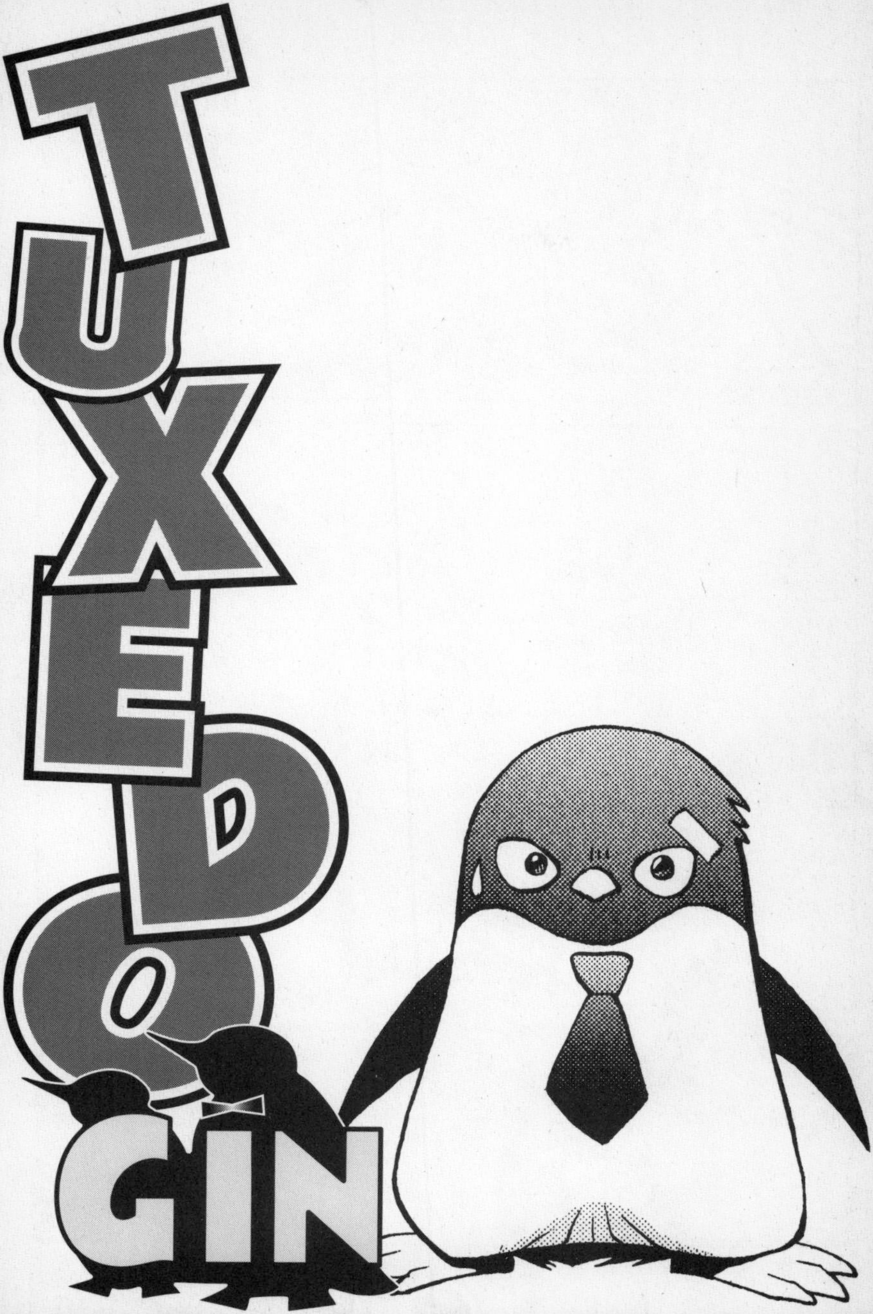
TUXEDO
GIN

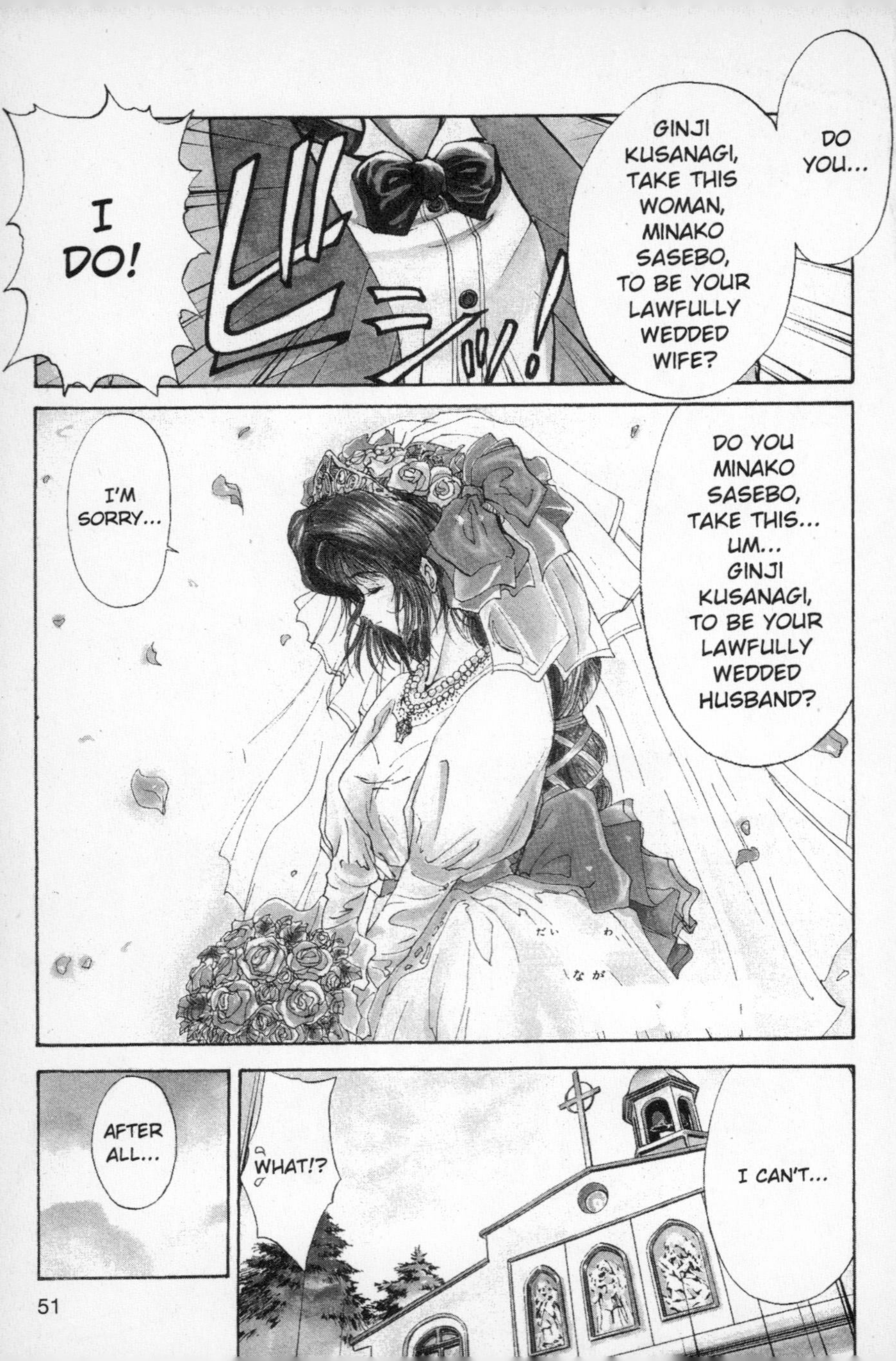

DO YOU...
GINJI KUSANAGI, TAKE THIS WOMAN, MINAKO SASEBO, TO BE YOUR LAWFULLY WEDDED WIFE?
I DO!
DO YOU MINAKO SASEBO, TAKE THIS... UM... GINJI KUSANAGI, TO BE YOUR LAWFULLY WEDDED HUSBAND?
I'M SORRY...
I CAN'T...
WHAT!?
AFTER ALL...

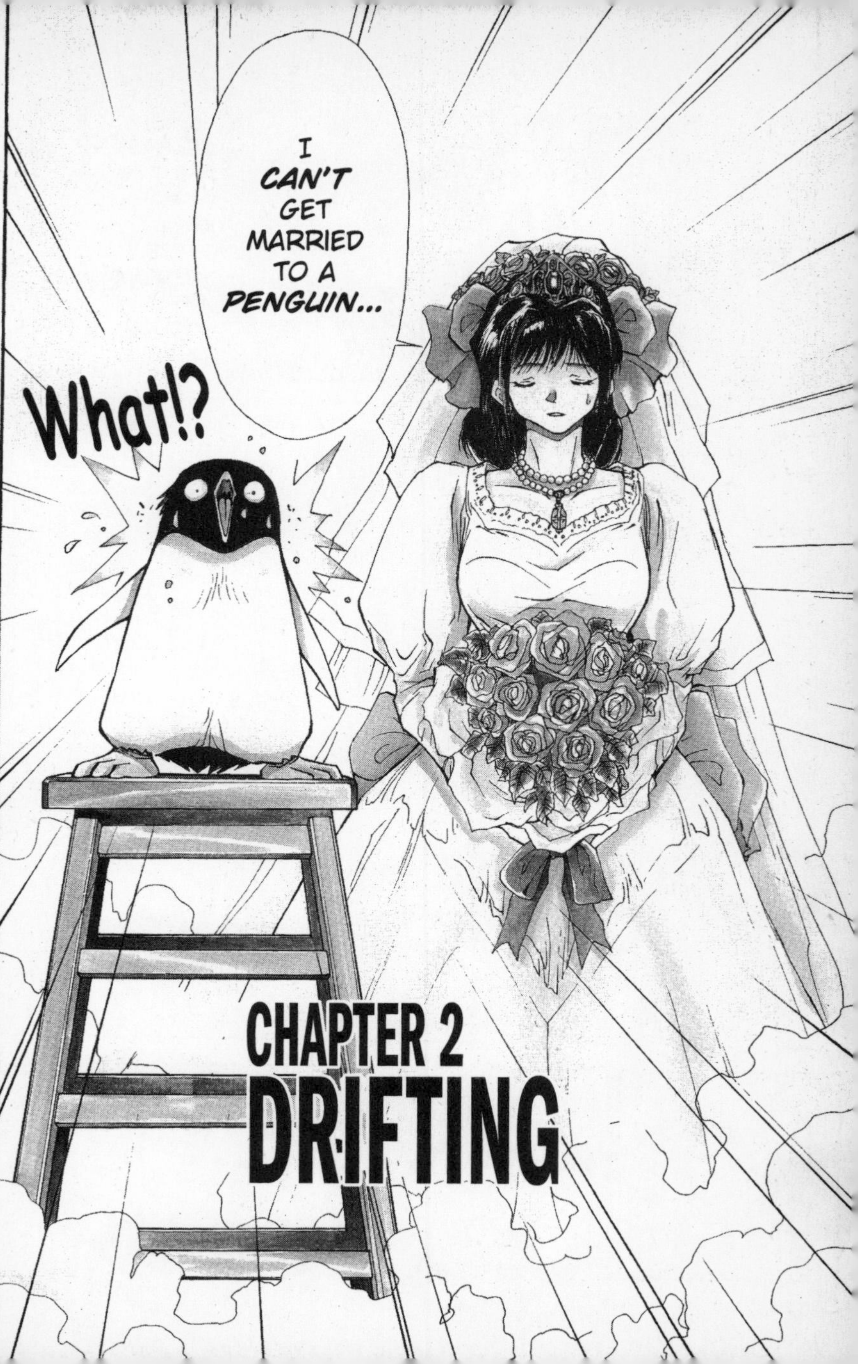
I CAN'T GET MARRIED TO A PENGUIN...
What!?
CHAPTER 2
DRIFTING

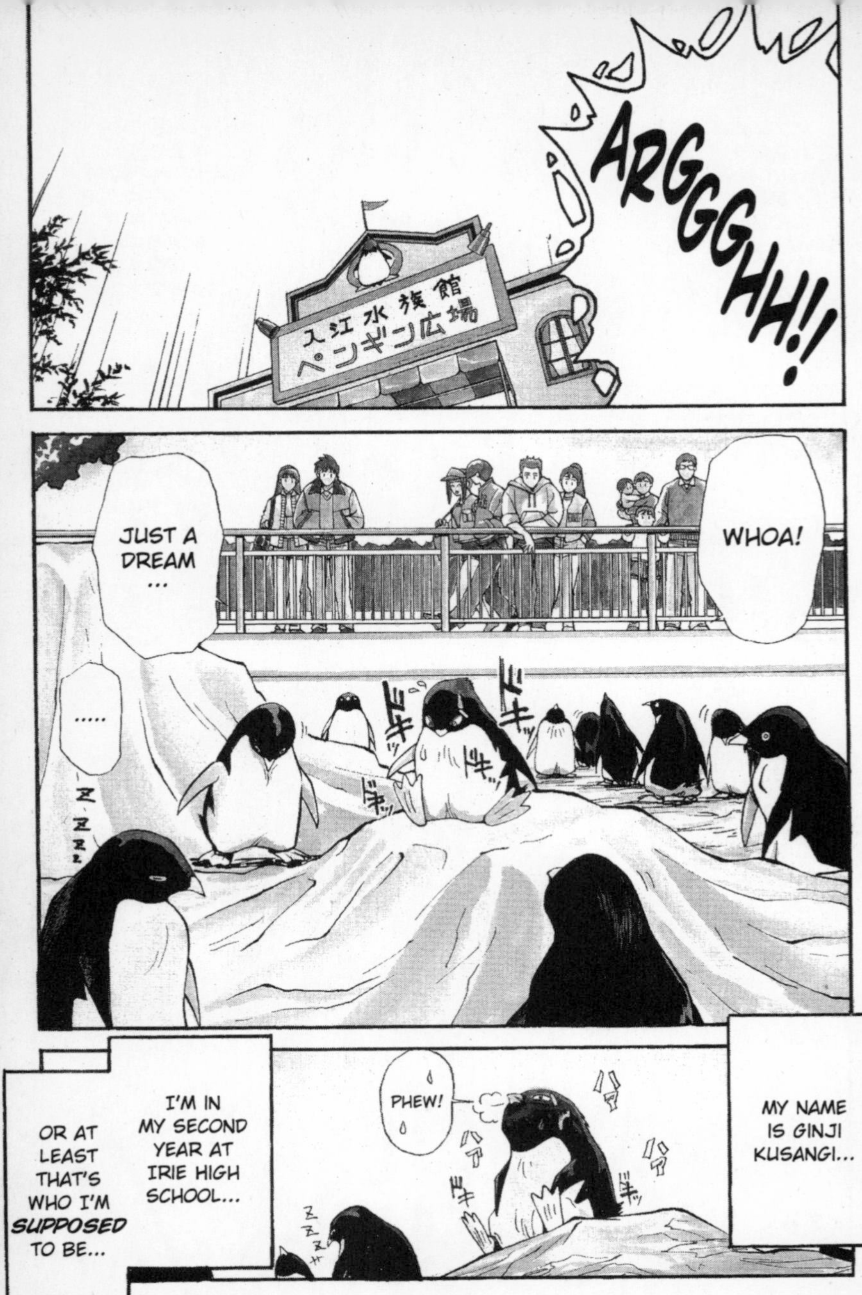
ARGGGHH!!
入江水族館
ペンギン広場
WHOA!
JUST A DREAM ...
.....
MY NAME IS GINJI KUSANGI...
PHEW!
I'M IN MY SECOND YEAR AT IRIE HIGH SCHOOL...
OR AT LEAST THAT'S WHO I'M *SUPPOSED* TO BE...

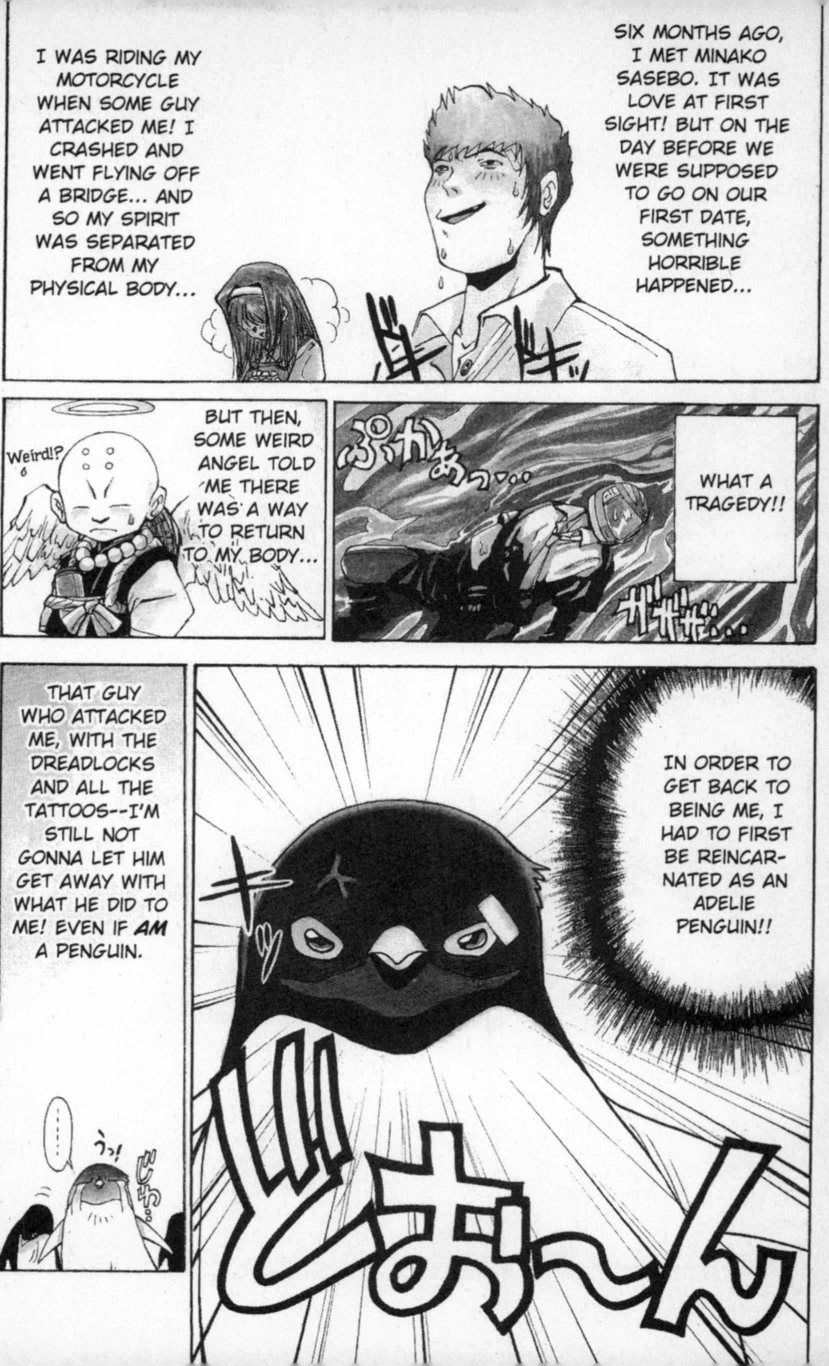

SIX MONTHS AGO, I MET MINAKO SASEBO. IT WAS LOVE AT FIRST SIGHT! BUT ON THE DAY BEFORE WE WERE SUPPOSED TO GO ON OUR FIRST DATE, SOMETHING HORRIBLE HAPPENED...
I WAS RIDING MY MOTORCYCLE WHEN SOME GUY ATTACKED ME! I CRASHED AND WENT FLYING OFF A BRIDGE... AND SO MY SPIRIT WAS SEPARATED FROM MY PHYSICAL BODY...
WHAT A TRAGEDY!!
ぷかあっ...
ザザザ...
BUT THEN, SOME WEIRD ANGEL TOLD ME THERE WAS A WAY TO RETURN TO MY BODY...
Weird!?
IN ORDER TO GET BACK TO BEING ME, I HAD TO FIRST BE REINCARNATED AS AN ADELIE PENGUIN!!
どぉ～ん
THAT GUY WHO ATTACKED ME, WITH THE DREADLOCKS AND ALL THE TATTOOS--I'M STILL NOT GONNA LET HIM GET AWAY WITH WHAT HE DID TO ME! EVEN IF ***AM*** A PENGUIN.
......
うっ!
じわっ

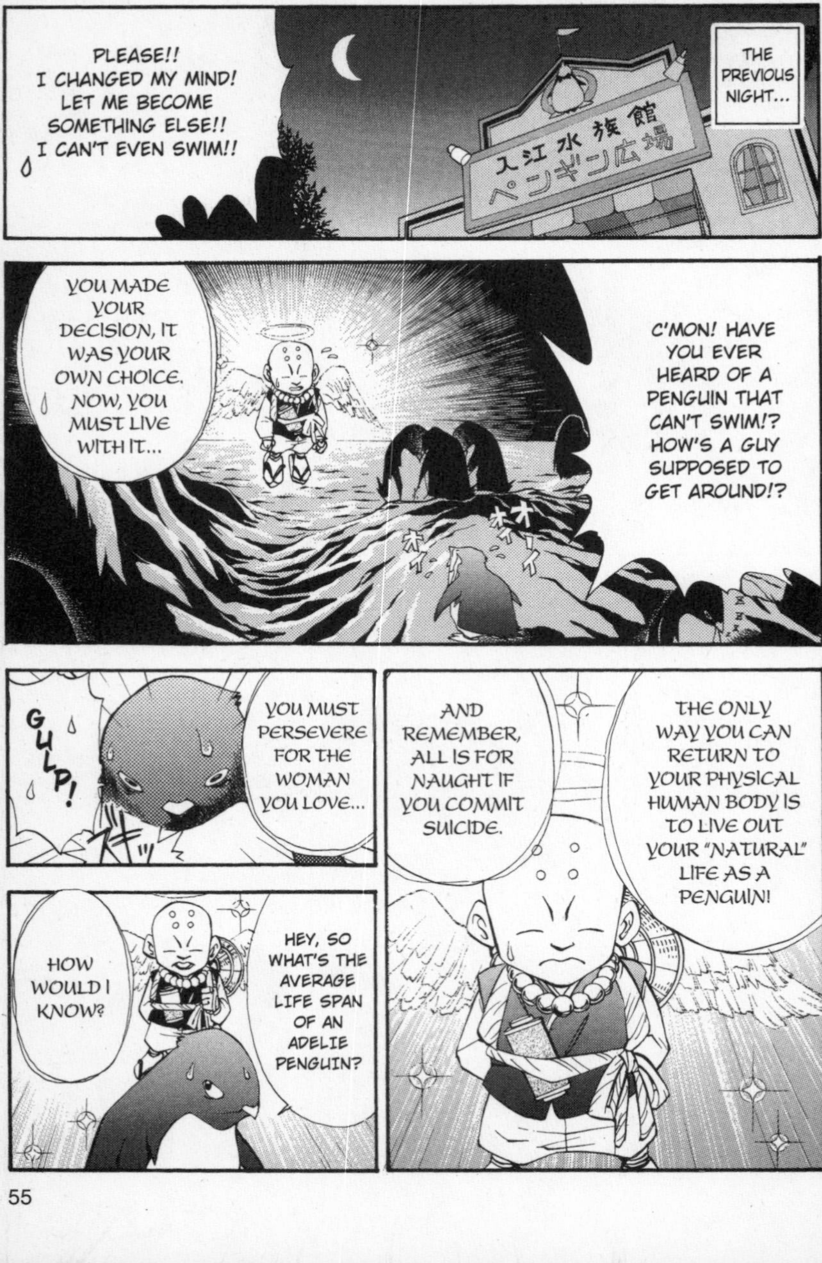
THE PREVIOUS NIGHT...
入江水族館
ペンギン広場
PLEASE!! I CHANGED MY MIND! LET ME BECOME SOMETHING ELSE!! I CAN'T EVEN SWIM!!
C'MON! HAVE YOU EVER HEARD OF A PENGUIN THAT CAN'T SWIM!? HOW'S A GUY SUPPOSED TO GET AROUND!?
YOU MADE YOUR DECISION, IT WAS YOUR OWN CHOICE. NOW, YOU MUST LIVE WITH IT...
THE ONLY WAY YOU CAN RETURN TO YOUR PHYSICAL HUMAN BODY IS TO LIVE OUT YOUR "NATURAL" LIFE AS A PENGUIN!
AND REMEMBER, ALL IS FOR NAUGHT IF YOU COMMIT SUICIDE.
YOU MUST PERSEVERE FOR THE WOMAN YOU LOVE...
GULP!
HEY, SO WHAT'S THE AVERAGE LIFE SPAN OF AN ADELIE PENGUIN?
HOW WOULD I KNOW?

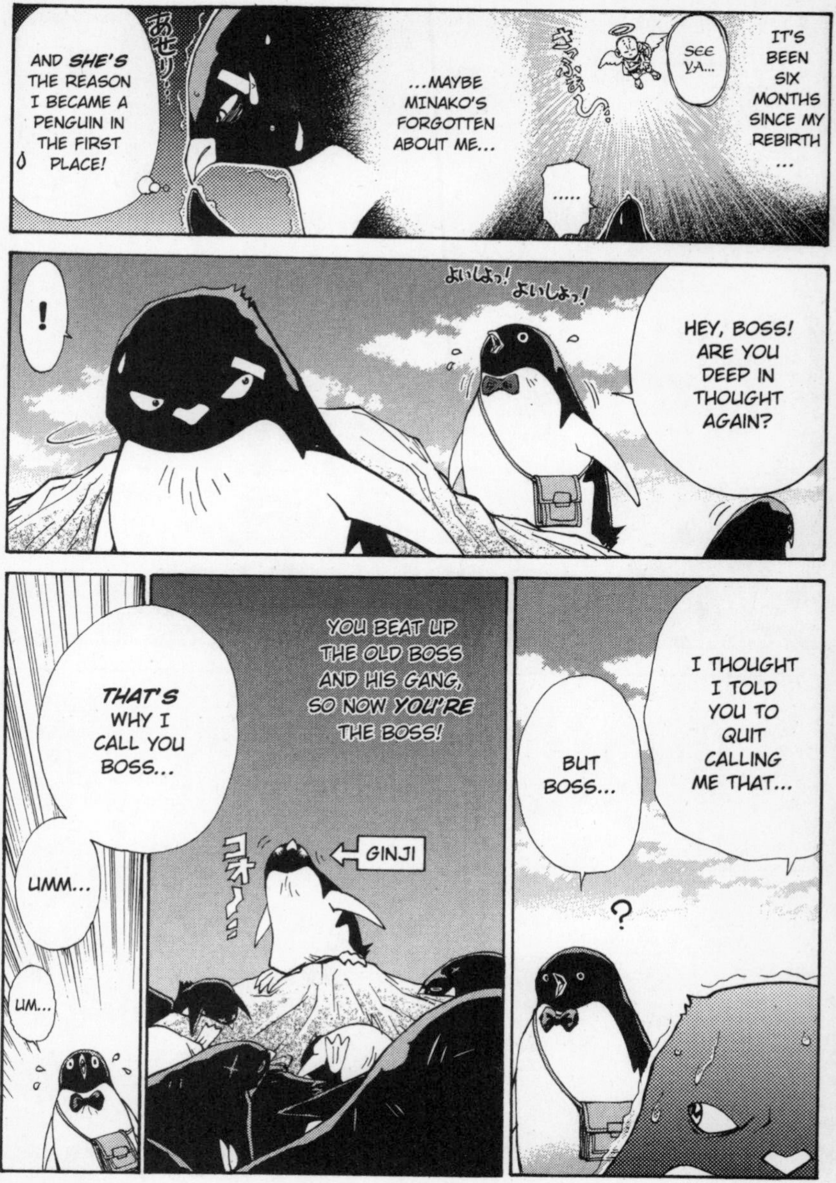
IT'S BEEN SIX MONTHS SINCE MY REBIRTH ...
SEE YA...
.....
...MAYBE MINAKO'S FORGOTTEN ABOUT ME...
あせり
AND SHE'S THE REASON I BECAME A PENGUIN IN THE FIRST PLACE!
HEY, BOSS! ARE YOU DEEP IN THOUGHT AGAIN?
よいしょっ! よいしょっ!
!
I THOUGHT I TOLD YOU TO QUIT CALLING ME THAT...
BUT BOSS...
?
YOU BEAT UP THE OLD BOSS AND HIS GANG, SO NOW YOU'RE THE BOSS!
GINJI
THAT'S WHY I CALL YOU BOSS...
UMM...
UM...

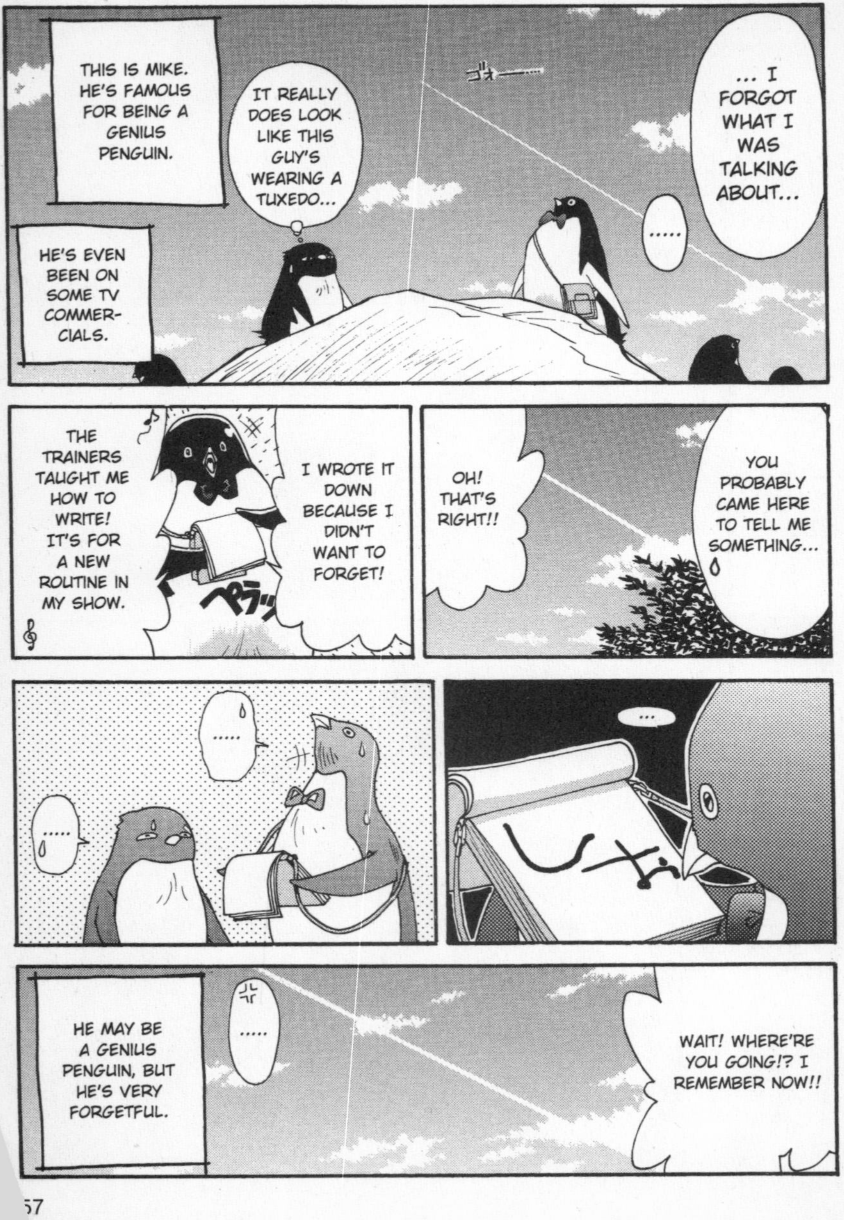
... I FORGOT WHAT I WAS TALKING ABOUT...
......
ゴォー......
IT REALLY DOES LOOK LIKE THIS GUY'S WEARING A TUXEDO...
THIS IS MIKE. HE'S FAMOUS FOR BEING A GENIUS PENGUIN.
HE'S EVEN BEEN ON SOME TV COMMER-CIALS.
YOU PROBABLY CAME HERE TO TELL ME SOMETHING...
OH! THAT'S RIGHT!!
I WROTE IT DOWN BECAUSE I DIDN'T WANT TO FORGET!
THE TRAINERS TAUGHT ME HOW TO WRITE! IT'S FOR A NEW ROUTINE IN MY SHOW.
ペラッ
...
......
......
WAIT! WHERE'RE YOU GOING!? I REMEMBER NOW!!
......
HE MAY BE A GENIUS PENGUIN, BUT HE'S VERY FORGETFUL.

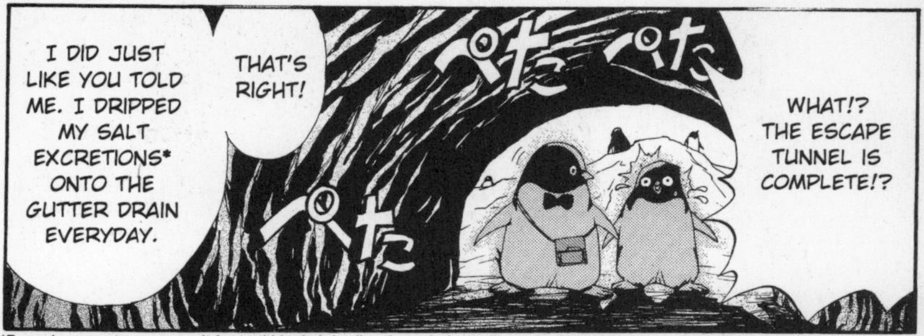
WHAT!? THE ESCAPE TUNNEL IS COMPLETE!?
ぺた
ぺた
THAT'S RIGHT!
I DID JUST LIKE YOU TOLD ME. I DRIPPED MY SALT EXCRETIONS* ONTO THE GUTTER DRAIN EVERYDAY.
ぺた

*Penguins excrete excess salt from within their bodies through ducts that pass through the nares (nostrils).

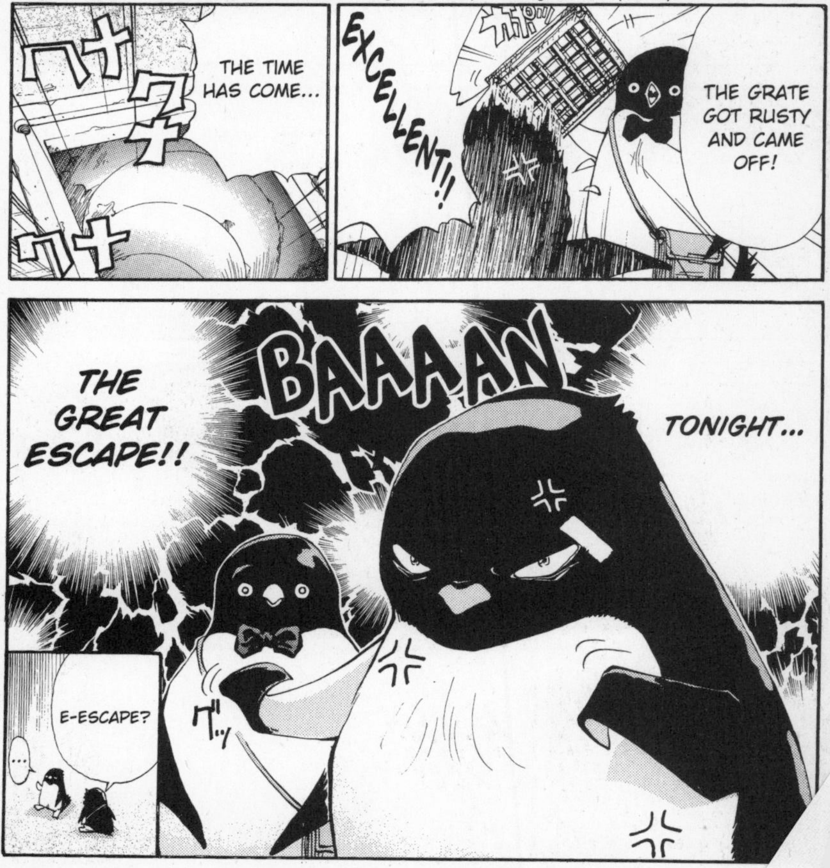
THE GRATE GOT RUSTY AND CAME OFF!
EXCELLENT!!
THE TIME HAS COME...
ワナワナ
ワナ
TONIGHT...
BAAAAAN
THE GREAT ESCAPE!!
E-ESCAPE?
...

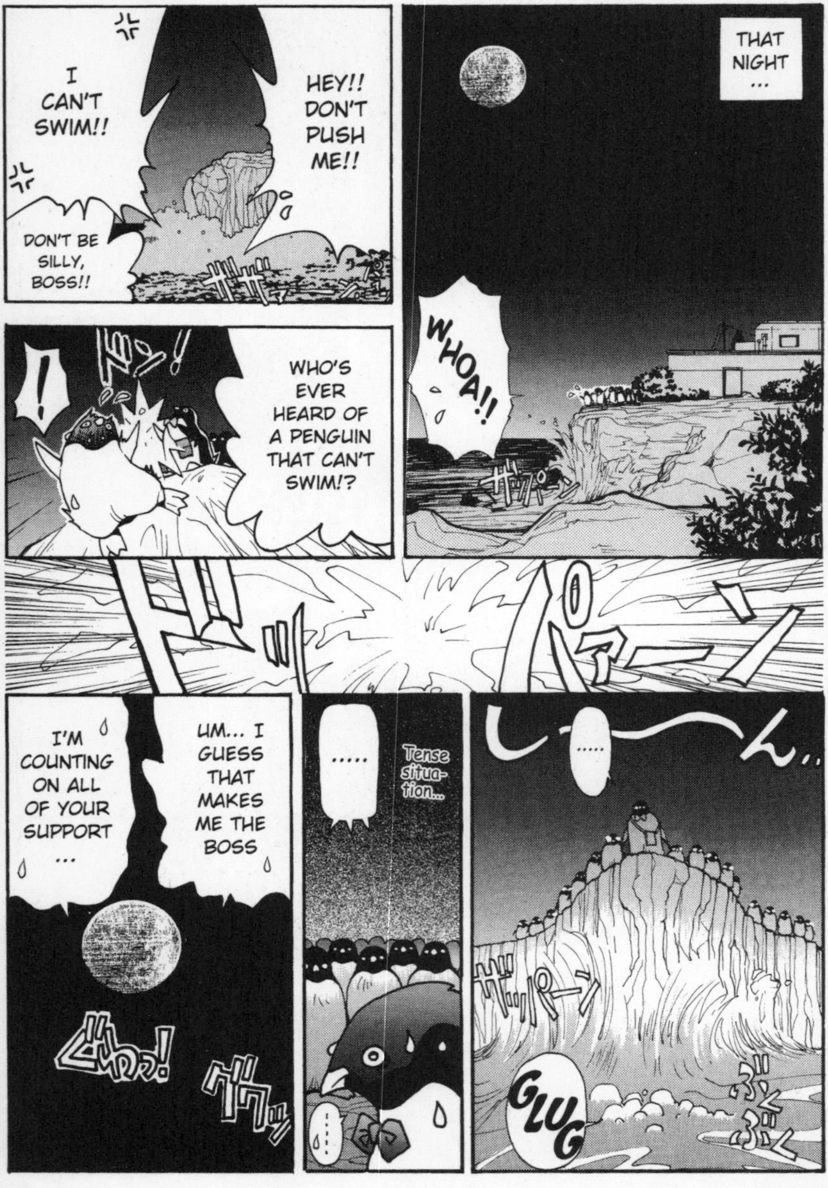
THAT NIGHT ...
WHOA!!
HEY!! DON'T PUSH ME!!
I CAN'T SWIM!!
DON'T BE SILLY, BOSS!!
WHO'S EVER HEARD OF A PENGUIN THAT CAN'T SWIM!?
.....
GLUG
.....
Tense situation...
UM... I GUESS THAT MAKES ME THE BOSS
I'M COUNTING ON ALL OF YOUR SUPPORT ...

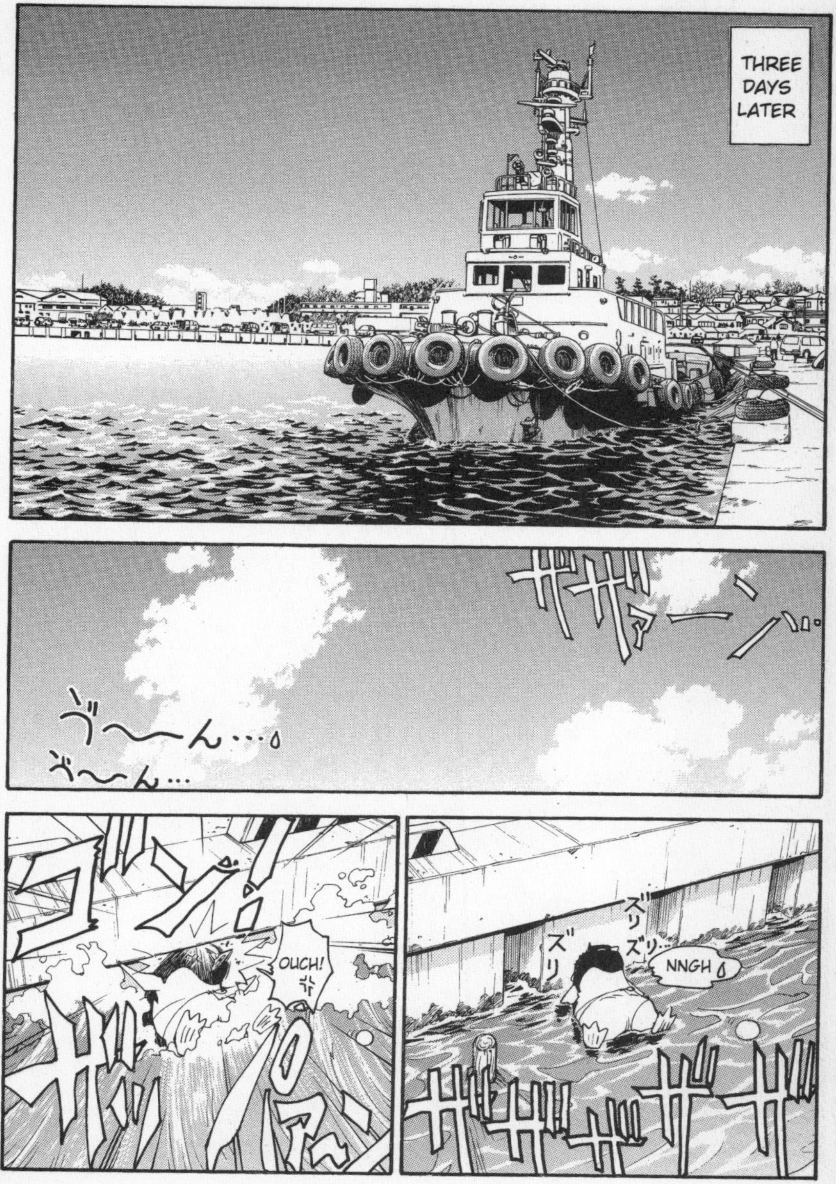
THREE DAYS LATER
NNGH
OUCH!

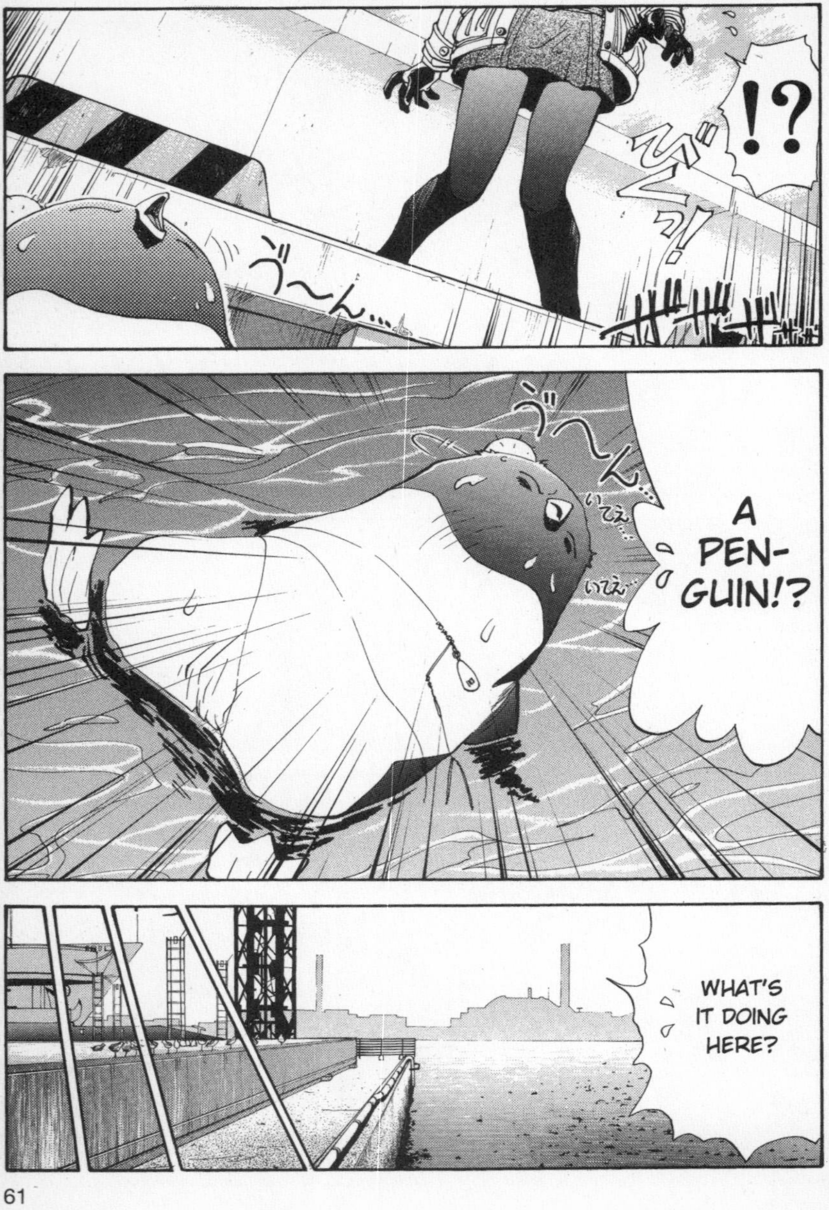

!?
びくっ!
う~ん…
う~ん…
いてぇ…
いてぇ…
A PEN-GUIN!?
WHAT'S IT DOING HERE?

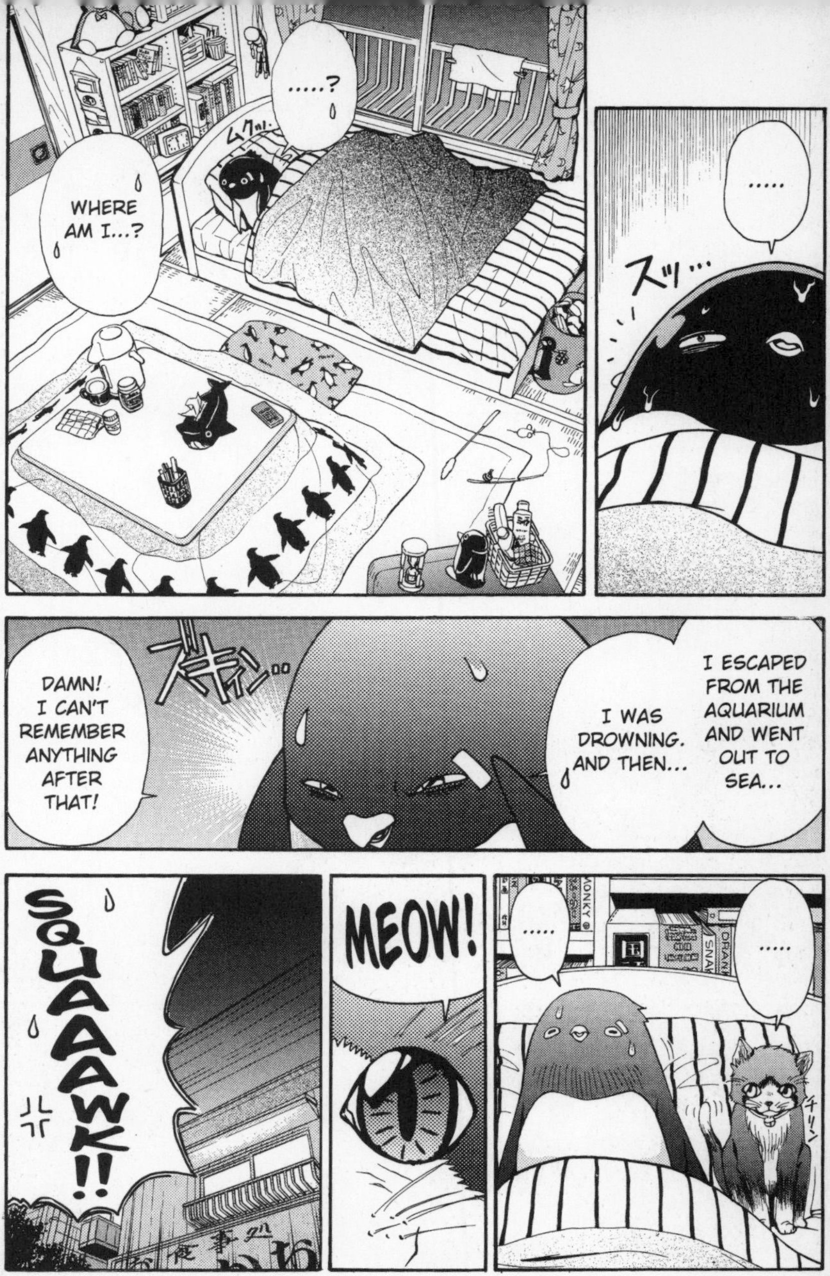
.....
.....?
WHERE AM I...?
I ESCAPED FROM THE AQUARIUM AND WENT OUT TO SEA...
I WAS DROWNING. AND THEN...
DAMN! I CAN'T REMEMBER ANYTHING AFTER THAT!
.....
.....
MEOW!
SQUAAAAWK!!

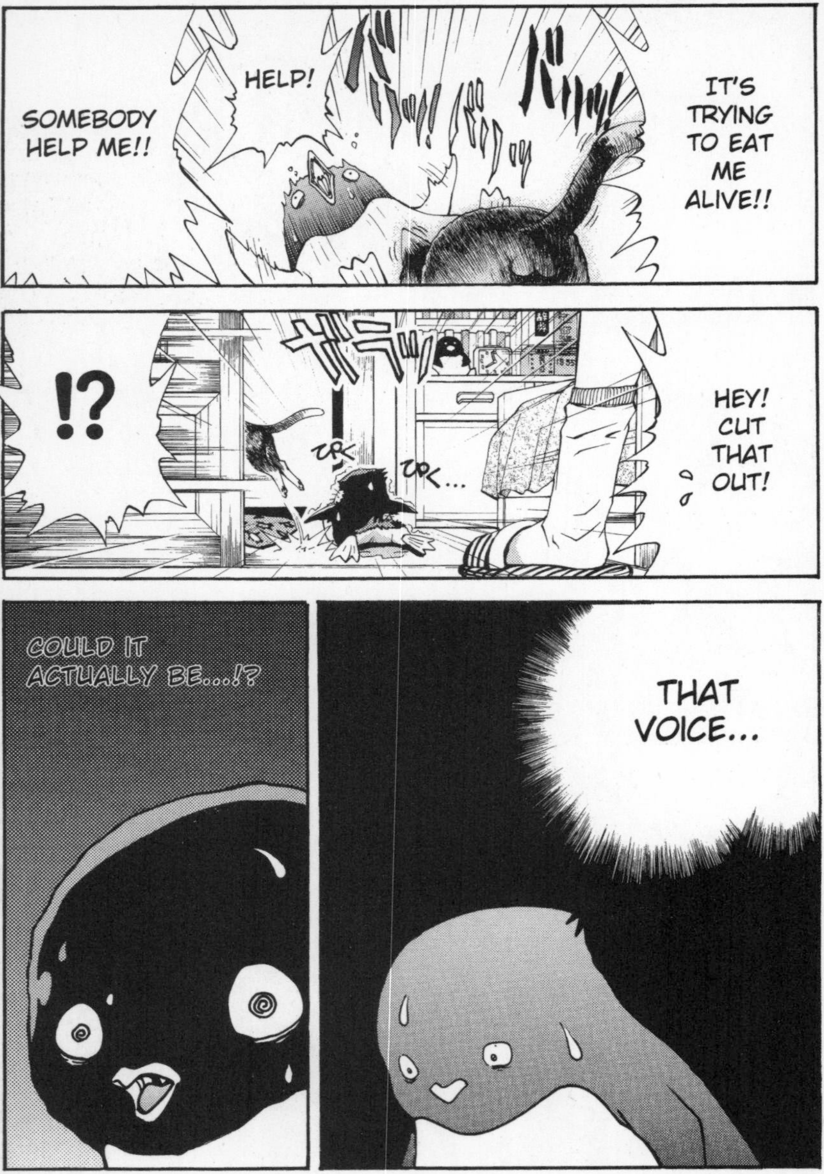
IT'S TRYING TO EAT ME ALIVE!!
HELP!
SOMEBODY HELP ME!!
HEY! CUT THAT OUT!
!?
THAT VOICE...
COULD IT ACTUALLY BE...!?

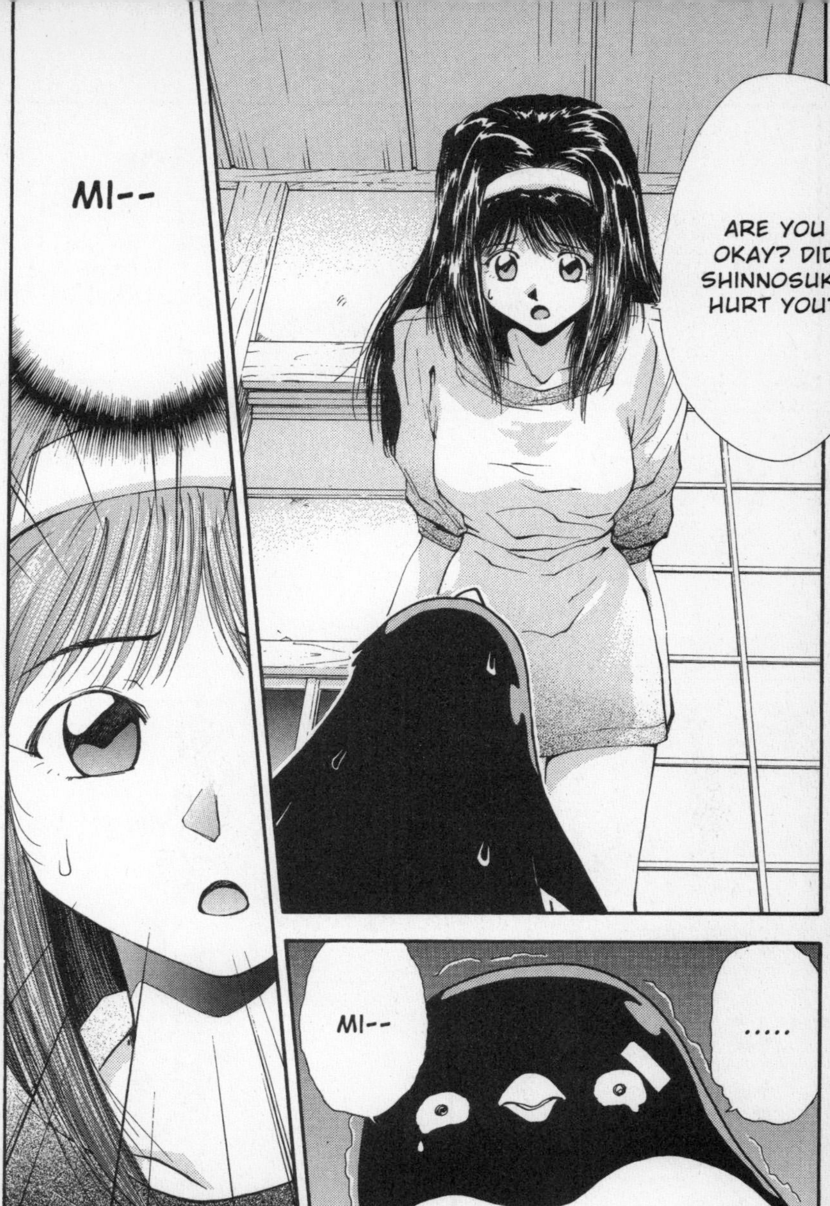
ARE YOU OKAY? DID SHINNOSUKE HURT YOU?
.....
MI--
MI--

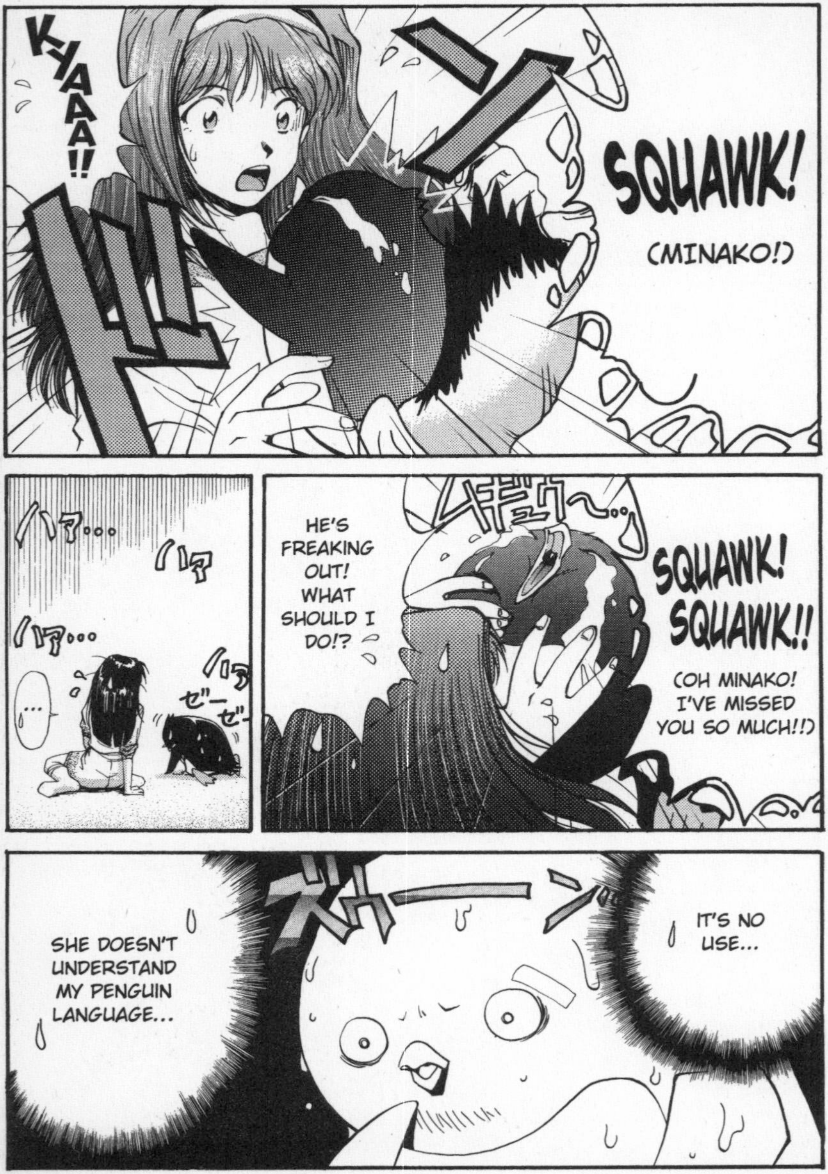
SQUAWK!
(MINAKO!)
KYAAA!!
SQUAWK! SQUAWK!!
(OH MINAKO! I'VE MISSED YOU SO MUCH!!)
HE'S FREAKING OUT! WHAT SHOULD I DO!?
ハァ...
ハァ
ハァ...
ハァ
ゼー ゼー
...
IT'S NO USE...
SHE DOESN'T UNDERSTAND MY PENGUIN LANGUAGE...

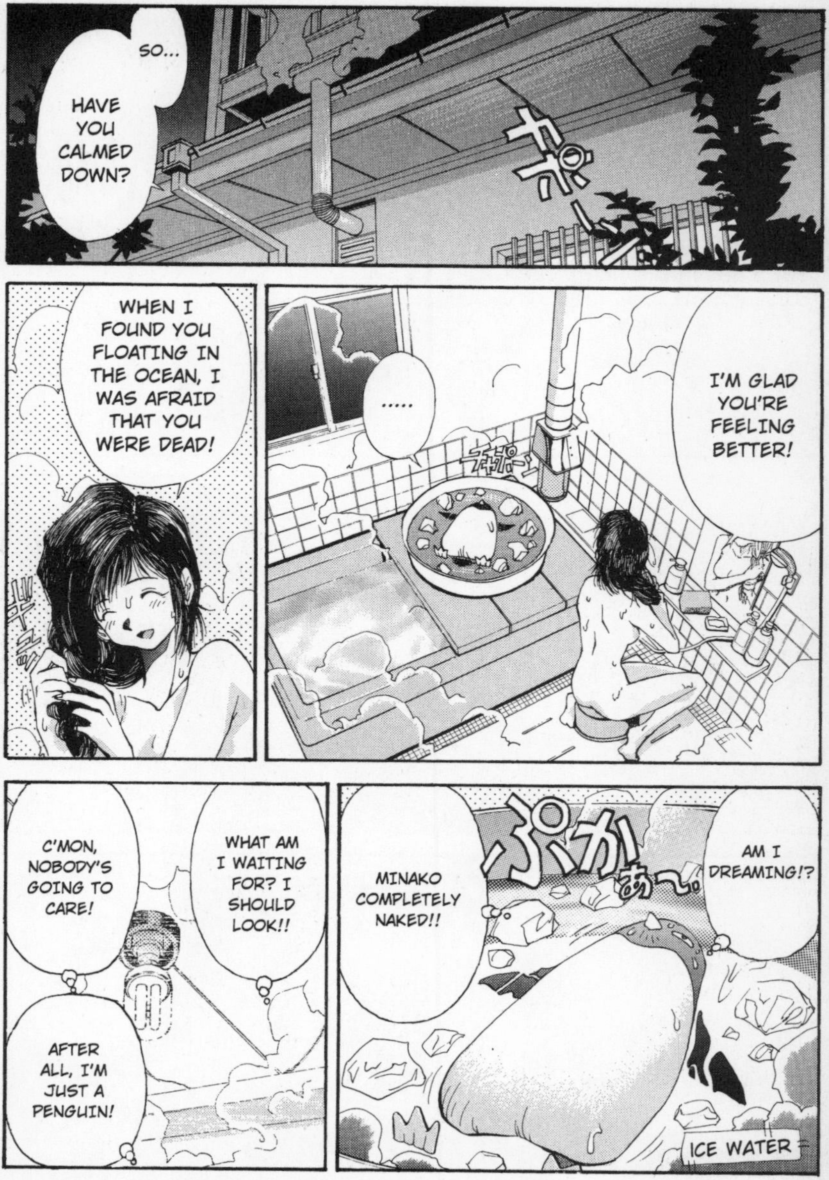
SO...
HAVE YOU CALMED DOWN?
チャポーン
I'M GLAD YOU'RE FEELING BETTER!
.....
WHEN I FOUND YOU FLOATING IN THE OCEAN, I WAS AFRAID THAT YOU WERE DEAD!
AM I DREAMING!?
MINAKO COMPLETELY NAKED!!
ぷかあ〜
ICE WATER
WHAT AM I WAITING FOR? I SHOULD LOOK!!
C'MON, NOBODY'S GOING TO CARE!
AFTER ALL, I'M JUST A PENGUIN!

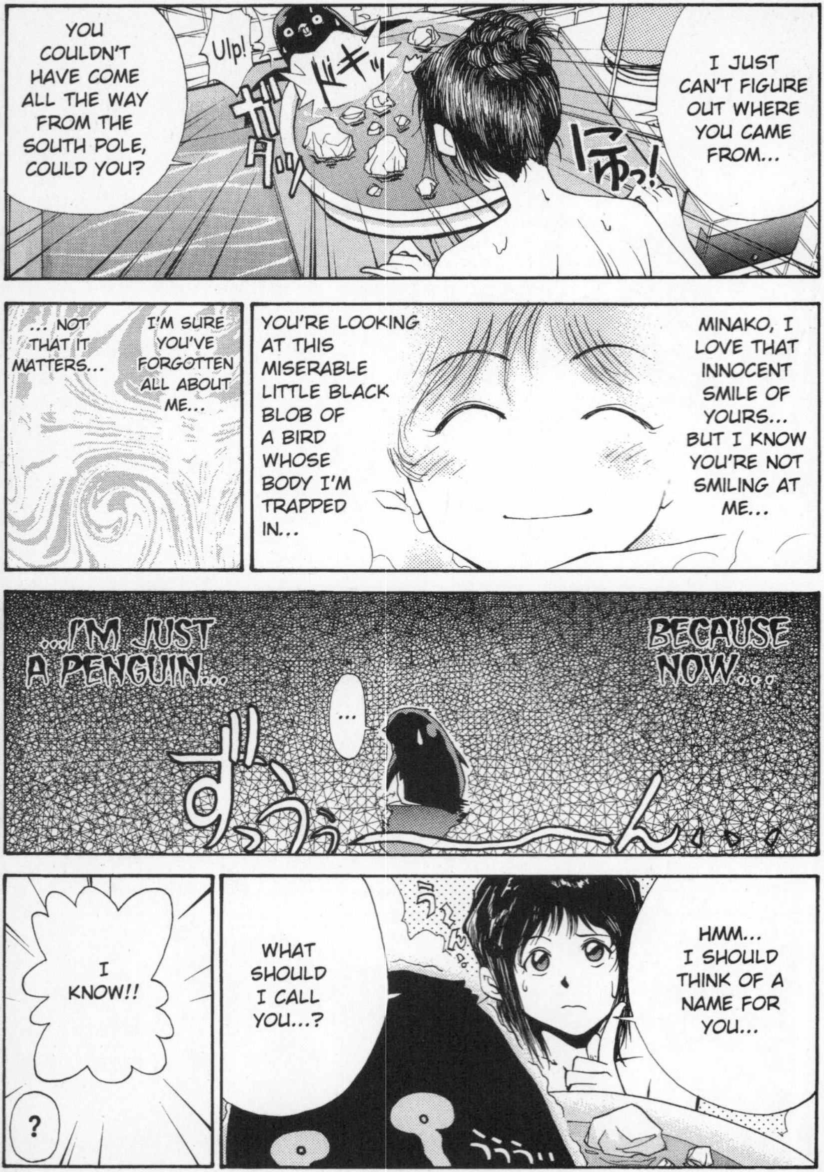
I JUST CAN'T FIGURE OUT WHERE YOU CAME FROM...
YOU COULDN'T HAVE COME ALL THE WAY FROM THE SOUTH POLE, COULD YOU?
Ulp!
ドキッ
MINAKO, I LOVE THAT INNOCENT SMILE OF YOURS... BUT I KNOW YOU'RE NOT SMILING AT ME...
YOU'RE LOOKING AT THIS MISERABLE LITTLE BLACK BLOB OF A BIRD WHOSE BODY I'M TRAPPED IN...
I'M SURE YOU'VE FORGOTTEN ALL ABOUT ME...
... NOT THAT IT MATTERS...
BECAUSE NOW...
...
...I'M JUST A PENGUIN...
HMM... I SHOULD THINK OF A NAME FOR YOU...
WHAT SHOULD I CALL YOU...?
I KNOW!!
?

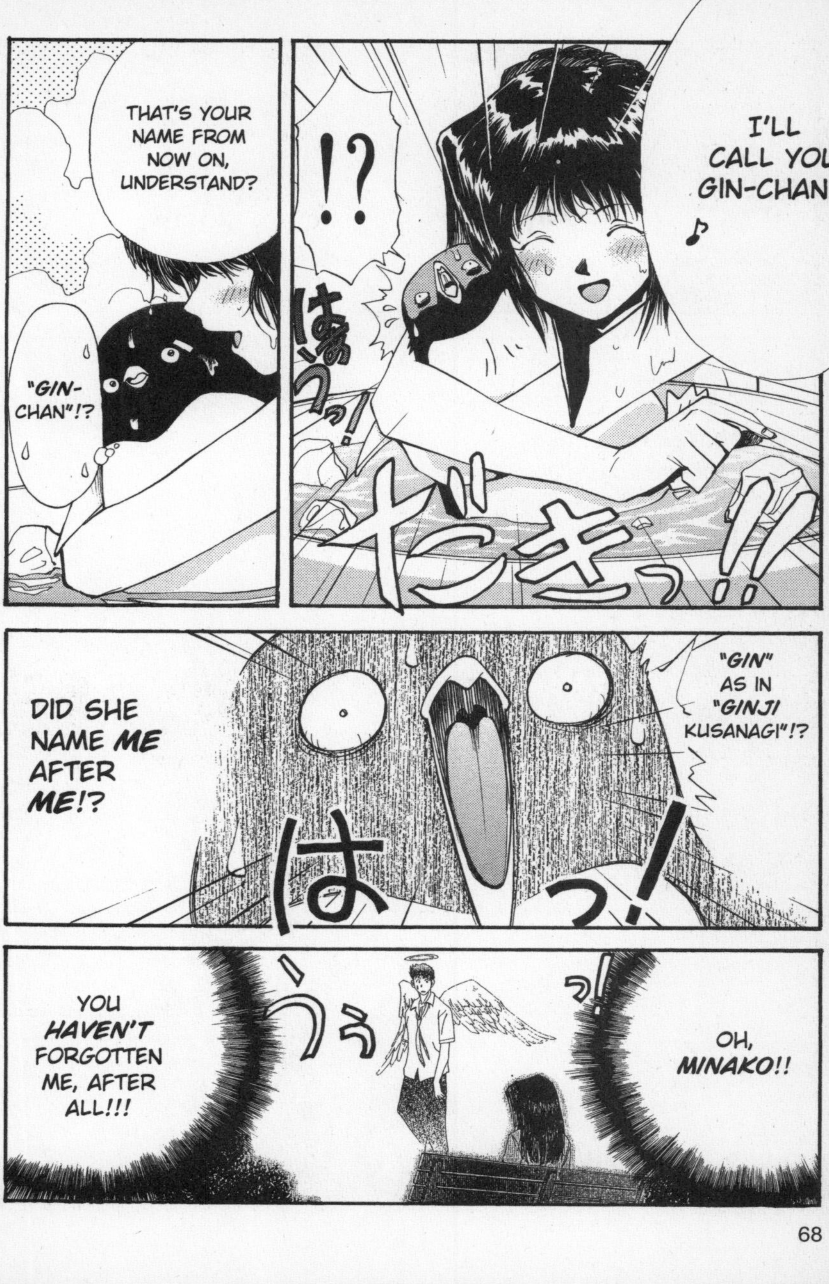
I'LL CALL YOU GIN-CHAN!! ♪
!?
はぁっ!
だきっ!!
THAT'S YOUR NAME FROM NOW ON, UNDERSTAND?
"GIN-CHAN"!?
"GIN" AS IN "GINJI KUSANAGI"!?
DID SHE NAME ME AFTER ME!?
はっ!
OH, MINAKO!!
うぅっ!
YOU HAVEN'T FORGOTTEN ME, AFTER ALL!!!

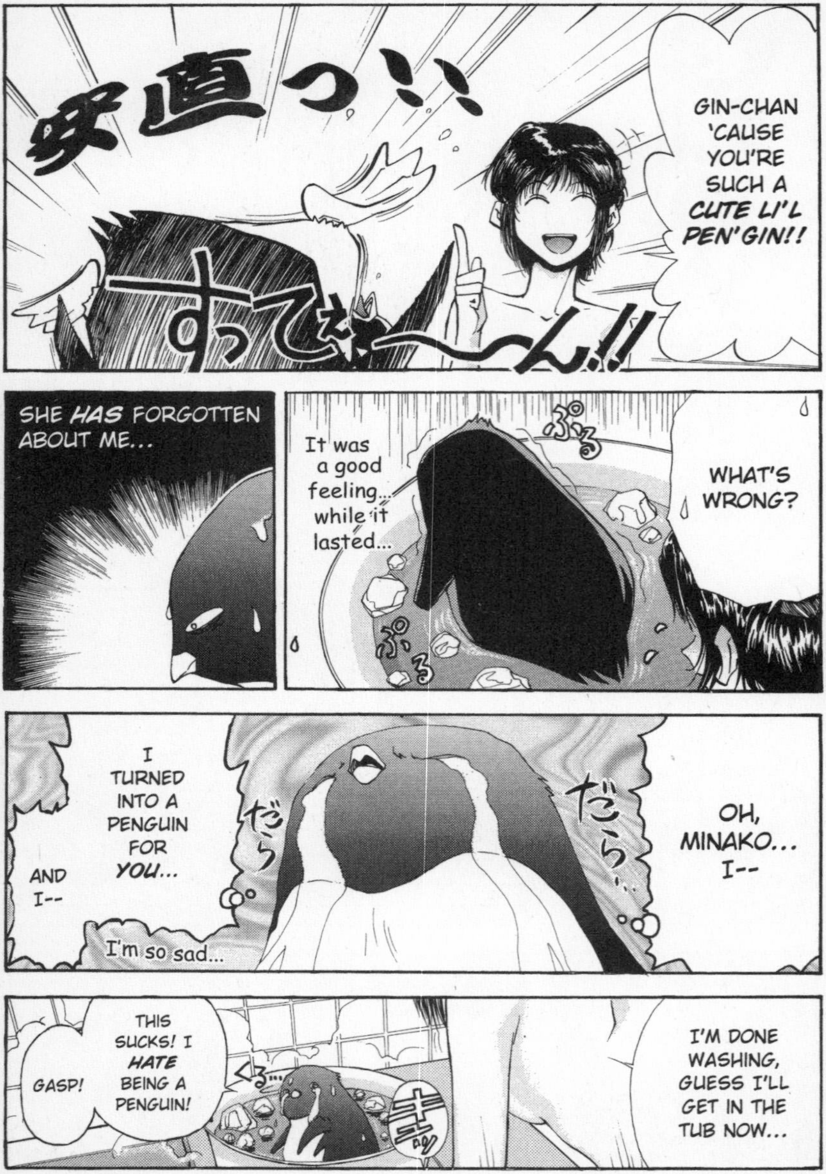
GIN-CHAN 'CAUSE YOU'RE SUCH A CUTE LI'L PEN'GIN!!
すてき〜〜ん!!
WHAT'S WRONG?
ぷる
It was a good feeling... while it lasted...
ぷる
SHE HAS FORGOTTEN ABOUT ME...
OH, MINAKO... I--
だら...
I TURNED INTO A PENGUIN FOR YOU...
AND I--
だら
I'm so sad...
I'M DONE WASHING, GUESS I'LL GET IN THE TUB NOW...
THIS SUCKS! I HATE BEING A PENGUIN!
くる...
GASP!

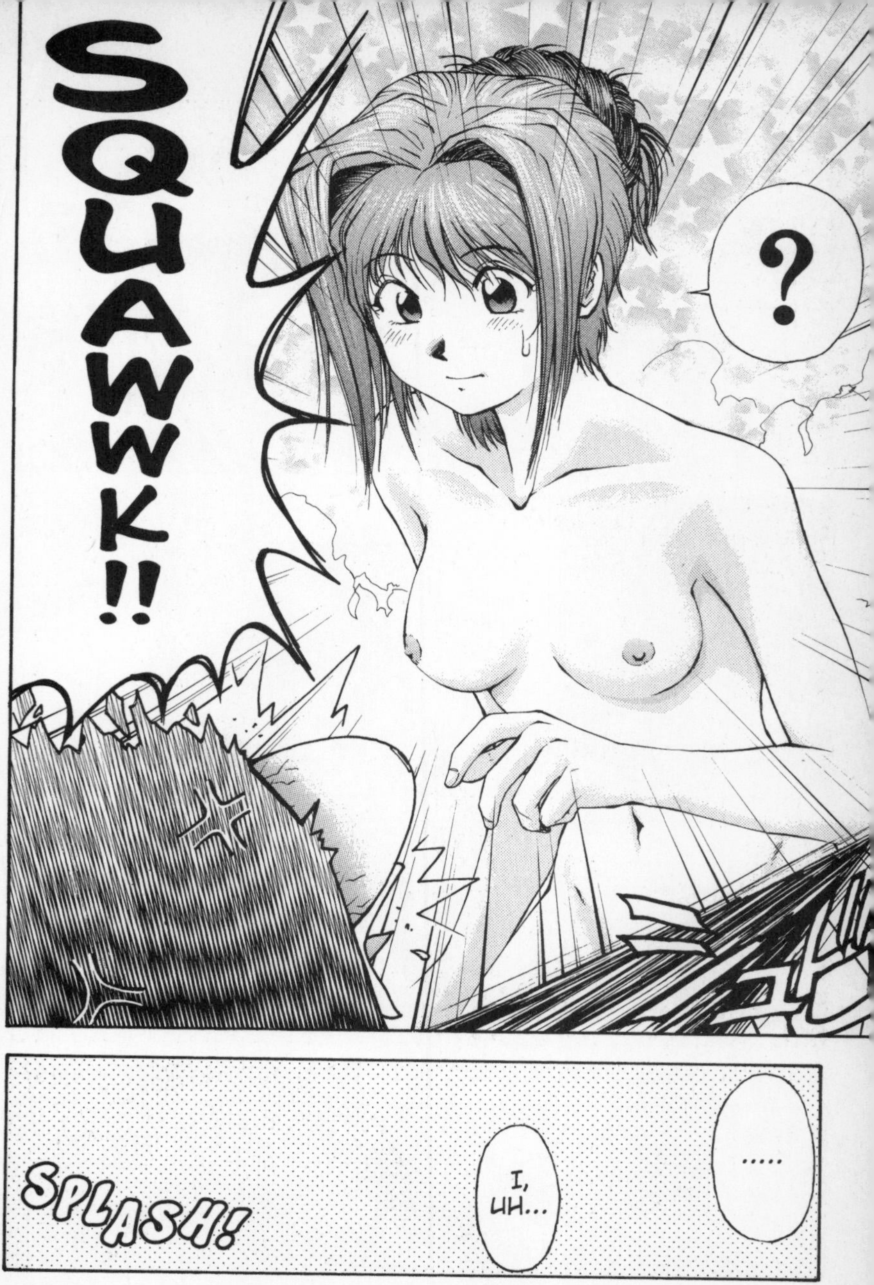
?
SQUAWK!!
.....
I, UH...
SPLASH!

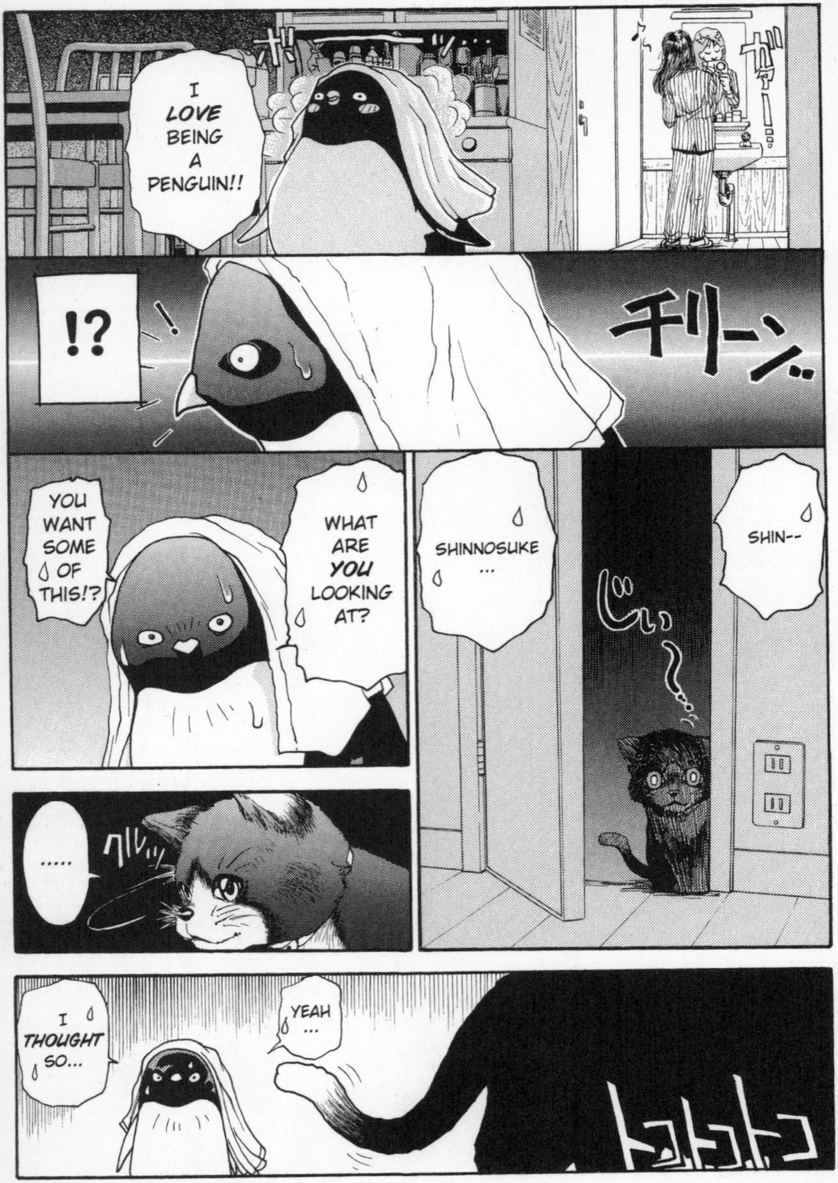
I *LOVE* BEING A PENGUIN!!
!?
チリーン
SHIN--
SHINNOSUKE ...
じぃ～
WHAT ARE *YOU* LOOKING AT?
YOU WANT SOME OF THIS!?
.....
クルッ
YEAH ...
I *THOUGHT* SO...
トコトコ

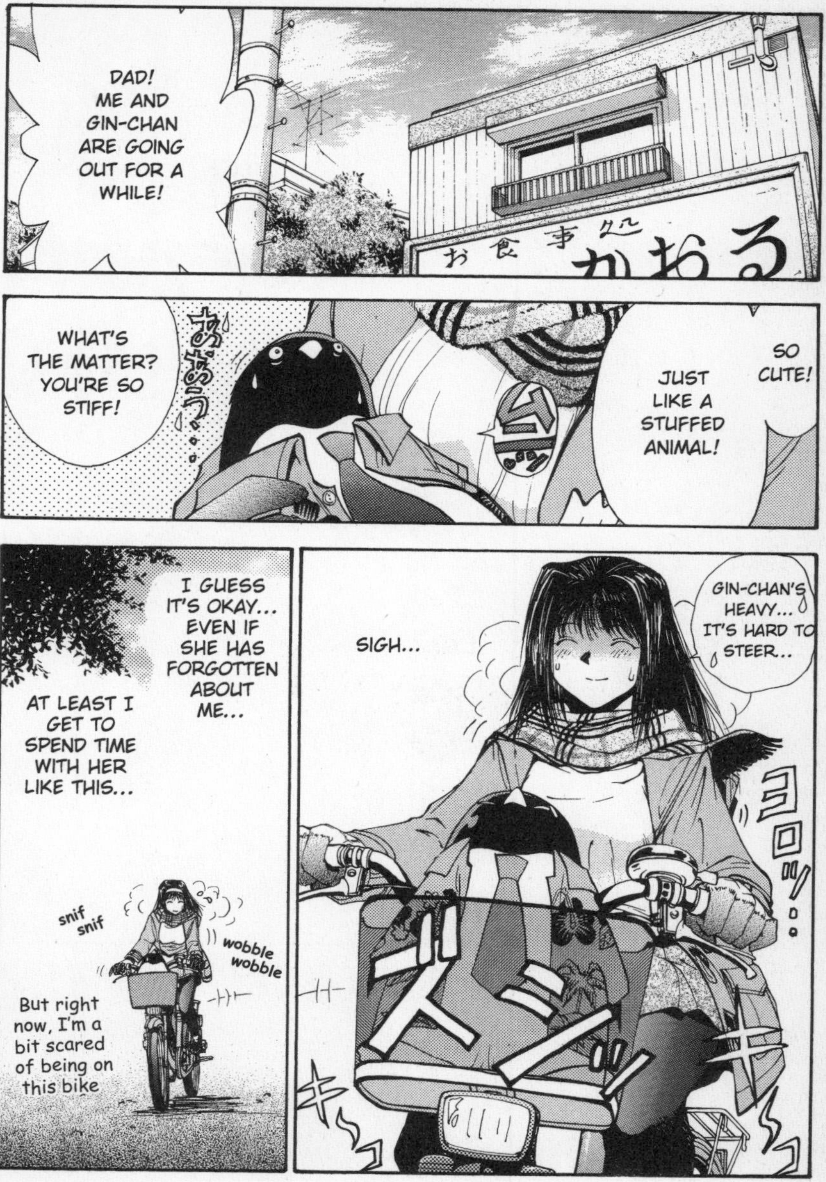
DAD! ME AND GIN-CHAN ARE GOING OUT FOR A WHILE!
お食事処
かおる
SO CUTE!
JUST LIKE A STUFFED ANIMAL!
WHAT'S THE MATTER? YOU'RE SO STIFF!
GIN-CHAN'S HEAVY... IT'S HARD TO STEER...
SIGH...
ヨロッ...
I GUESS IT'S OKAY... EVEN IF SHE HAS FORGOTTEN ABOUT ME...
AT LEAST I GET TO SPEND TIME WITH HER LIKE THIS...
snif snif
wobble wobble
But right now, I'm a bit scared of being on this bike

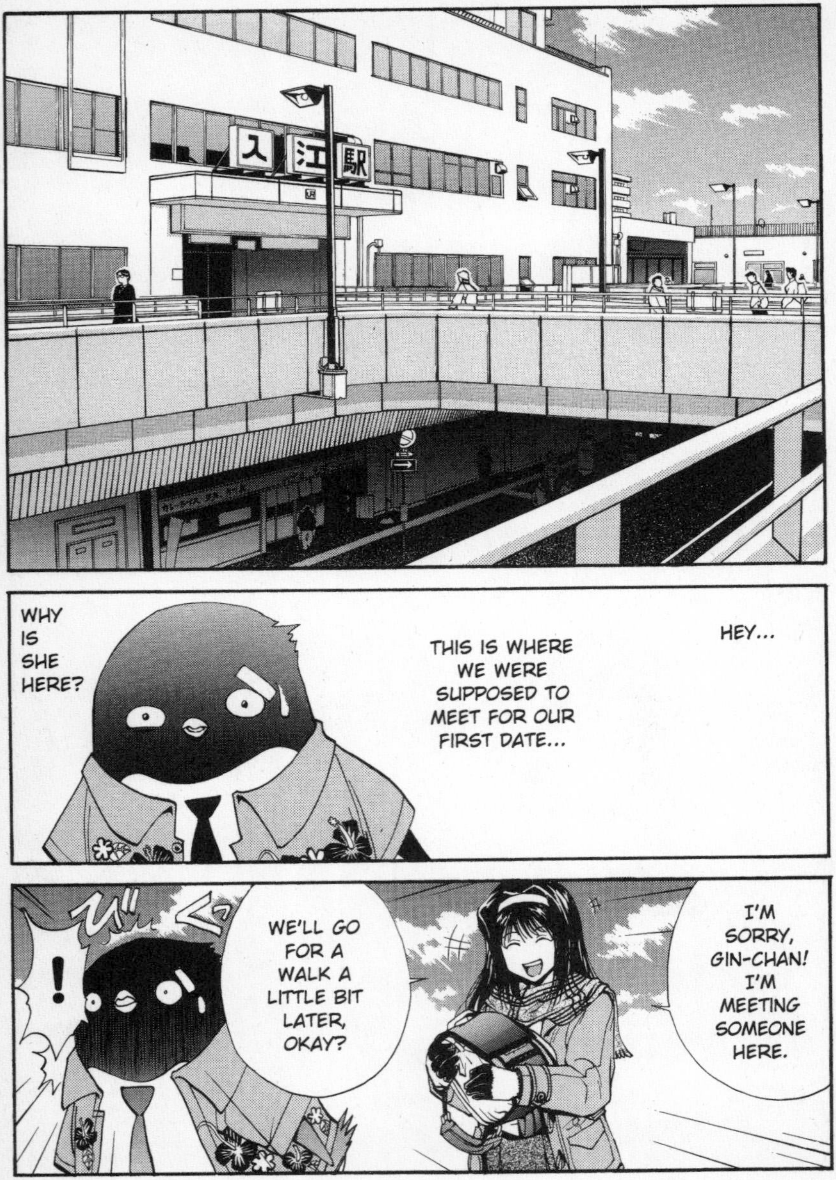
入江駅
HEY...
THIS IS WHERE WE WERE SUPPOSED TO MEET FOR OUR FIRST DATE...
WHY IS SHE HERE?
I'M SORRY, GIN-CHAN! I'M MEETING SOMEONE HERE.
WE'LL GO FOR A WALK A LITTLE BIT LATER, OKAY?
びくっ
!

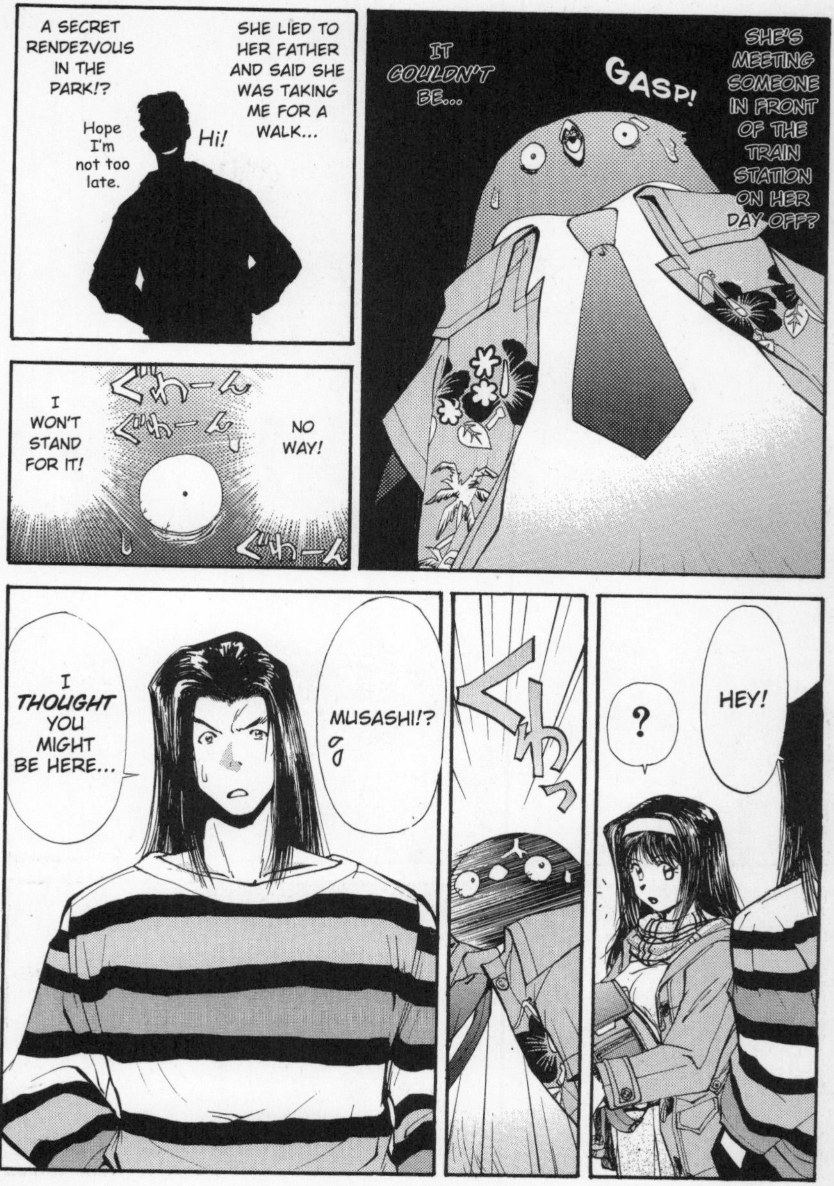
SHE'S MEETING SOMEONE IN FRONT OF THE TRAIN STATION ON HER DAY OFF?
GASP!
IT COULDN'T BE...
SHE LIED TO HER FATHER AND SAID SHE WAS TAKING ME FOR A WALK...
A SECRET RENDEZVOUS IN THE PARK!?
Hi!
Hope I'm not too late.
NO WAY!
ぐわーん
ぐわーん
I WON'T STAND FOR IT!
ぐわーん
HEY!
?
くわっ
MUSASHI!?
I *THOUGHT* YOU MIGHT BE HERE...

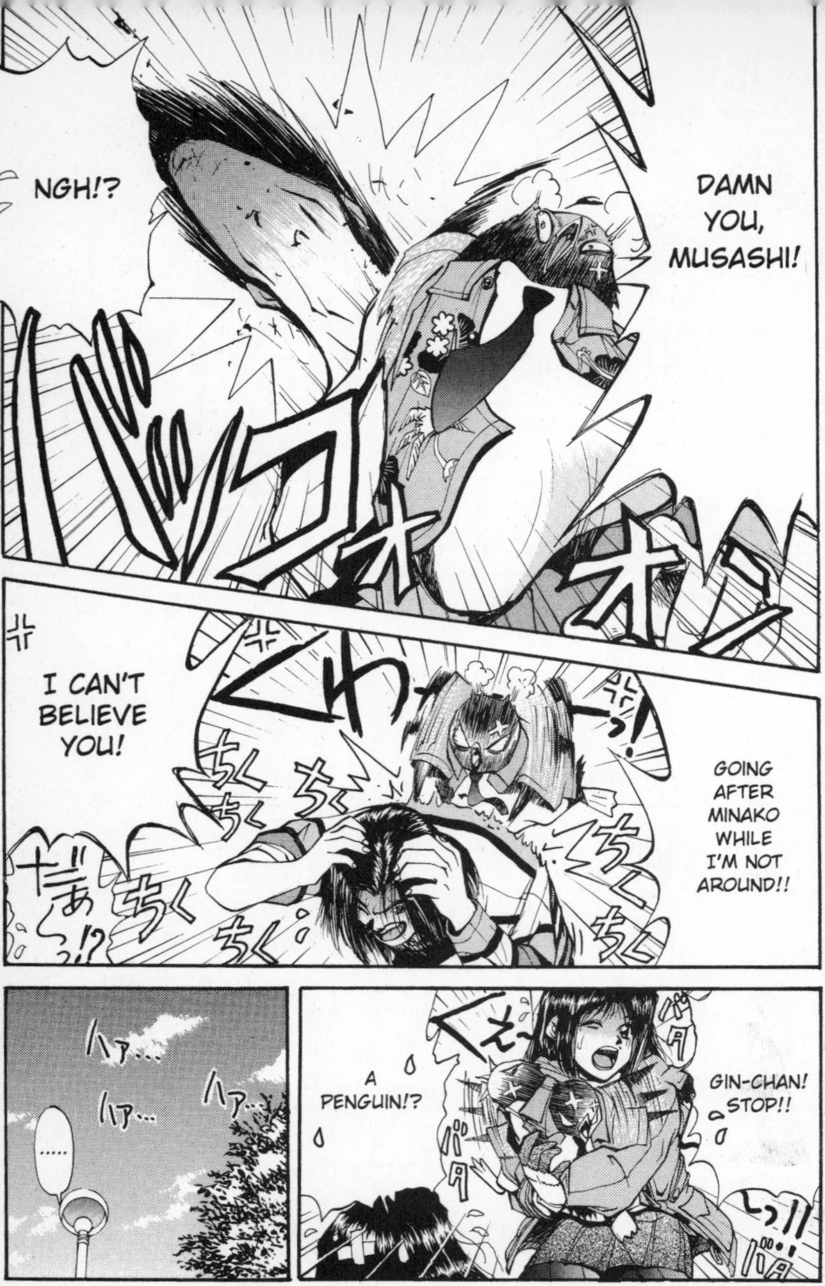
DAMN YOU, MUSASHI!
NGH!?
I CAN'T BELIEVE YOU!
GOING AFTER MINAKO WHILE I'M NOT AROUND!!
ちくちく
GIN-CHAN! STOP!!
A PENGUIN!?
ハァ... ハァ...
......

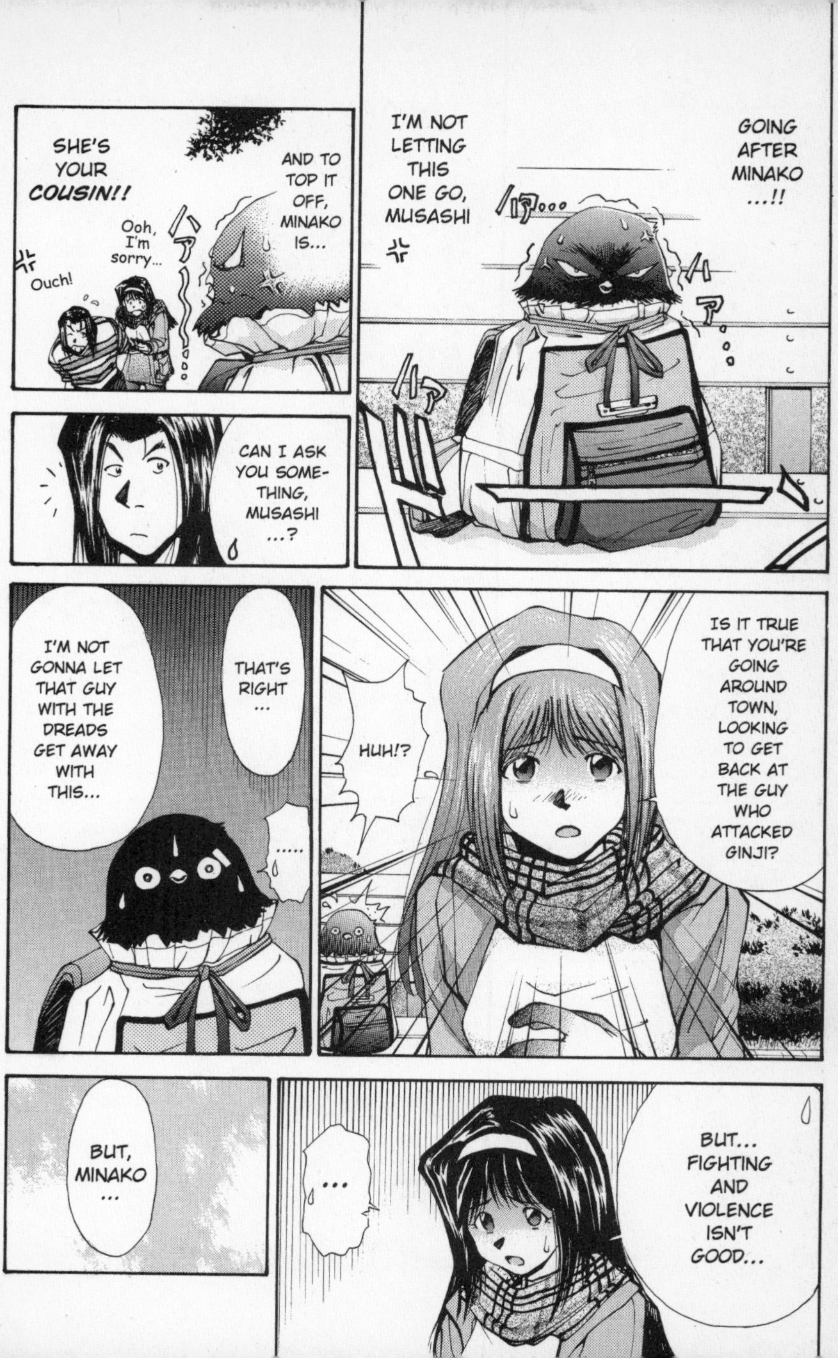
GOING AFTER MINAKO ...!!
I'M NOT LETTING THIS ONE GO, MUSASHI
AND TO TOP IT OFF, MINAKO IS...
SHE'S YOUR **COUSIN!!**
Ooh, I'm sorry...
Ouch!
CAN I ASK YOU SOME-THING, MUSASHI ...?
IS IT TRUE THAT YOU'RE GOING AROUND TOWN, LOOKING TO GET BACK AT THE GUY WHO ATTACKED GINJI?
HUH!?
THAT'S RIGHT ...
I'M NOT GONNA LET THAT GUY WITH THE DREADS GET AWAY WITH THIS...
.....
BUT... FIGHTING AND VIOLENCE ISN'T GOOD...
...
BUT, MINAKO ...

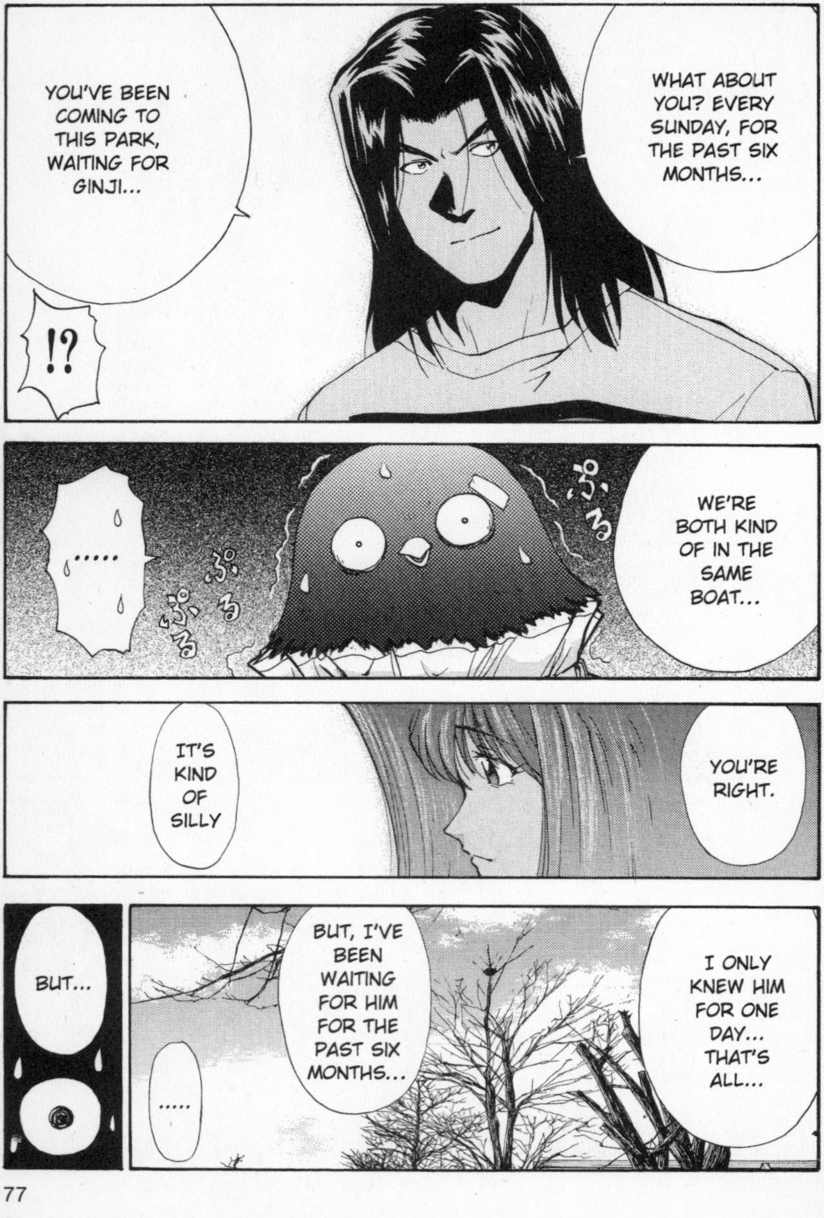
WHAT ABOUT YOU? EVERY SUNDAY, FOR THE PAST SIX MONTHS...
YOU'VE BEEN COMING TO THIS PARK, WAITING FOR GINJI...
!?
WE'RE BOTH KIND OF IN THE SAME BOAT...
ぷる
ぷる
ぷる
.....
YOU'RE RIGHT.
IT'S KIND OF SILLY
I ONLY KNEW HIM FOR ONE DAY... THAT'S ALL...
BUT, I'VE BEEN WAITING FOR HIM FOR THE PAST SIX MONTHS...
.....
BUT...

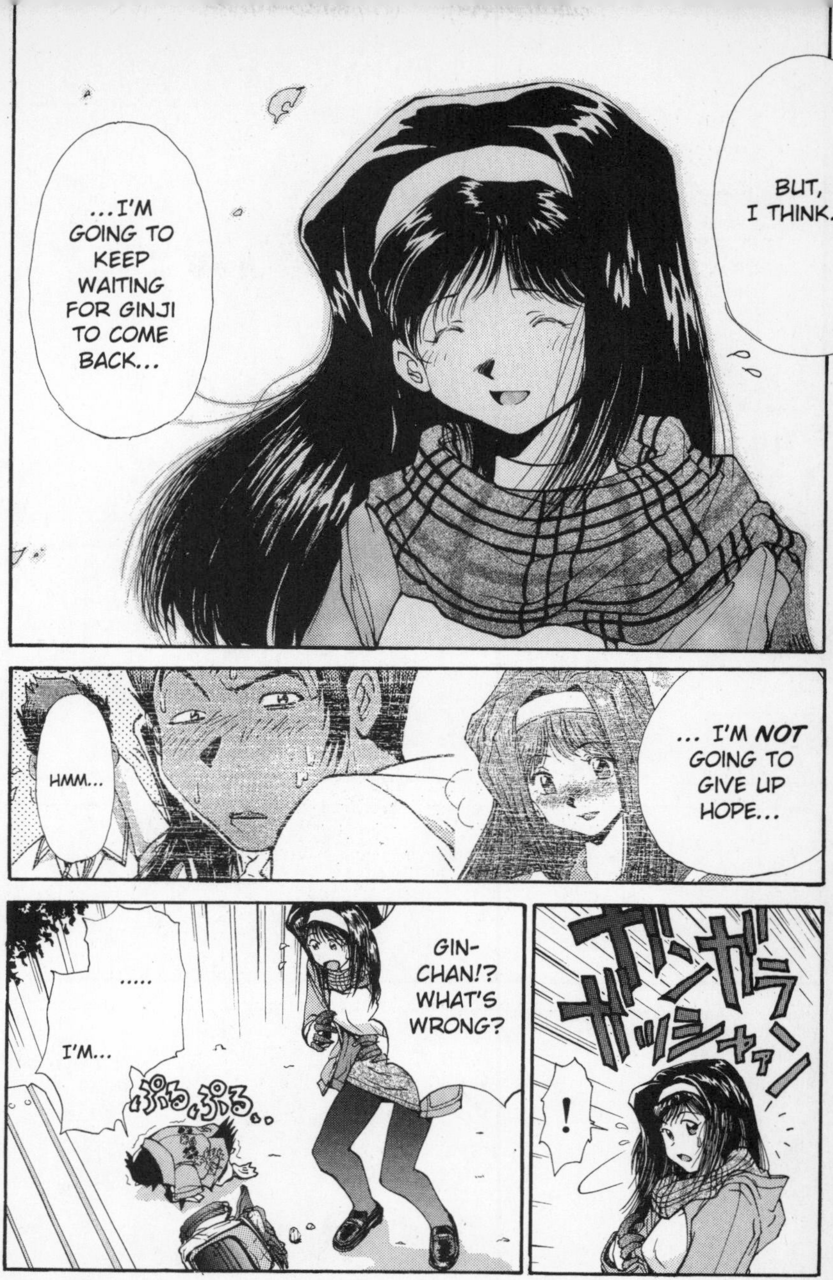
BUT, I THINK...
...I'M GOING TO KEEP WAITING FOR GINJI TO COME BACK...
... I'M **NOT** GOING TO GIVE UP HOPE...
HMM...
ガンガラ
ガッシャァン
!
GIN-CHAN!? WHAT'S WRONG?
.....
I'M...
ぷるぷる..

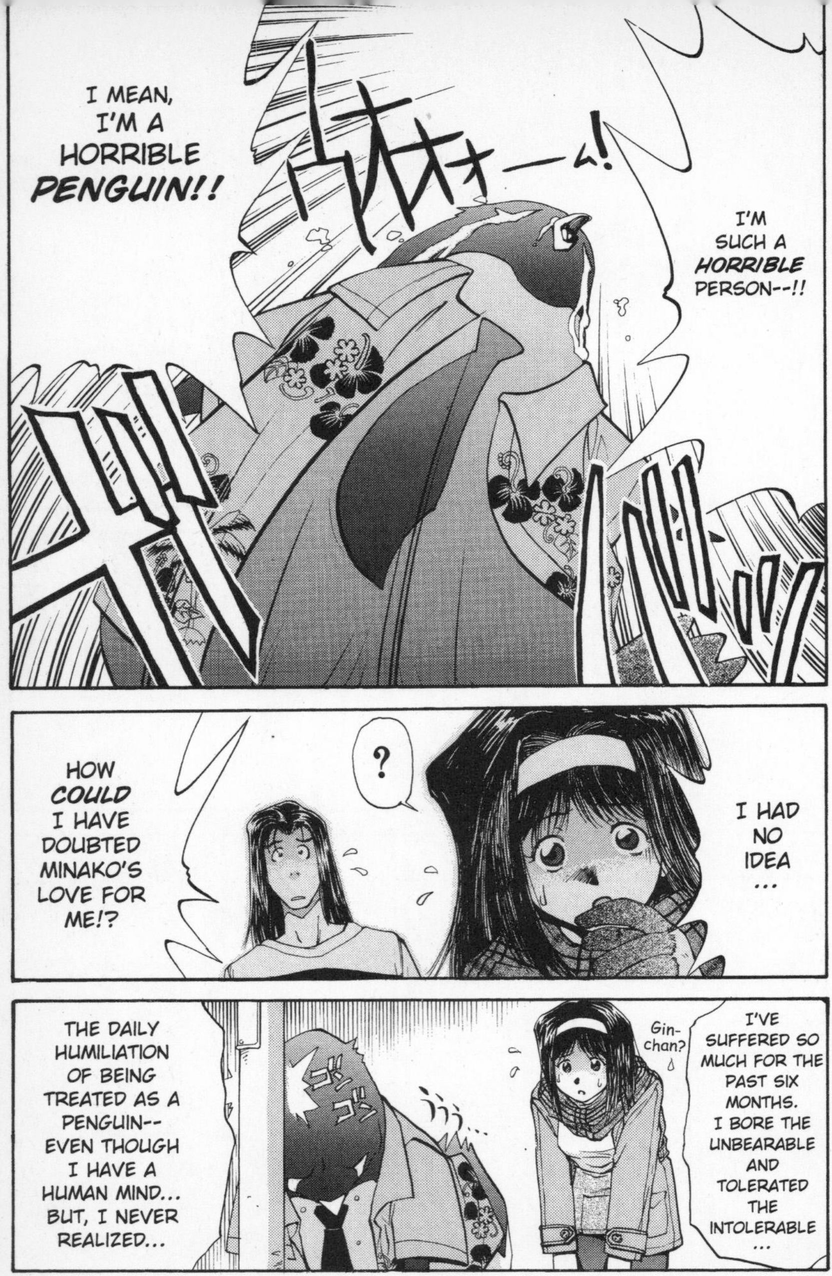
I'M SUCH A HORRIBLE PERSON--!!
I MEAN, I'M A HORRIBLE PENGUIN!!
I HAD NO IDEA ...
?
HOW COULD I HAVE DOUBTED MINAKO'S LOVE FOR ME!?
I'VE SUFFERED SO MUCH FOR THE PAST SIX MONTHS. I BORE THE UNBEARABLE AND TOLERATED THE INTOLERABLE ...
Gin-chan?
ううう…
THE DAILY HUMILIATION OF BEING TREATED AS A PENGUIN-- EVEN THOUGH I HAVE A HUMAN MIND... BUT, I NEVER REALIZED...

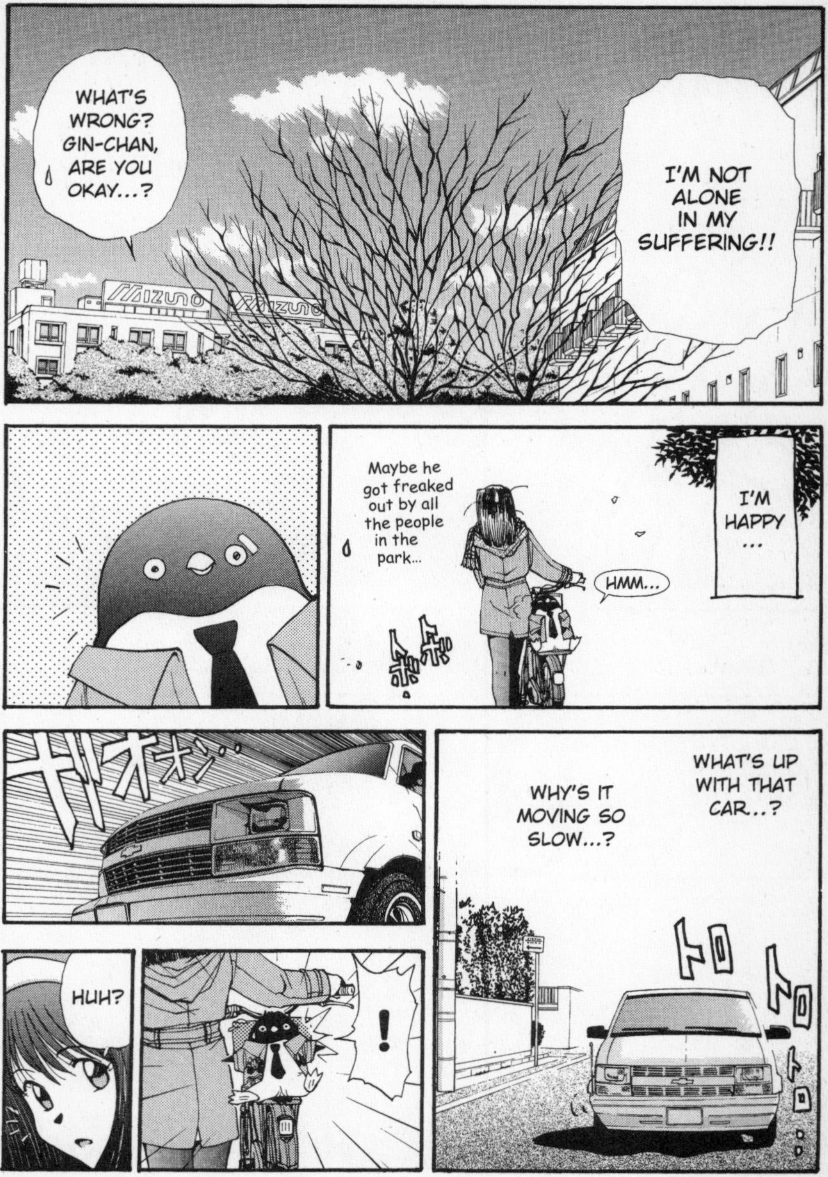
I'M NOT ALONE IN MY SUFFERING!!
WHAT'S WRONG? GIN-CHAN, ARE YOU OKAY...?
I'M HAPPY ...
HMM...
Maybe he got freaked out by all the people in the park...
WHAT'S UP WITH THAT CAR...?
WHY'S IT MOVING SO SLOW...?
!
HUH?

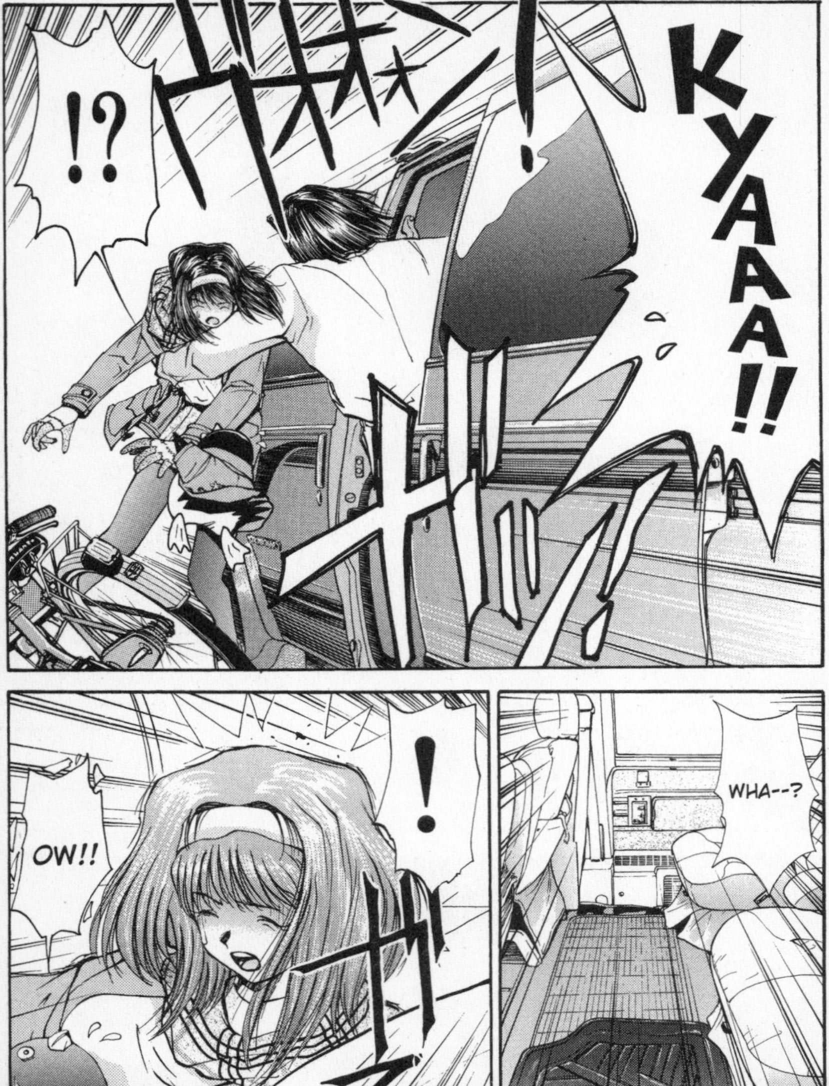
KYAAA!!
!?
WHA--?
!
OW!!

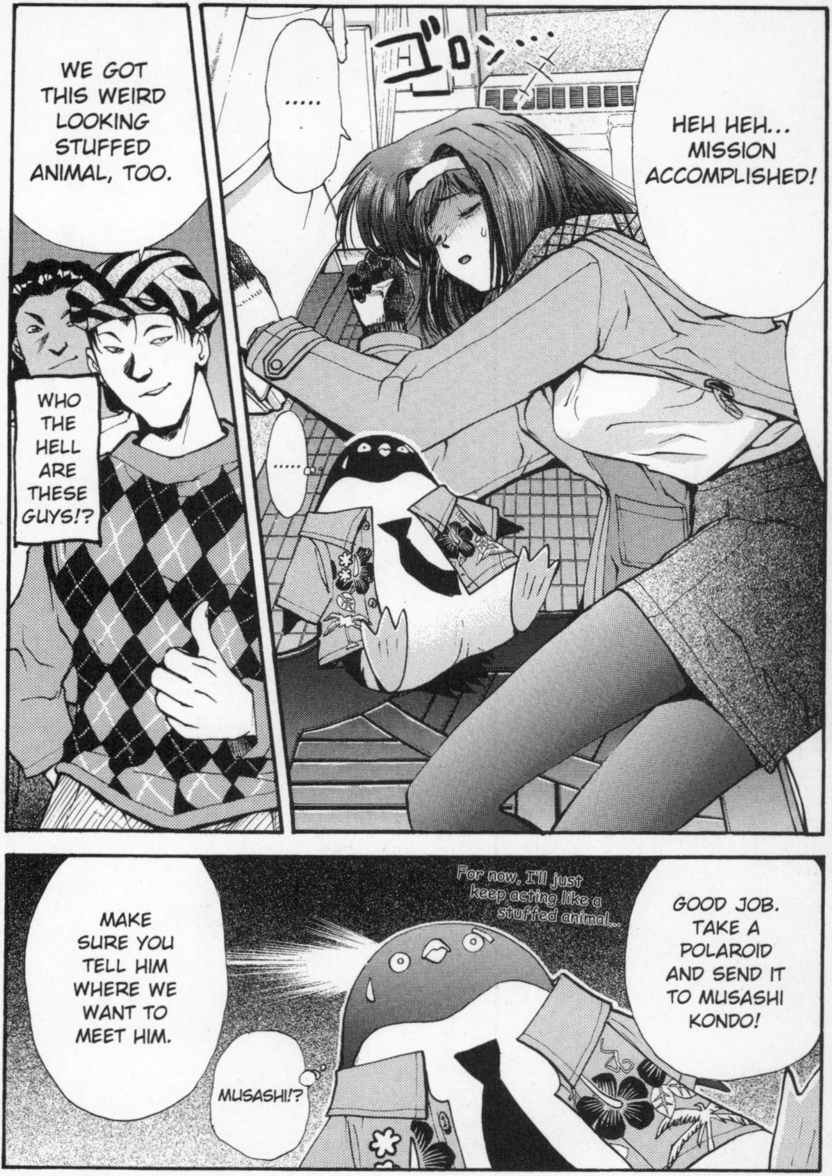
ゴロン...
.....
HEH HEH... MISSION ACCOMPLISHED!
.....
WE GOT THIS WEIRD LOOKING STUFFED ANIMAL, TOO.
WHO THE HELL ARE THESE GUYS!?
GOOD JOB. TAKE A POLAROID AND SEND IT TO MUSASHI KONDO!
For now, I'll just keep acting like a stuffed animal...
MAKE SURE YOU TELL HIM WHERE WE WANT TO MEET HIM.
MUSASHI!?

MUSASHI MUST'VE GOTTEN HIMSELF INTO SOME TROUBLE, AGAIN!

BUT THESE GUYS PISS ME OFF!

How could they treat my Minako like this!?

WHO'S THE BOSS HERE? I'LL BEAT THE CRAP OUT OF HIM!!

BUT...

NOBODY BETTER LAY A HAND ON THE GIRL. WE NEED HER...

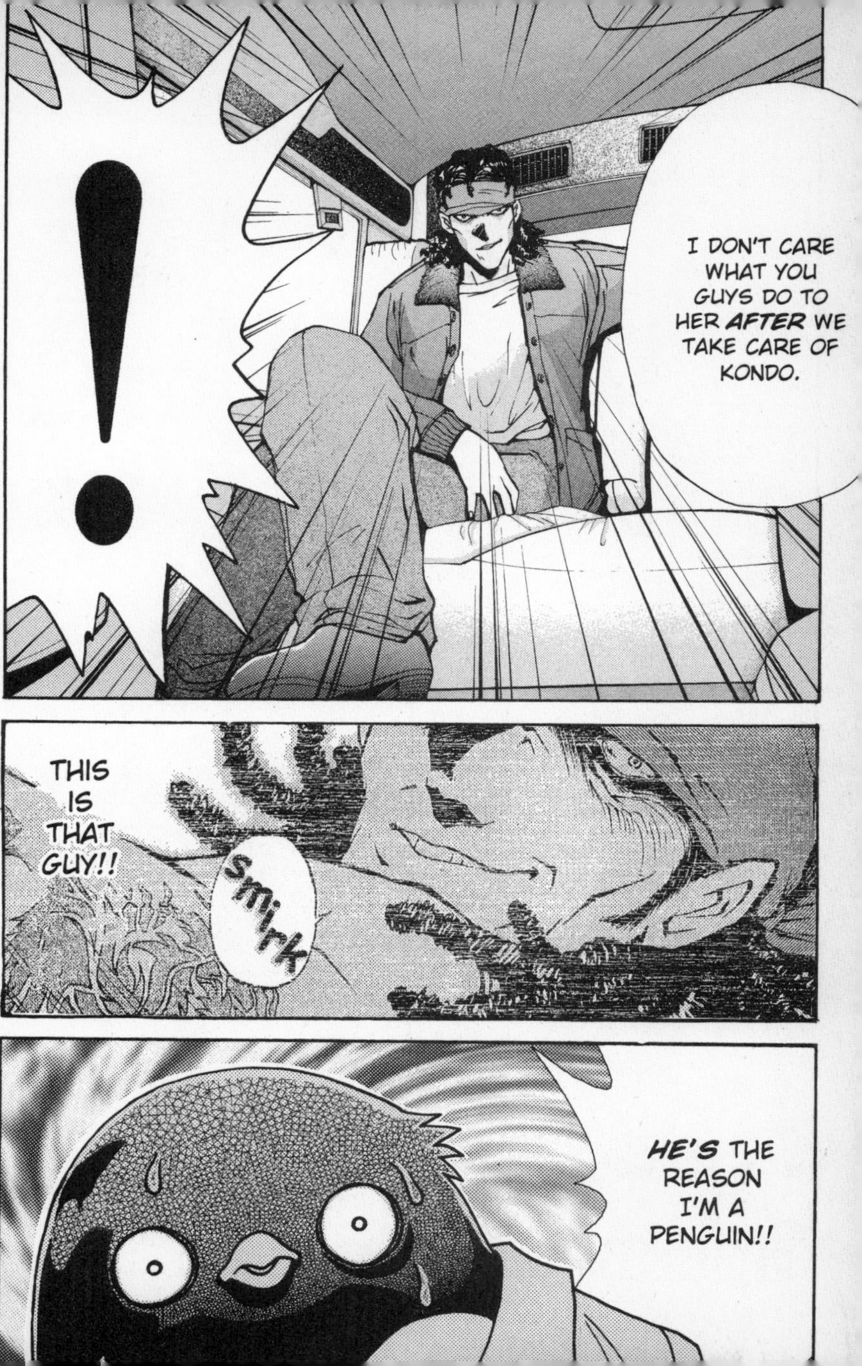
I DON'T CARE WHAT YOU GUYS DO TO HER *AFTER* WE TAKE CARE OF KONDO.
!
THIS IS THAT GUY!!
Smirk
HE'S THE REASON I'M A PENGUIN!!

CHAPTER 3
FRIENDS

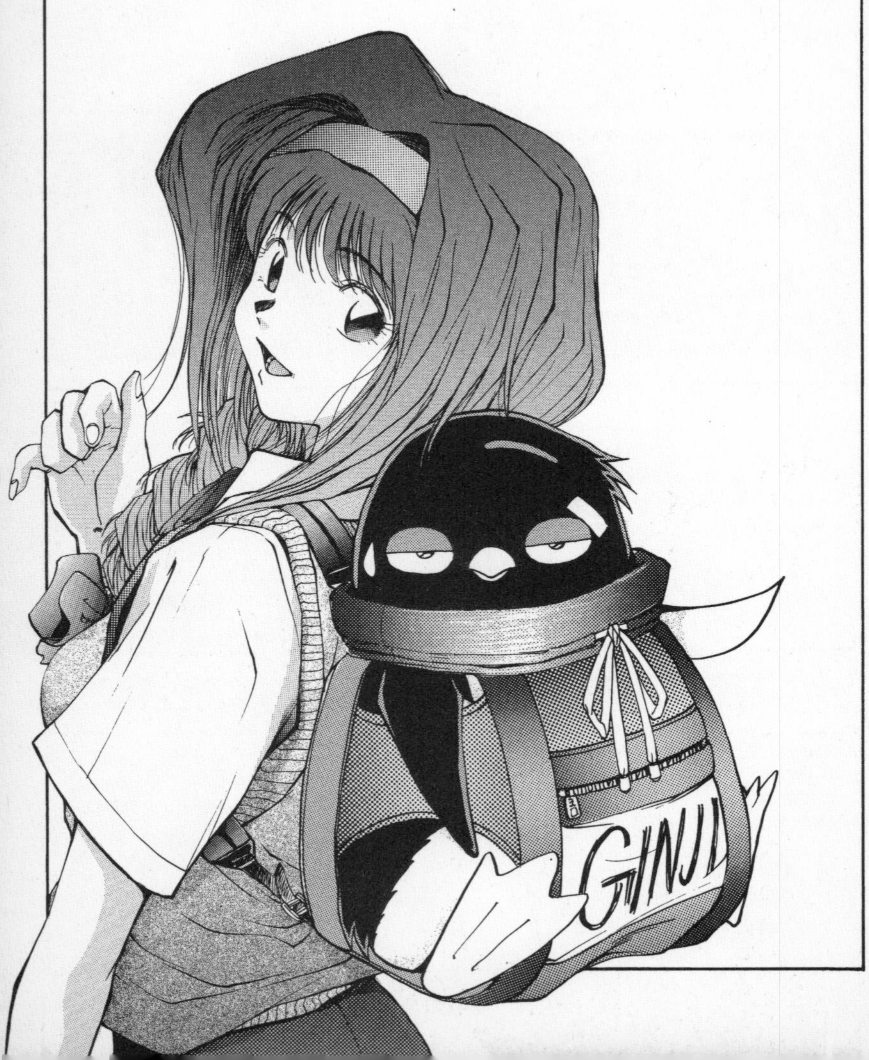
GINJI

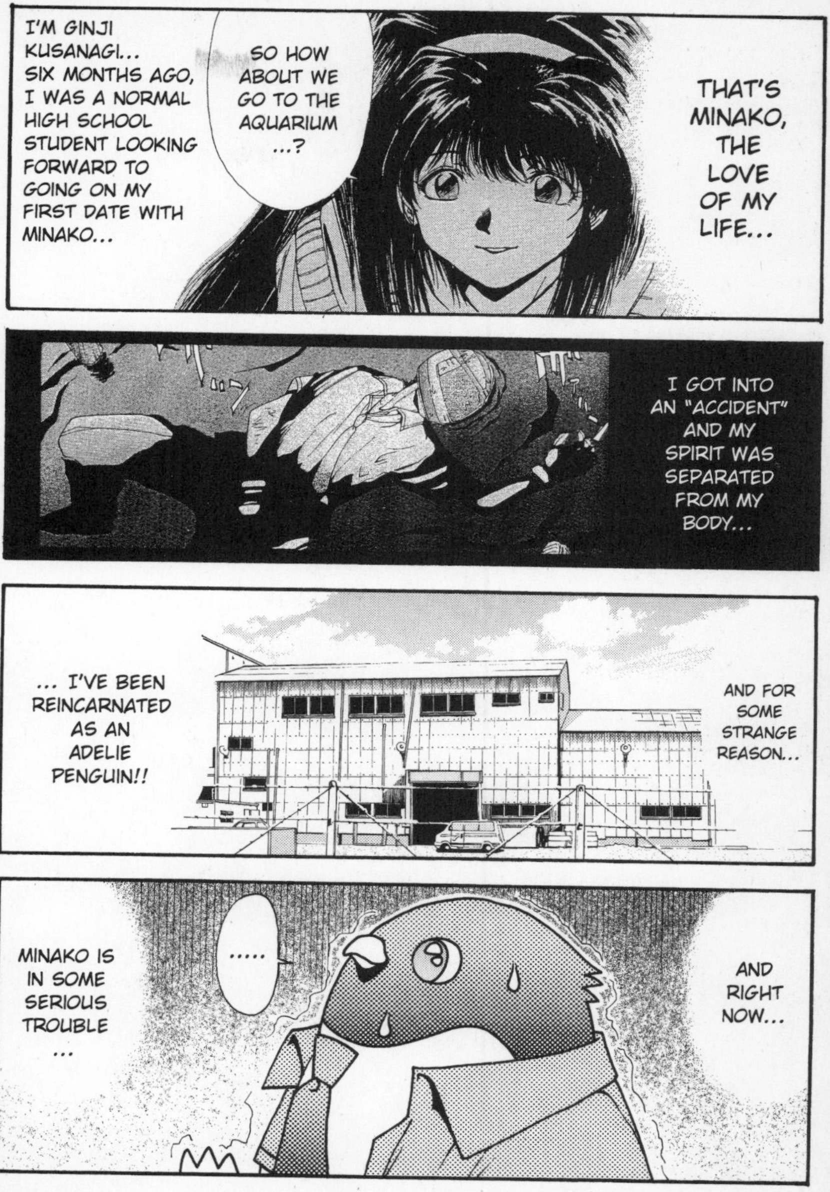
THAT'S MINAKO, THE LOVE OF MY LIFE...
SO HOW ABOUT WE GO TO THE AQUARIUM ...?
I'M GINJI KUSANAGI... SIX MONTHS AGO, I WAS A NORMAL HIGH SCHOOL STUDENT LOOKING FORWARD TO GOING ON MY FIRST DATE WITH MINAKO...
I GOT INTO AN "ACCIDENT" AND MY SPIRIT WAS SEPARATED FROM MY BODY...
AND FOR SOME STRANGE REASON...
... I'VE BEEN REINCARNATED AS AN ADELIE PENGUIN!!
AND RIGHT NOW...
.....
MINAKO IS IN SOME SERIOUS TROUBLE ...

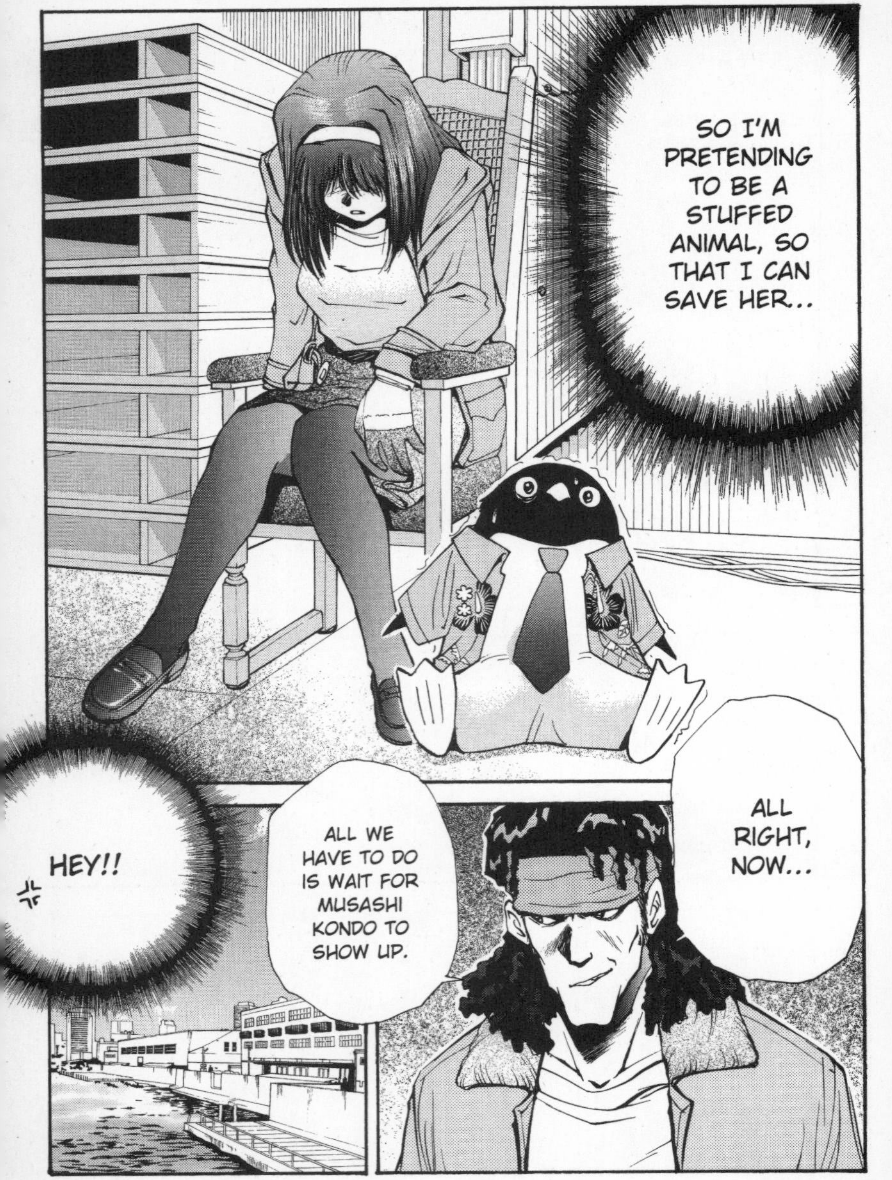
SO I'M PRETENDING TO BE A STUFFED ANIMAL, SO THAT I CAN SAVE HER...
ALL RIGHT, NOW...
ALL WE HAVE TO DO IS WAIT FOR MUSASHI KONDO TO SHOW UP.
HEY!!

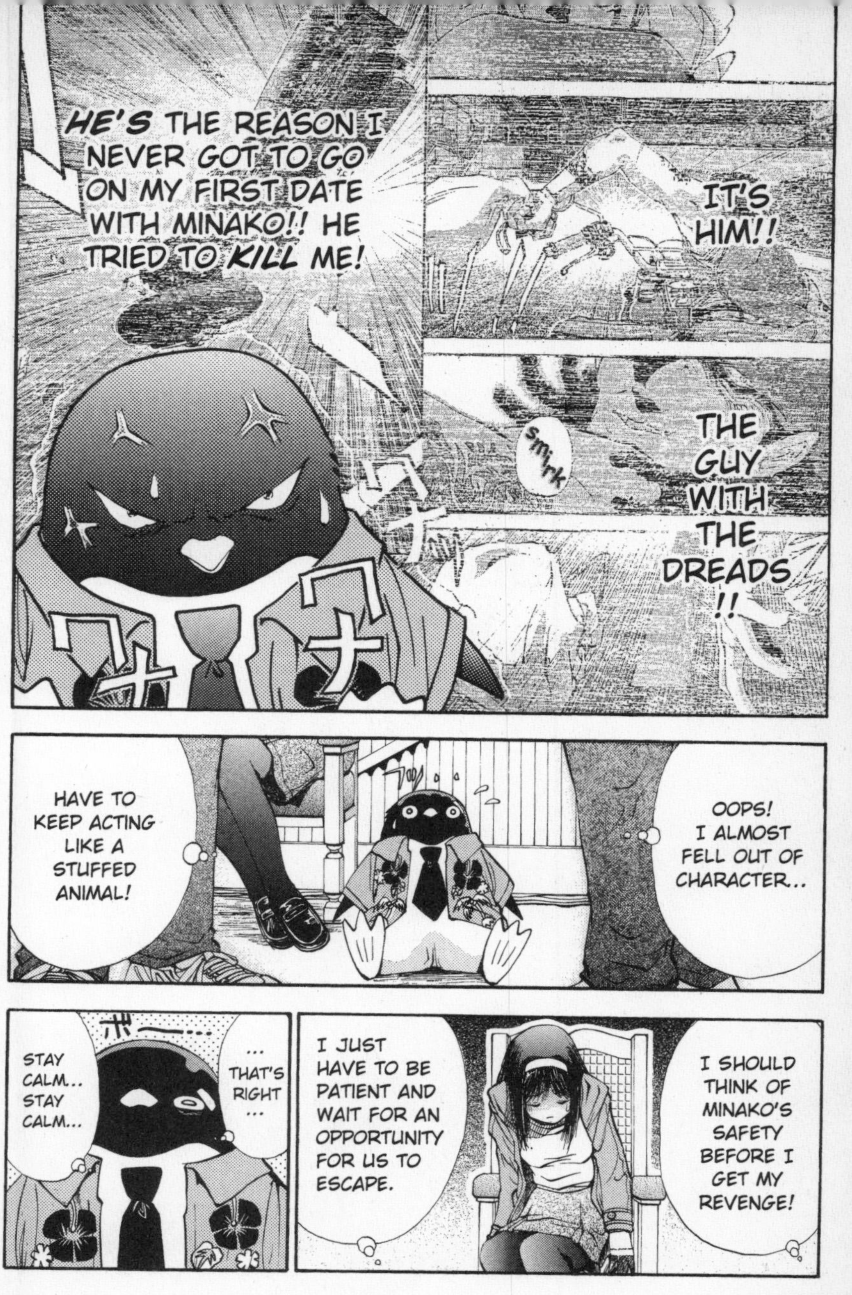
IT'S HIM!!
smirk
THE GUY WITH THE DREADS!!
HE'S THE REASON I NEVER GOT TO GO ON MY FIRST DATE WITH MINAKO!! HE TRIED TO KILL ME!
OOPS! I ALMOST FELL OUT OF CHARACTER...
HAVE TO KEEP ACTING LIKE A STUFFED ANIMAL!
I SHOULD THINK OF MINAKO'S SAFETY BEFORE I GET MY REVENGE!
I JUST HAVE TO BE PATIENT AND WAIT FOR AN OPPORTUNITY FOR US TO ESCAPE.
... THAT'S RIGHT ...
STAY CALM... STAY CALM...

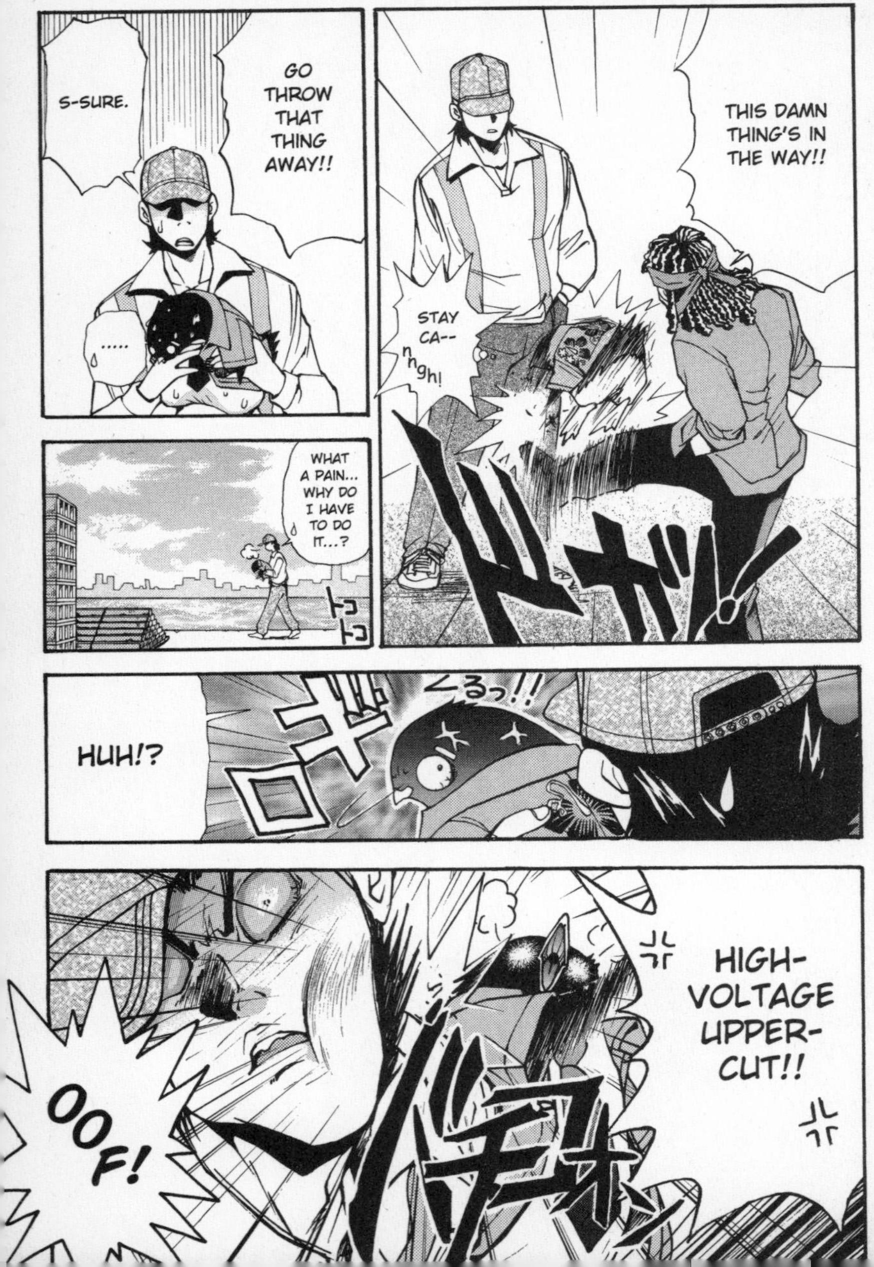
THIS DAMN THING'S IN THE WAY!!
STAY CA-- nngh!
GO THROW THAT THING AWAY!!
S-SURE.
.....
WHAT A PAIN... WHY DO I HAVE TO DO IT...?
くるっ!!
ギロ
HUH!?
HIGH-VOLTAGE UPPER-CUT!!
OOF!

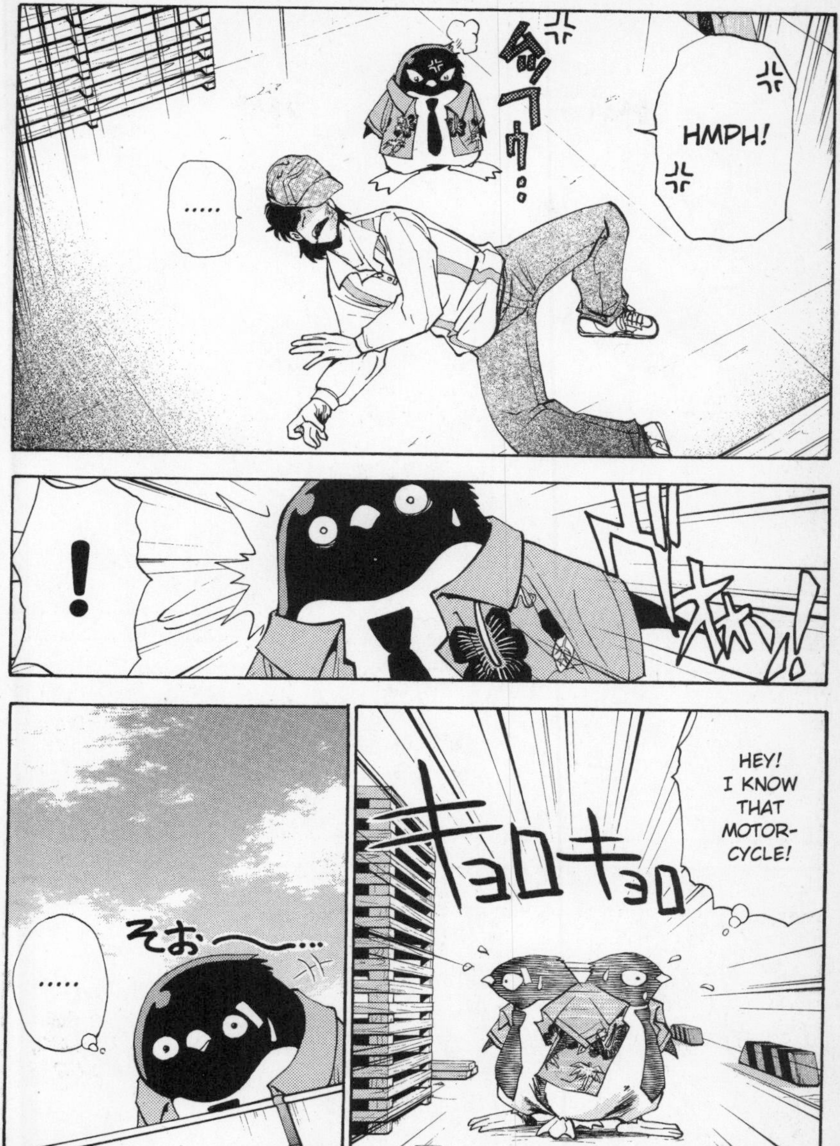
HMPH!
ムッフゥ..
.....
!
HEY! I KNOW THAT MOTOR-CYCLE!
キョロキョロ
そおーー....
.....

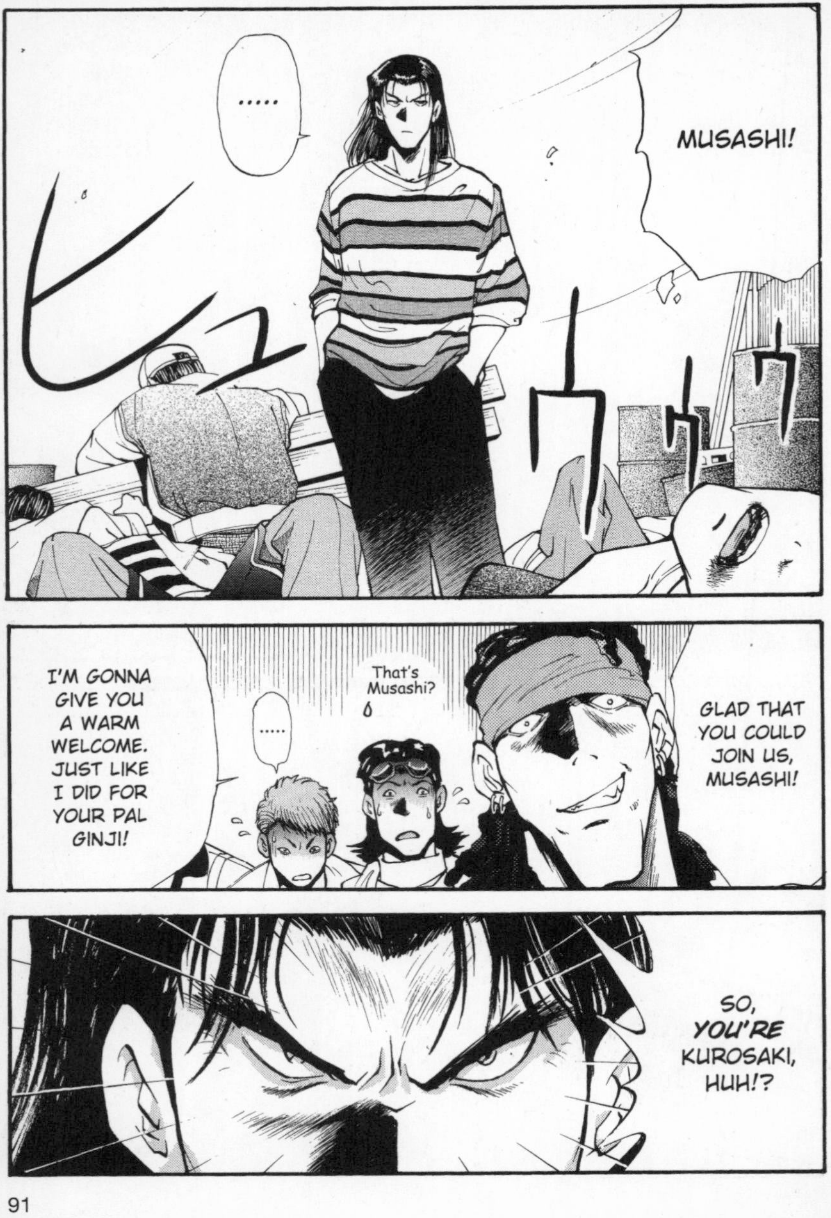
MUSASHI!
.....
GLAD THAT YOU COULD JOIN US, MUSASHI!
That's Musashi?
.....
I'M GONNA GIVE YOU A WARM WELCOME. JUST LIKE I DID FOR YOUR PAL GINJI!
SO, *YOU'RE* KUROSAKI, HUH!?

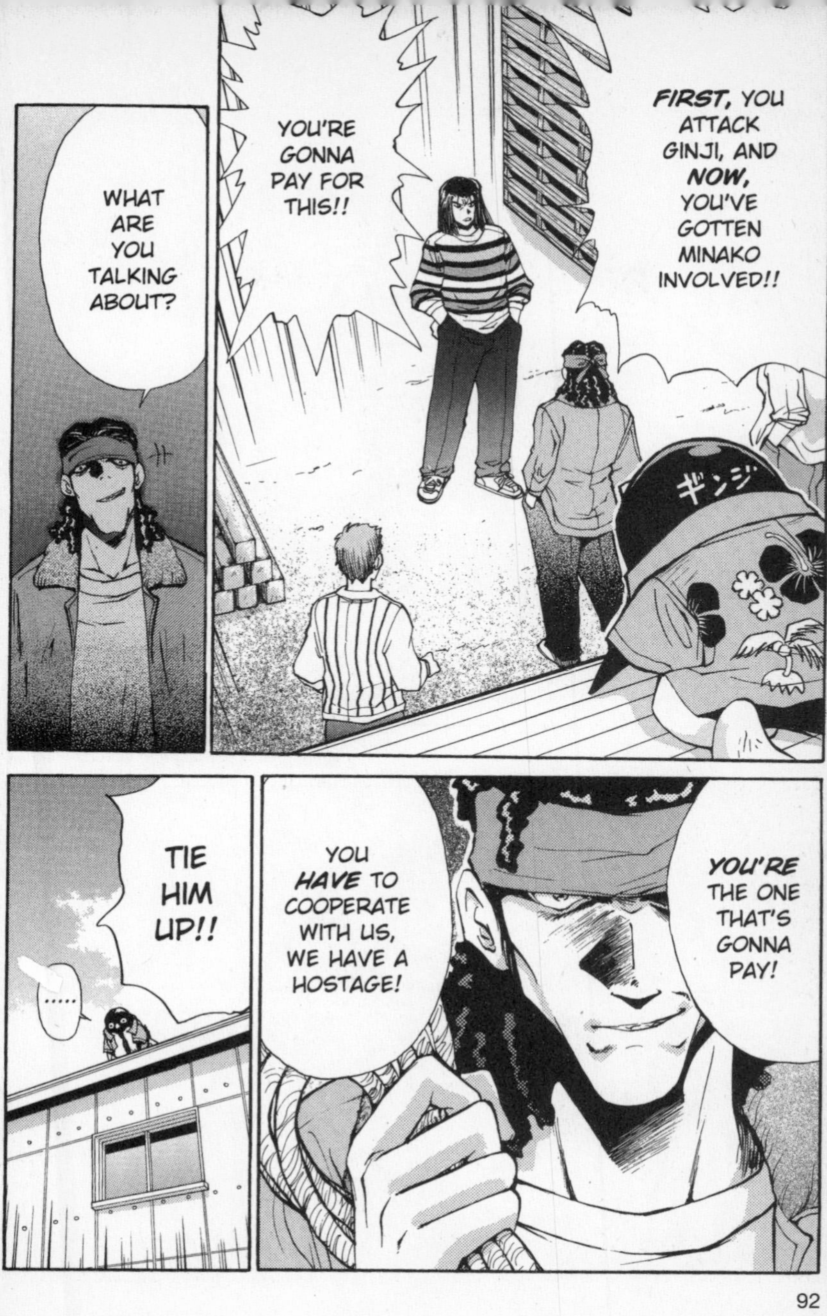
FIRST, YOU ATTACK GINJI, AND NOW, YOU'VE GOTTEN MINAKO INVOLVED!!
YOU'RE GONNA PAY FOR THIS!!
ギンジ
WHAT ARE YOU TALKING ABOUT?
YOU'RE THE ONE THAT'S GONNA PAY!
YOU HAVE TO COOPERATE WITH US, WE HAVE A HOSTAGE!
TIE HIM UP!!
......

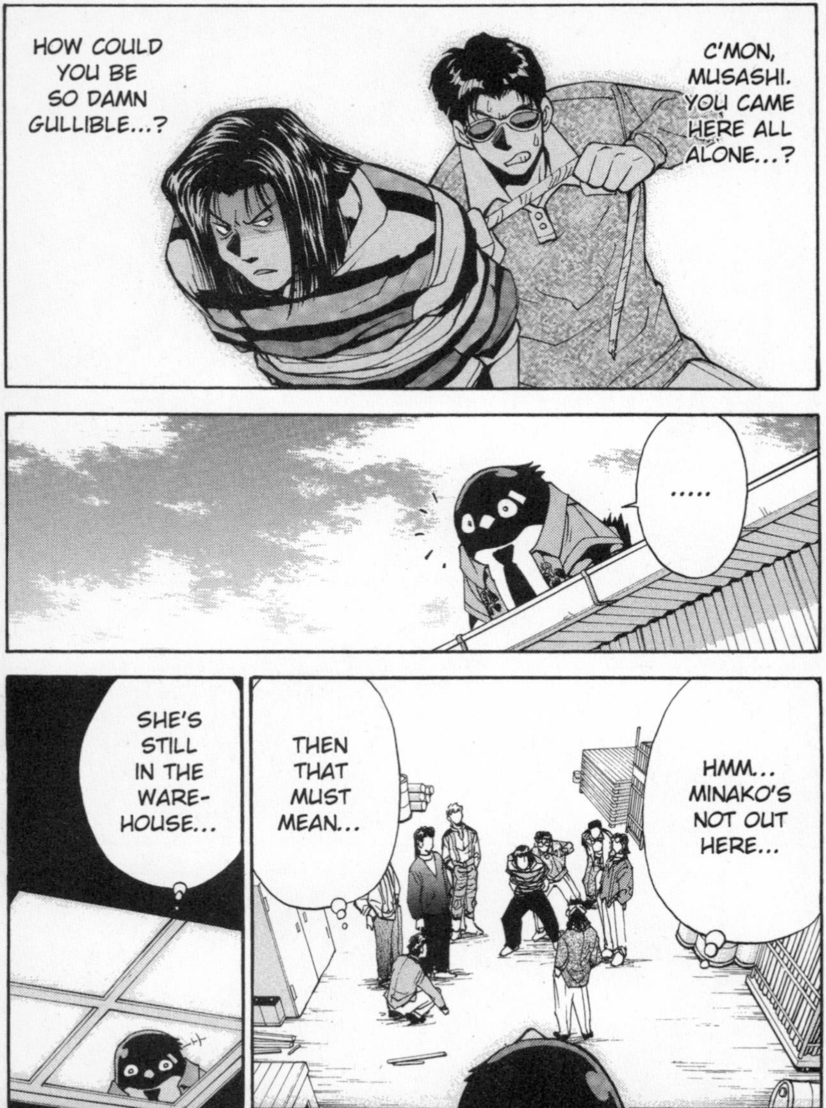
C'MON, MUSASHI. YOU CAME HERE ALL ALONE...?
HOW COULD YOU BE SO DAMN GULLIBLE...?
.....
HMM... MINAKO'S NOT OUT HERE...
THEN THAT MUST MEAN...
SHE'S STILL IN THE WARE-HOUSE...

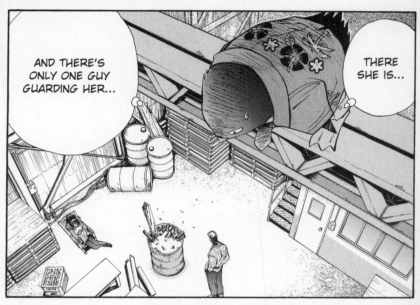

THERE SHE IS...
AND THERE'S ONLY ONE GUY GUARDING HER...
THIS IS MY CHANCE TO RESCUE MINAKO!!
.....
HMPH! WHY DO I HAVE TO STAND GUARD HERE BY MYSELF?
BUT IT'S NOT ALL BAD...
AFTER ALL...

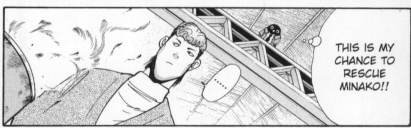

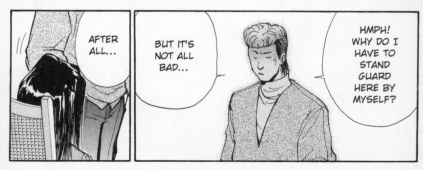

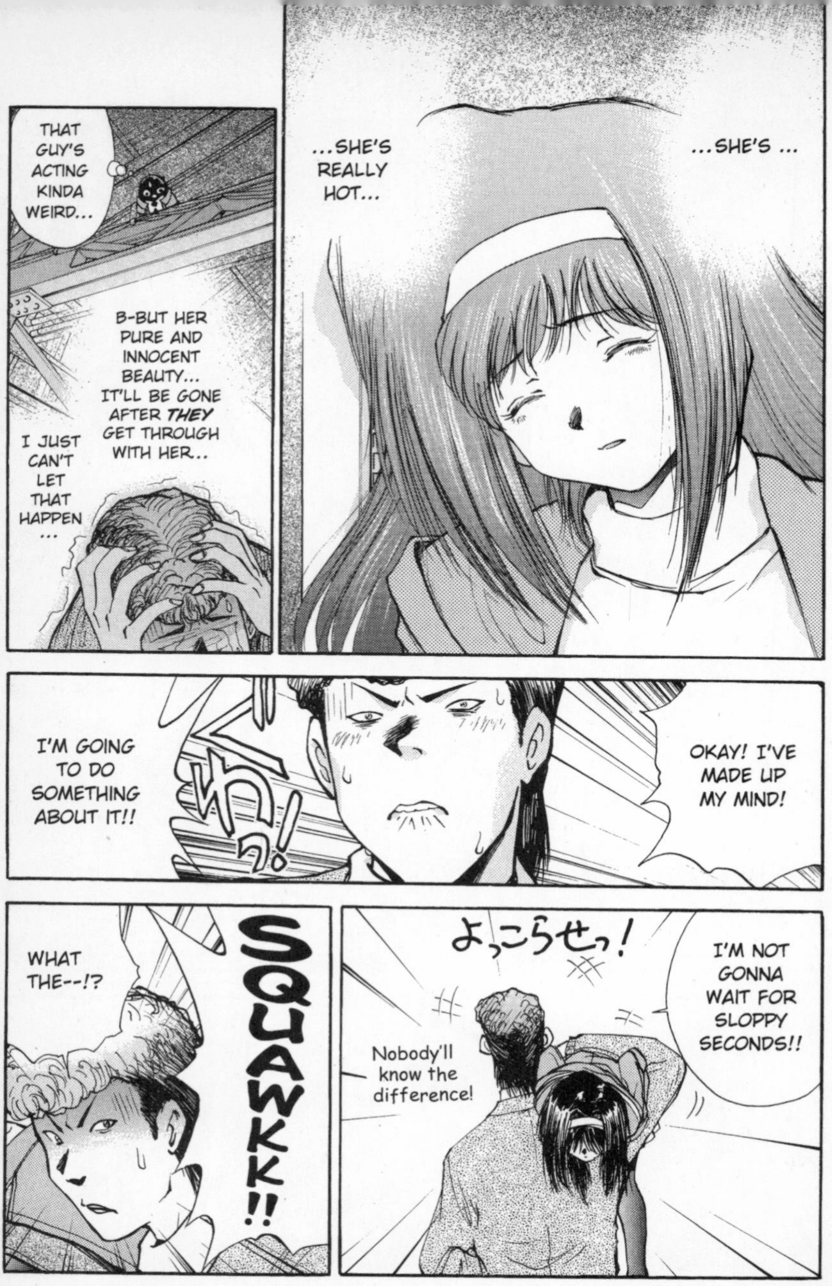
...SHE'S ...
...SHE'S REALLY HOT...
THAT GUY'S ACTING KINDA WEIRD...
B-BUT HER PURE AND INNOCENT BEAUTY... IT'LL BE GONE AFTER *THEY* GET THROUGH WITH HER...
I JUST CAN'T LET THAT HAPPEN ...
OKAY! I'VE MADE UP MY MIND!
わっ!
I'M GOING TO DO SOMETHING ABOUT IT!!
よっこらせっ!
I'M NOT GONNA WAIT FOR SLOPPY SECONDS!!
Nobody'll know the difference!
SQUAWKK!!
WHAT THE--!?

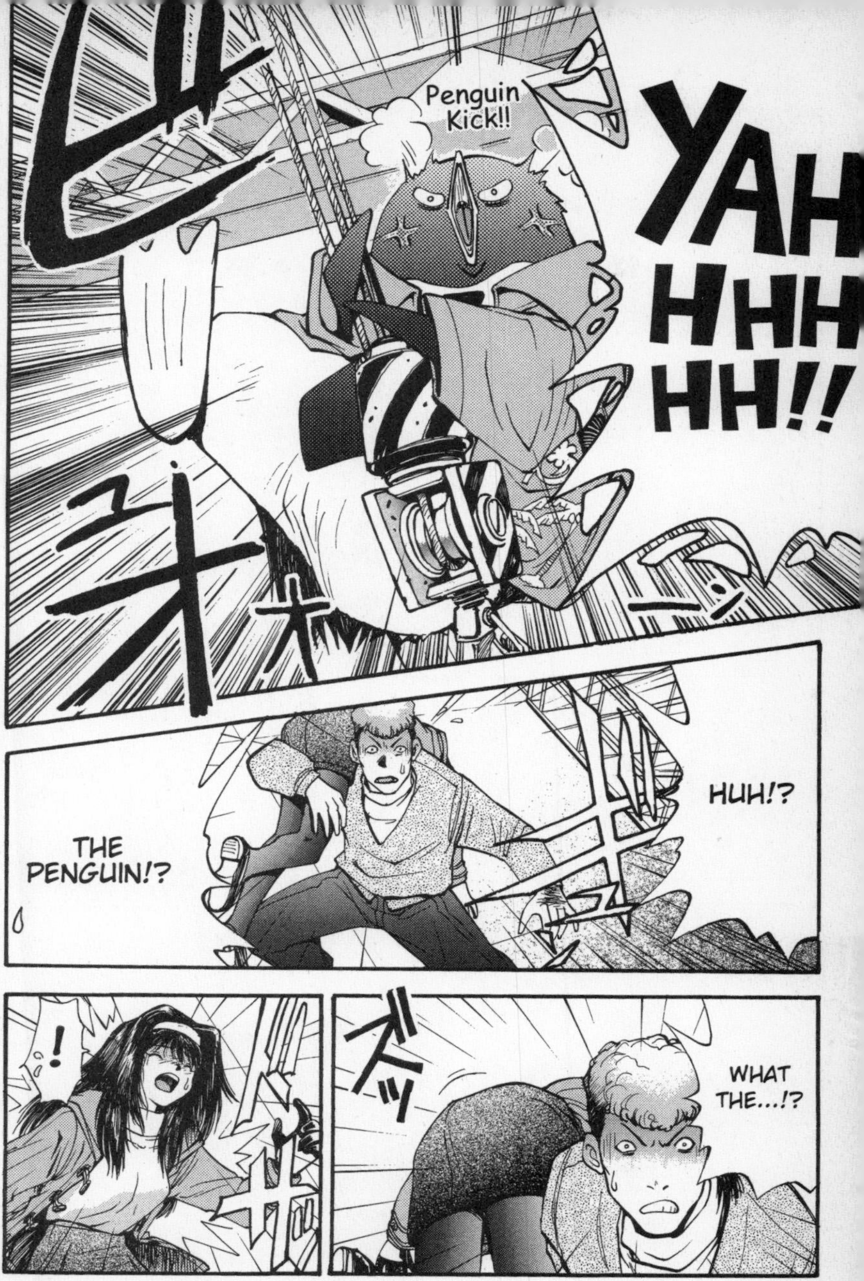
YAHHHHHH!!
Penguin Kick!!
HUH!?
THE PENGUIN!?
WHAT THE...!?
!

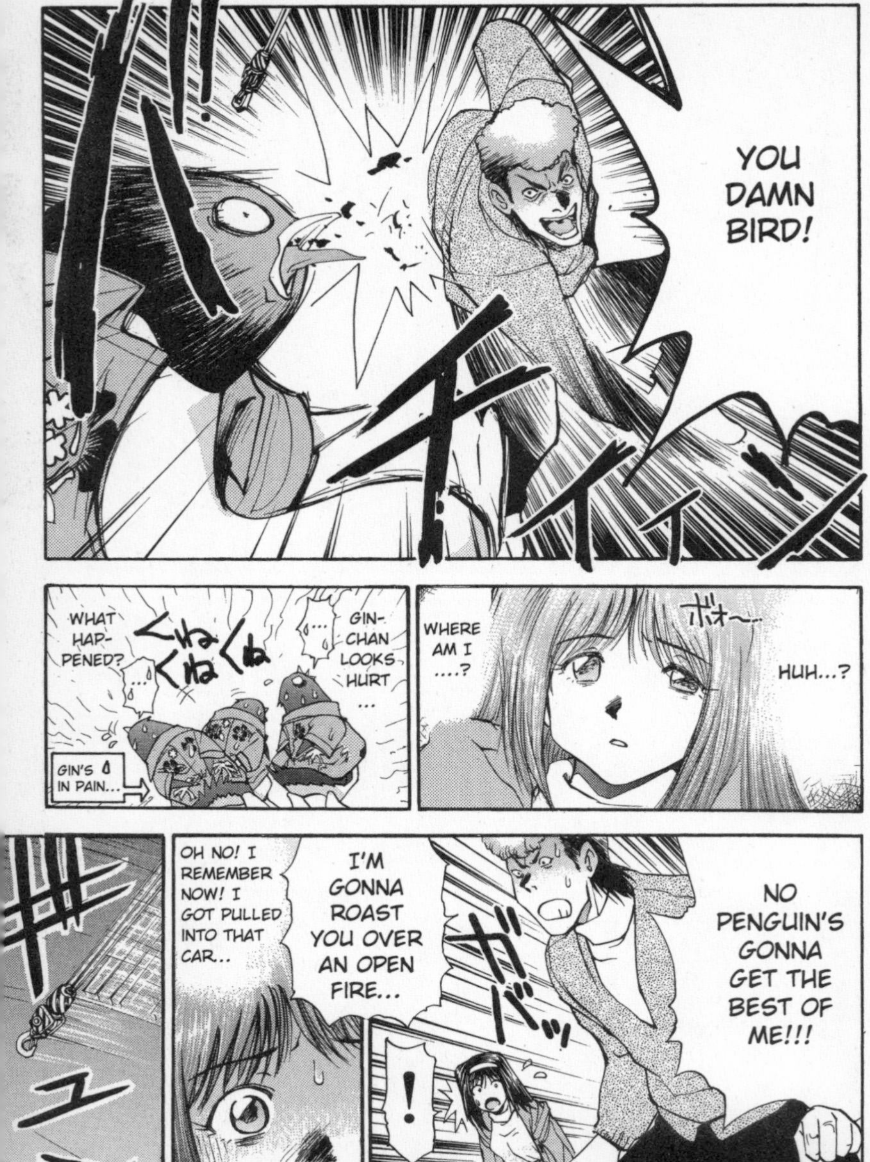
YOU DAMN BIRD!
ボオ〜…
HUH...?
WHERE AM I ....?
GIN-CHAN LOOKS HURT ...
くねくね くねくね
WHAT HAPPENED?
GIN'S IN PAIN...
NO PENGUIN'S GONNA GET THE BEST OF ME!!!
I'M GONNA ROAST YOU OVER AN OPEN FIRE...
OH NO! I REMEMBER NOW! I GOT PULLED INTO THAT CAR...
!

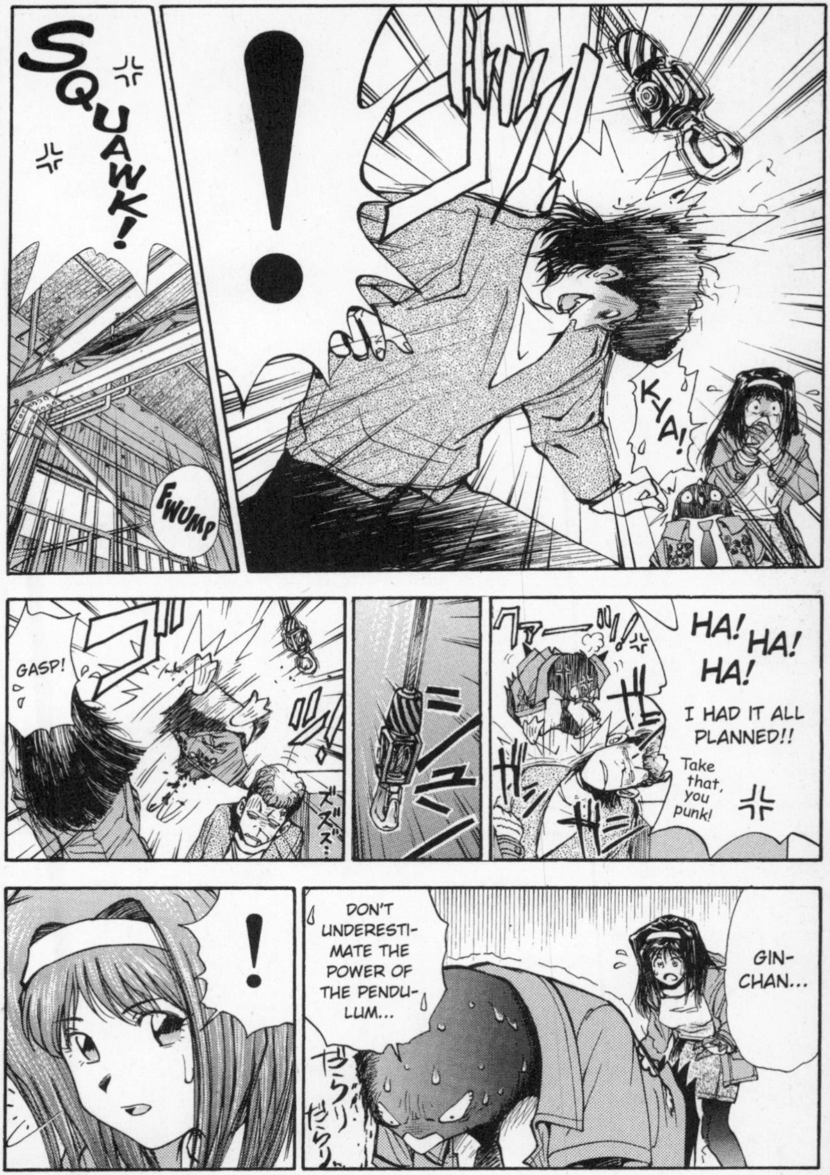
!
KYA!
SQUAWK!
FWUMP
HA! HA! HA!
I HAD IT ALL PLANNED!!
Take that, you punk!
GASP!
GIN-CHAN...
DON'T UNDERESTIMATE THE POWER OF THE PENDULUM...
!

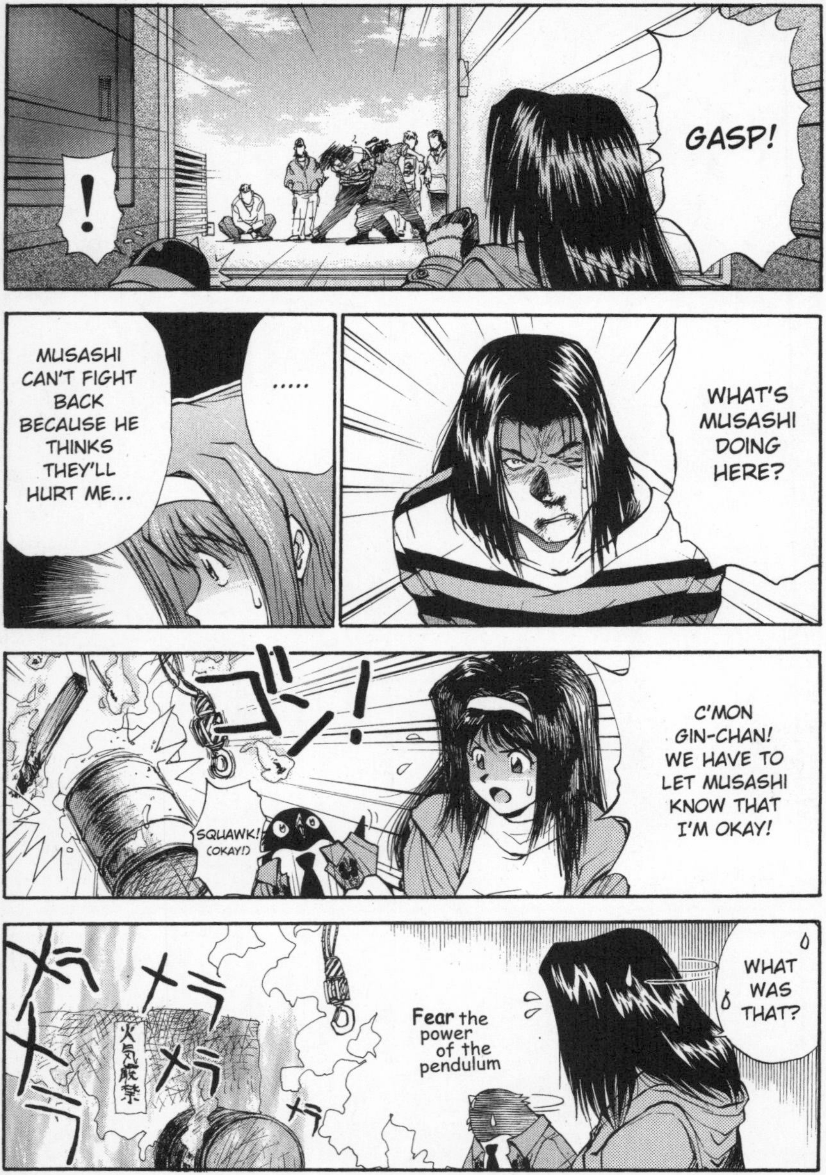
GASP!
!
WHAT'S MUSASHI DOING HERE?
.....
MUSASHI CAN'T FIGHT BACK BECAUSE HE THINKS THEY'LL HURT ME...
C'MON GIN-CHAN! WE HAVE TO LET MUSASHI KNOW THAT I'M OKAY!
ゴン!
SQUAWK!
(OKAY!)
WHAT WAS THAT?
Fear the power of the pendulum
メラ メラ
火気厳禁

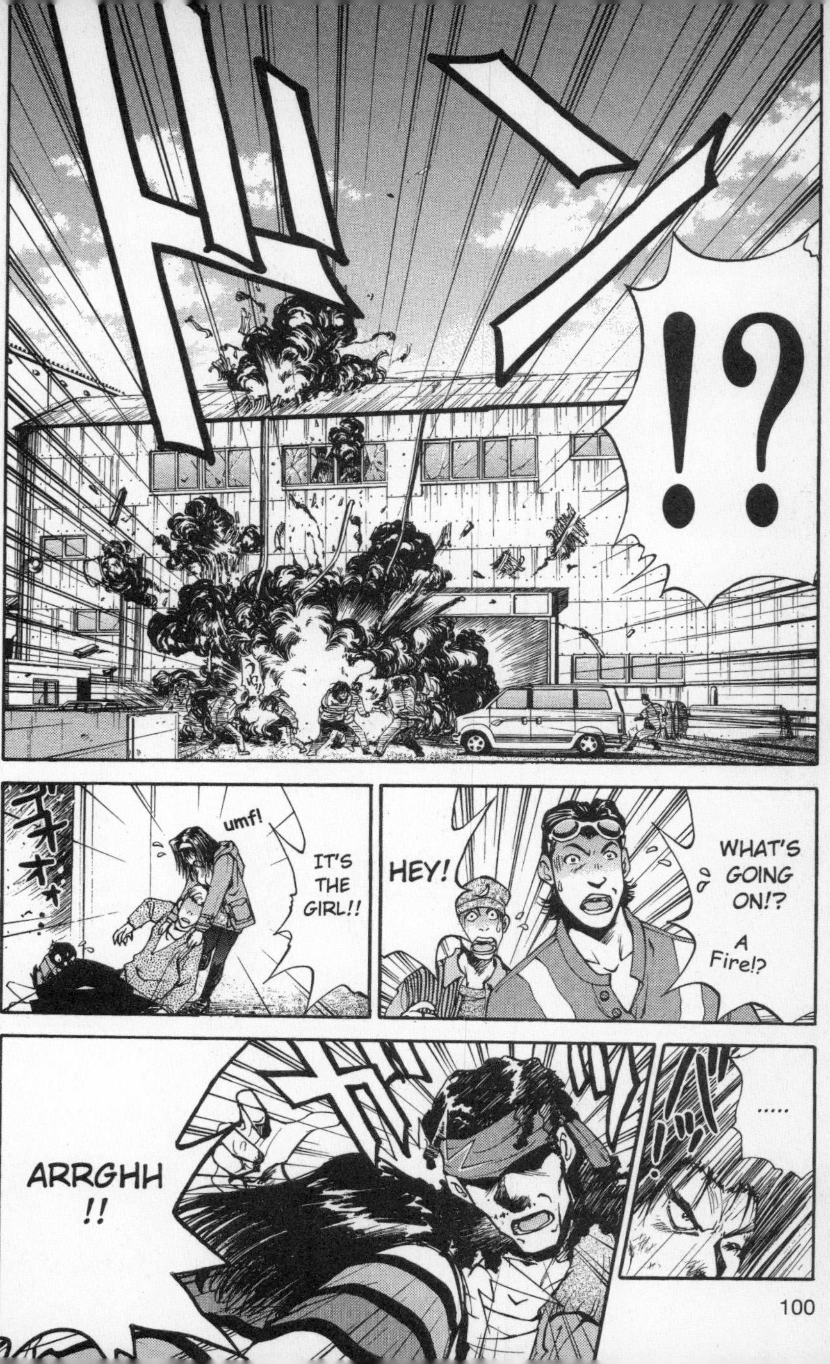
!?
WHAT'S GOING ON!?
A Fire!?
HEY!
IT'S THE GIRL!!
umf!
.....
ARRGHH !!

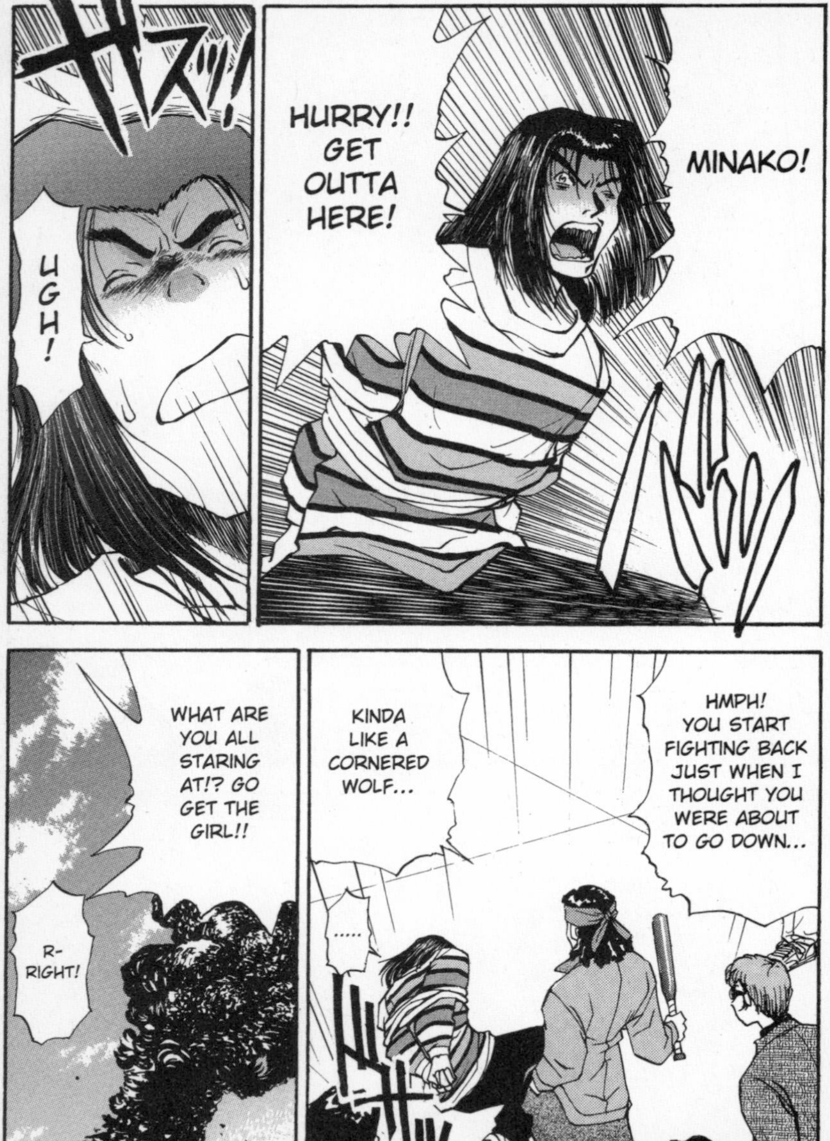
MINAKO!
HURRY!! GET OUTTA HERE!
ザスッ!
UGH!
HMPH! YOU START FIGHTING BACK JUST WHEN I THOUGHT YOU WERE ABOUT TO GO DOWN...
KINDA LIKE A CORNERED WOLF...
.....
WHAT ARE YOU ALL STARING AT!? GO GET THE GIRL!!
R-RIGHT!

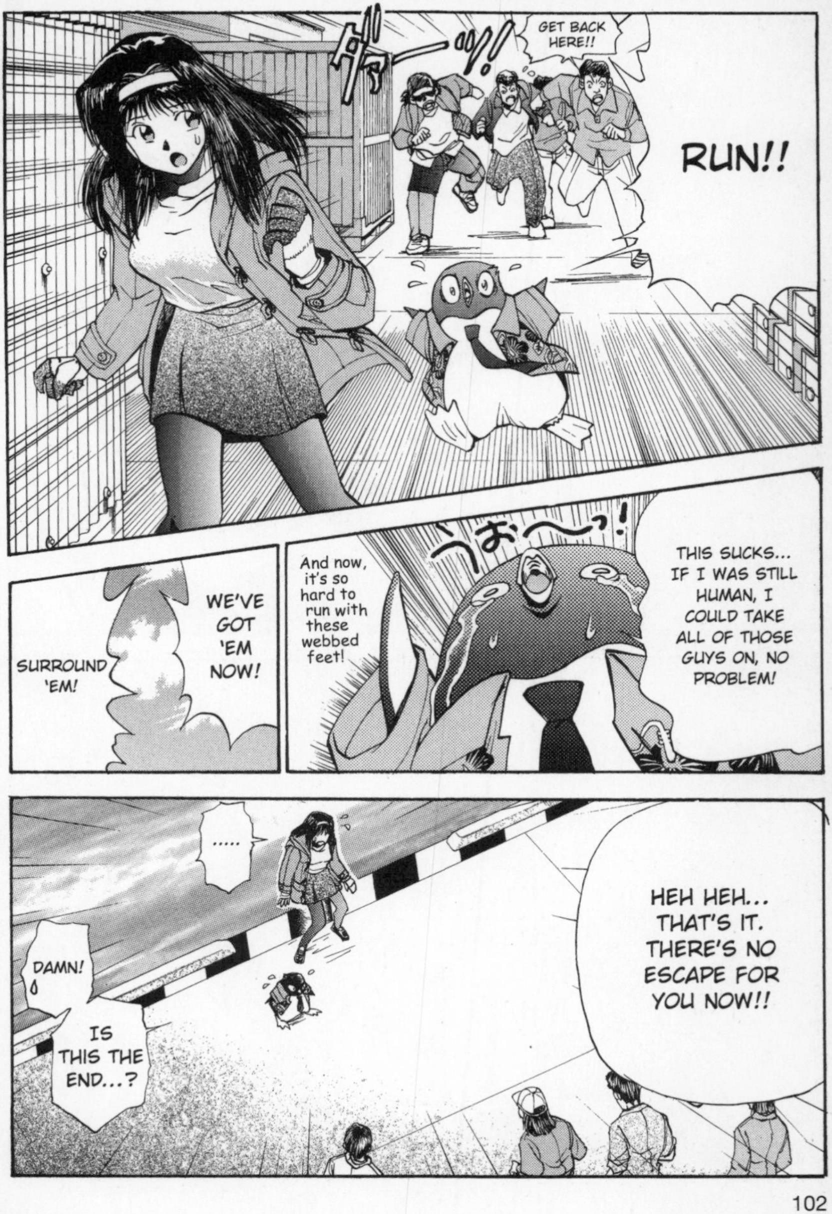
GET BACK HERE!!
RUN!!
うお〜っ!
THIS SUCKS... IF I WAS STILL HUMAN, I COULD TAKE ALL OF THOSE GUYS ON, NO PROBLEM!
And now, it's so hard to run with these webbed feet!
WE'VE GOT 'EM NOW!
SURROUND 'EM!
HEH HEH... THAT'S IT. THERE'S NO ESCAPE FOR YOU NOW!!
......
DAMN!
IS THIS THE END...?

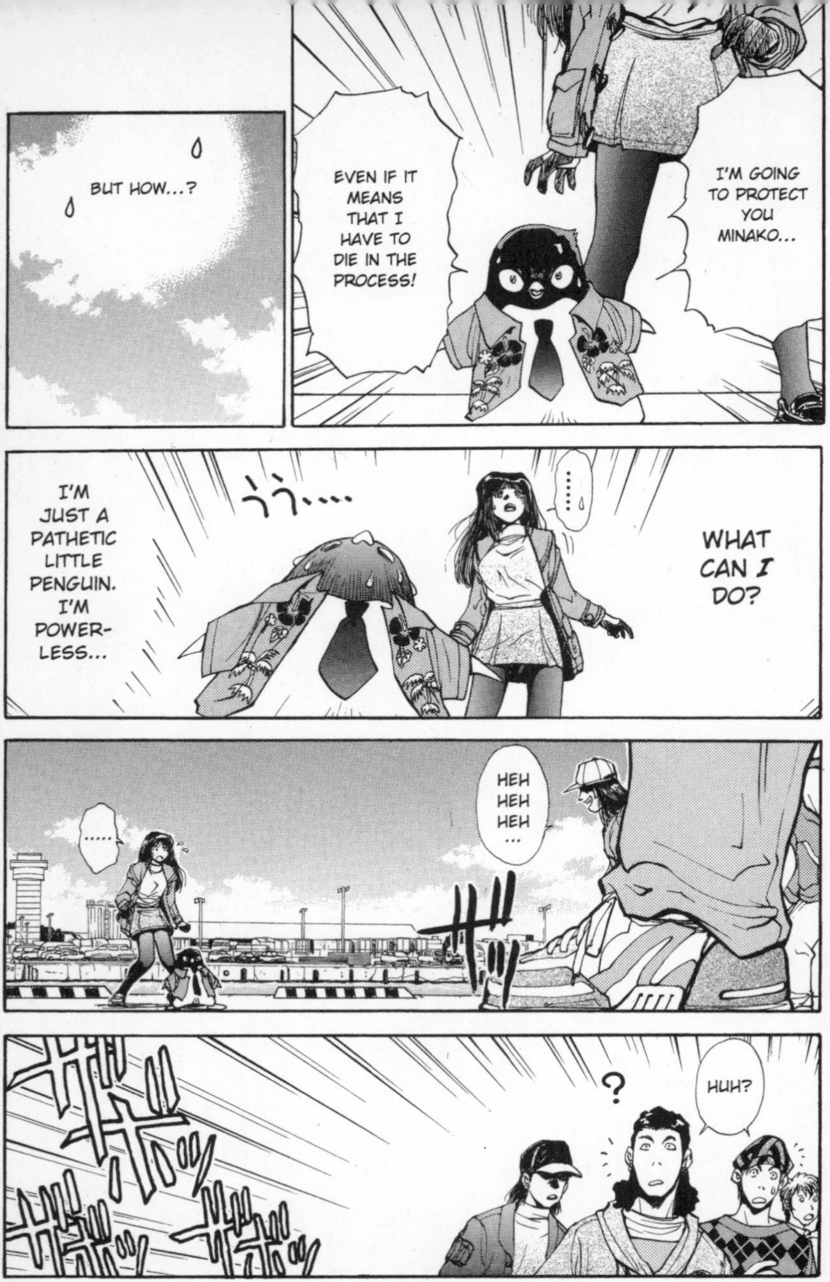
I'M GOING TO PROTECT YOU MINAKO...
EVEN IF IT MEANS THAT I HAVE TO DIE IN THE PROCESS!
BUT HOW...?
WHAT CAN I DO?
......
うう...
I'M JUST A PATHETIC LITTLE PENGUIN. I'M POWERLESS...
HEH HEH HEH ...
......
HUH?
?

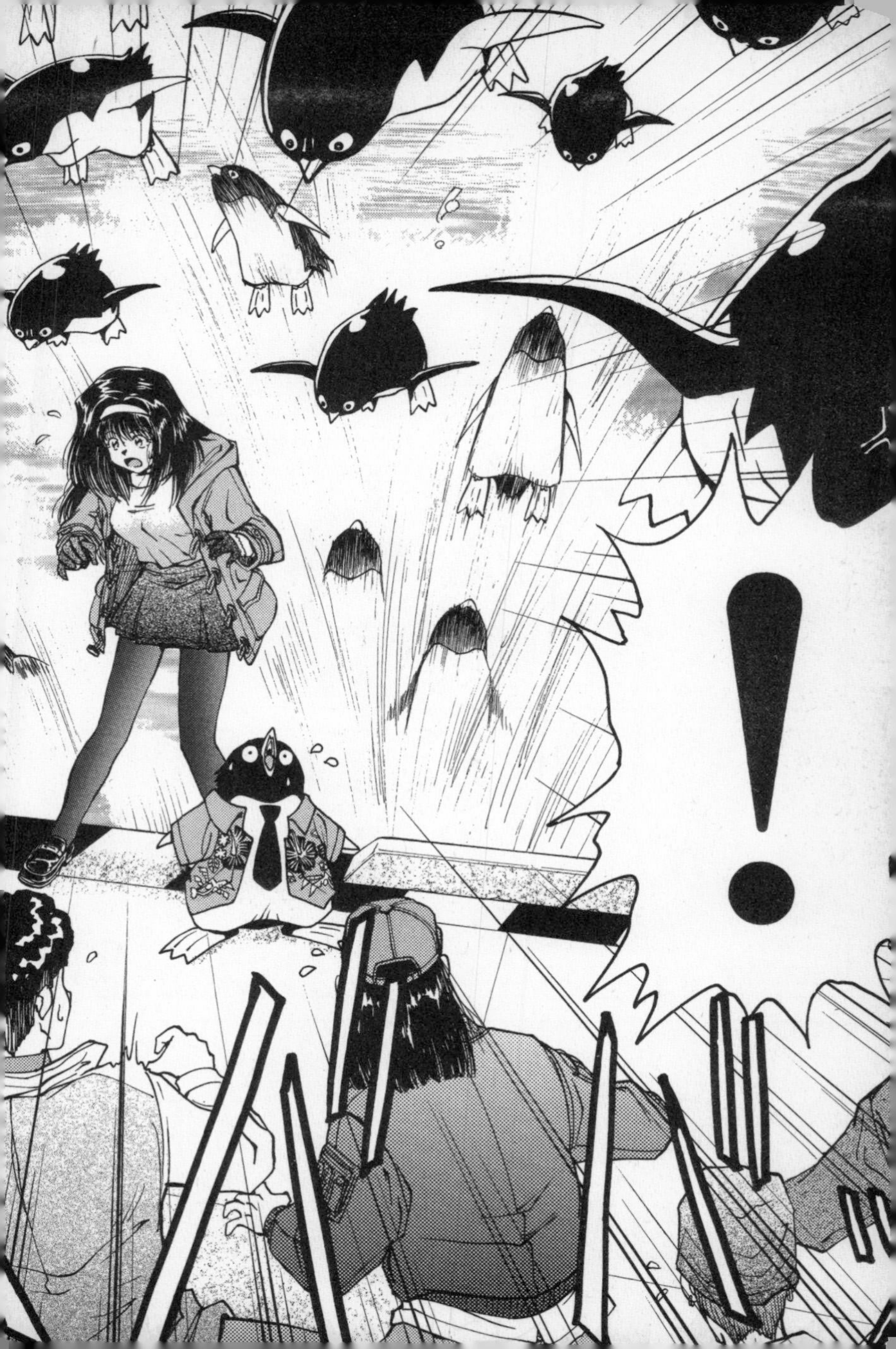
!

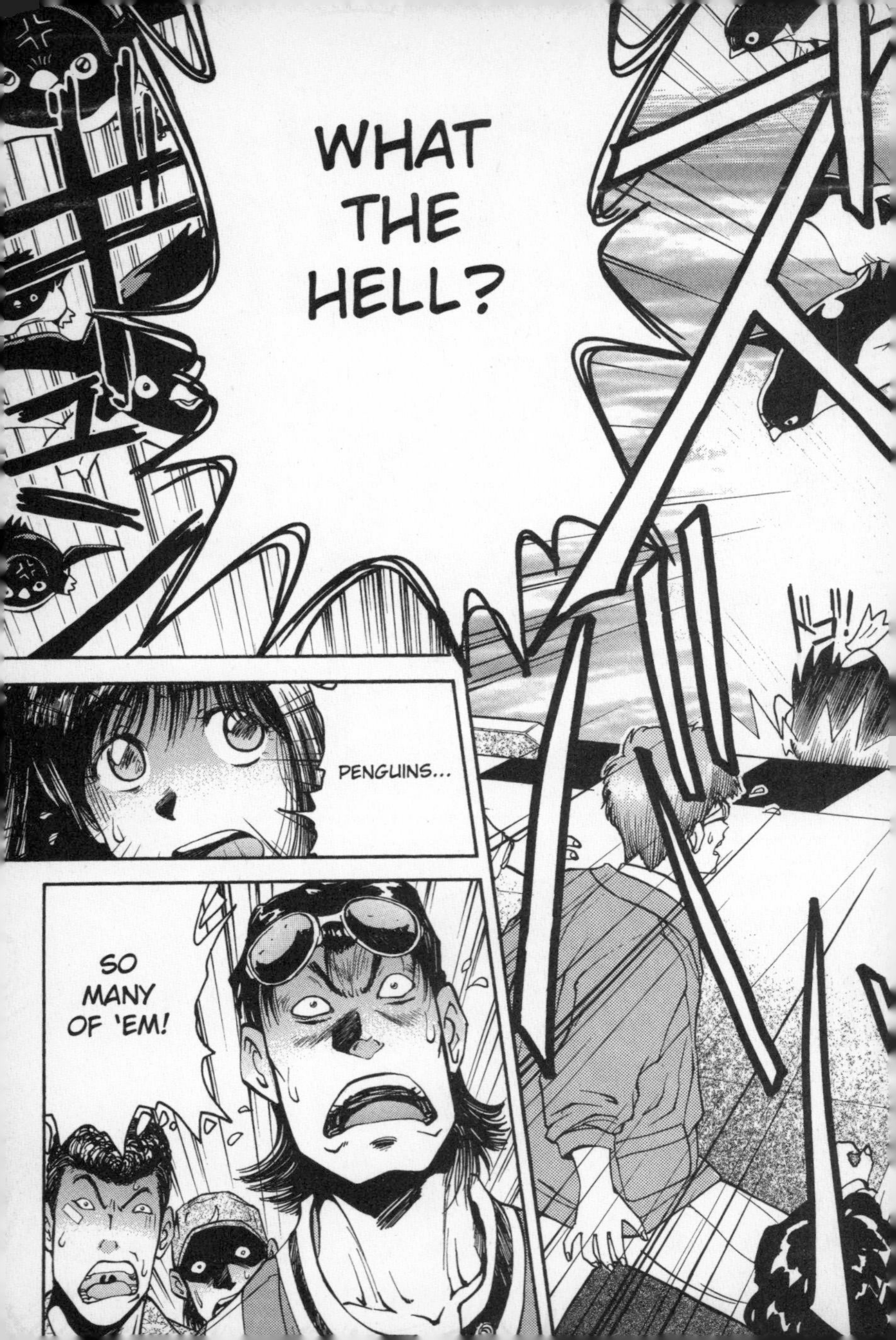
WHAT THE HELL?
PENGUINS...
SO MANY OF 'EM!

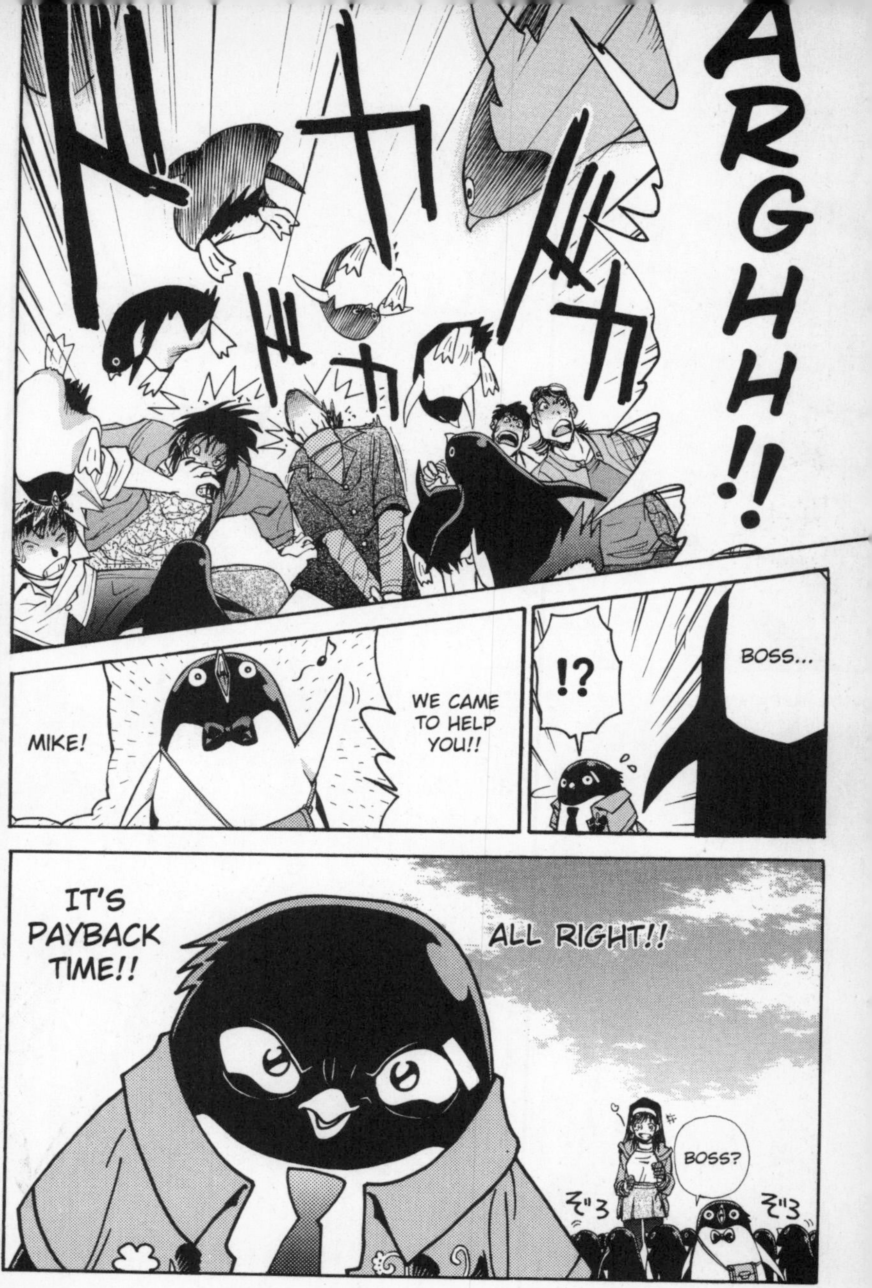
ARGH!!
BOSS...
!?
WE CAME TO HELP YOU!!
MIKE!
ALL RIGHT!!
IT'S PAYBACK TIME!!
BOSS?
ぞろ
ぞろ

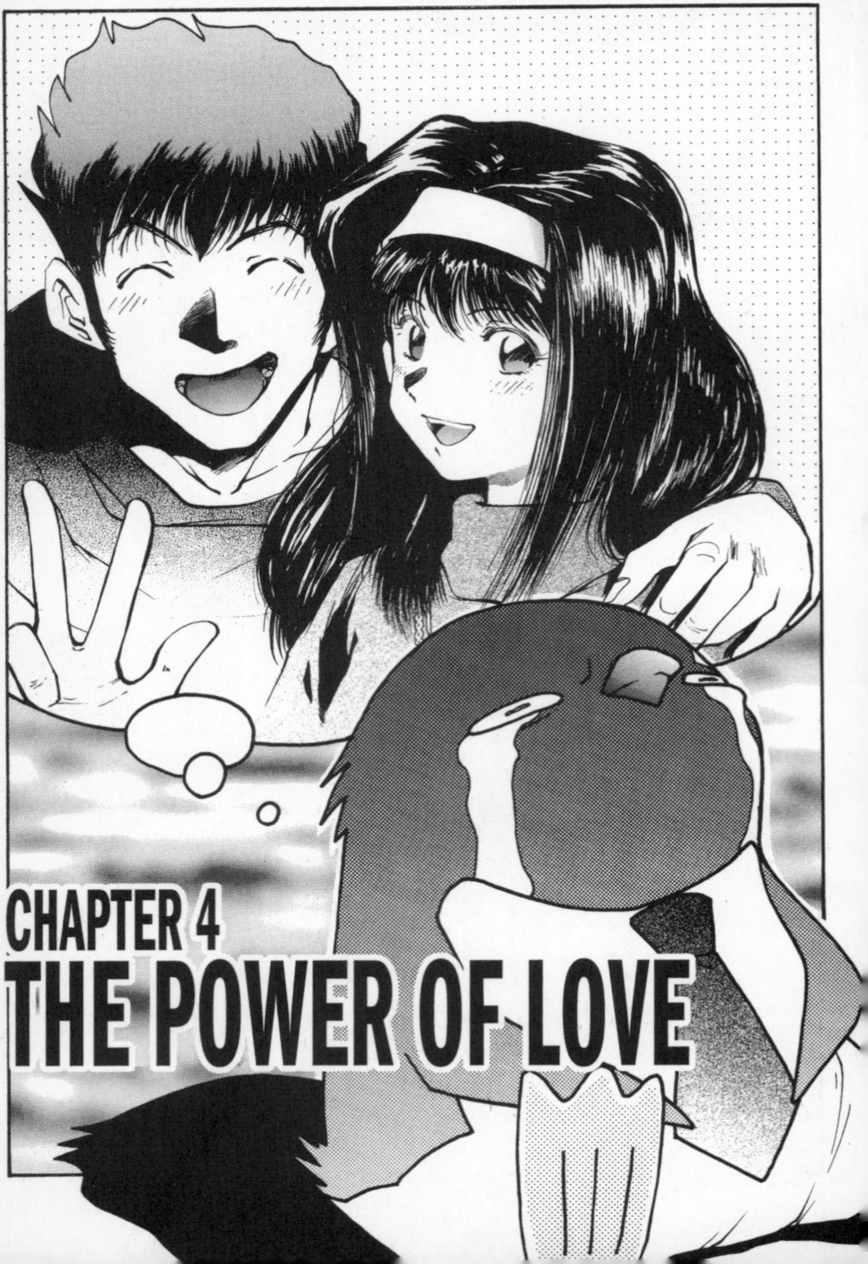
CHAPTER 4
THE POWER OF LOVE

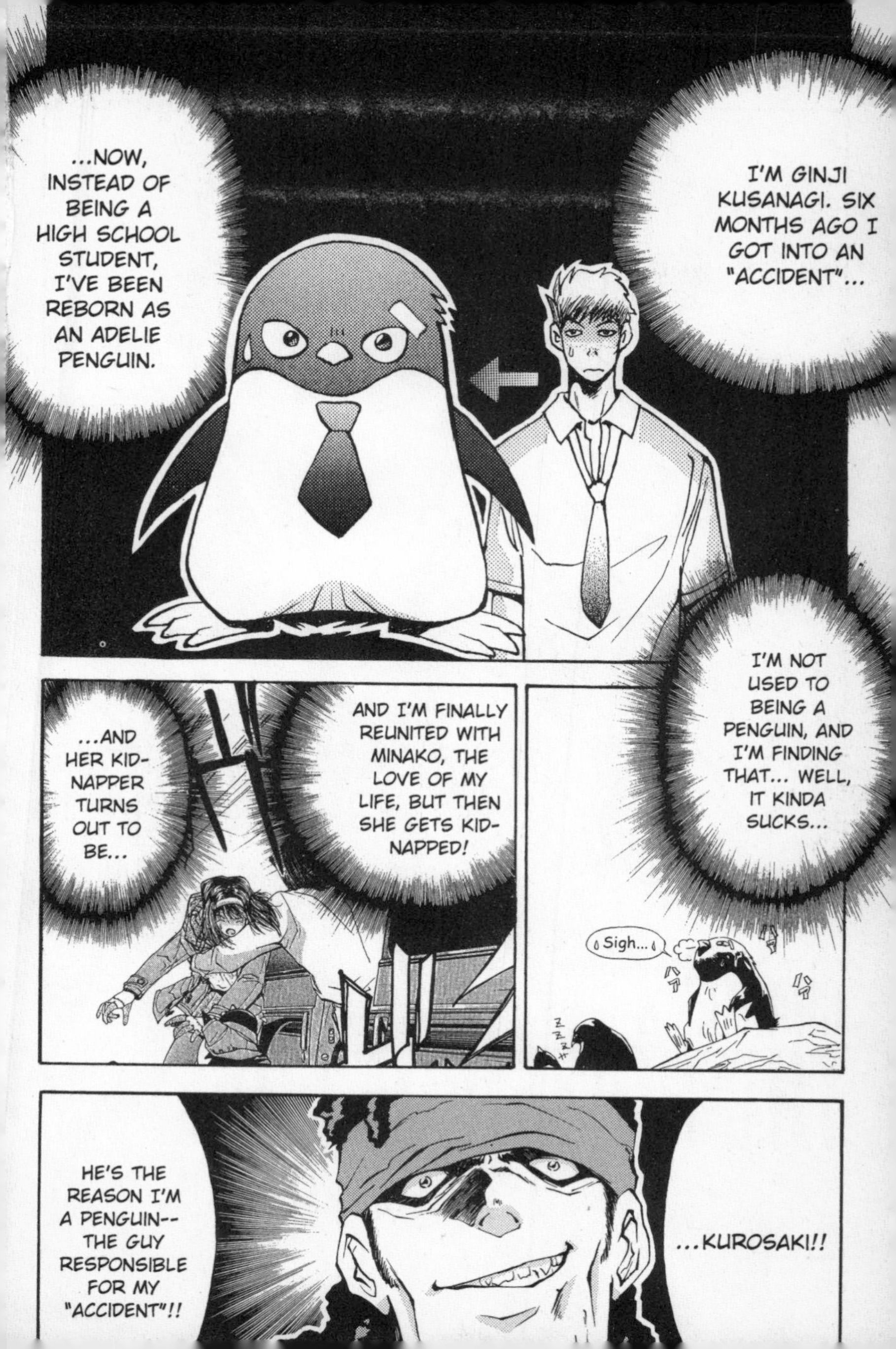
I'M GINJI KUSANAGI. SIX MONTHS AGO I GOT INTO AN "ACCIDENT"...
...NOW, INSTEAD OF BEING A HIGH SCHOOL STUDENT, I'VE BEEN REBORN AS AN ADELIE PENGUIN.
I'M NOT USED TO BEING A PENGUIN, AND I'M FINDING THAT... WELL, IT KINDA SUCKS...
Sigh...
AND I'M FINALLY REUNITED WITH MINAKO, THE LOVE OF MY LIFE, BUT THEN SHE GETS KID-NAPPED!
...AND HER KID-NAPPER TURNS OUT TO BE...
HE'S THE REASON I'M A PENGUIN-- THE GUY RESPONSIBLE FOR MY "ACCIDENT"!!
...KUROSAKI!!

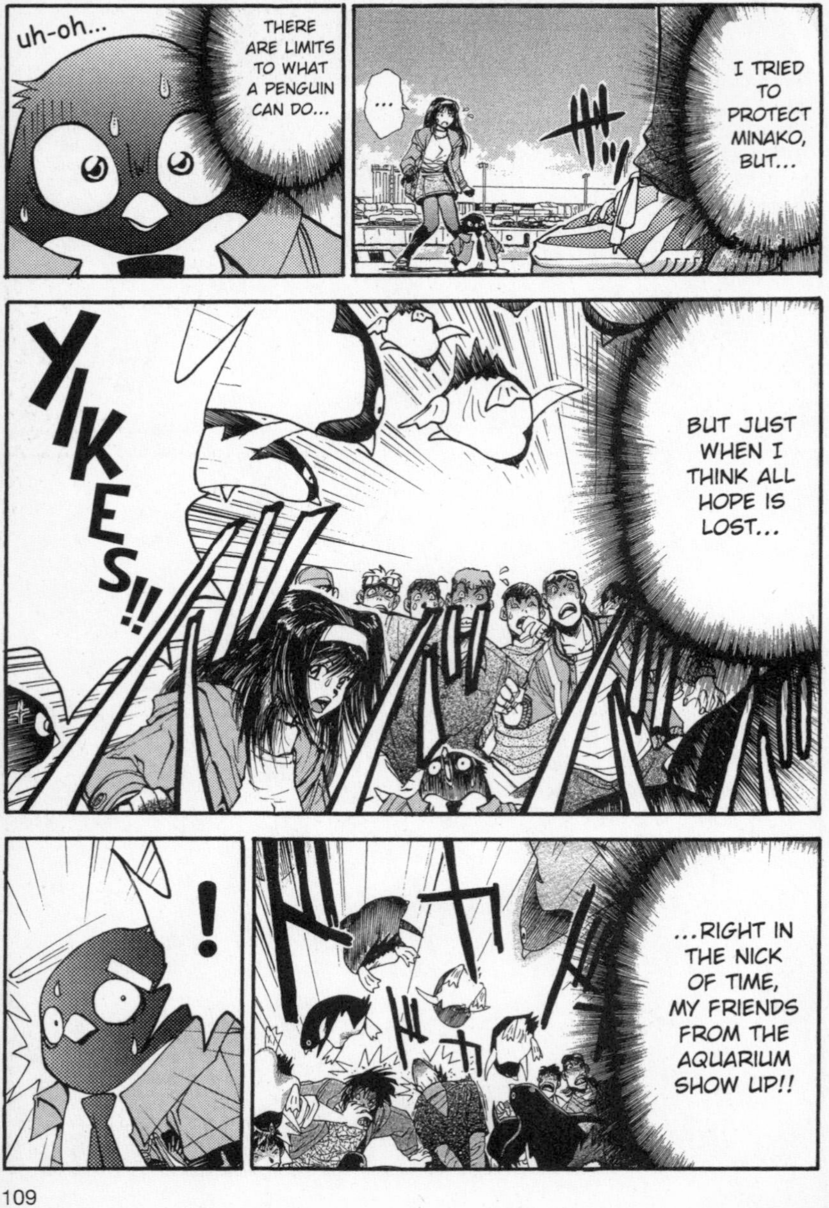
I TRIED TO PROTECT MINAKO, BUT...
...
THERE ARE LIMITS TO WHAT A PENGUIN CAN DO...
uh-oh...
BUT JUST WHEN I THINK ALL HOPE IS LOST...
YIKES!!
...RIGHT IN THE NICK OF TIME, MY FRIENDS FROM THE AQUARIUM SHOW UP!!
!

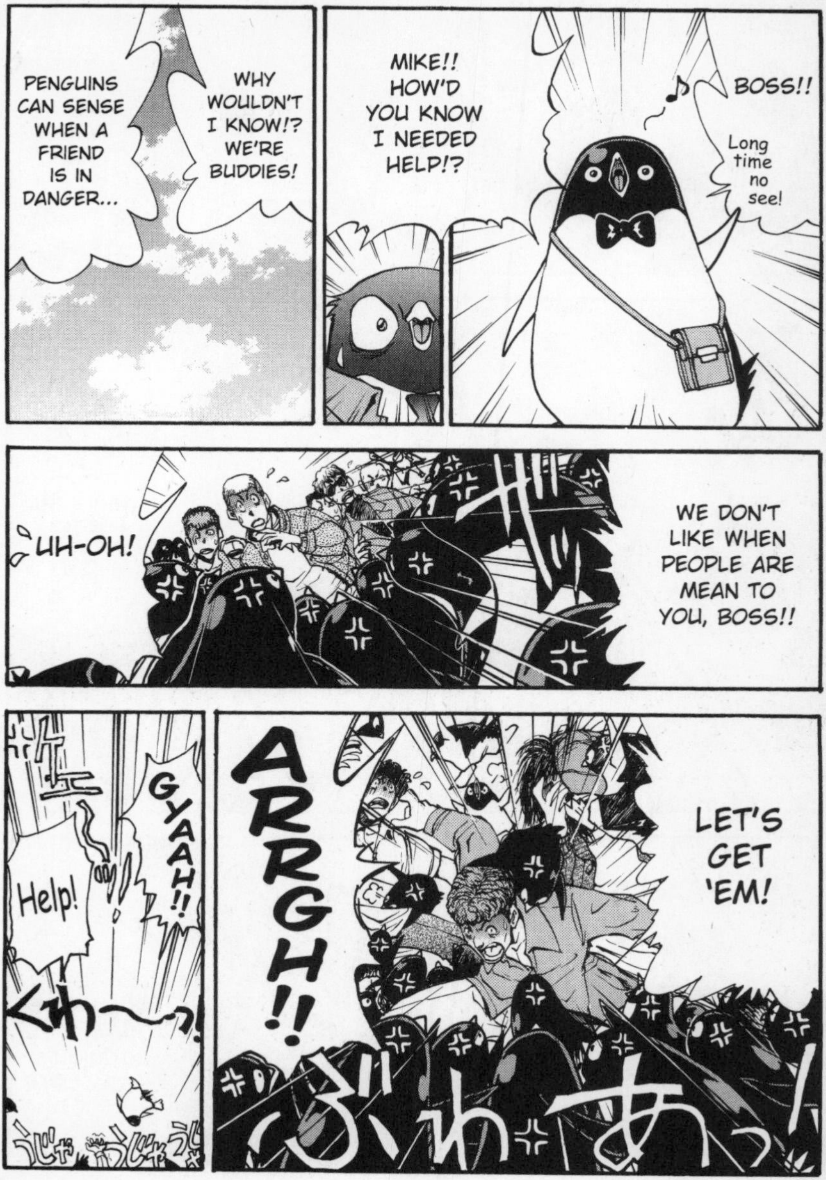

BOSS!!
Long time no see!
MIKE!! HOW'D YOU KNOW I NEEDED HELP!?
WHY WOULDN'T I KNOW!? WE'RE BUDDIES!
PENGUINS CAN SENSE WHEN A FRIEND IS IN DANGER...
WE DON'T LIKE WHEN PEOPLE ARE MEAN TO YOU, BOSS!!
UH-OH!
LET'S GET 'EM!
ARRGH!!
ぶわあっ!
GYAAH!!
Help!
くわ〜っ!

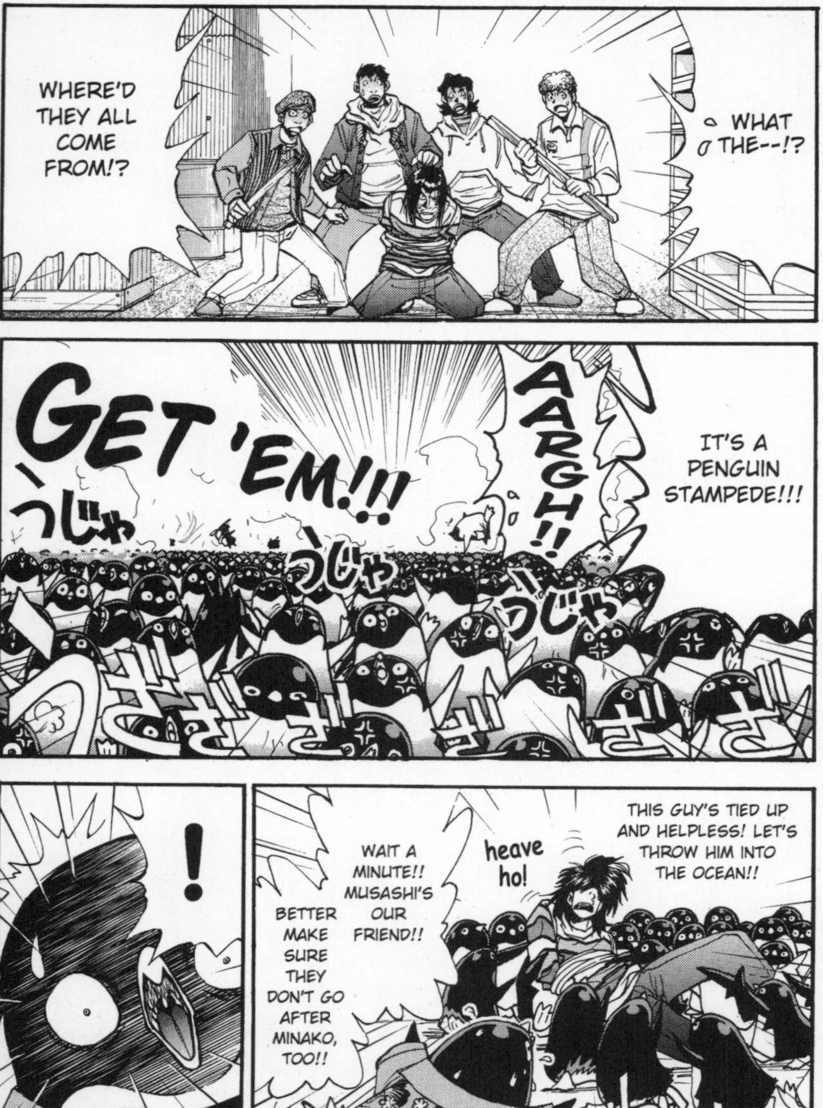
WHAT THE--!?
WHERE'D THEY ALL COME FROM!?
IT'S A PENGUIN STAMPEDE!!!
AARGH!!
GET 'EM!!!
うじゃ
うじゃ
うじゃ
THIS GUY'S TIED UP AND HELPLESS! LET'S THROW HIM INTO THE OCEAN!!
heave ho!
WAIT A MINUTE!! MUSASHI'S OUR FRIEND!!
BETTER MAKE SURE THEY DON'T GO AFTER MINAKO, TOO!!
わらわら
!

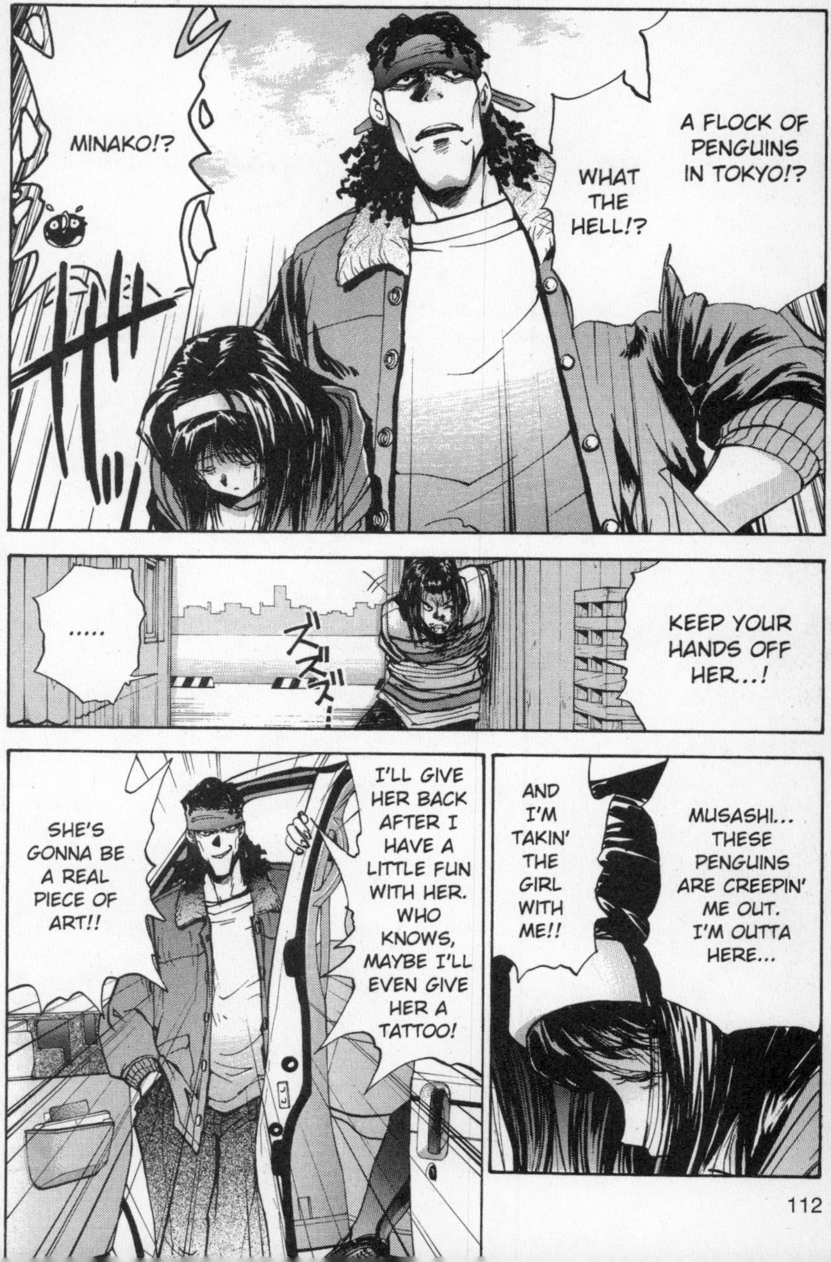
A FLOCK OF PENGUINS IN TOKYO!?
WHAT THE HELL!?
MINAKO!?
KEEP YOUR HANDS OFF HER...!
ズズズ
.....
MUSASHI... THESE PENGUINS ARE CREEPIN' ME OUT. I'M OUTTA HERE...
AND I'M TAKIN' THE GIRL WITH ME!!
I'LL GIVE HER BACK AFTER I HAVE A LITTLE FUN WITH HER. WHO KNOWS, MAYBE I'LL EVEN GIVE HER A TATTOO!
SHE'S GONNA BE A REAL PIECE OF ART!!

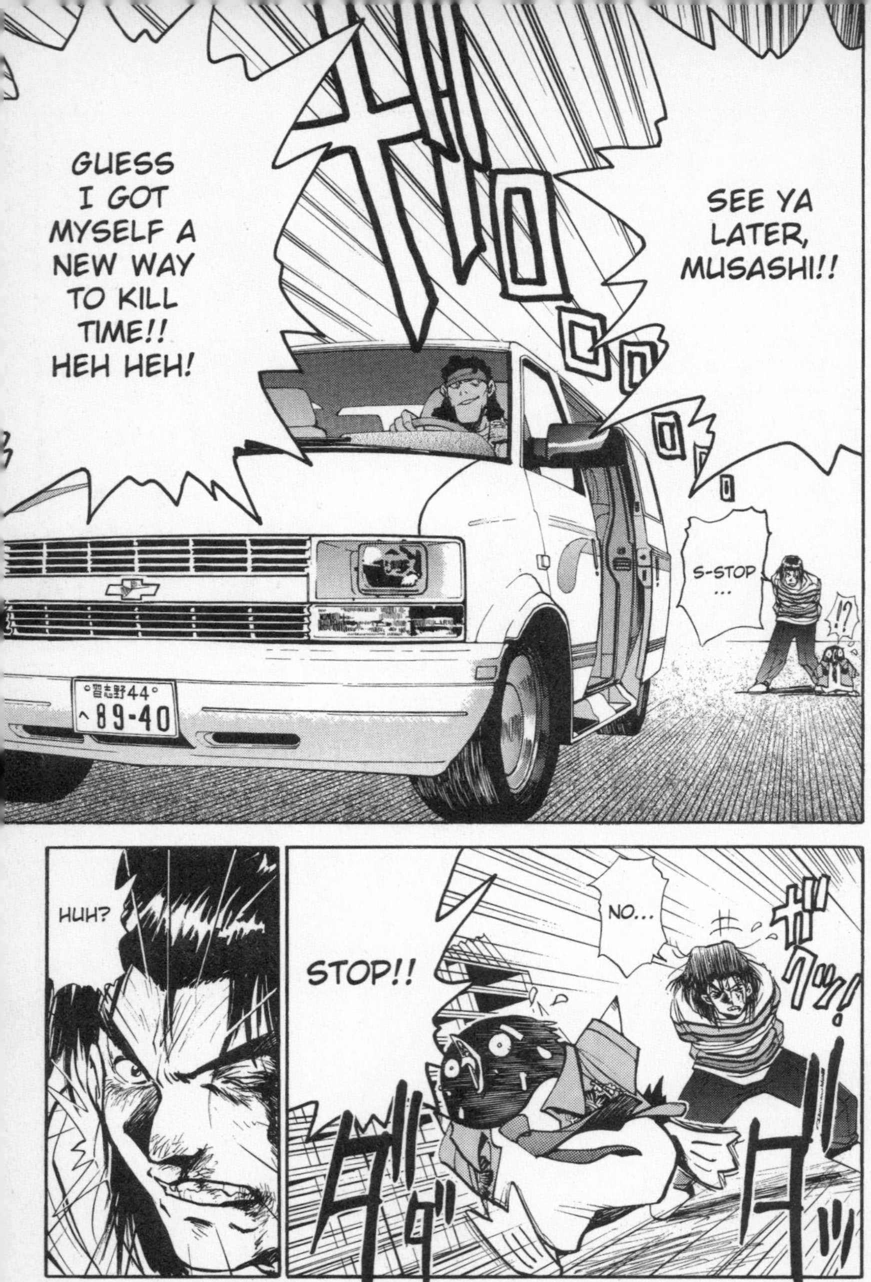
SEE YA LATER, MUSASHI!!
GUESS I GOT MYSELF A NEW WAY TO KILL TIME!! HEH HEH!
習志野44
へ 89-40
S-STOP ...
!?
NO...
STOP!!
HUH?

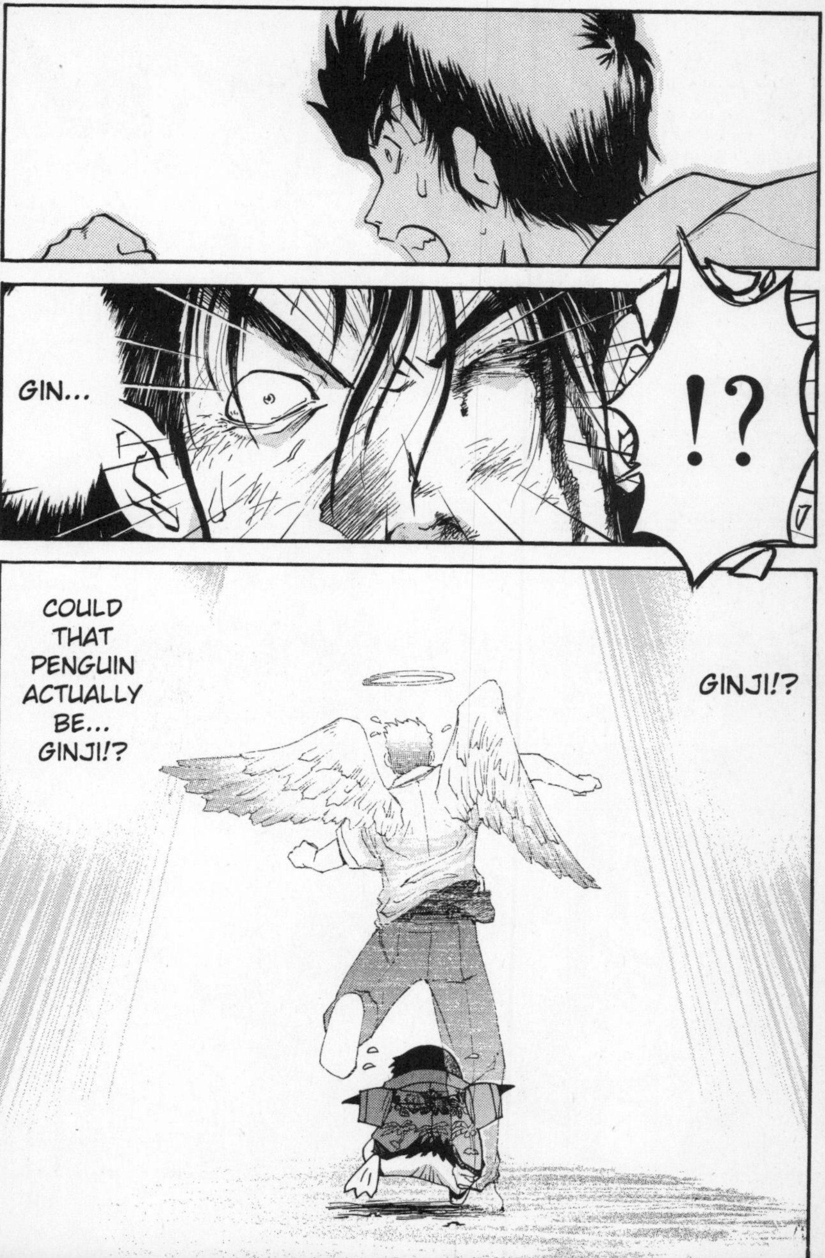
!?
GIN...
GINJI!?
COULD THAT PENGUIN ACTUALLY BE... GINJI!?

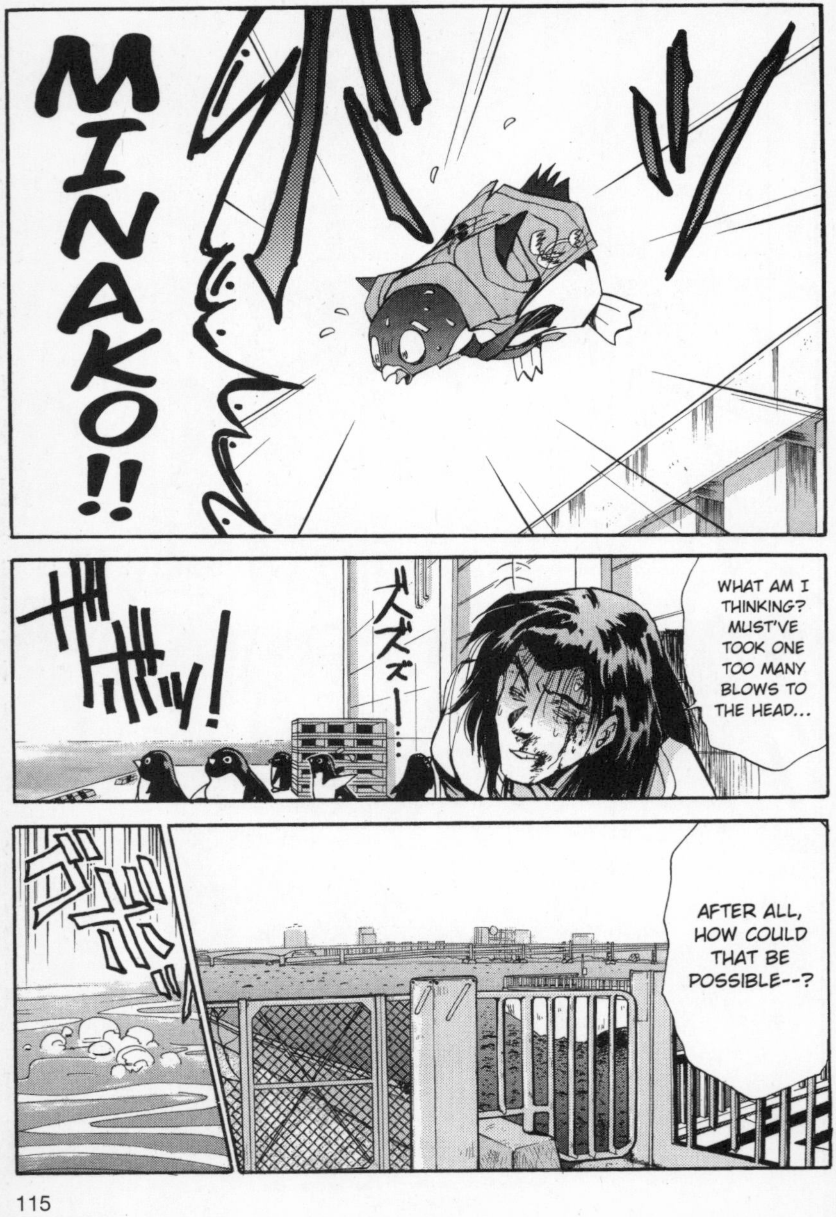
MINAKO!!
WHAT AM I THINKING? MUST'VE TOOK ONE TOO MANY BLOWS TO THE HEAD...
AFTER ALL, HOW COULD THAT BE POSSIBLE--?

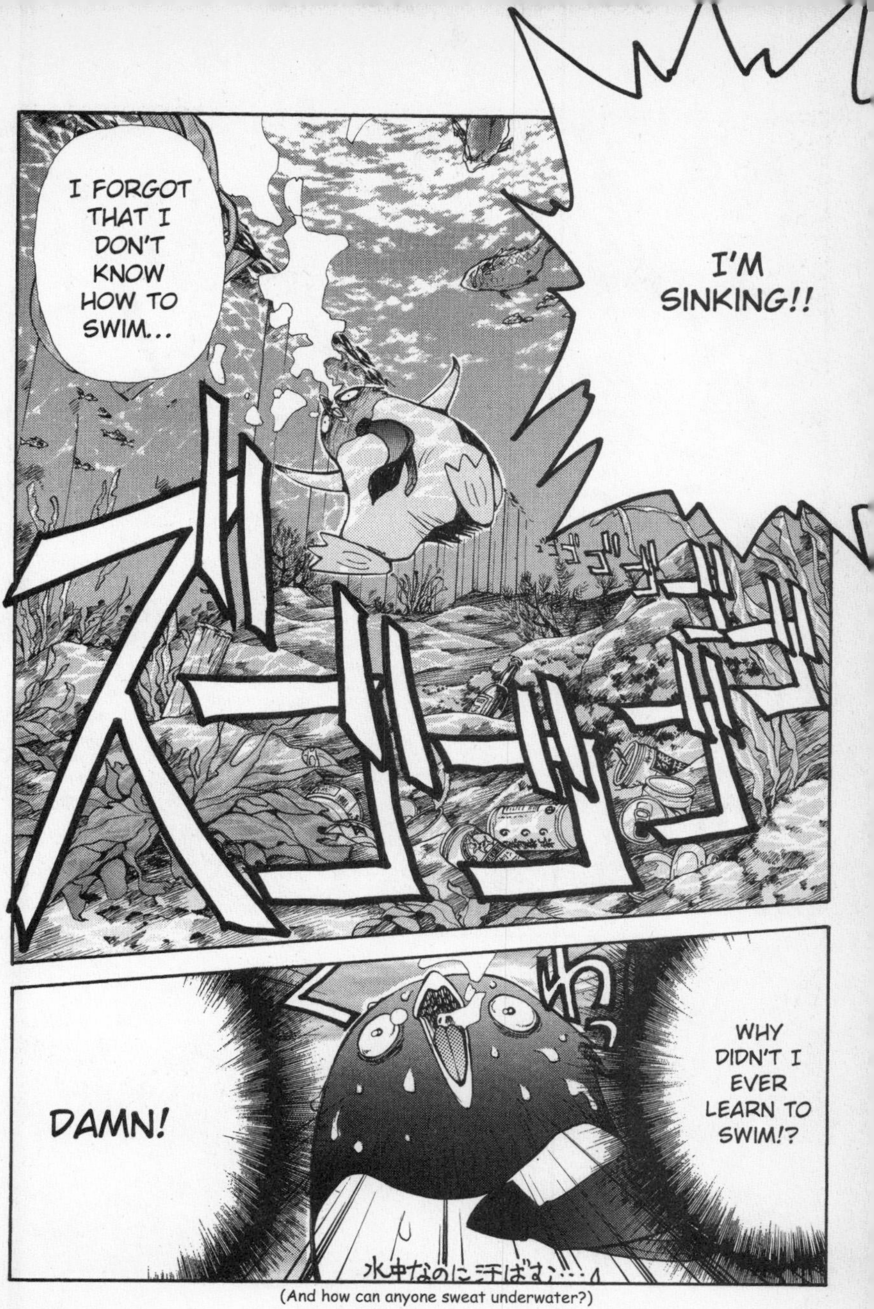
I'M SINKING!!
I FORGOT THAT I DON'T KNOW HOW TO SWIM...
WHY DIDN'T I EVER LEARN TO SWIM!?
DAMN!
水中なのに汗ばむ…
(And how can anyone sweat underwater?)

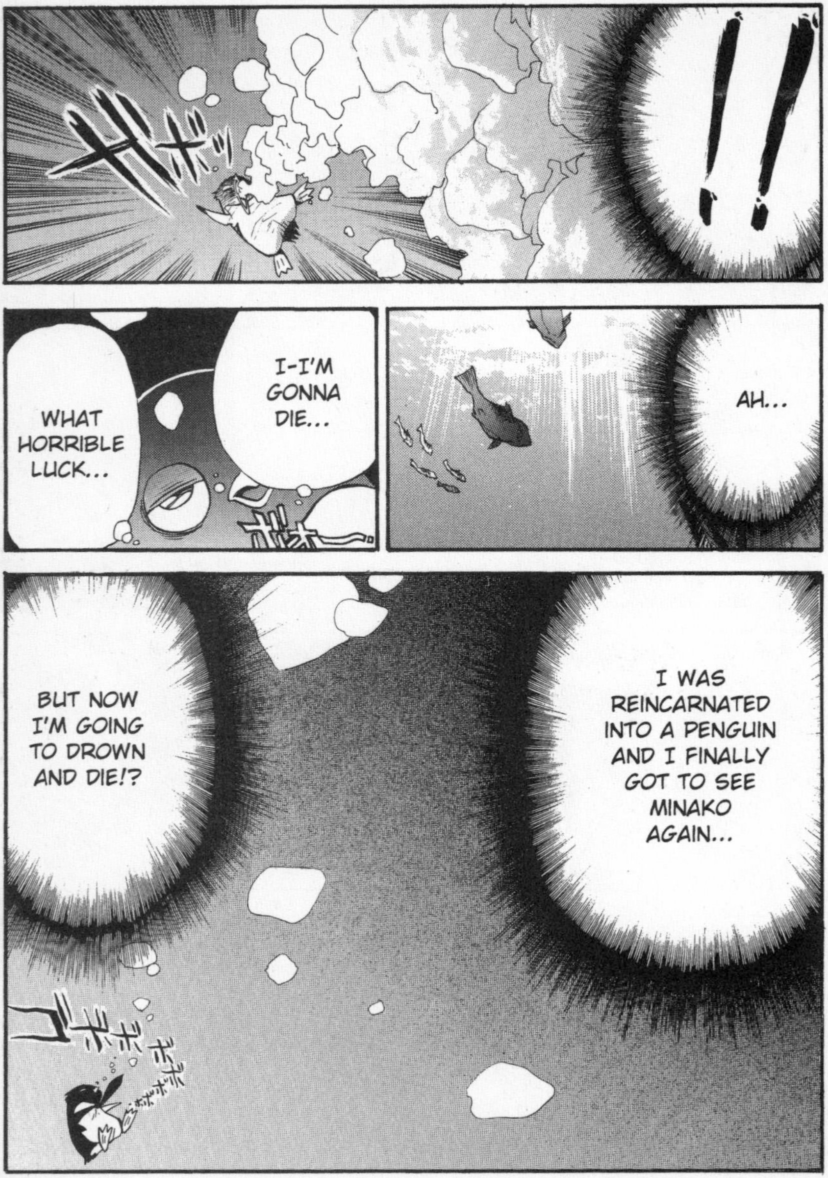
!!
AH...
I-I'M GONNA DIE...
WHAT HORRIBLE LUCK...
I WAS REINCARNATED INTO A PENGUIN AND I FINALLY GOT TO SEE MINAKO AGAIN...
BUT NOW I'M GOING TO DROWN AND DIE!?

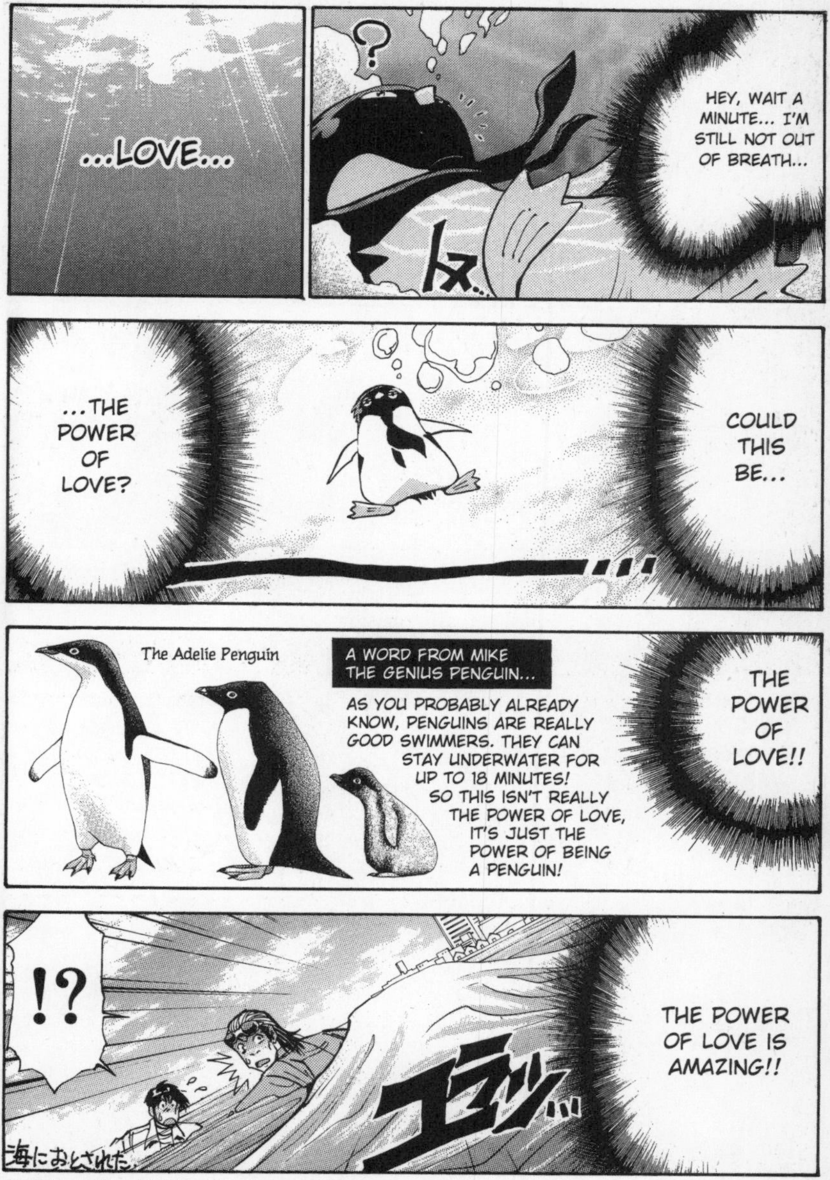
HEY, WAIT A MINUTE... I'M STILL NOT OUT OF BREATH...
...LOVE...
COULD THIS BE...
...THE POWER OF LOVE?
THE POWER OF LOVE!!
A WORD FROM MIKE THE GENIUS PENGUIN...
AS YOU PROBABLY ALREADY KNOW, PENGUINS ARE REALLY GOOD SWIMMERS. THEY CAN STAY UNDERWATER FOR UP TO 18 MINUTES! SO THIS ISN'T REALLY THE POWER OF LOVE, IT'S JUST THE POWER OF BEING A PENGUIN!
The Adelie Penguin
THE POWER OF LOVE IS AMAZING!!
!?
海におとされた
(THESE GUYS GOT THROWN INTO THE SEA.)

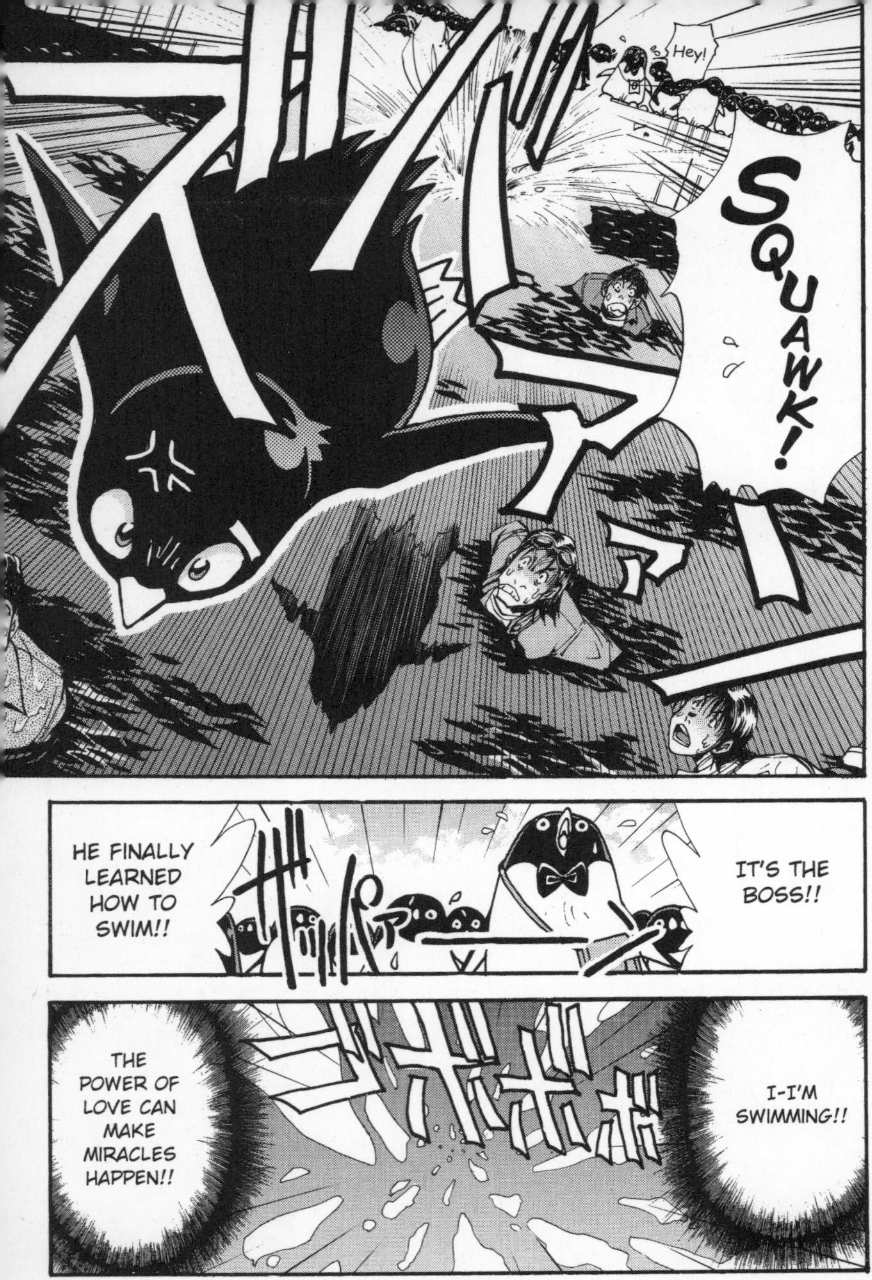
Hey!
SQUAWK!
IT'S THE BOSS!!
HE FINALLY LEARNED HOW TO SWIM!!
I-I'M SWIMMING!!
THE POWER OF LOVE CAN MAKE MIRACLES HAPPEN!!

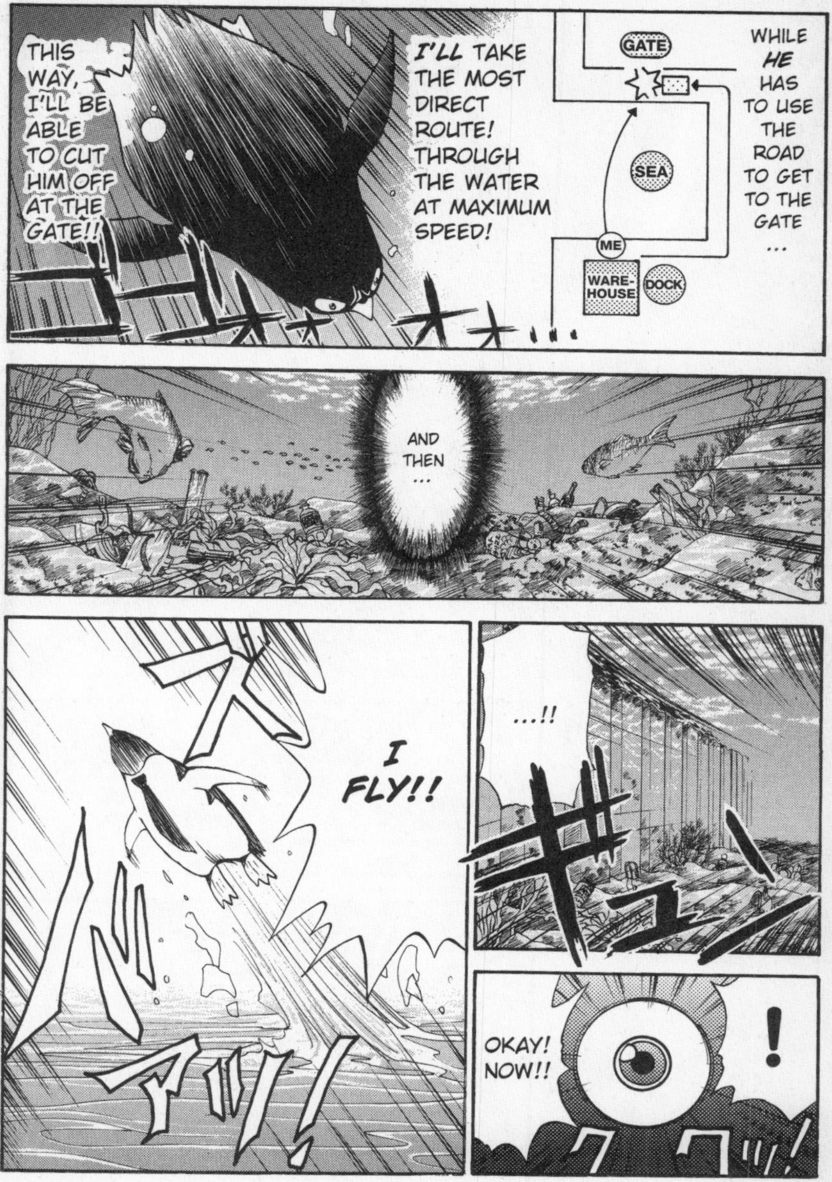
WHILE HE HAS TO USE THE ROAD TO GET TO THE GATE ...
GATE
SEA
ME
WARE-HOUSE
DOCK
I'LL TAKE THE MOST DIRECT ROUTE! THROUGH THE WATER AT MAXIMUM SPEED!
THIS WAY, I'LL BE ABLE TO CUT HIM OFF AT THE GATE!!
AND THEN ...
...!!
OKAY! NOW!!
!
I FLY!!

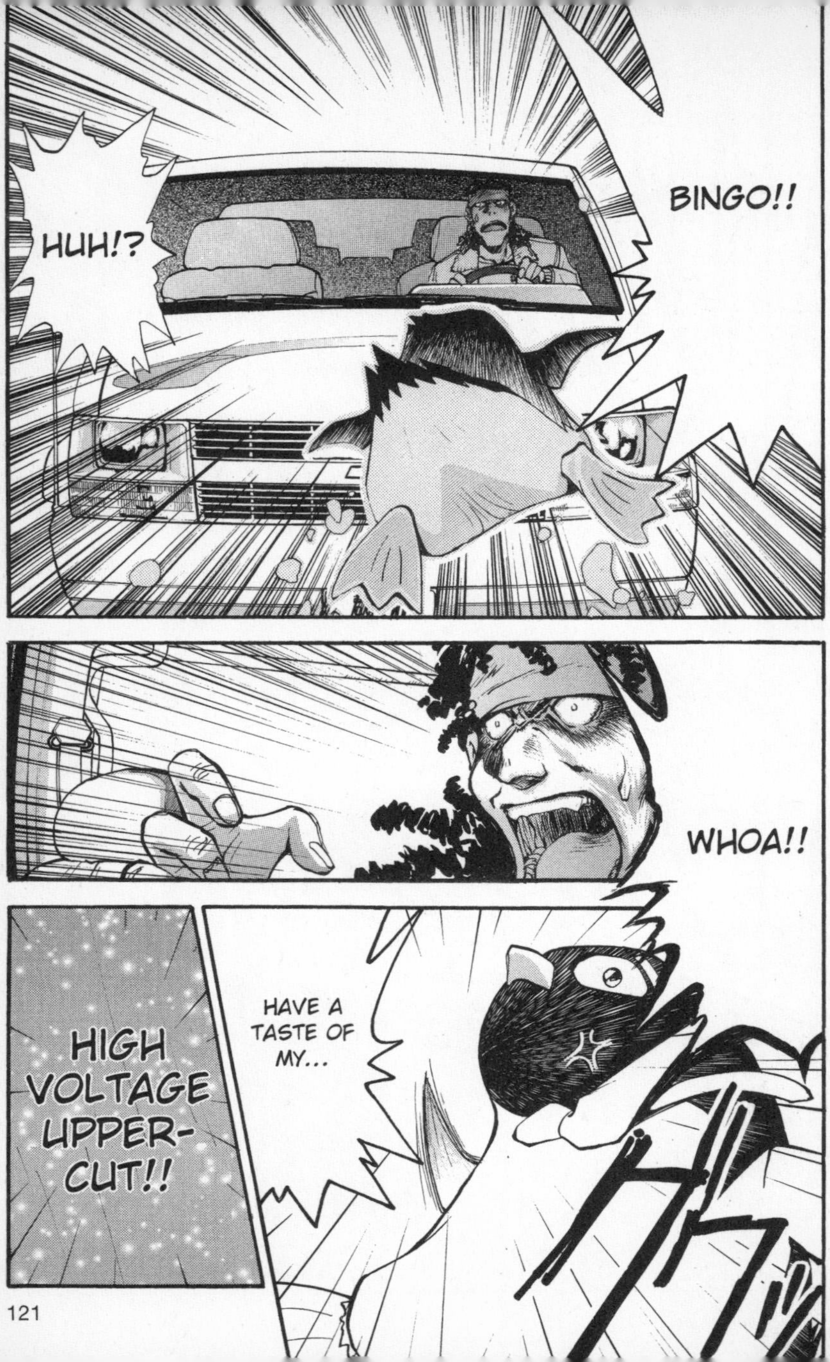
BINGO!!
HUH!?
WHOA!!
HAVE A TASTE OF MY...
HIGH VOLTAGE UPPER-CUT!!

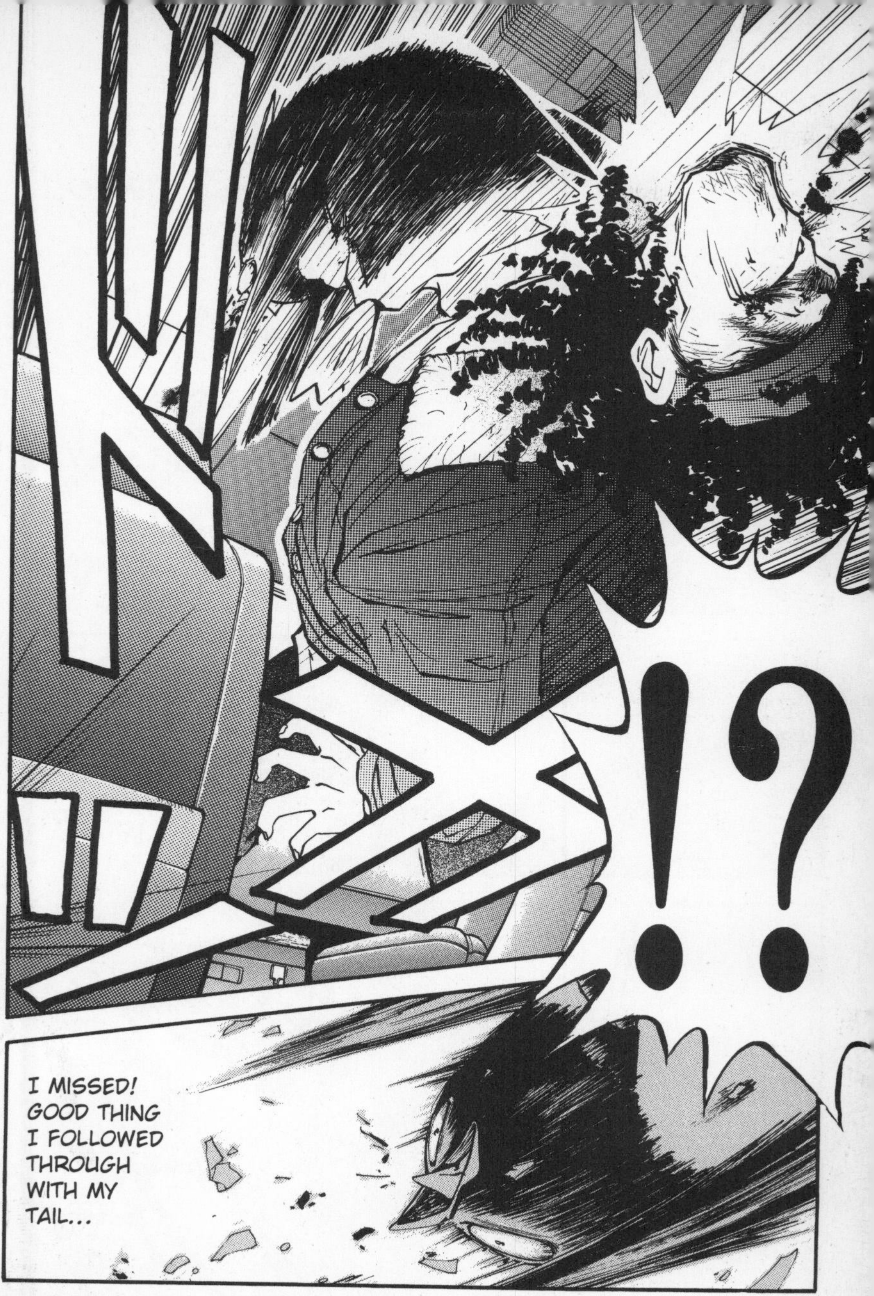
!?
I MISSED! GOOD THING I FOLLOWED THROUGH WITH MY TAIL...

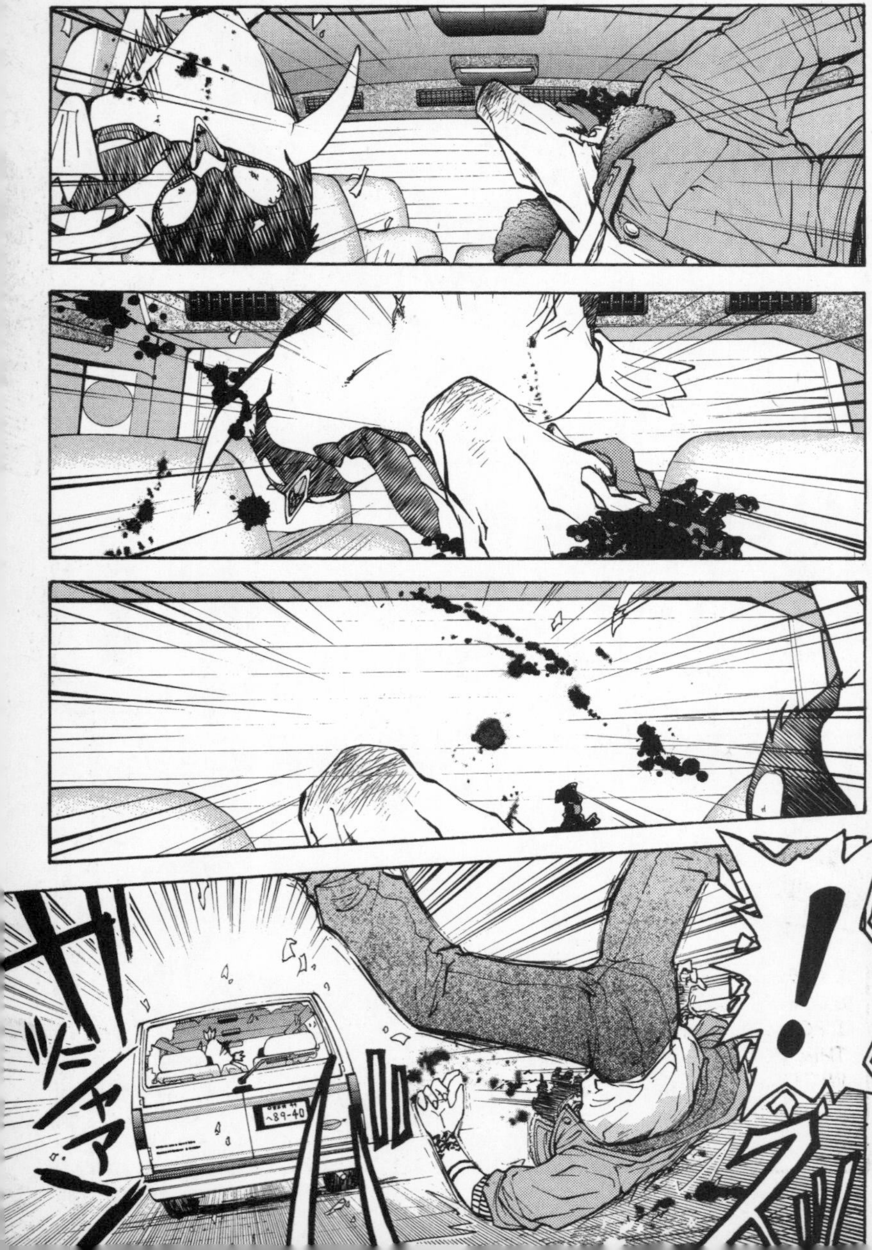
!
ガッシャアー
へ89-40

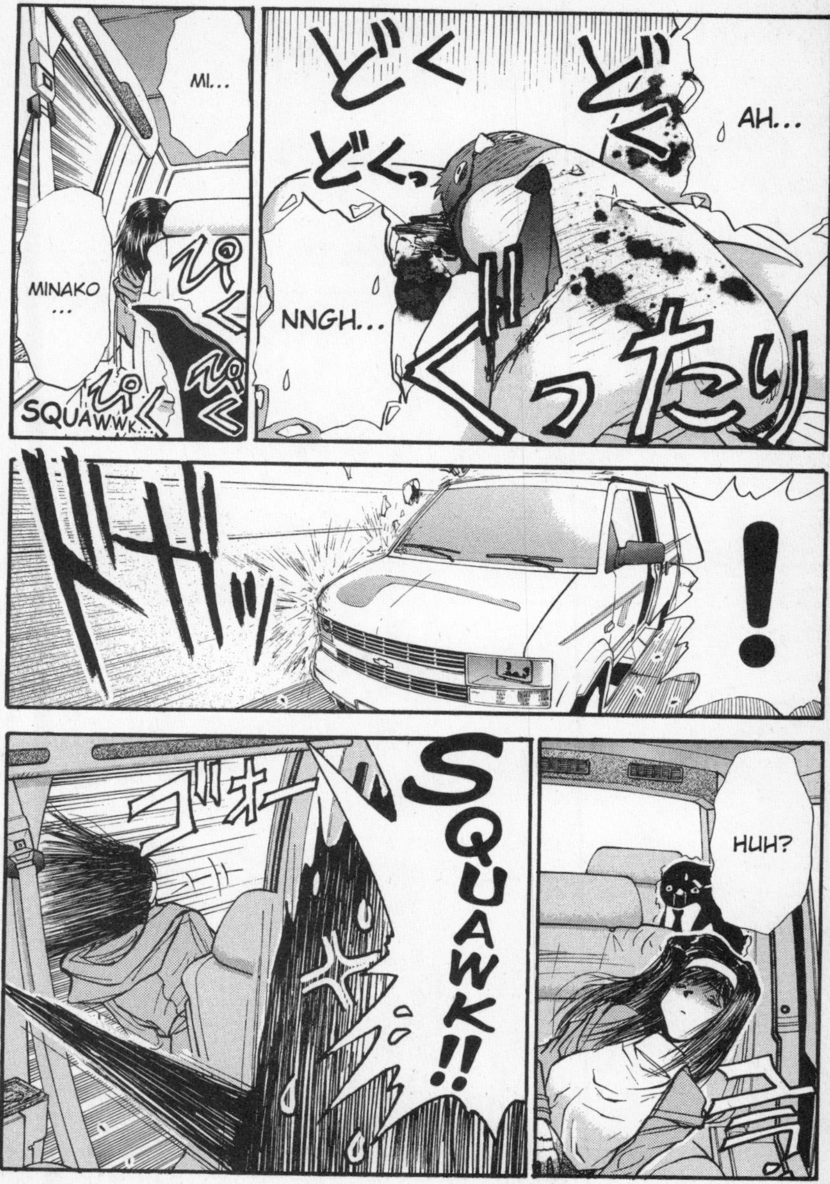

どく
どく
どくっ
AH...
NNGH...
ぐったり
MI...
MINAKO ...
ぴくぴくぴく
SQUAWWK
ドザザッ
!
HUH?
SQUAWK!!
ゴォー

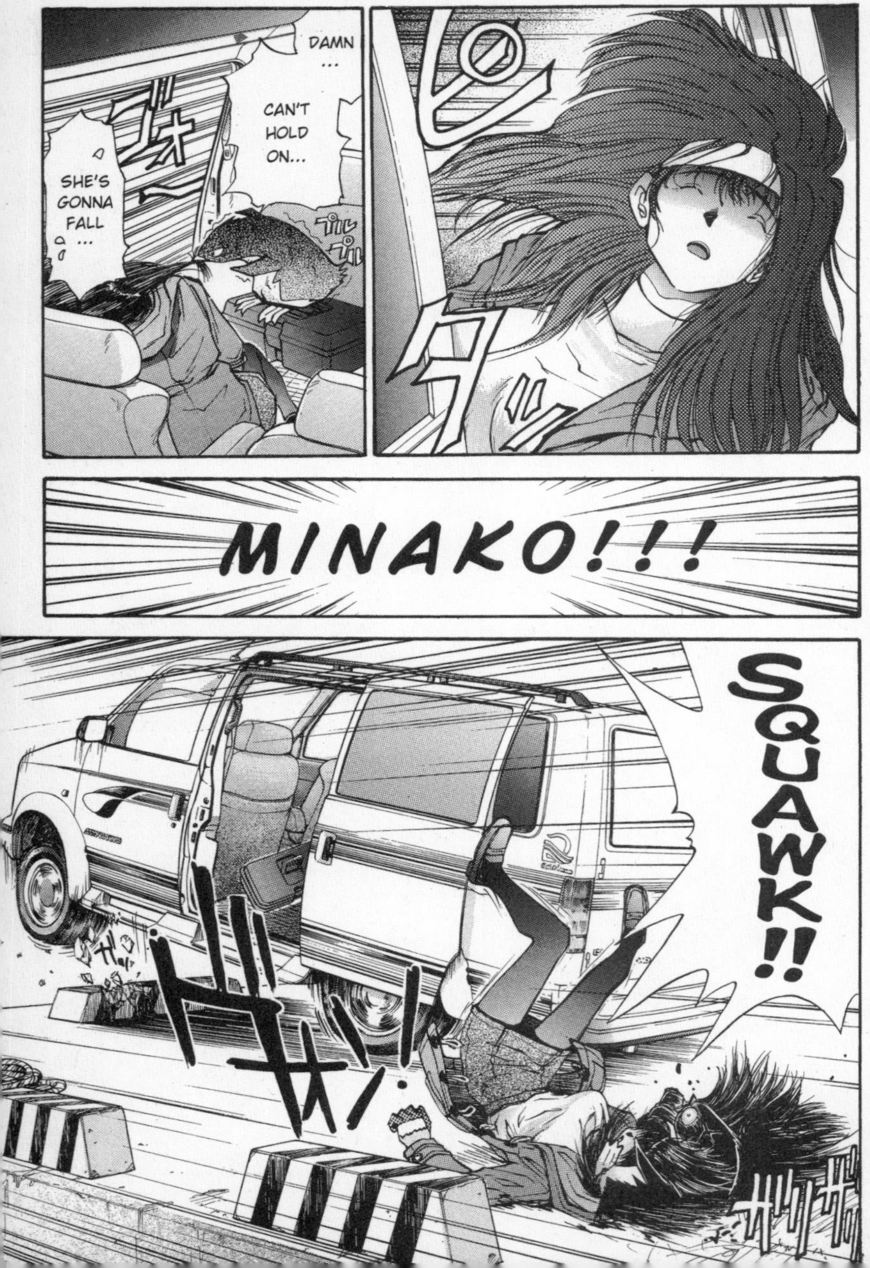
DAMN ...
CAN'T HOLD ON...
SHE'S GONNA FALL ...
MINAKO!!!
SQUAWK!!

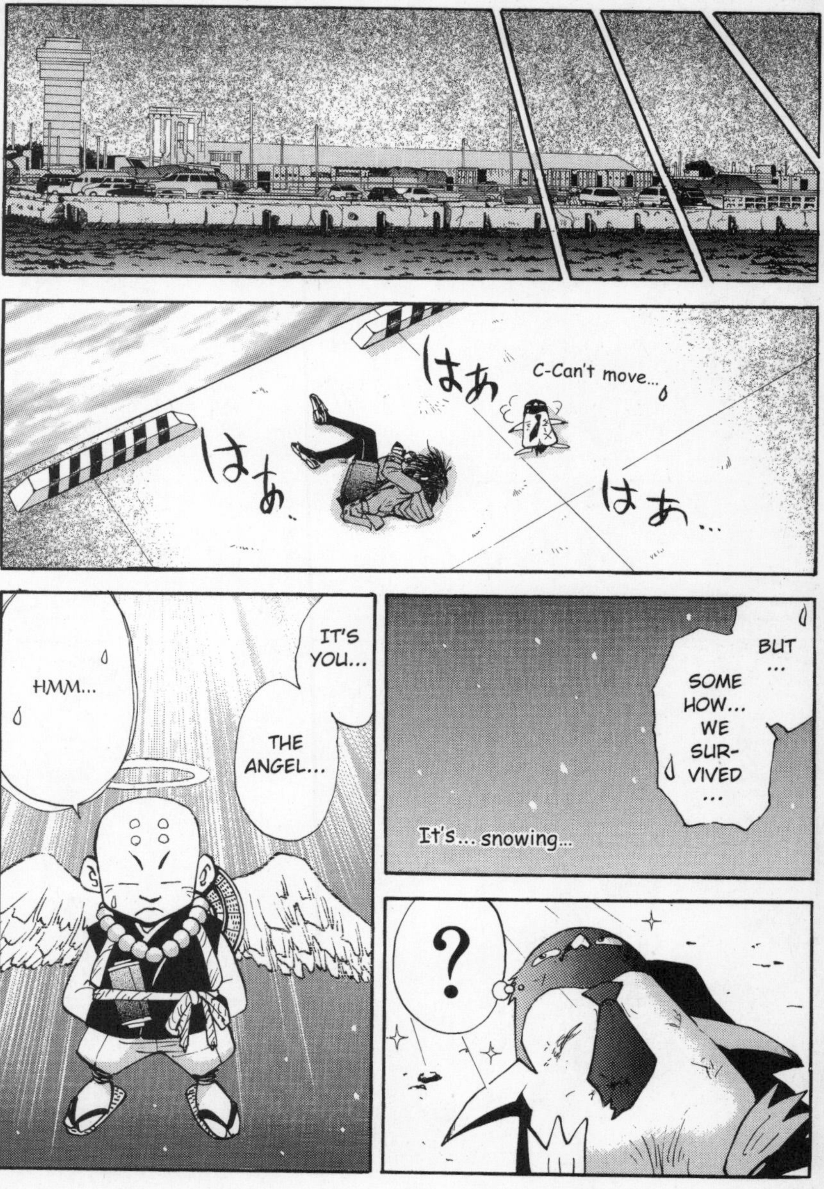
C-Can't move...
はぁ
はぁ...
はぁ..
BUT... SOME HOW... WE SUR-VIVED...
It's... snowing...
?
IT'S YOU...
THE ANGEL...
HMM...

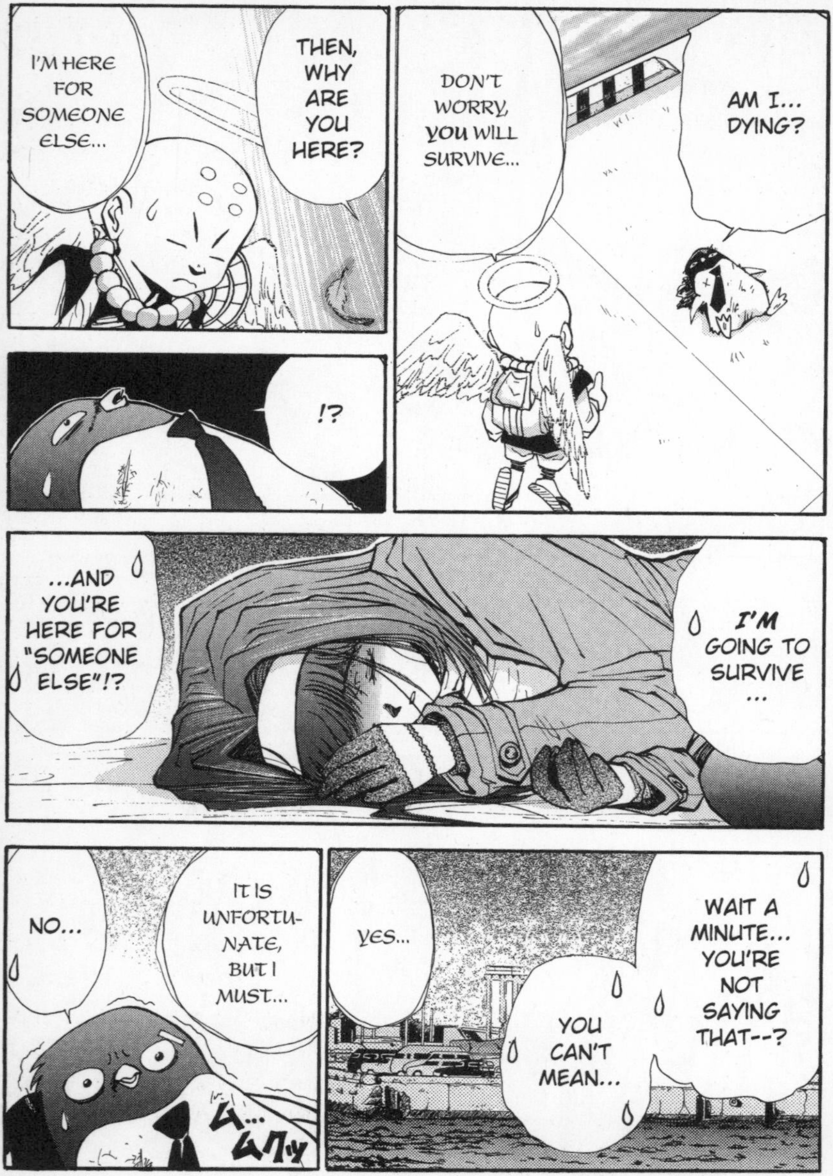
AM I... DYING?
DON'T WORRY, YOU WILL SURVIVE...
THEN, WHY ARE YOU HERE?
I'M HERE FOR SOMEONE ELSE...
!?
I'M GOING TO SURVIVE ...
...AND YOU'RE HERE FOR "SOMEONE ELSE"!?
WAIT A MINUTE... YOU'RE NOT SAYING THAT--?
YOU CAN'T MEAN...
YES...
IT IS UNFORTUNATE, BUT I MUST...
NO...

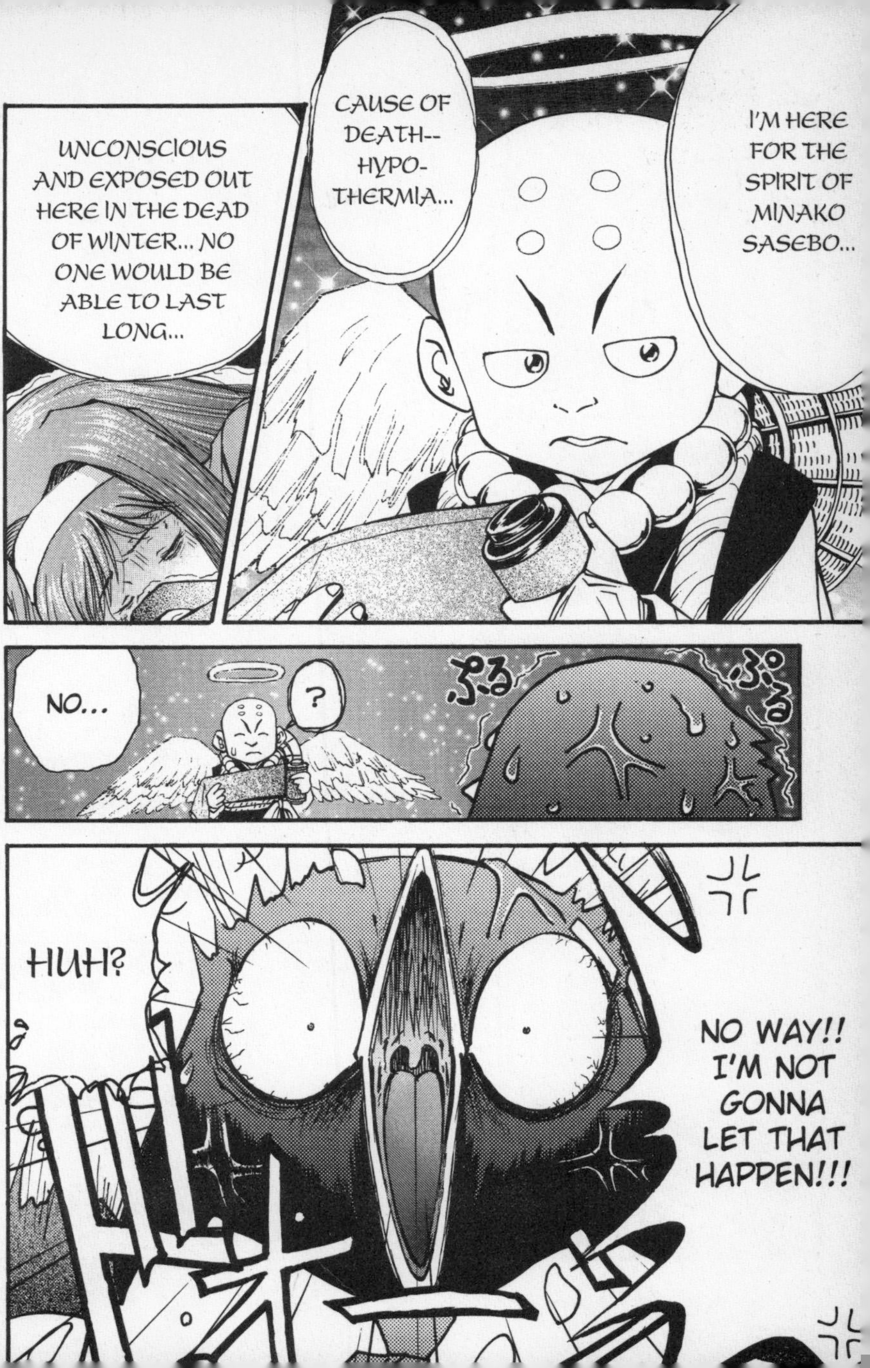
I'M HERE FOR THE SPIRIT OF MINAKO SASEBO...
CAUSE OF DEATH-- HYPO-THERMIA...
UNCONSCIOUS AND EXPOSED OUT HERE IN THE DEAD OF WINTER... NO ONE WOULD BE ABLE TO LAST LONG...
ぷる
ぷる
?
NO...
NO WAY!! I'M NOT GONNA LET THAT HAPPEN!!!
HUH?

CHAPTER 5
WHAT A MAN'S GOTTA DO...

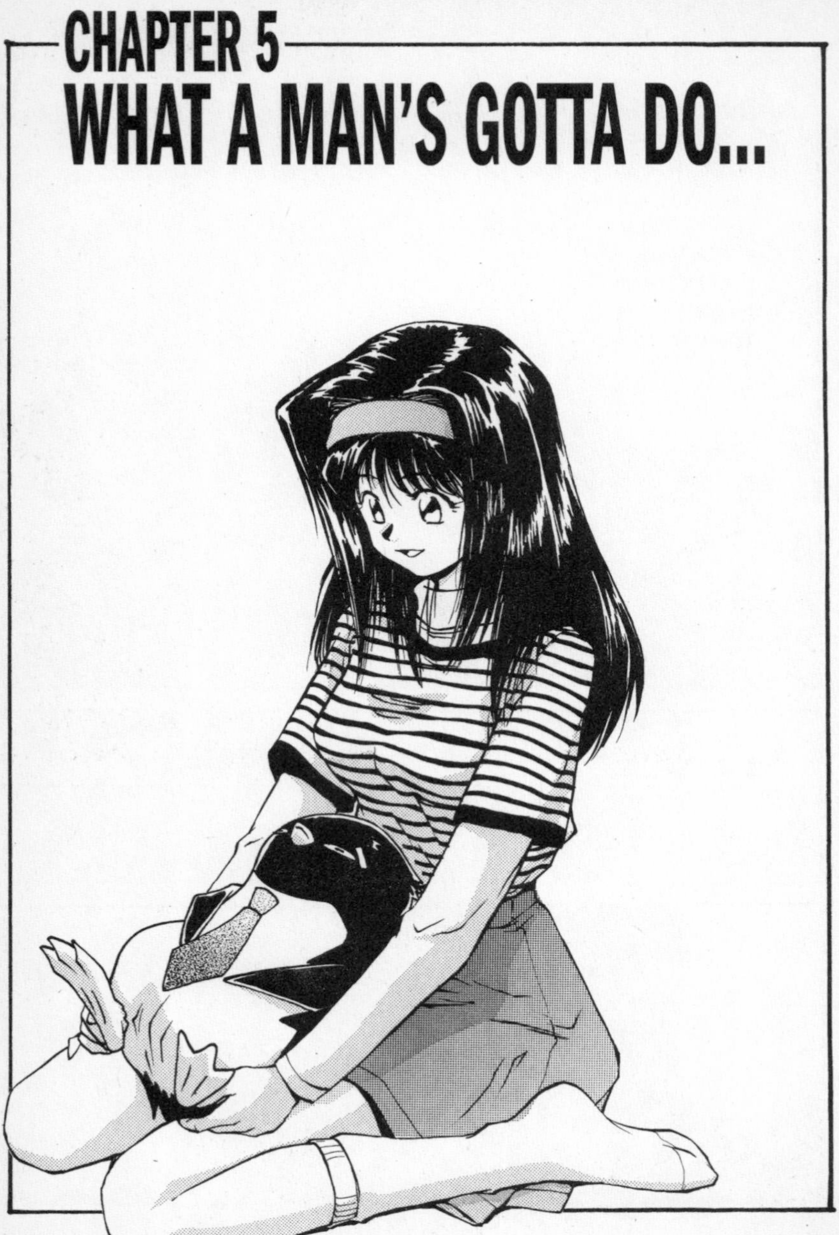

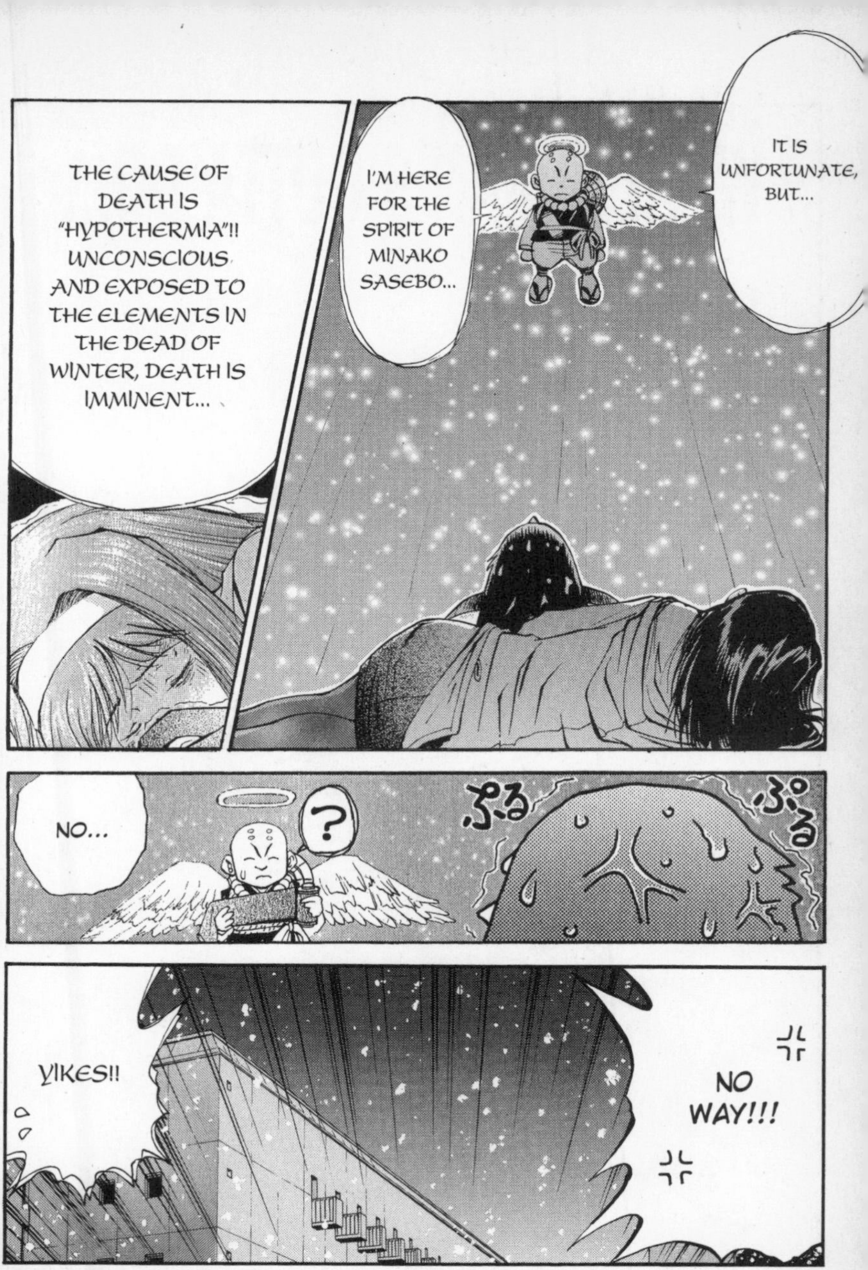
IT IS UNFORTUNATE, BUT...
I'M HERE FOR THE SPIRIT OF MINAKO SASEBO...
THE CAUSE OF DEATH IS "HYPOTHERMIA"!! UNCONSCIOUS AND EXPOSED TO THE ELEMENTS IN THE DEAD OF WINTER, DEATH IS IMMINENT...
ぷる ぷる
?
NO...
NO WAY!!!
YIKES!!

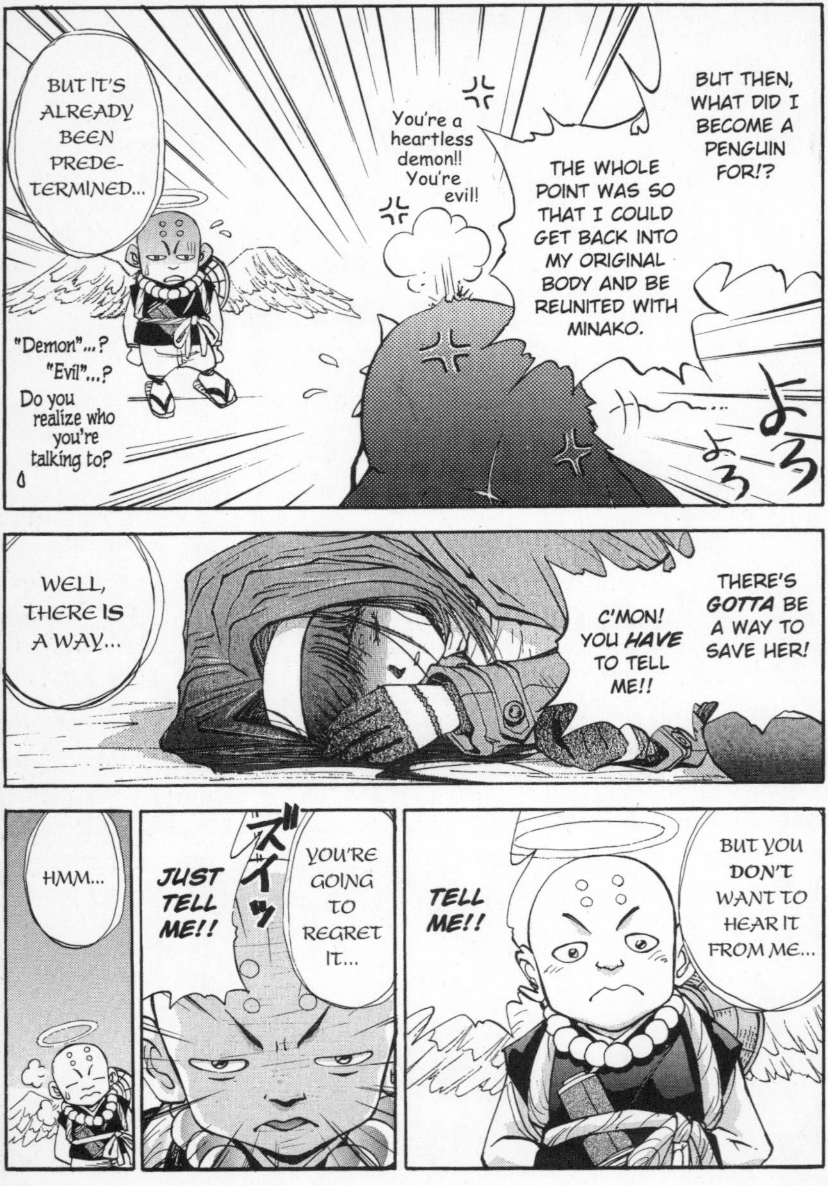
BUT THEN, WHAT DID I BECOME A PENGUIN FOR!?
THE WHOLE POINT WAS SO THAT I COULD GET BACK INTO MY ORIGINAL BODY AND BE REUNITED WITH MINAKO.
よろよろ
You're a heartless demon!! You're evil!
BUT IT'S ALREADY BEEN PREDE-TERMINED...
"Demon"...? "Evil"...? Do you realize who you're talking to?
THERE'S GOTTA BE A WAY TO SAVE HER!
C'MON! YOU HAVE TO TELL ME!!
WELL, THERE IS A WAY...
BUT YOU DON'T WANT TO HEAR IT FROM ME...
TELL ME!!
YOU'RE GOING TO REGRET IT...
ズイッ
JUST TELL ME!!
HMM...

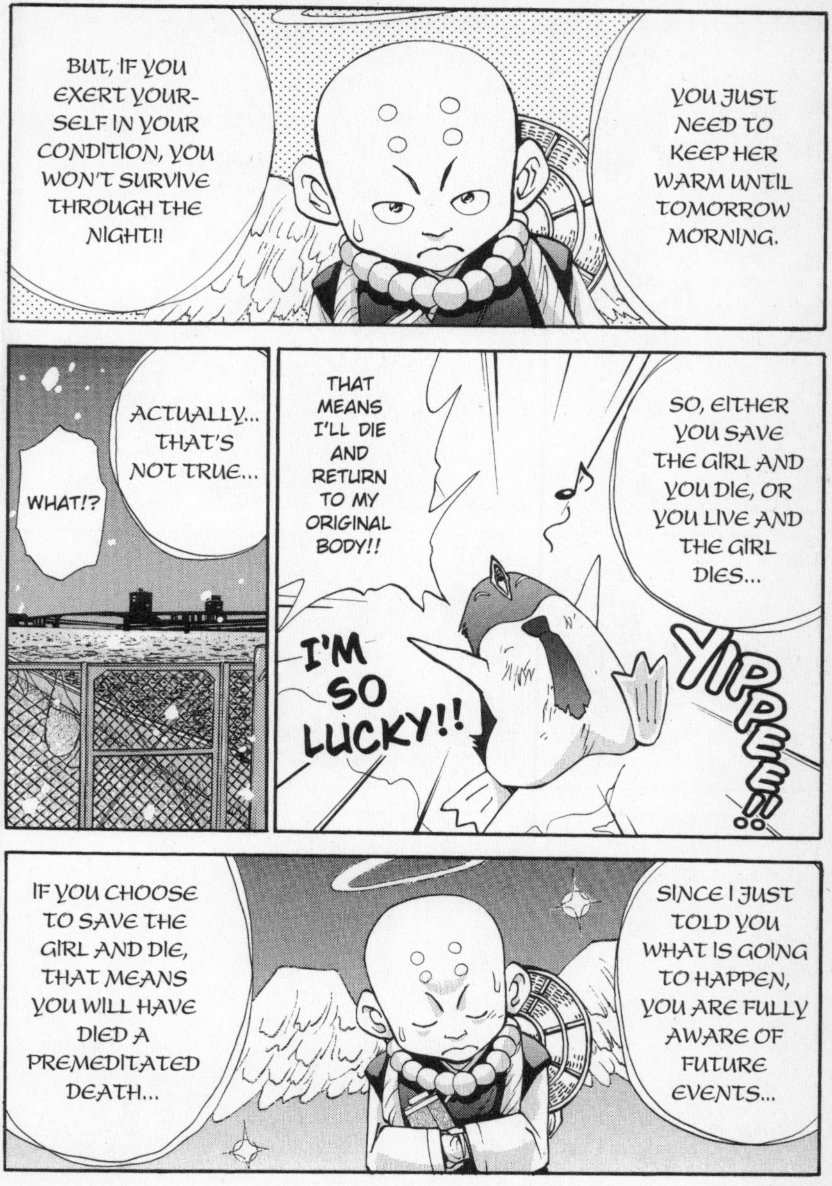
YOU JUST NEED TO KEEP HER WARM UNTIL TOMORROW MORNING.
BUT, IF YOU EXERT YOUR-SELF IN YOUR CONDITION, YOU WON'T SURVIVE THROUGH THE NIGHT!!
SO, EITHER YOU SAVE THE GIRL AND YOU DIE, OR YOU LIVE AND THE GIRL DIES...
YIPPEE!!
THAT MEANS I'LL DIE AND RETURN TO MY ORIGINAL BODY!!
I'M SO LUCKY!!
ACTUALLY... THAT'S NOT TRUE...
WHAT!?
SINCE I JUST TOLD YOU WHAT IS GOING TO HAPPEN, YOU ARE FULLY AWARE OF FUTURE EVENTS...
IF YOU CHOOSE TO SAVE THE GIRL AND DIE, THAT MEANS YOU WILL HAVE DIED A PREMEDITATED DEATH...

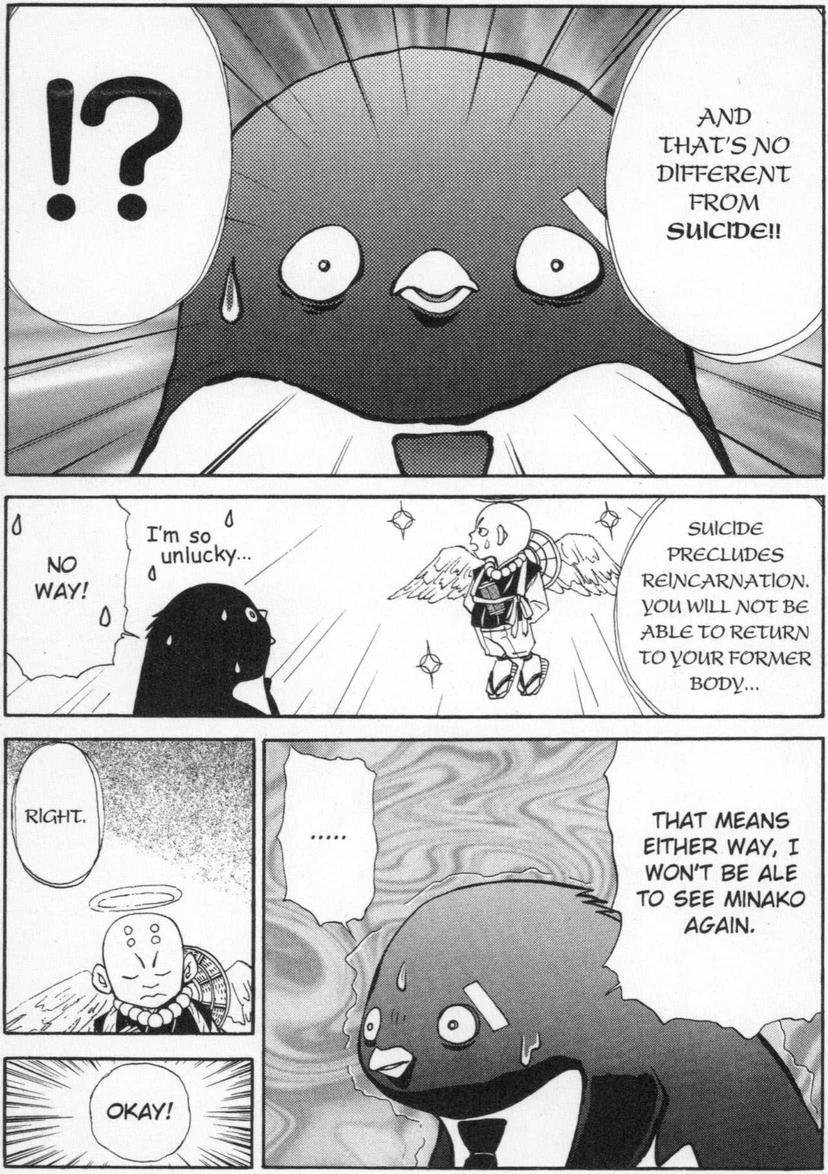
AND THAT'S NO DIFFERENT FROM SUICIDE!!
!?
SUICIDE PRECLUDES REINCARNATION. YOU WILL NOT BE ABLE TO RETURN TO YOUR FORMER BODY...
I'm so unlucky...
NO WAY!
THAT MEANS EITHER WAY, I WON'T BE ALE TO SEE MINAKO AGAIN.
.....
RIGHT.
OKAY!

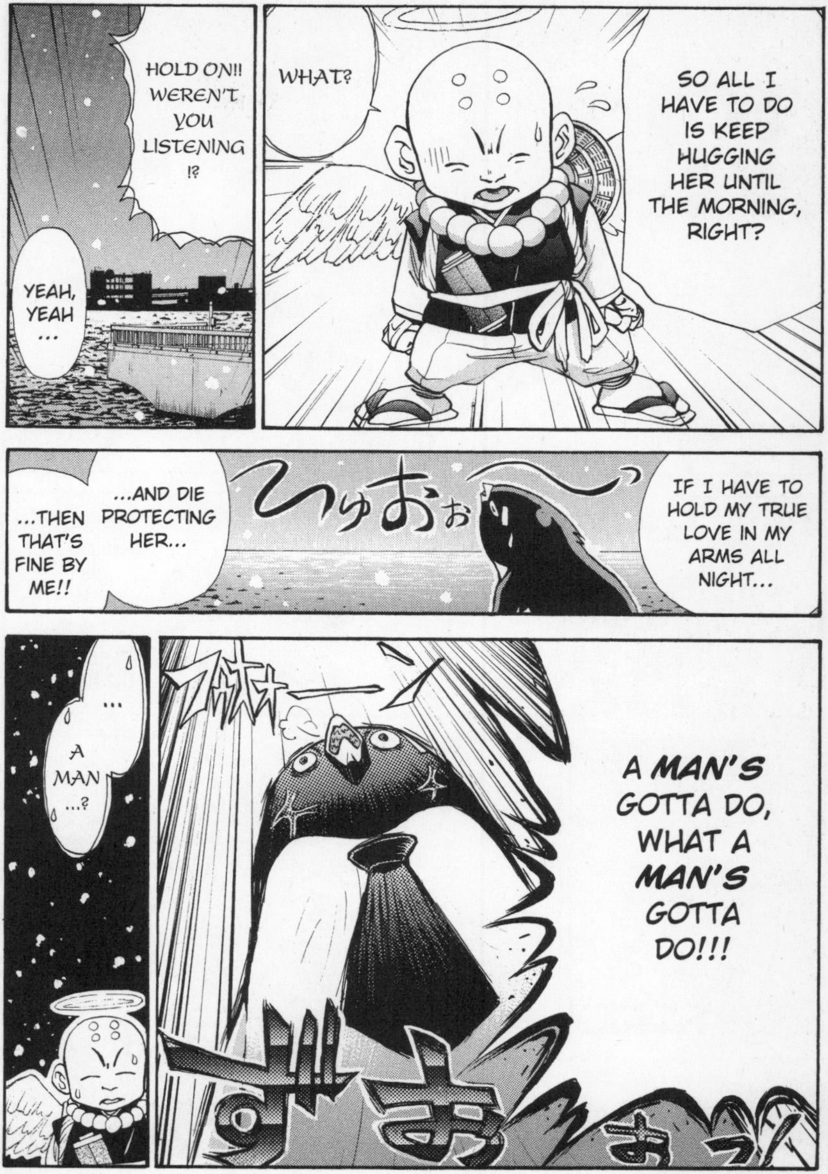
SO ALL I HAVE TO DO IS KEEP HUGGING HER UNTIL THE MORNING, RIGHT?
WHAT?
HOLD ON!! WEREN'T YOU LISTENING !?
YEAH, YEAH ...
IF I HAVE TO HOLD MY TRUE LOVE IN MY ARMS ALL NIGHT...
ひゅおぉ
...AND DIE PROTECTING HER...
...THEN THAT'S FINE BY ME!!
A MAN'S GOTTA DO, WHAT A MAN'S GOTTA DO!!!
ずおおっ
... A MAN ...?

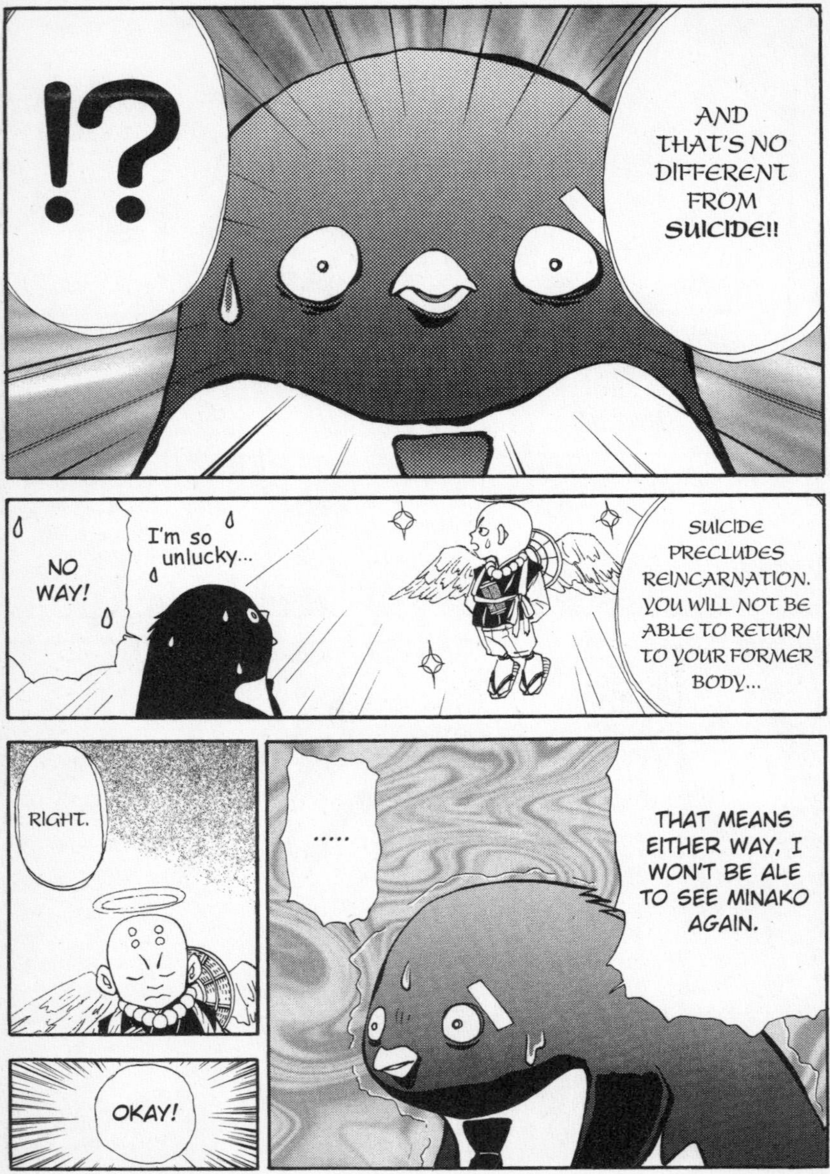
AND THAT'S NO DIFFERENT FROM SUICIDE!!
!?
SUICIDE PRECLUDES REINCARNATION. YOU WILL NOT BE ABLE TO RETURN TO YOUR FORMER BODY...
I'm so unlucky...
NO WAY!
THAT MEANS EITHER WAY, I WON'T BE ALE TO SEE MINAKO AGAIN.
.....
RIGHT.
OKAY!

HOLD ON!! WEREN'T YOU LISTENING !?

YEAH, YEAH ...

WHAT?

SO ALL I HAVE TO DO IS KEEP HUGGING HER UNTIL THE MORNING, RIGHT?

...THEN THAT'S FINE BY ME!!

...AND DIE PROTECTING HER...

IF I HAVE TO HOLD MY TRUE LOVE IN MY ARMS ALL NIGHT...

...

A MAN ...?

A *MAN'S* GOTTA DO, WHAT A *MAN'S* GOTTA DO!!!

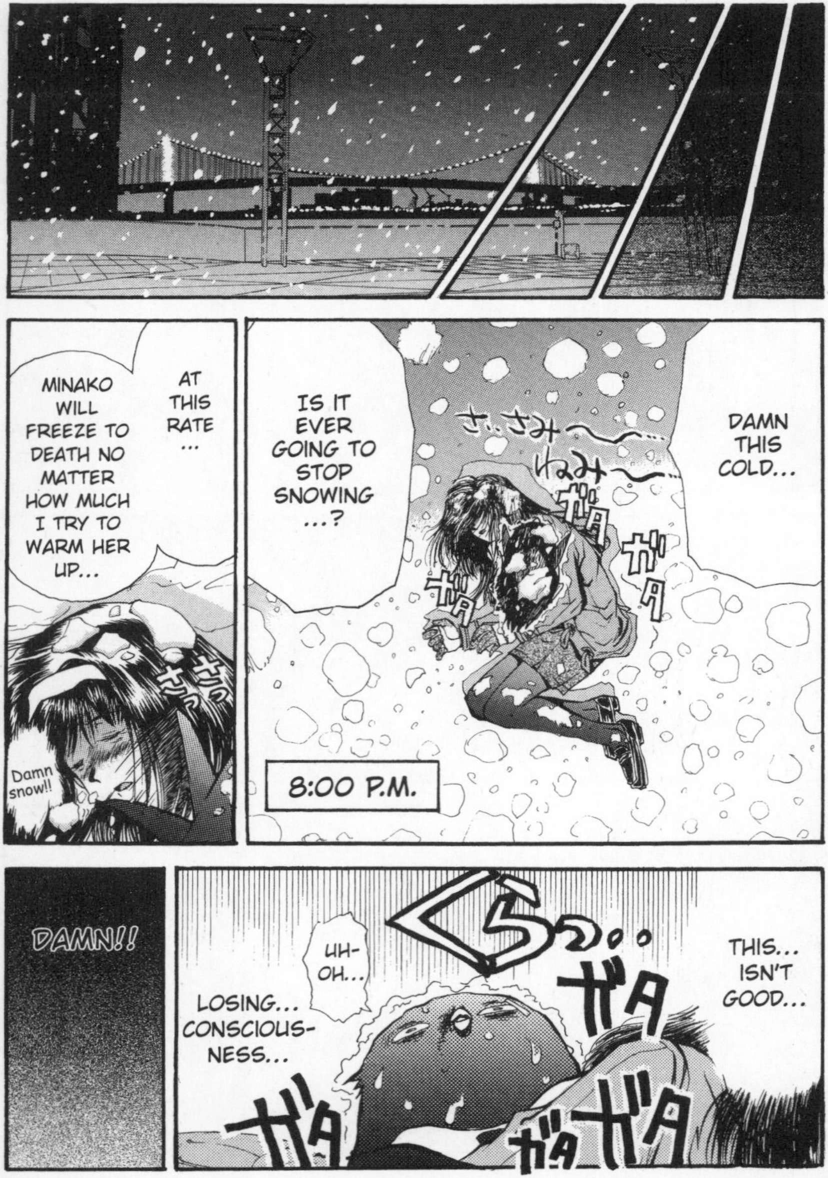
DAMN THIS COLD...
IS IT EVER GOING TO STOP SNOWING...?
8:00 P.M.
AT THIS RATE ...
MINAKO WILL FREEZE TO DEATH NO MATTER HOW MUCH I TRY TO WARM HER UP...
Damn snow!!
THIS... ISN'T GOOD...
UH-OH...
LOSING... CONSCIOUS-NESS...
DAMN!!

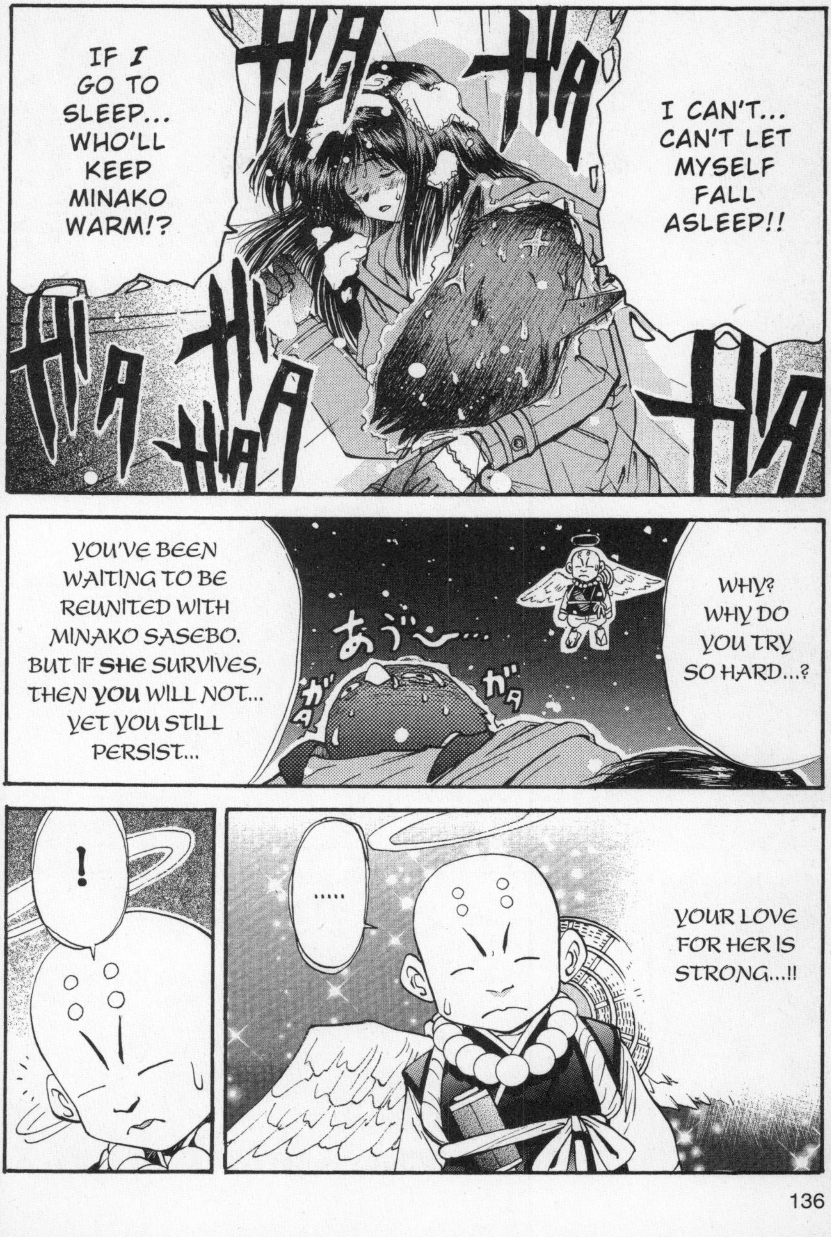

I CAN'T... CAN'T LET MYSELF FALL ASLEEP!!
IF I GO TO SLEEP... WHO'LL KEEP MINAKO WARM!?
ガタ ガタ
ガタ ガタ ガタ ガタ
WHY? WHY DO YOU TRY SO HARD...?
あう～…
ガタ ガタ
YOU'VE BEEN WAITING TO BE REUNITED WITH MINAKO SASEBO. BUT IF SHE SURVIVES, THEN YOU WILL NOT... YET YOU STILL PERSIST...
YOUR LOVE FOR HER IS STRONG...!!
.....
!

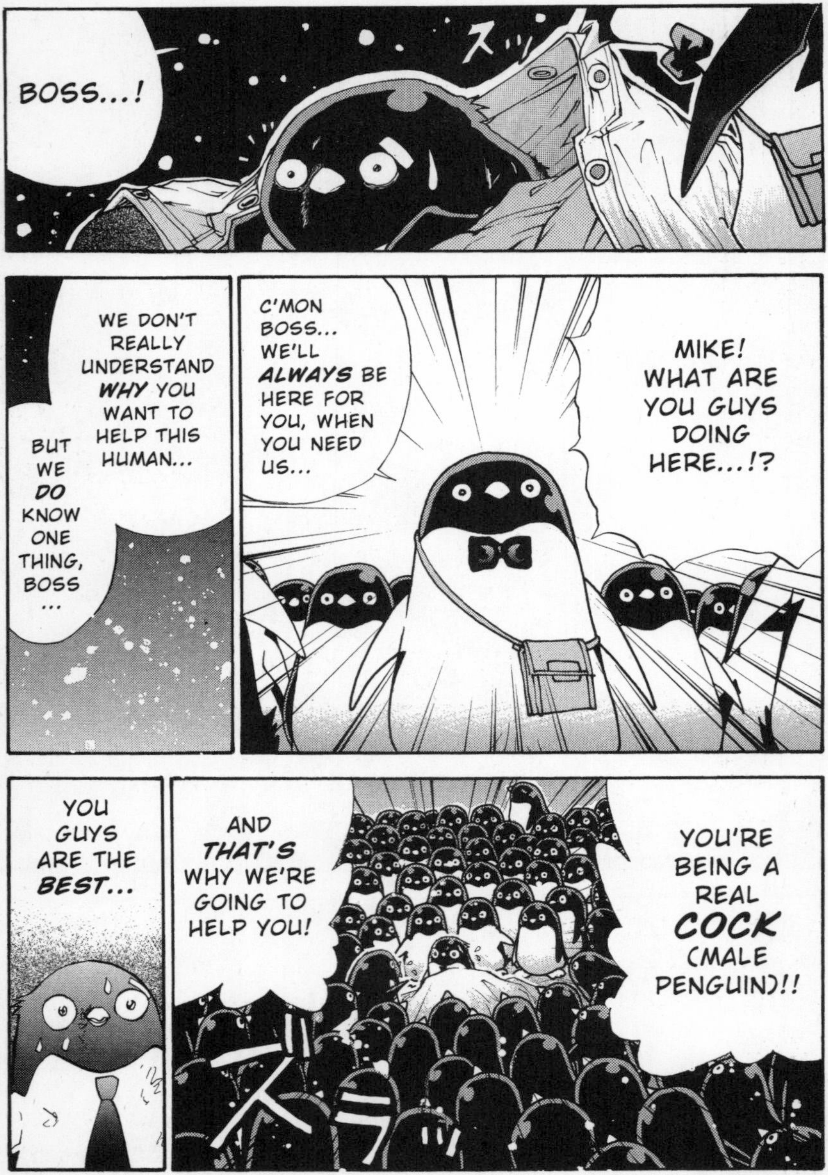

スッ
BOSS...!
MIKE! WHAT ARE YOU GUYS DOING HERE...!?
C'MON BOSS... WE'LL ***ALWAYS*** BE HERE FOR YOU, WHEN YOU NEED US...
WE DON'T REALLY UNDERSTAND ***WHY*** YOU WANT TO HELP THIS HUMAN...
BUT WE ***DO*** KNOW ONE THING, BOSS...
YOU'RE BEING A REAL **COCK** (MALE PENGUIN)!!
AND ***THAT'S*** WHY WE'RE GOING TO HELP YOU!
YOU GUYS ARE THE ***BEST...***

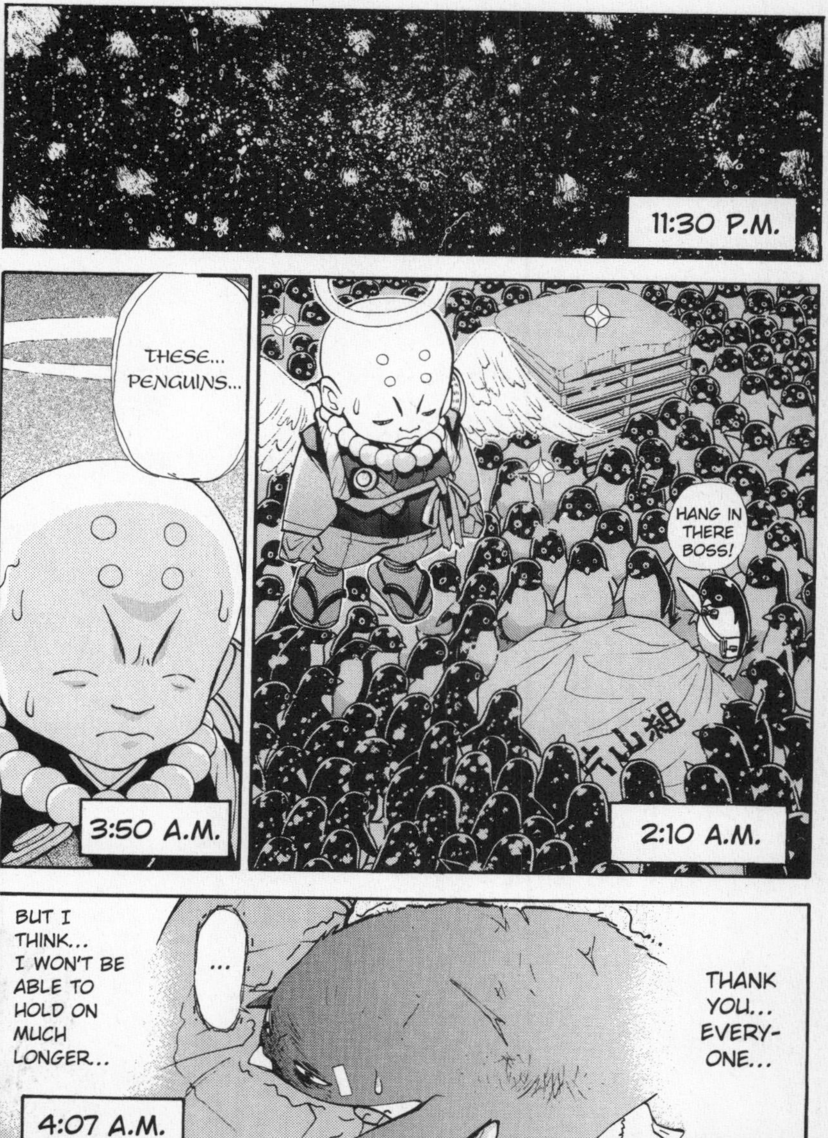
11:30 P.M.
2:10 A.M.
HANG IN THERE BOSS!
THESE... PENGUINS...
3:50 A.M.
THANK YOU... EVERY-ONE...
...
BUT I THINK... I WON'T BE ABLE TO HOLD ON MUCH LONGER...
4:07 A.M.

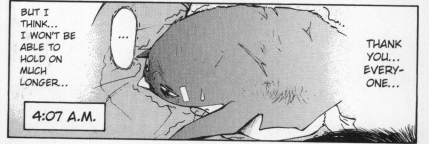

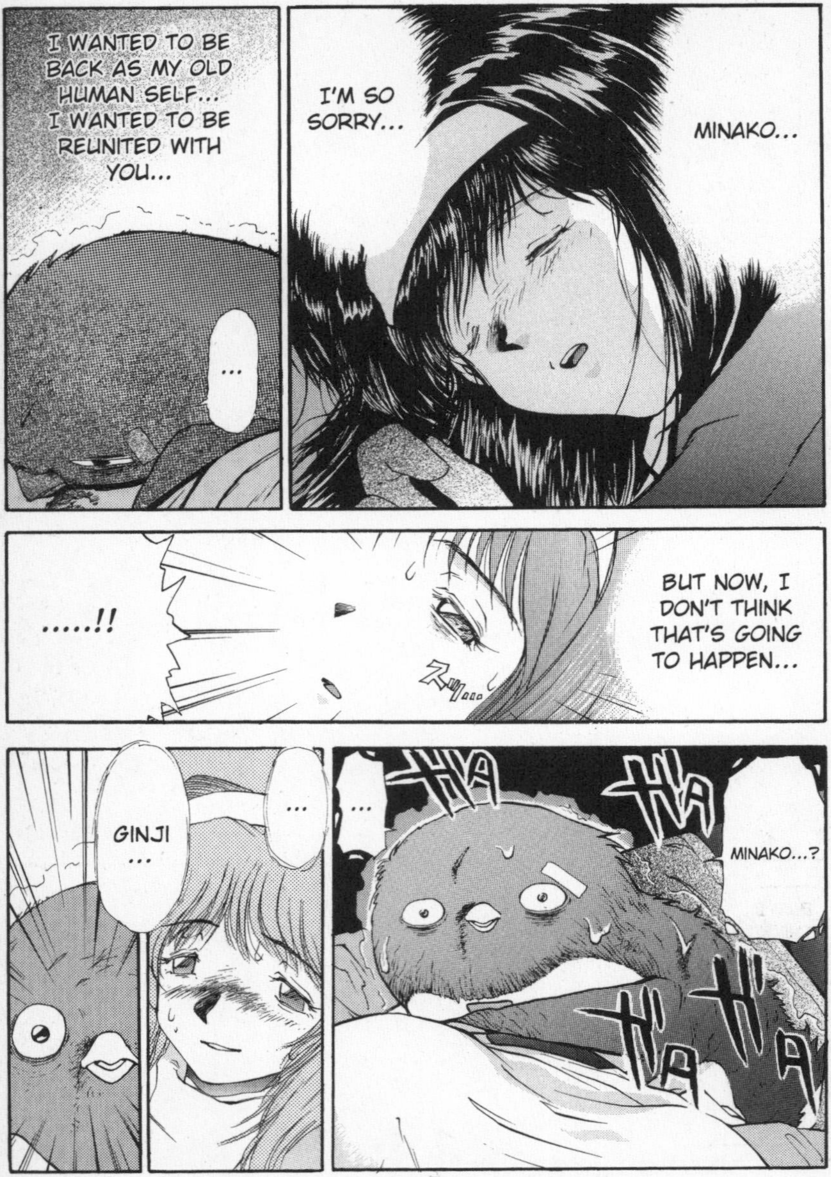
MINAKO...
I'M SO SORRY...
I WANTED TO BE BACK AS MY OLD HUMAN SELF... I WANTED TO BE REUNITED WITH YOU...
...
BUT NOW, I DON'T THINK THAT'S GOING TO HAPPEN...
スッ...
.....!!
HA HA
MINAKO...?
HA HA HA HA
...
...
GINJI ...

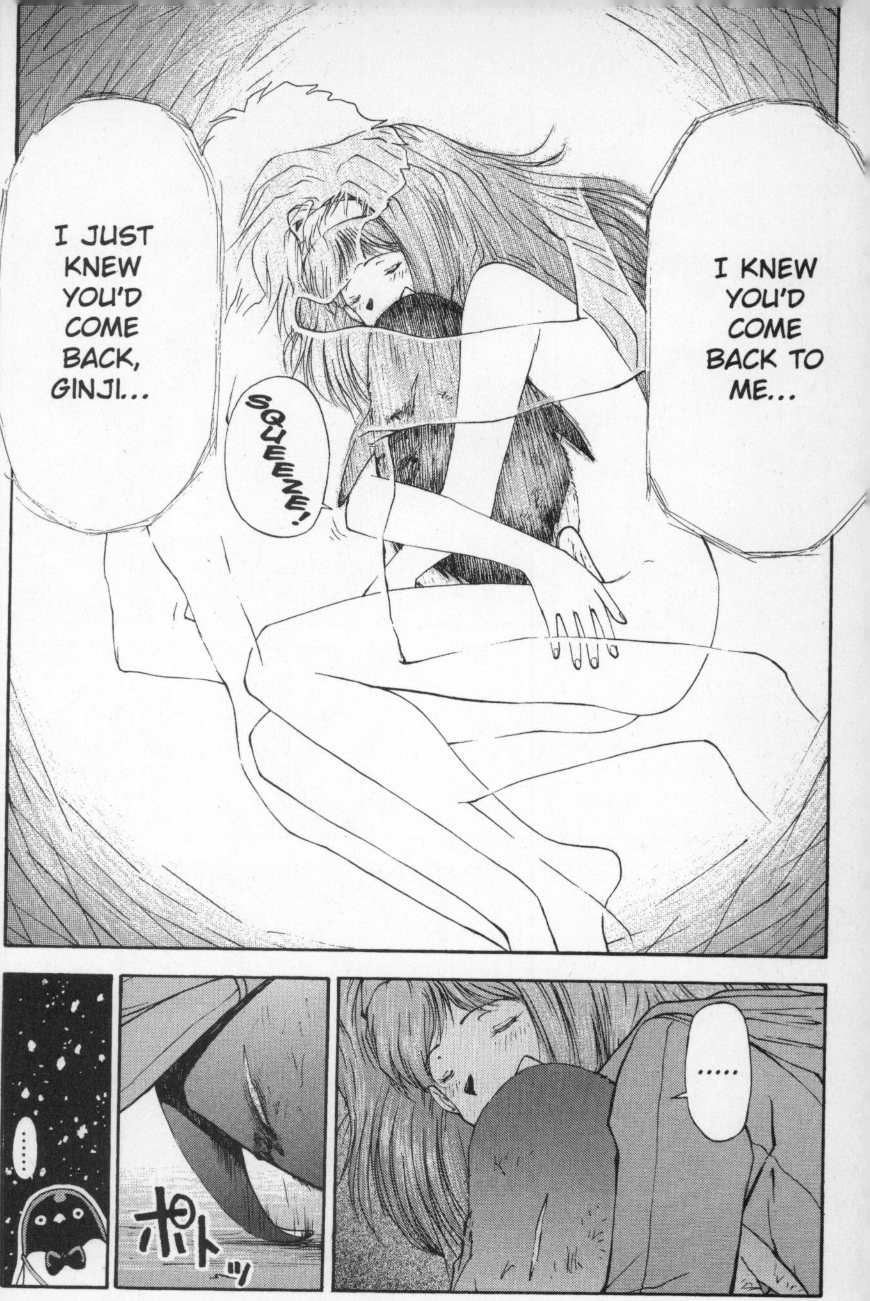
I KNEW YOU'D COME BACK TO ME...
SQUEEZE!
I JUST KNEW YOU'D COME BACK, GINJI...
......
ポトッ
......

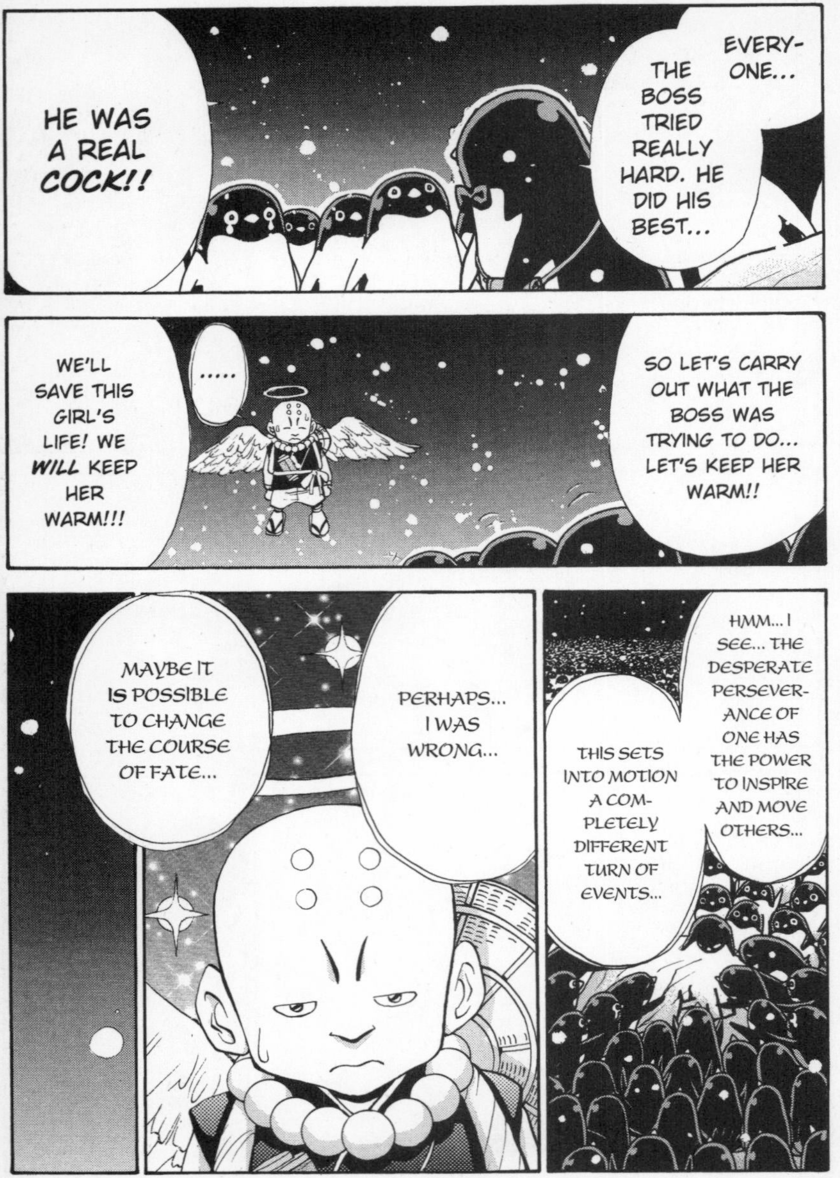
EVERY-ONE... THE BOSS TRIED REALLY HARD. HE DID HIS BEST...
HE WAS A REAL COCK!!
SO LET'S CARRY OUT WHAT THE BOSS WAS TRYING TO DO... LET'S KEEP HER WARM!!
......
WE'LL SAVE THIS GIRL'S LIFE! WE WILL KEEP HER WARM!!!
HMM... I SEE... THE DESPERATE PERSEVER-ANCE OF ONE HAS THE POWER TO INSPIRE AND MOVE OTHERS...
THIS SETS INTO MOTION A COM-PLETELY DIFFERENT TURN OF EVENTS...
PERHAPS... I WAS WRONG...
MAYBE IT IS POSSIBLE TO CHANGE THE COURSE OF FATE...

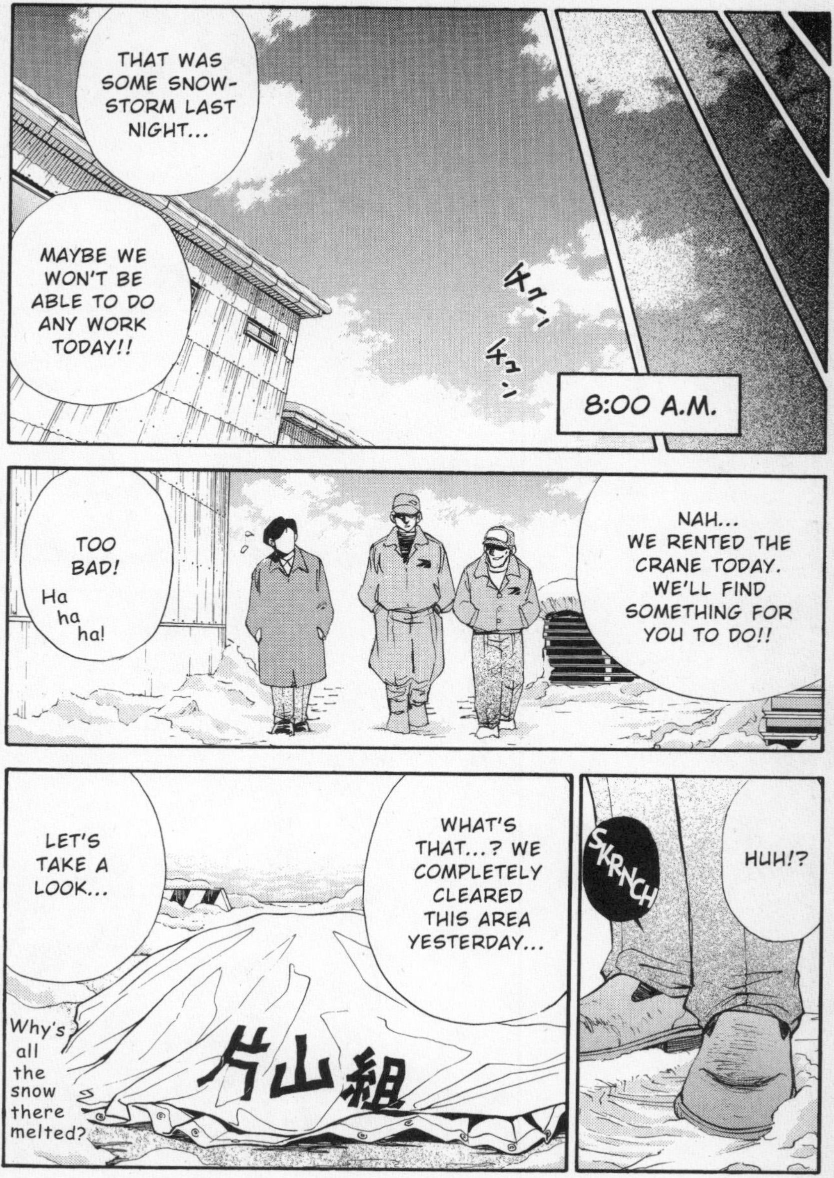
8:00 A.M.
チュン チュン
THAT WAS SOME SNOW-STORM LAST NIGHT...
MAYBE WE WON'T BE ABLE TO DO ANY WORK TODAY!!
NAH... WE RENTED THE CRANE TODAY. WE'LL FIND SOMETHING FOR YOU TO DO!!
TOO BAD!
Ha ha ha!
HUH!?
SKRNCH
WHAT'S THAT...? WE COMPLETELY CLEARED THIS AREA YESTERDAY...
LET'S TAKE A LOOK...
片山組
Why's all the snow there melted?

IT'S A
PERSON!!

CALL AN
AMBU-
LANCE!!

SHE'S
ALIVE
!!

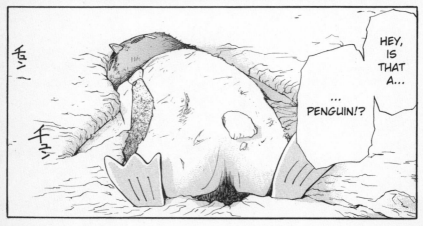

HEY,
IS
THAT
A...

...PENGUIN!?

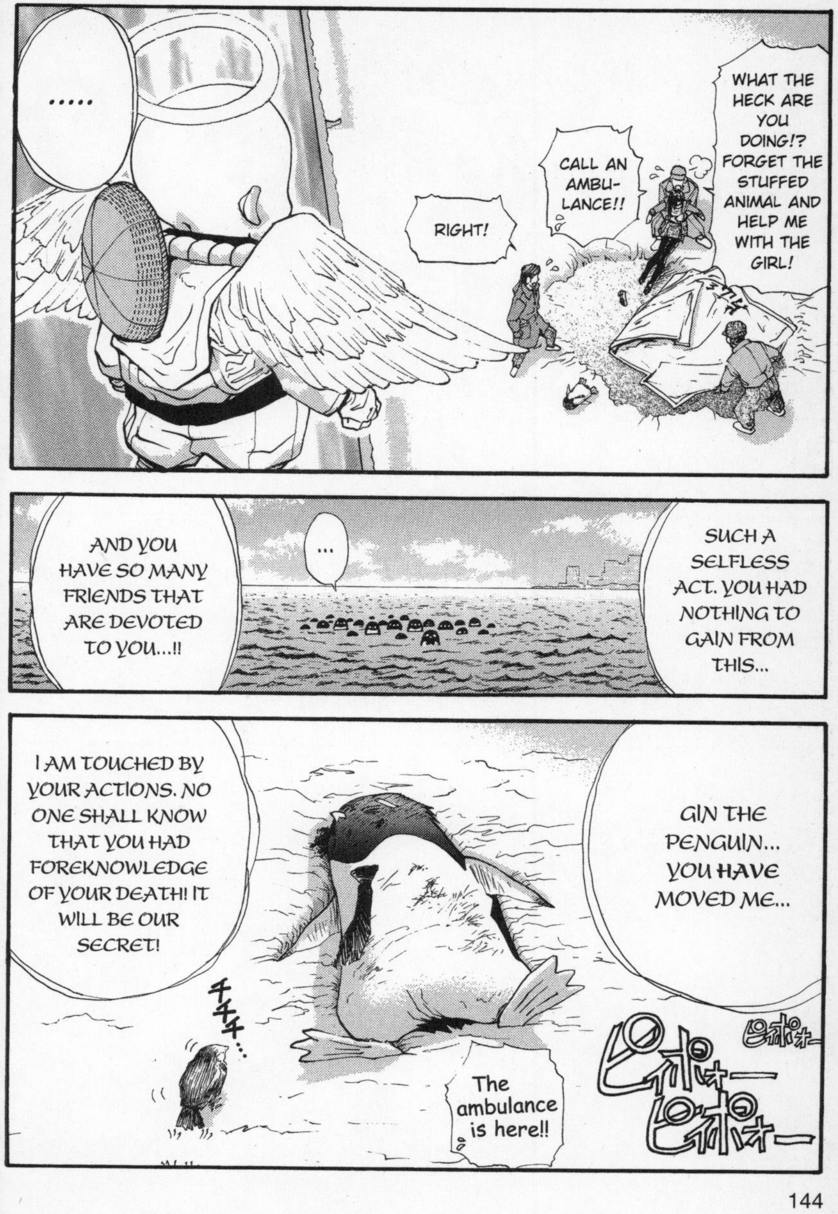
WHAT THE HECK ARE YOU DOING!? FORGET THE STUFFED ANIMAL AND HELP ME WITH THE GIRL!
CALL AN AMBULANCE!!
RIGHT!
.....
SUCH A SELFLESS ACT. YOU HAD NOTHING TO GAIN FROM THIS...
...
AND YOU HAVE SO MANY FRIENDS THAT ARE DEVOTED TO YOU...!!
GIN THE PENGUIN... YOU HAVE MOVED ME...
I AM TOUCHED BY YOUR ACTIONS. NO ONE SHALL KNOW THAT YOU HAD FOREKNOWLEDGE OF YOUR DEATH! IT WILL BE OUR SECRET!
The ambulance is here!!
チチチ...

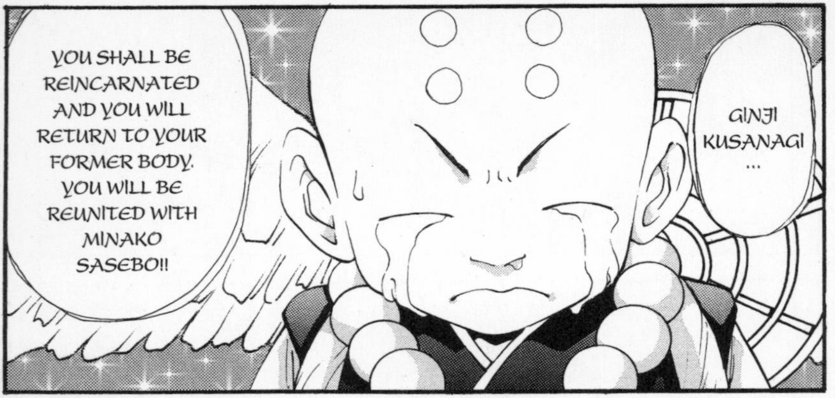
GINJI KUSANAGI ...
YOU SHALL BE REINCARNATED AND YOU WILL RETURN TO YOUR FORMER BODY. YOU WILL BE REUNITED WITH MINAKO SASEBO!!

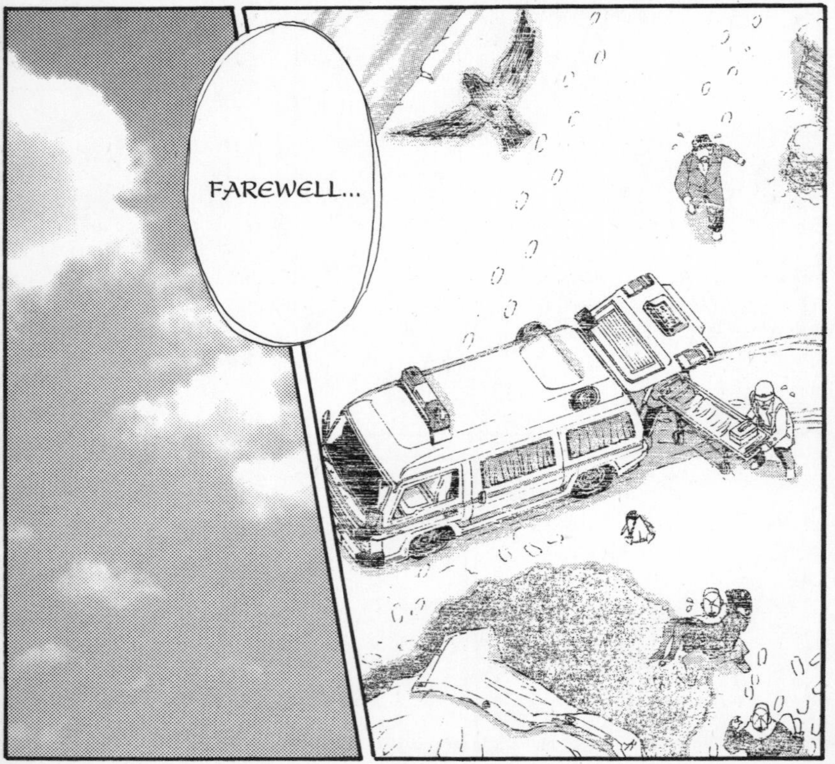
FAREWELL...

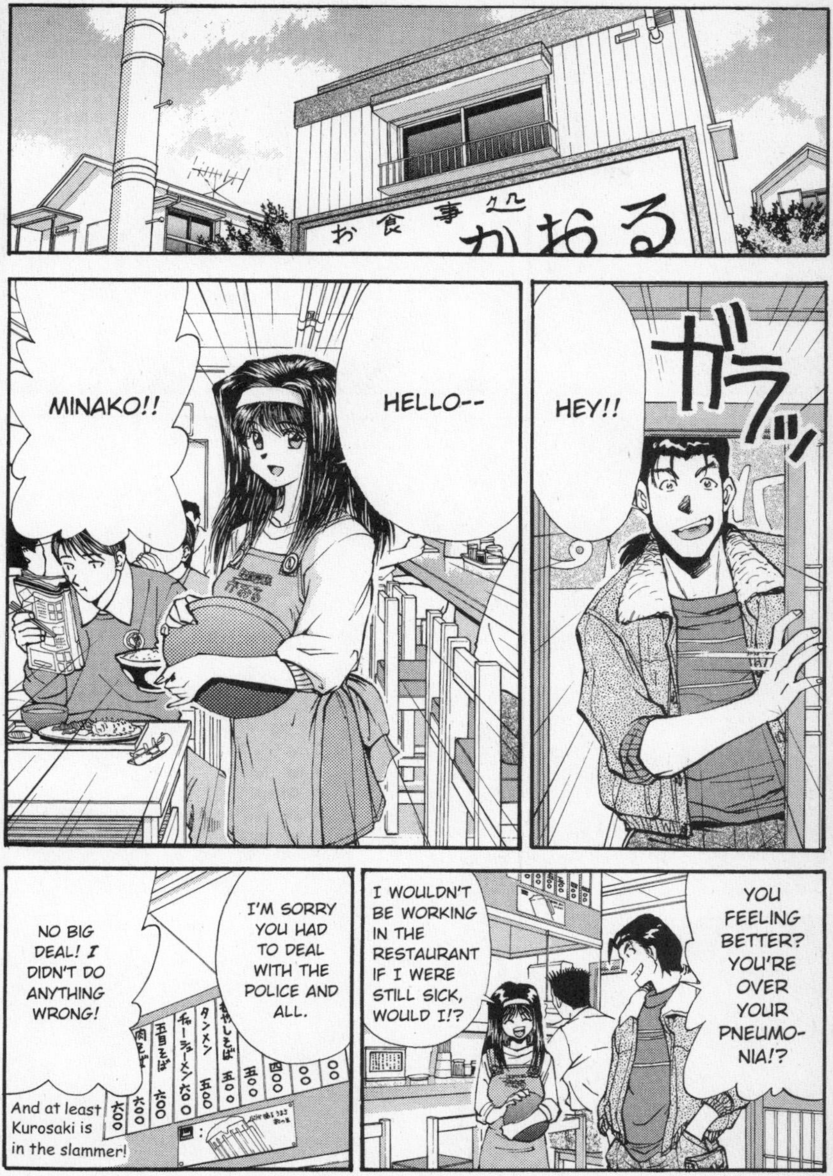
お食事処
かおる
ガラッ
HEY!!
HELLO--
MINAKO!!
YOU FEELING BETTER? YOU'RE OVER YOUR PNEUMONIA!?
I WOULDN'T BE WORKING IN THE RESTAURANT IF I WERE STILL SICK, WOULD I!?
I'M SORRY YOU HAD TO DEAL WITH THE POLICE AND ALL.
NO BIG DEAL! I DIDN'T DO ANYTHING WRONG!
And at least Kurosaki is in the slammer!

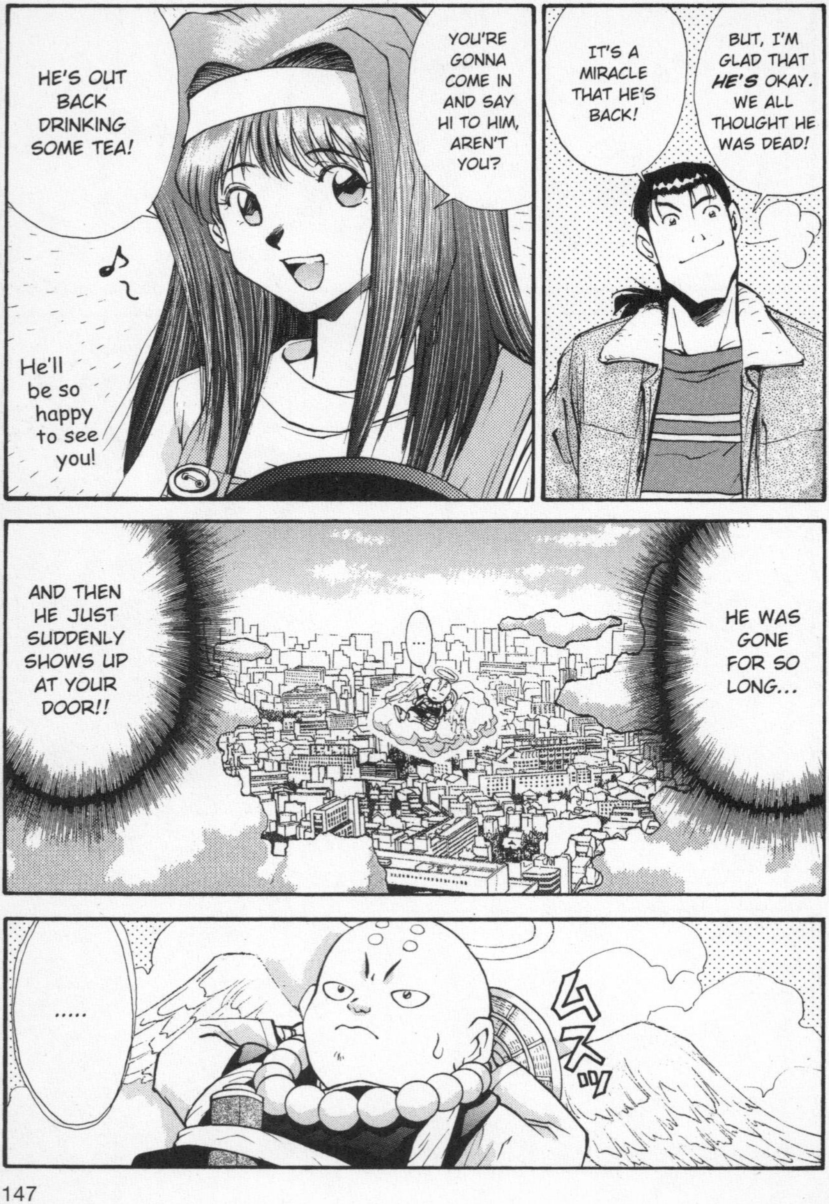
BUT, I'M GLAD THAT **HE'S** OKAY. WE ALL THOUGHT HE WAS DEAD!
IT'S A MIRACLE THAT HE'S BACK!
YOU'RE GONNA COME IN AND SAY HI TO HIM, AREN'T YOU?
HE'S OUT BACK DRINKING SOME TEA!
He'll be so happy to see you!
HE WAS GONE FOR SO LONG...
...
AND THEN HE JUST SUDDENLY SHOWS UP AT YOUR DOOR!!
ムスッ
.....

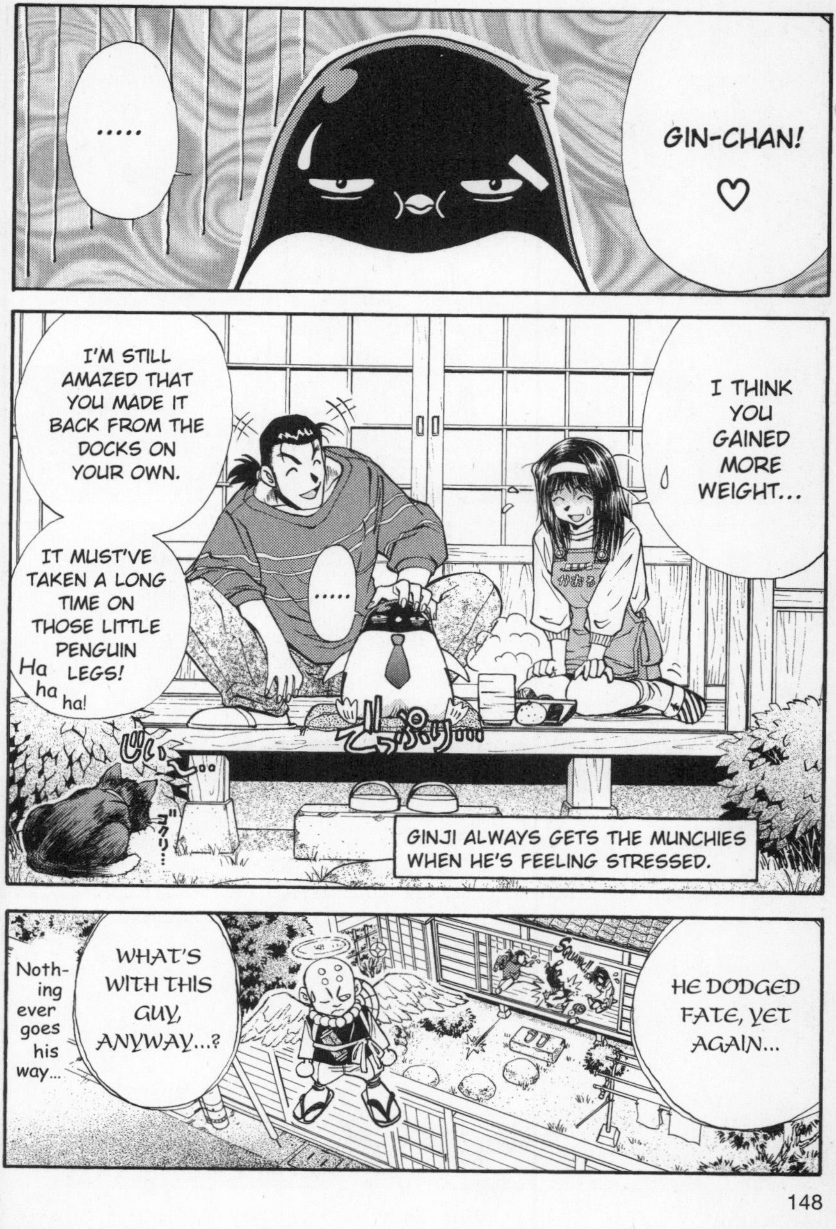
GIN-CHAN! ♡
.....
I THINK YOU GAINED MORE WEIGHT...
I'M STILL AMAZED THAT YOU MADE IT BACK FROM THE DOCKS ON YOUR OWN.
IT MUST'VE TAKEN A LONG TIME ON THOSE LITTLE PENGUIN LEGS!
Ha ha ha!
.....
ゴクリ...
GINJI ALWAYS GETS THE MUNCHIES WHEN HE'S FEELING STRESSED.
HE DODGED FATE, YET AGAIN...
WHAT'S WITH THIS GUY, ANYWAY...?
Nothing ever goes his way...

CHAPTER 6
THE WRONG ATTITUDE

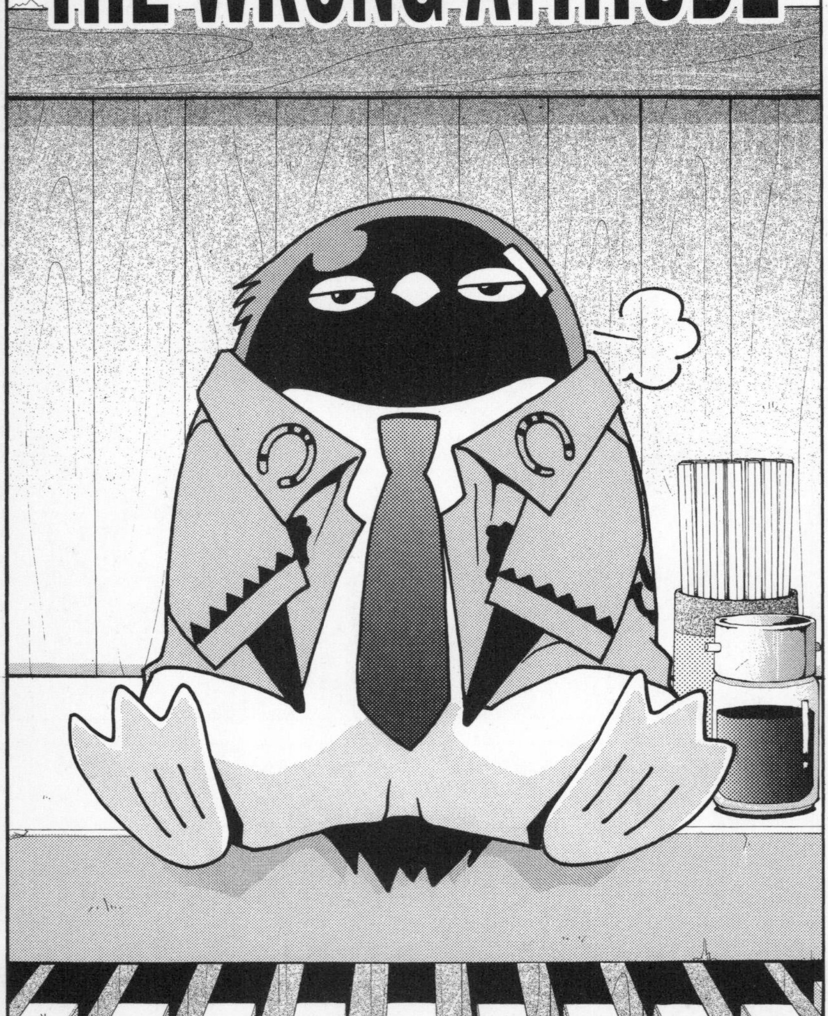

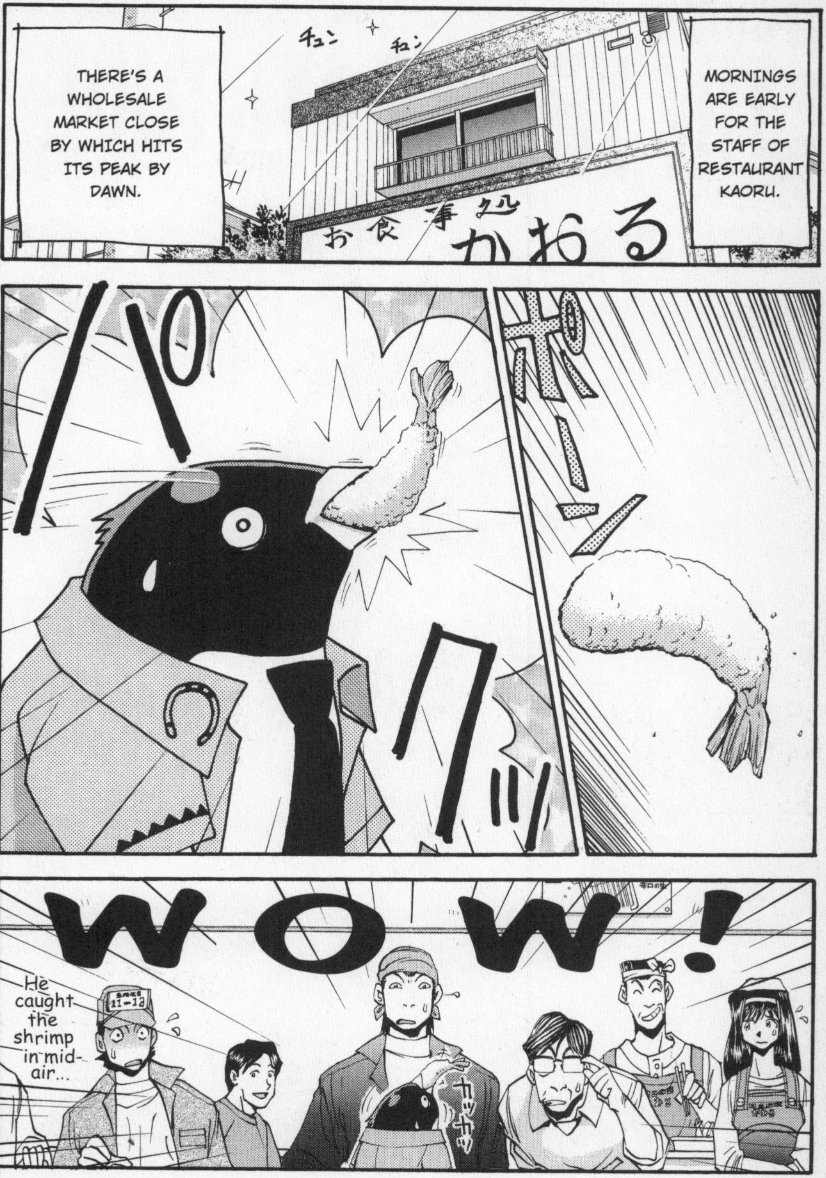
MORNINGS ARE EARLY FOR THE STAFF OF RESTAURANT KAORU.
チュン チュン
お食事処 かおる
THERE'S A WHOLESALE MARKET CLOSE BY WHICH HITS ITS PEAK BY DAWN.
ポーン
パクッ
WOW!
He caught the shrimp in mid-air...

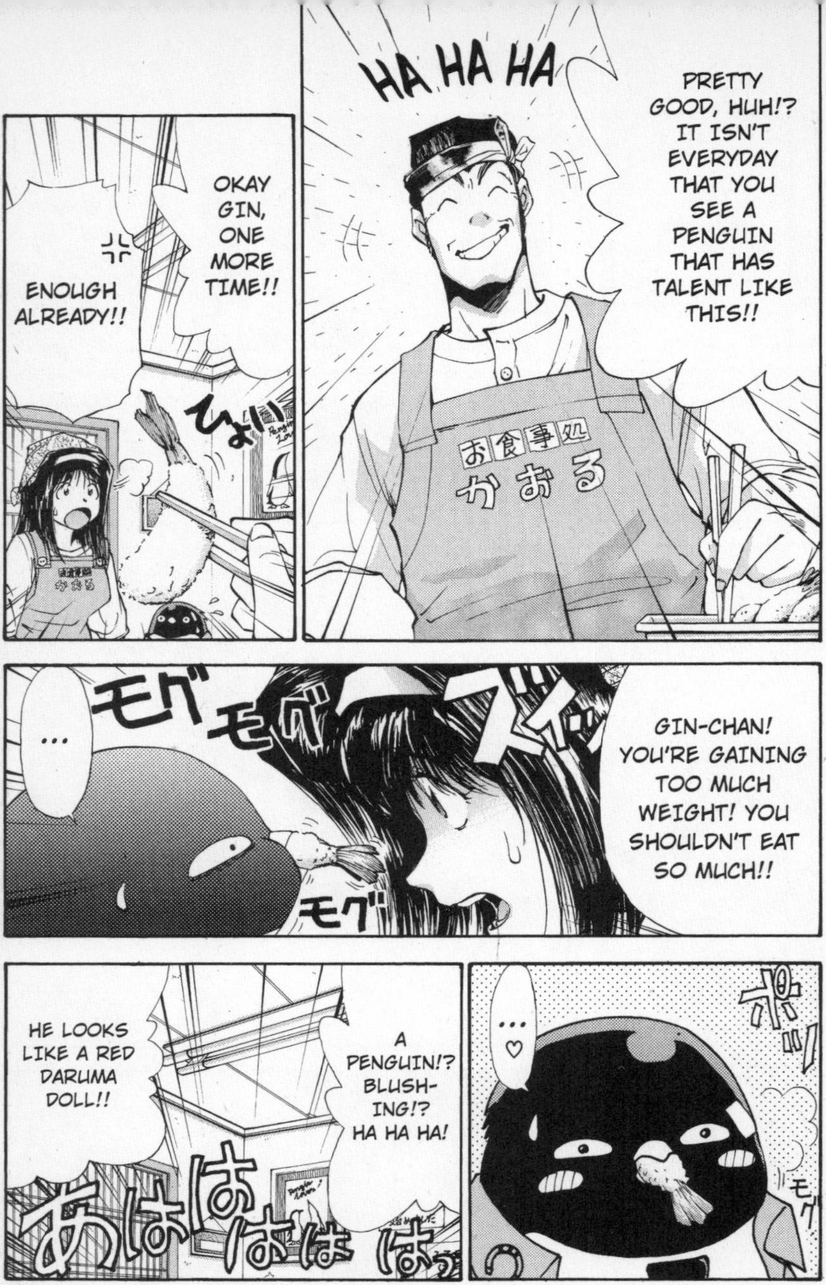
HA HA HA
PRETTY GOOD, HUH!? IT ISN'T EVERYDAY THAT YOU SEE A PENGUIN THAT HAS TALENT LIKE THIS!!
お食事処
かおる
OKAY GIN, ONE MORE TIME!!
ENOUGH ALREADY!!
ひょい
GIN-CHAN! YOU'RE GAINING TOO MUCH WEIGHT! YOU SHOULDN'T EAT SO MUCH!!
ズイッ
モグモグ
...
モグ
... ♡
ポッ
モグ
A PENGUIN!? BLUSH-ING!? HA HA HA!
HE LOOKS LIKE A RED DARUMA DOLL!!
あはははははっ

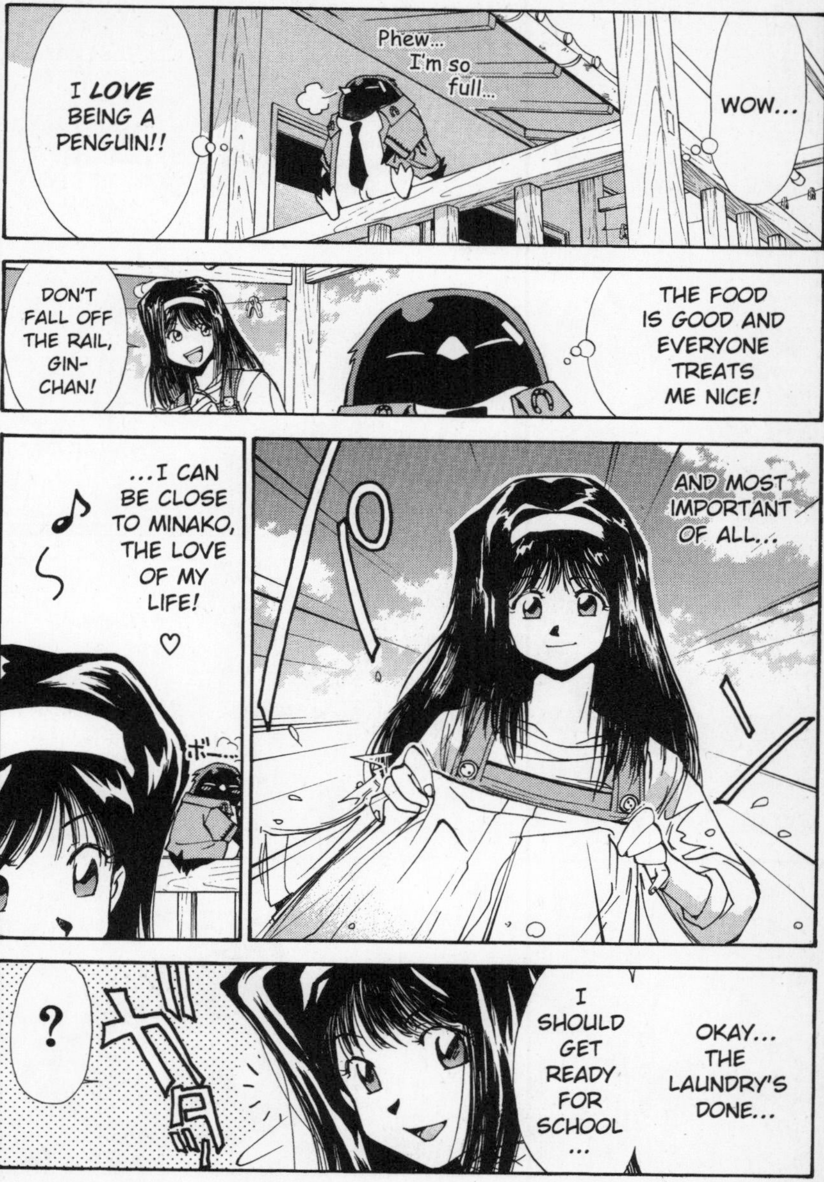
WOW...
Phew... I'm so full...
I LOVE BEING A PENGUIN!!
THE FOOD IS GOOD AND EVERYONE TREATS ME NICE!
DON'T FALL OFF THE RAIL, GIN-CHAN!
AND MOST IMPORTANT OF ALL...
...I CAN BE CLOSE TO MINAKO, THE LOVE OF MY LIFE!
♪
♡
ボー...
OKAY... THE LAUNDRY'S DONE...
I SHOULD GET READY FOR SCHOOL...
?

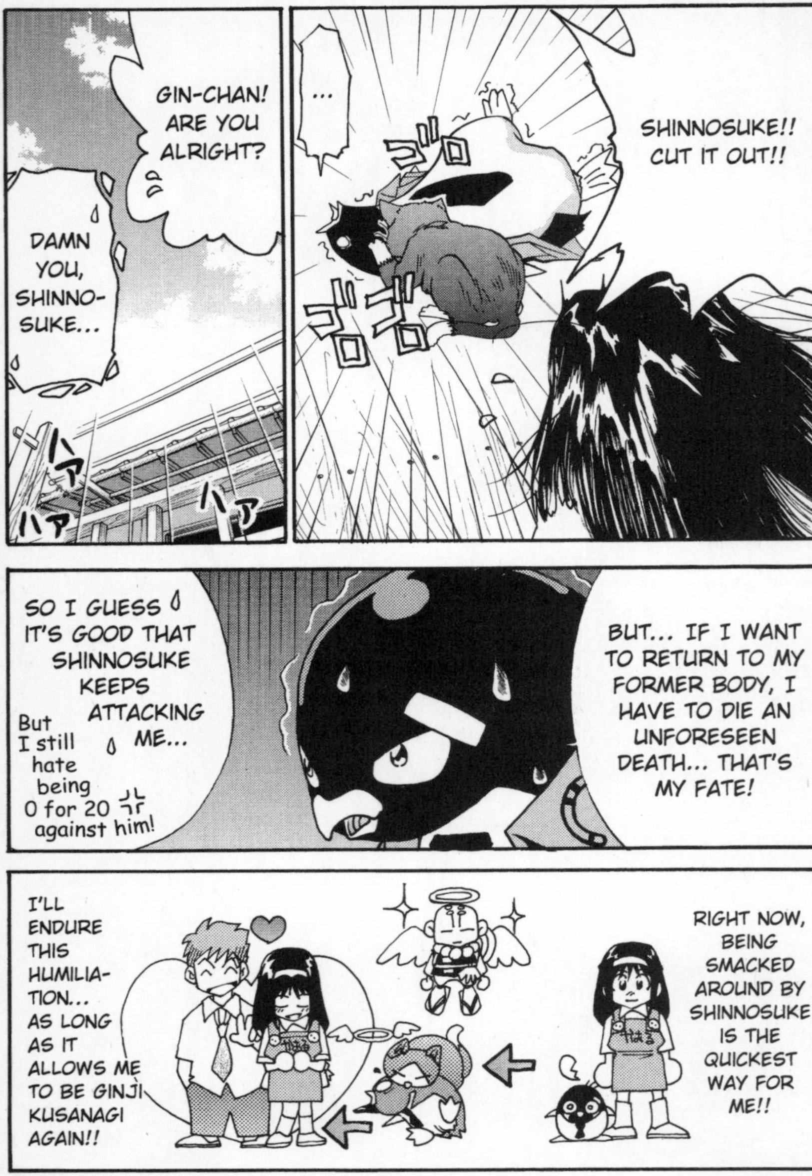
SHINNOSUKE!! CUT IT OUT!!
ゴロ
...
ゴロゴロ
GIN-CHAN! ARE YOU ALRIGHT?
DAMN YOU, SHINNO-SUKE...
ハア
ハア
ハア
BUT... IF I WANT TO RETURN TO MY FORMER BODY, I HAVE TO DIE AN UNFORESEEN DEATH... THAT'S MY FATE!
SO I GUESS IT'S GOOD THAT SHINNOSUKE KEEPS ATTACKING ME...
But I still hate being 0 for 20 against him!
RIGHT NOW, BEING SMACKED AROUND BY SHINNOSUKE IS THE QUICKEST WAY FOR ME!!
I'LL ENDURE THIS HUMILIA-TION... AS LONG AS IT ALLOWS ME TO BE GINJI KUSANAGI AGAIN!!

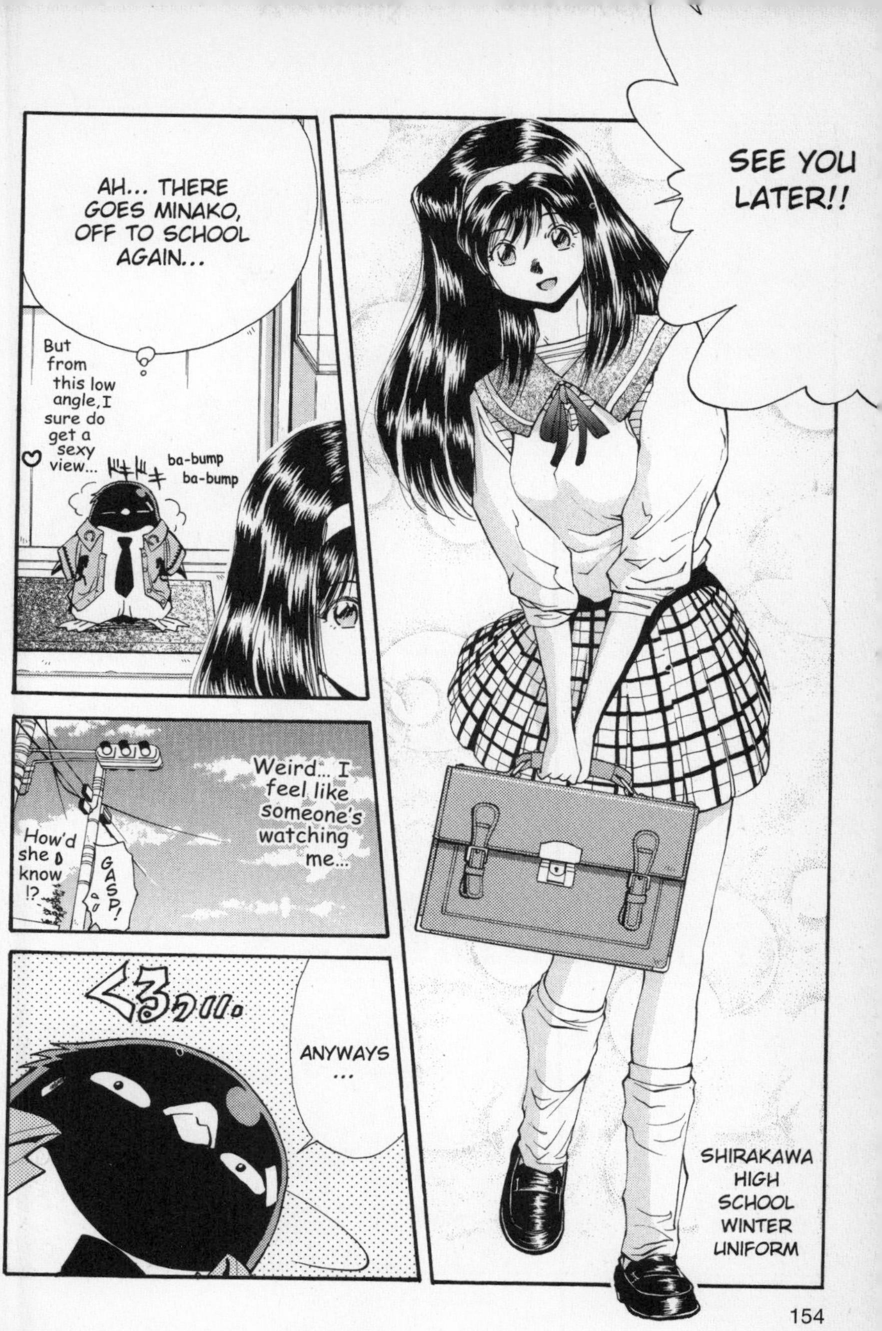
SEE YOU LATER!!
SHIRAKAWA HIGH SCHOOL WINTER UNIFORM
AH... THERE GOES MINAKO, OFF TO SCHOOL AGAIN...
But from this low angle, I sure do get a sexy view...
ドキドキ
ba-bump ba-bump
Weird... I feel like someone's watching me...
GASP!
How'd she know!?
くるっ
ANYWAYS...

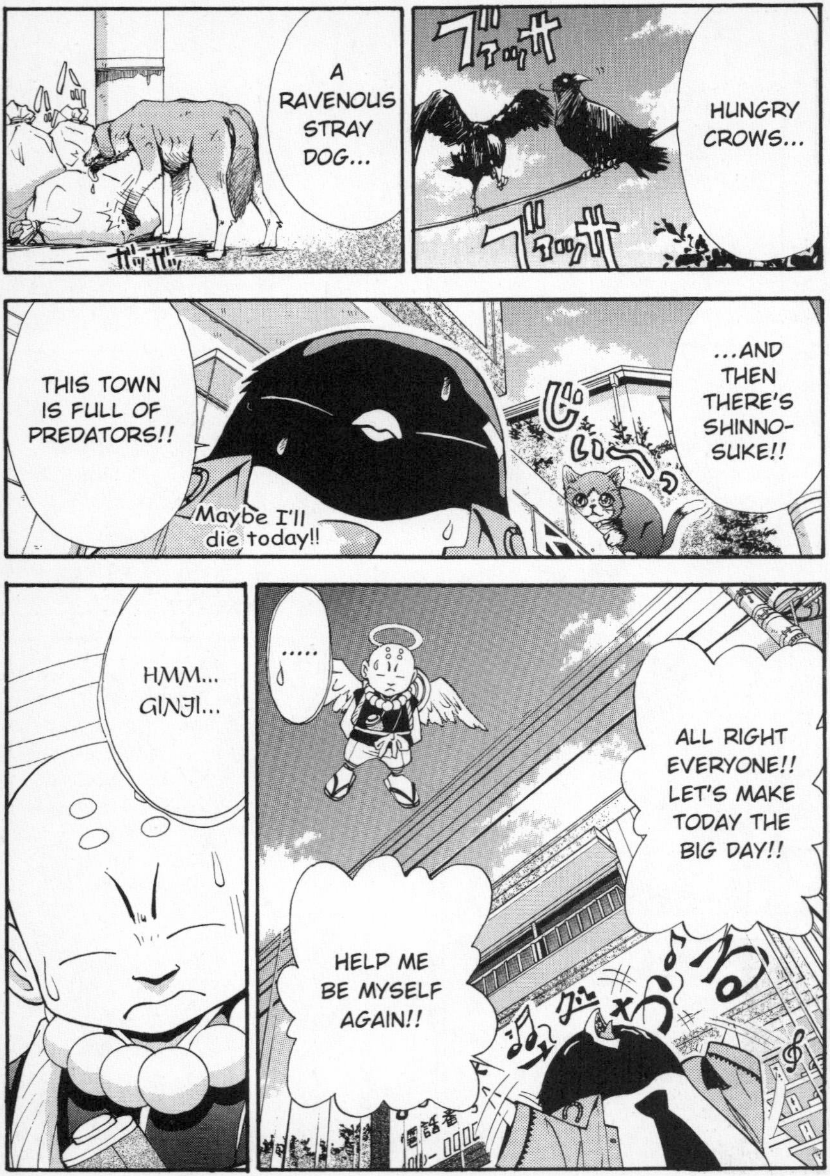
HUNGRY CROWS...
A RAVENOUS STRAY DOG...
...AND THEN THERE'S SHINNO-SUKE!!
THIS TOWN IS FULL OF PREDATORS!!
Maybe I'll die today!!
.....
ALL RIGHT EVERYONE!! LET'S MAKE TODAY THE BIG DAY!!
HELP ME BE MYSELF AGAIN!!
HMM... GINJI...

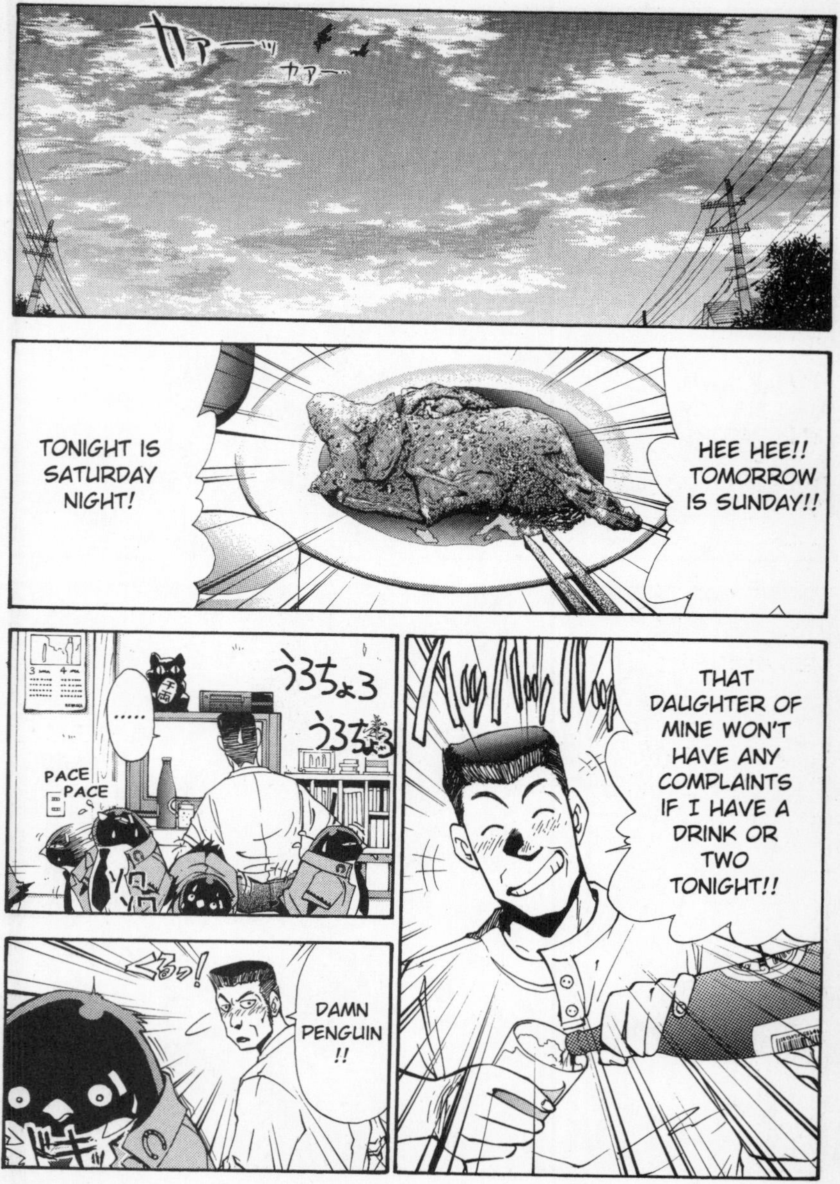
カァーッ
カァー
HEE HEE!! TOMORROW IS SUNDAY!!
TONIGHT IS SATURDAY NIGHT!
THAT DAUGHTER OF MINE WON'T HAVE ANY COMPLAINTS IF I HAVE A DRINK OR TWO TONIGHT!!
うろちょろ
うろちょろ
......
PACE PACE
ソワソワ
DAMN PENGUIN !!
くるっ!
ドキ

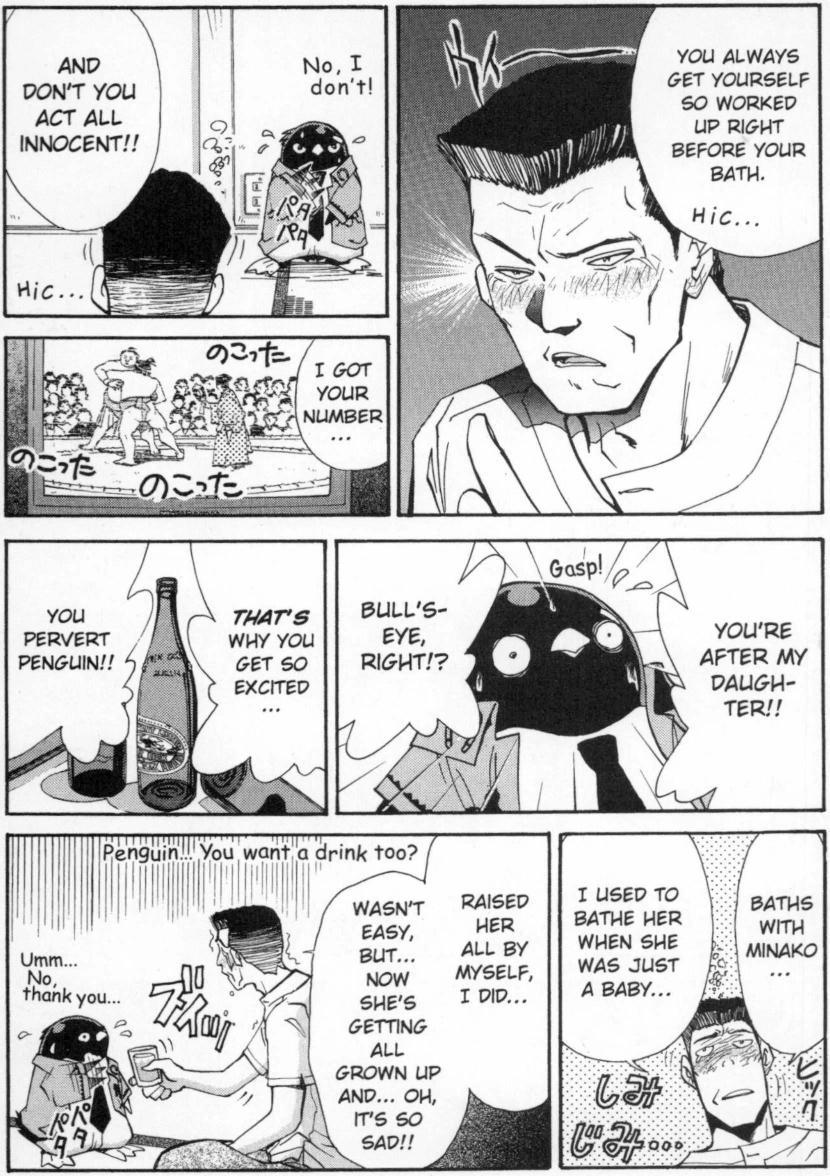
YOU ALWAYS GET YOURSELF SO WORKED UP RIGHT BEFORE YOUR BATH.
Hic...
No, I don't!
AND DON'T YOU ACT ALL INNOCENT!!
パタパタ
Hic...
I GOT YOUR NUMBER...
のこった
のこった
のこった
YOU'RE AFTER MY DAUGHTER!!
Gasp!
BULL'S-EYE, RIGHT!?
THAT'S WHY YOU GET SO EXCITED...
YOU PERVERT PENGUIN!!
BATHS WITH MINAKO...
I USED TO BATHE HER WHEN SHE WAS JUST A BABY...
ヒック
しみじみ...
RAISED HER ALL BY MYSELF, I DID...
WASN'T EASY, BUT... NOW SHE'S GETTING ALL GROWN UP AND... OH, IT'S SO SAD!!
Penguin... You want a drink too?
Umm... No, thank you...
パタパタ

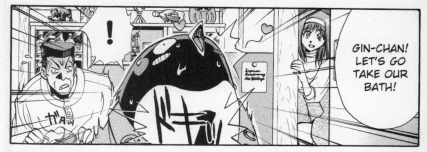

GIN-CHAN! LET'S GO TAKE OUR BATH!
COMING!
SKRNCH
WAIT A MINUTE ...
DIDN'T YOU HEAR A WORD I SAID!?
I'M NOT GONNA LET SOME PERVERT PENGUIN OGLE OVER MY DAUGHTER TAKING A BATH!! NO WAY!
SQUAWK!!
DAD, YOU'RE DRUNK AGAIN!!
SORRY GIN-CHAN!
Dad can sometimes be a mean drunk...

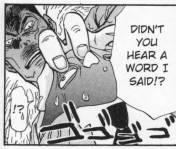

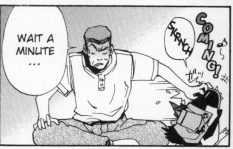

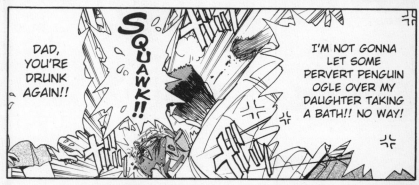

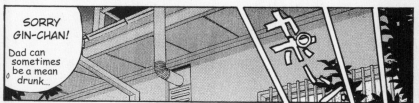

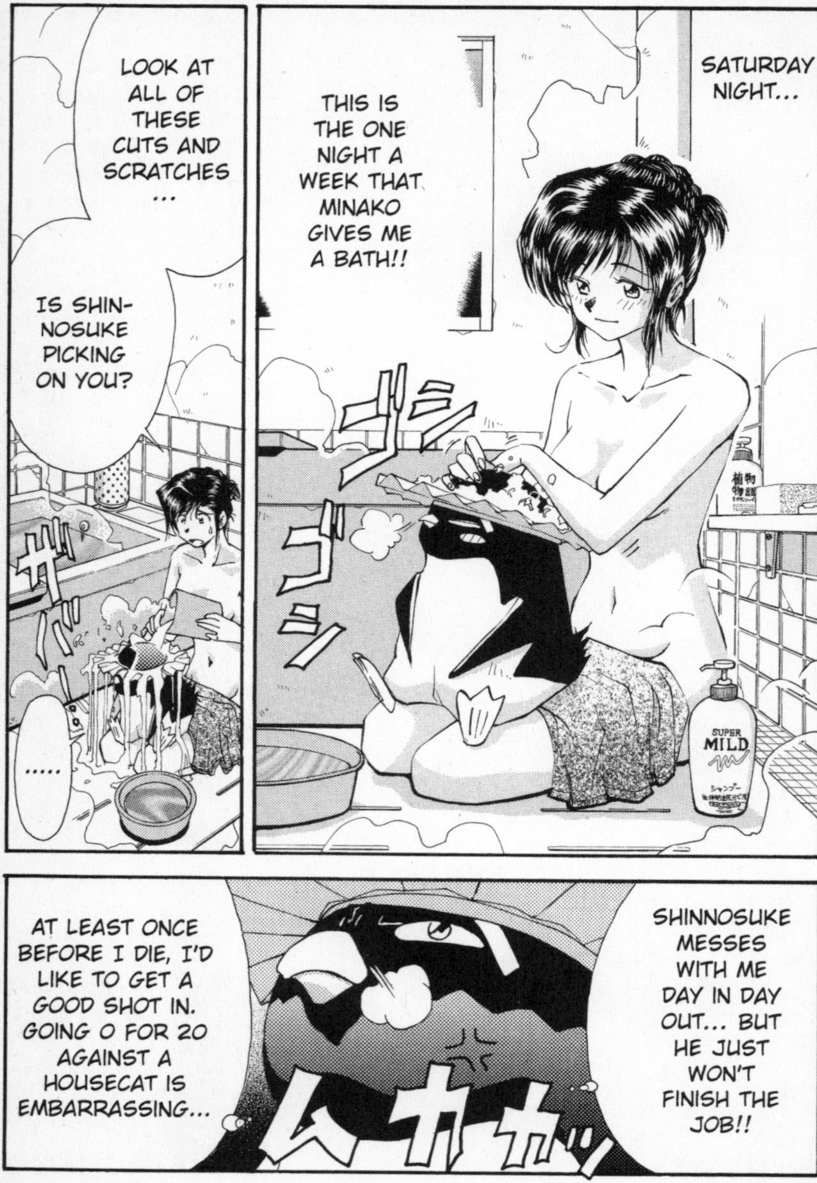
SATURDAY NIGHT...
THIS IS THE ONE NIGHT A WEEK THAT MINAKO GIVES ME A BATH!!
SUPER MILD
LOOK AT ALL OF THESE CUTS AND SCRATCHES ...
IS SHIN-NOSUKE PICKING ON YOU?
.....
SHINNOSUKE MESSES WITH ME DAY IN DAY OUT... BUT HE JUST WON'T FINISH THE JOB!!
AT LEAST ONCE BEFORE I DIE, I'D LIKE TO GET A GOOD SHOT IN. GOING 0 FOR 20 AGAINST A HOUSECAT IS EMBARRASSING...

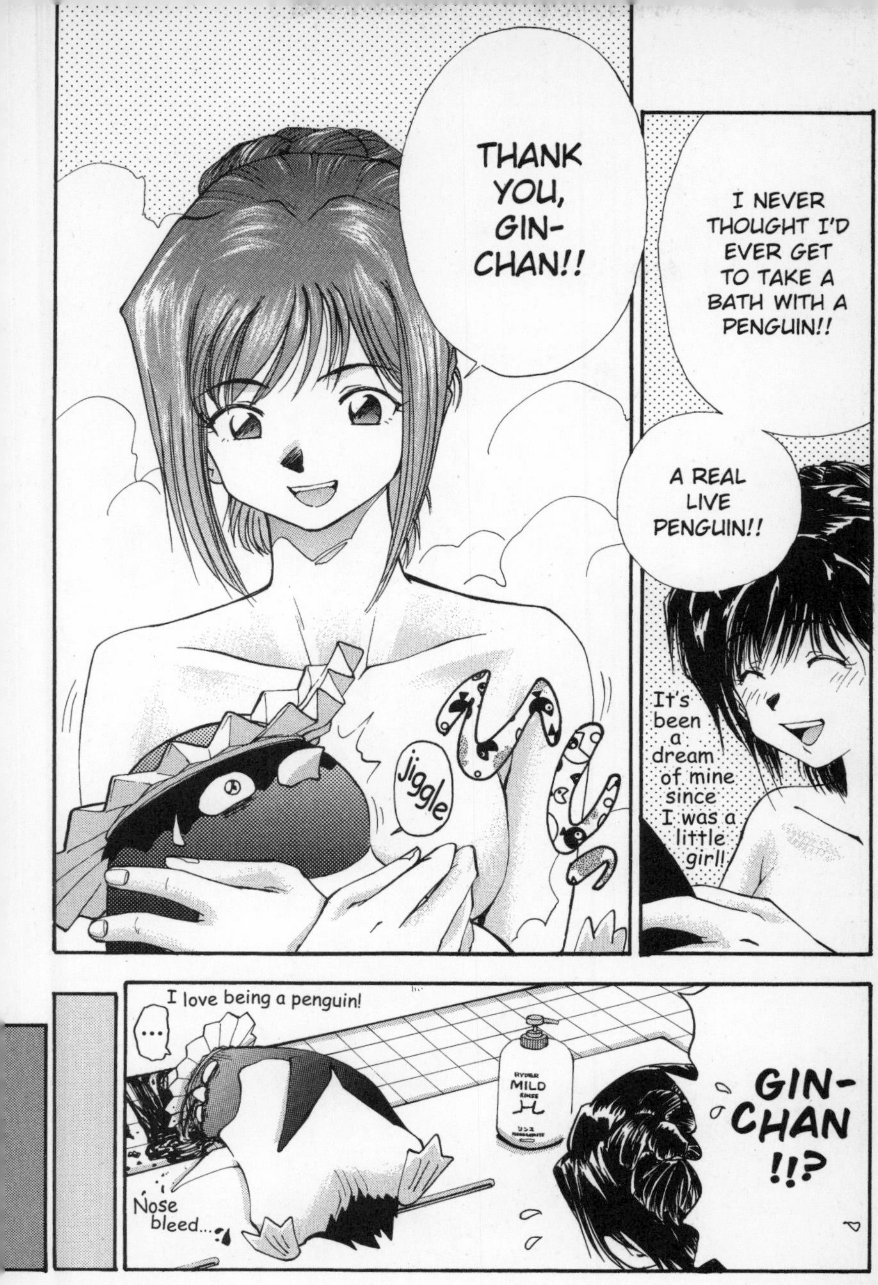
I NEVER THOUGHT I'D EVER GET TO TAKE A BATH WITH A PENGUIN!!
A REAL LIVE PENGUIN!!
It's been a dream of mine since I was a little girl!
THANK YOU, GIN-CHAN!!
jiggle
GIN-CHAN!!?
MILD
I love being a penguin!
...
Nose bleed...

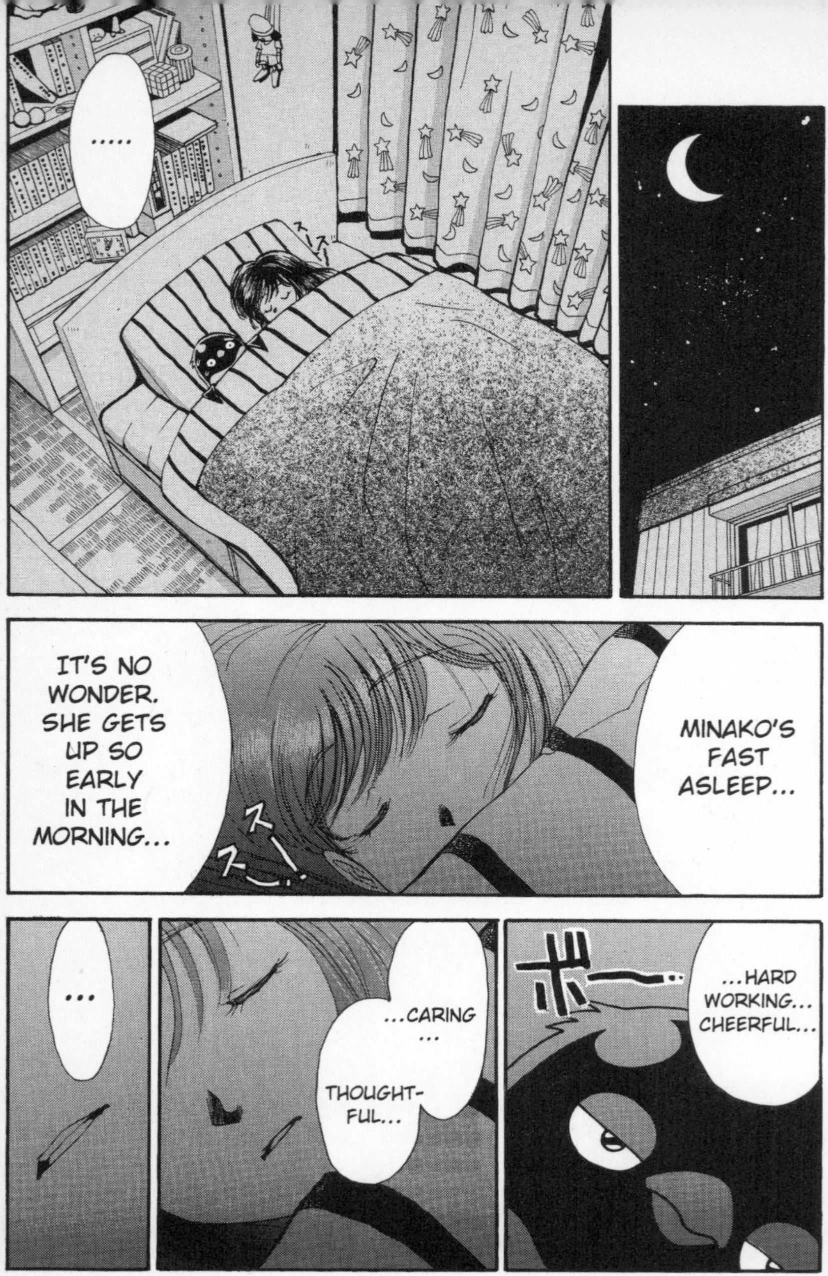
.....
MINAKO'S FAST ASLEEP...
IT'S NO WONDER. SHE GETS UP SO EARLY IN THE MORNING...
スースー
ボー
...HARD WORKING... CHEERFUL...
...CARING ...
THOUGHT-FUL...
...

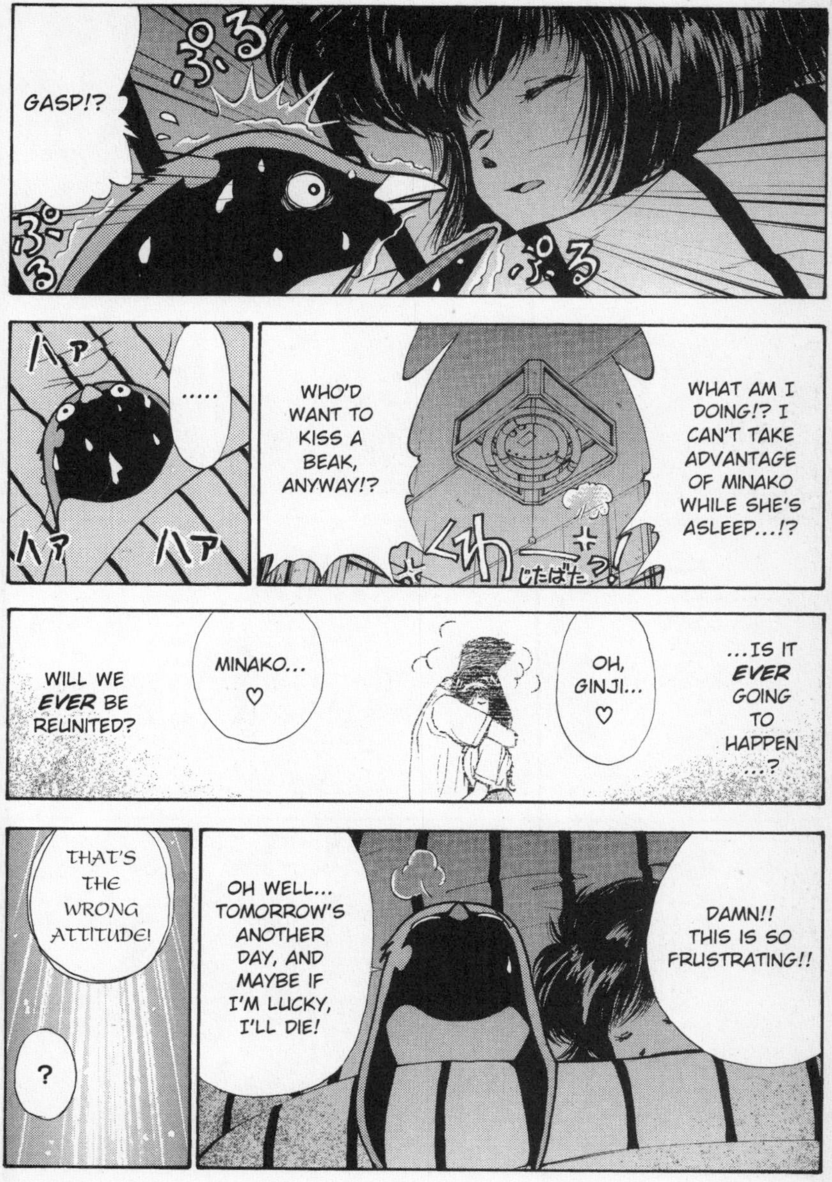
GASP!?
ぷる
ぷる
ぷる
WHAT AM I DOING!? I CAN'T TAKE ADVANTAGE OF MINAKO WHILE SHE'S ASLEEP...!?
WHO'D WANT TO KISS A BEAK, ANYWAY!?
くわーっ
じたばた
.....
ハァ
ハァ
ハァ
...IS IT EVER GOING TO HAPPEN...?
OH, GINJI... ♡
MINAKO... ♡
WILL WE EVER BE REUNITED?
DAMN!! THIS IS SO FRUSTRATING!!
OH WELL... TOMORROW'S ANOTHER DAY, AND MAYBE IF I'M LUCKY, I'LL DIE!
THAT'S THE WRONG ATTITUDE!
?

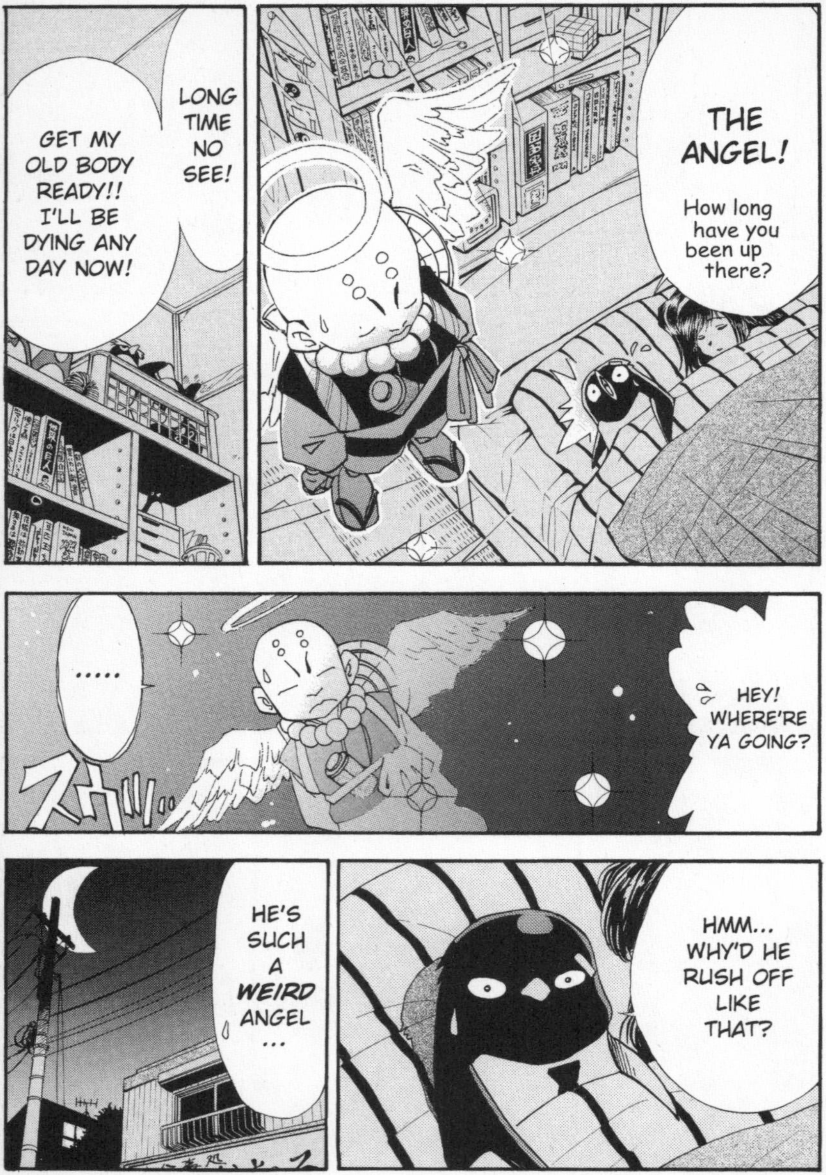
THE ANGEL!
How long have you been up there?
LONG TIME NO SEE!
GET MY OLD BODY READY!! I'LL BE DYING ANY DAY NOW!
HEY! WHERE'RE YA GOING?
.....
HMM... WHY'D HE RUSH OFF LIKE THAT?
HE'S SUCH A WEIRD ANGEL...

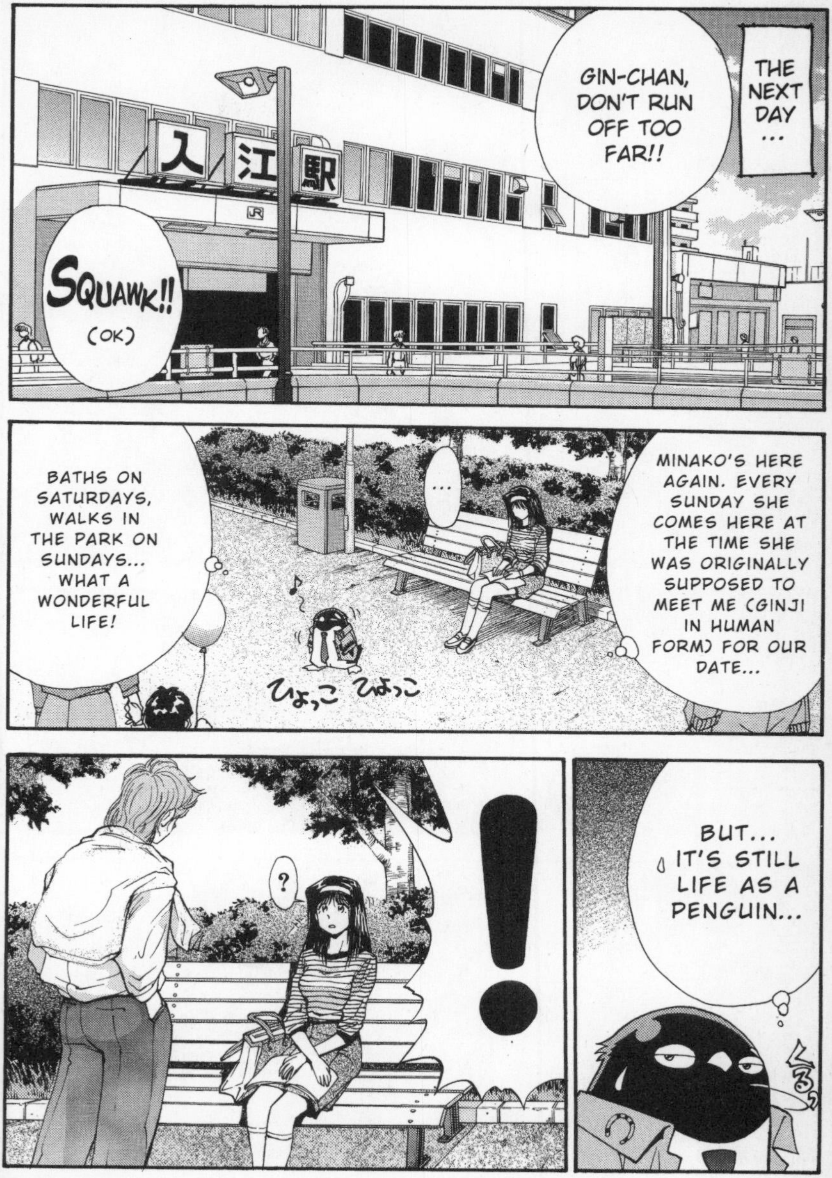
THE NEXT DAY...
GIN-CHAN, DON'T RUN OFF TOO FAR!!
入江駅
JR
SQUAWK!!
(OK)
MINAKO'S HERE AGAIN. EVERY SUNDAY SHE COMES HERE AT THE TIME SHE WAS ORIGINALLY SUPPOSED TO MEET ME (GINJI IN HUMAN FORM) FOR OUR DATE...
...
BATHS ON SATURDAYS, WALKS IN THE PARK ON SUNDAYS... WHAT A WONDERFUL LIFE!
ひょっこ ひょっこ
BUT... IT'S STILL LIFE AS A PENGUIN...
くるっ
!
?

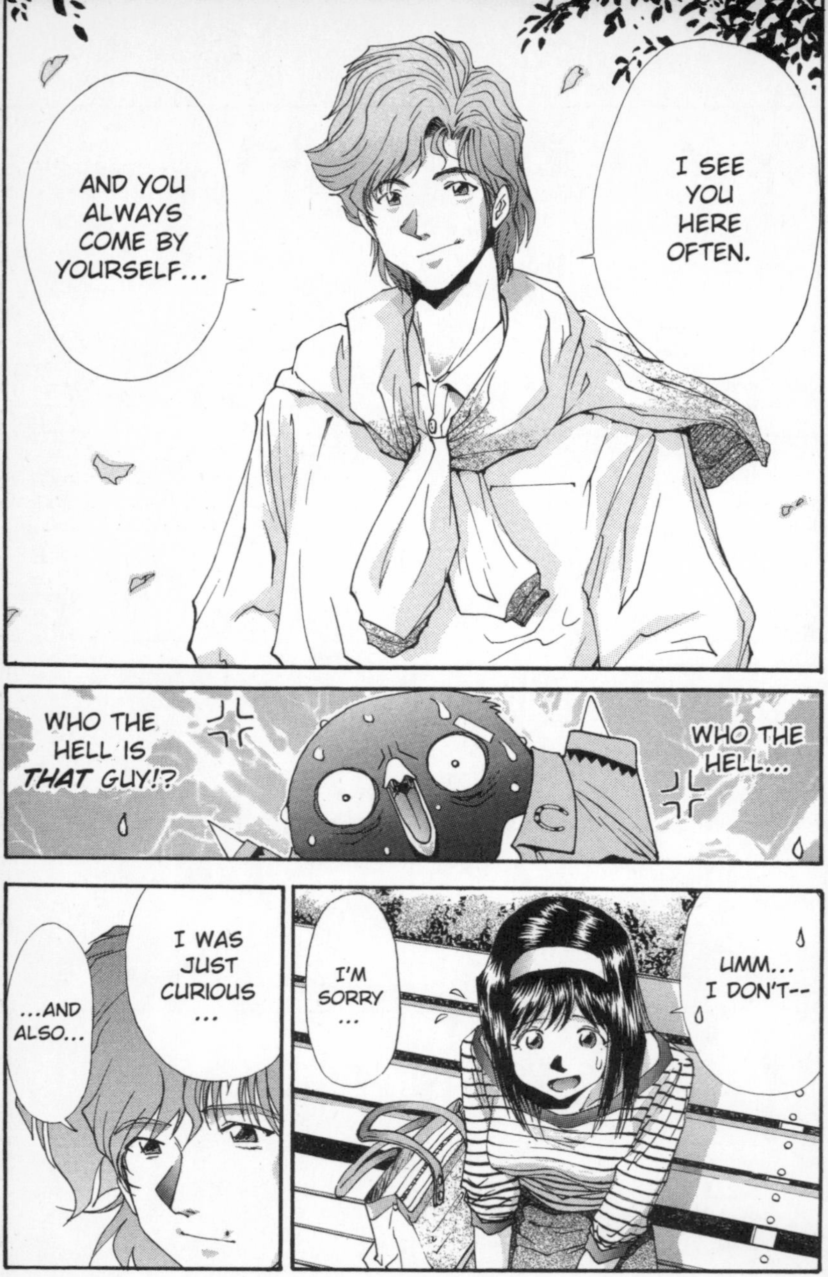
I SEE YOU HERE OFTEN.
AND YOU ALWAYS COME BY YOURSELF...
WHO THE HELL...
WHO THE HELL IS *THAT* GUY!?
UMM... I DON'T--
I'M SORRY ...
I WAS JUST CURIOUS ...
...AND ALSO...

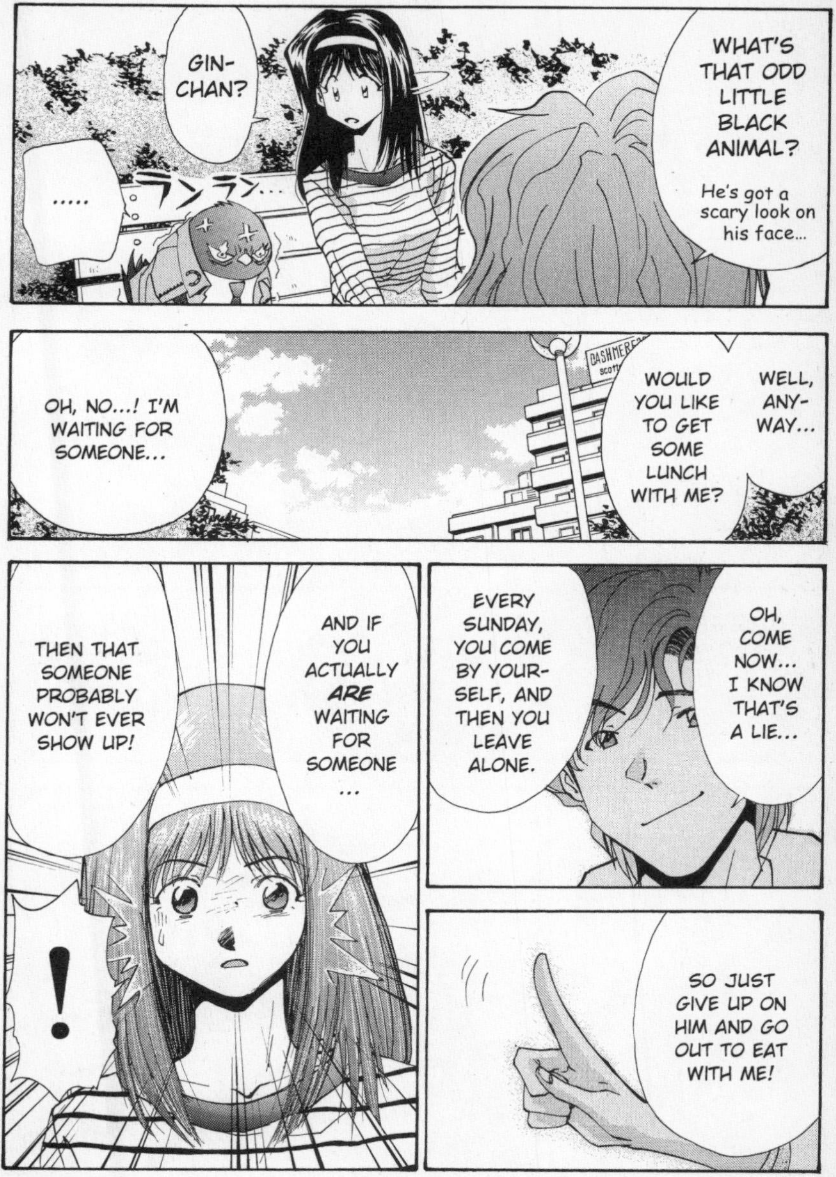
WHAT'S THAT ODD LITTLE BLACK ANIMAL?
He's got a scary look on his face...
GIN-CHAN?
ランラン...
.....
WELL, ANY-WAY...
WOULD YOU LIKE TO GET SOME LUNCH WITH ME?
OH, NO...! I'M WAITING FOR SOMEONE...
OH, COME NOW... I KNOW THAT'S A LIE...
EVERY SUNDAY, YOU COME BY YOUR-SELF, AND THEN YOU LEAVE ALONE.
SO JUST GIVE UP ON HIM AND GO OUT TO EAT WITH ME!
AND IF YOU ACTUALLY *ARE* WAITING FOR SOMEONE ...
THEN THAT SOMEONE PROBABLY WON'T EVER SHOW UP!
!

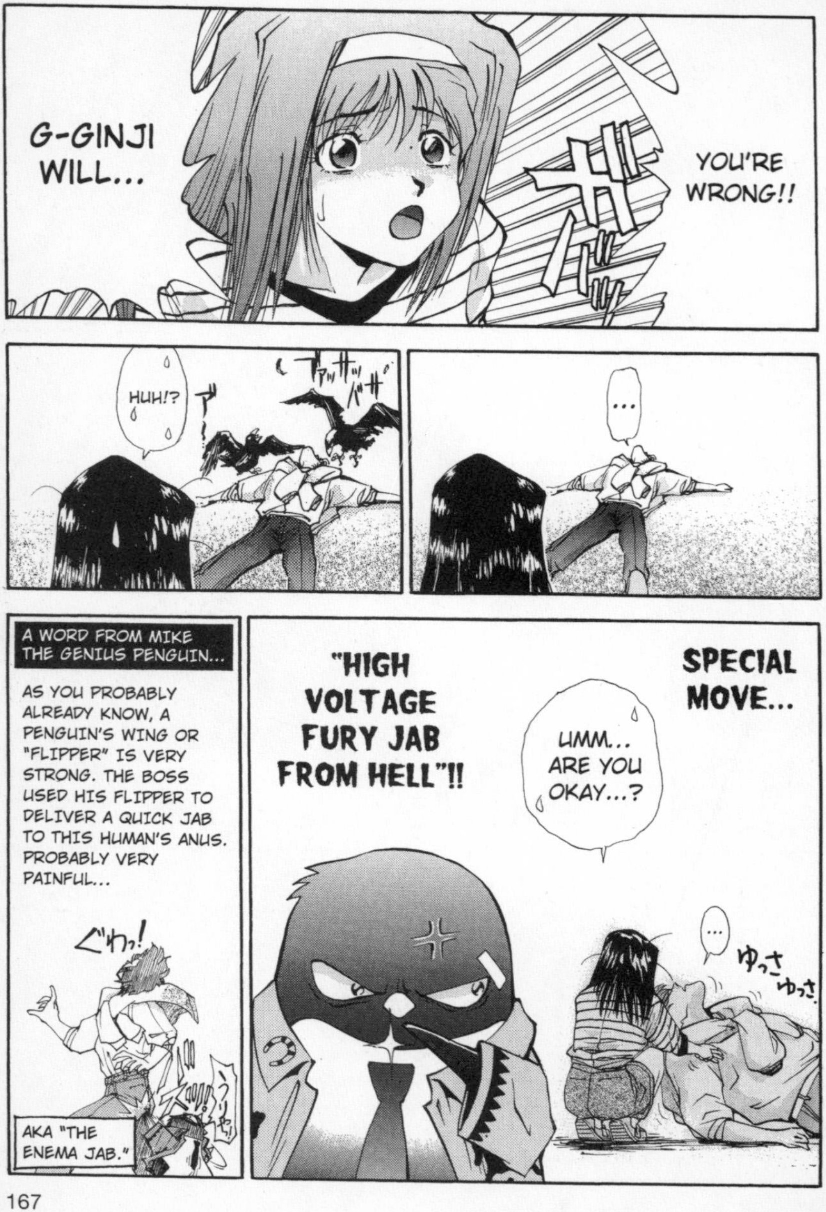
YOU'RE WRONG!!
G-GINJI WILL...
...
HUH!?
SPECIAL MOVE...
"HIGH VOLTAGE FURY JAB FROM HELL"!!
UMM... ARE YOU OKAY...?
...
ゆっさゆっさ
A WORD FROM MIKE THE GENIUS PENGUIN...
AS YOU PROBABLY ALREADY KNOW, A PENGUIN'S WING OR "FLIPPER" IS VERY STRONG. THE BOSS USED HIS FLIPPER TO DELIVER A QUICK JAB TO THIS HUMAN'S ANUS. PROBABLY VERY PAINFUL...
ぐわっ!
AKA "THE ENEMA JAB."

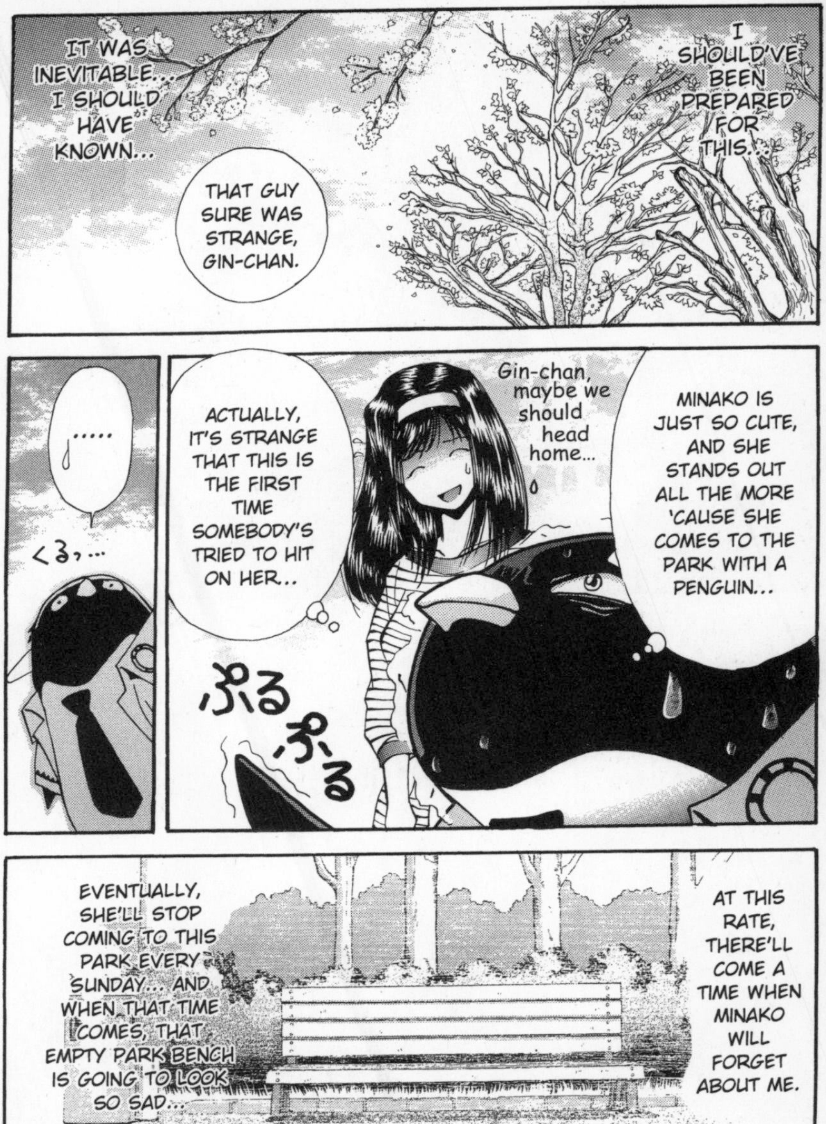
I SHOULD'VE BEEN PREPARED FOR THIS...
IT WAS INEVITABLE... I SHOULD HAVE KNOWN...
THAT GUY SURE WAS STRANGE, GIN-CHAN.
MINAKO IS JUST SO CUTE, AND SHE STANDS OUT ALL THE MORE 'CAUSE SHE COMES TO THE PARK WITH A PENGUIN...
Gin-chan, maybe we should head home...
ACTUALLY, IT'S STRANGE THAT THIS IS THE FIRST TIME SOMEBODY'S TRIED TO HIT ON HER...
ぷるぷる
.....
くるっ...
AT THIS RATE, THERE'LL COME A TIME WHEN MINAKO WILL FORGET ABOUT ME.
EVENTUALLY, SHE'LL STOP COMING TO THIS PARK EVERY SUNDAY... AND WHEN THAT TIME COMES, THAT EMPTY PARK BENCH IS GOING TO LOOK SO SAD...

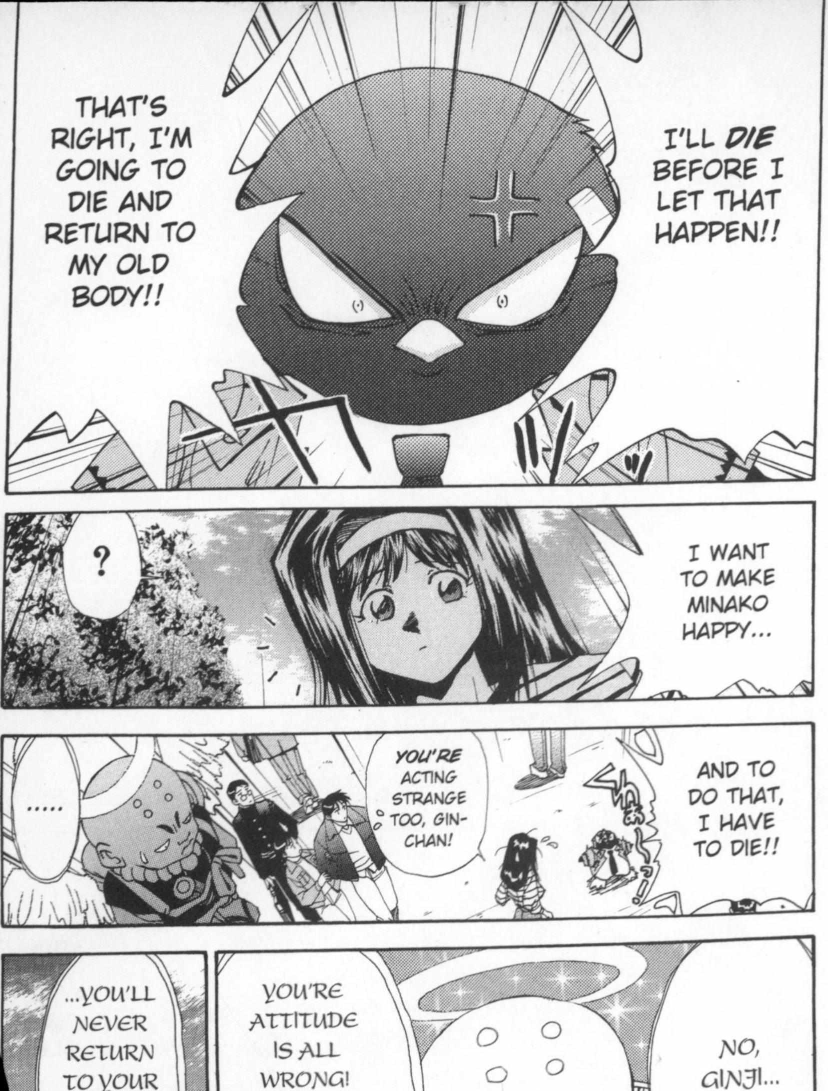
I'LL DIE BEFORE I LET THAT HAPPEN!!
THAT'S RIGHT, I'M GOING TO DIE AND RETURN TO MY OLD BODY!!
I WANT TO MAKE MINAKO HAPPY...
?
AND TO DO THAT, I HAVE TO DIE!!
YOU'RE ACTING STRANGE TOO, GIN-CHAN!
.....
NO, GINJI...
YOU'RE ATTITUDE IS ALL WRONG! IF YOU CONTINUE ALONG THIS LINE OF THOUGHT...
...YOU'LL NEVER RETURN TO YOUR FORMER BODY...!!

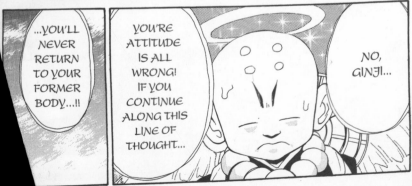

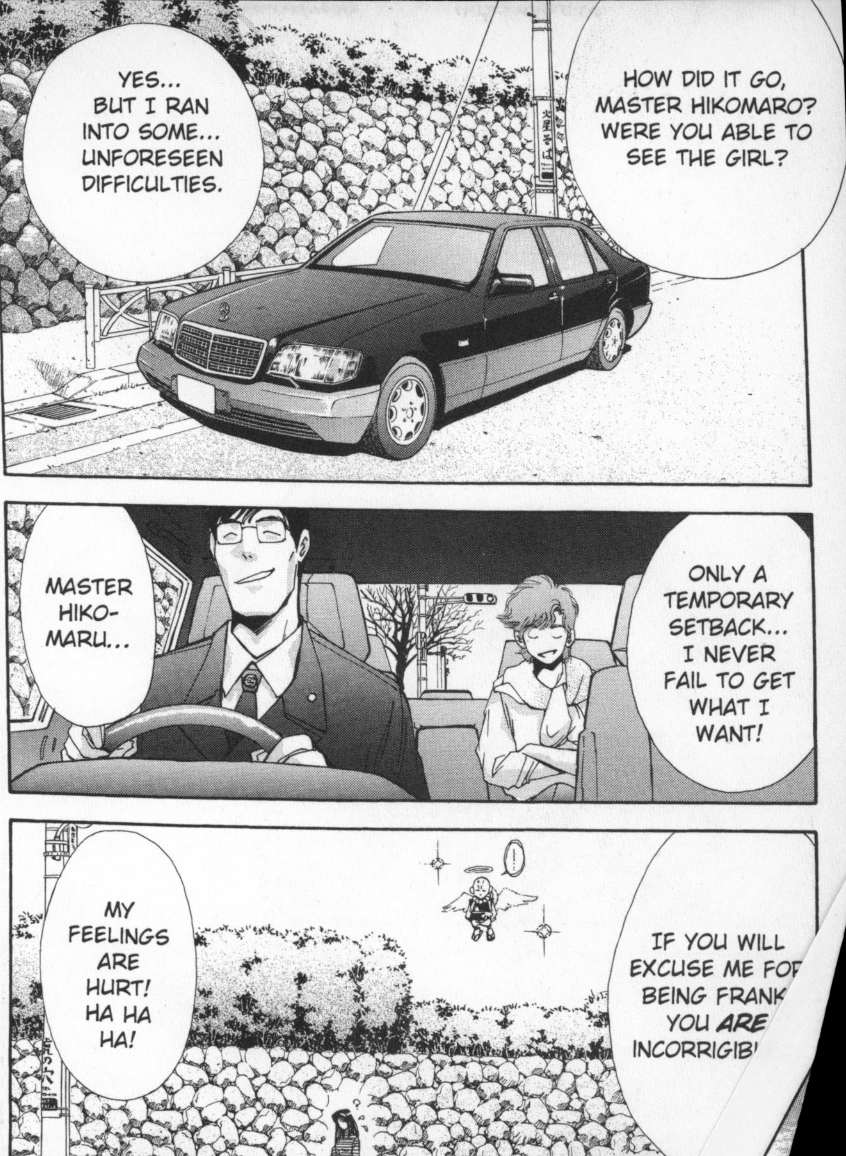
HOW DID IT GO, MASTER HIKOMARO? WERE YOU ABLE TO SEE THE GIRL?
YES... BUT I RAN INTO SOME... UNFORESEEN DIFFICULTIES.
ONLY A TEMPORARY SETBACK... I NEVER FAIL TO GET WHAT I WANT!
MASTER HIKO-MARU...
IF YOU WILL EXCUSE ME FO BEING FRANK YOU ARE INCORRIGIB
!
MY FEELINGS ARE HURT! HA HA HA!

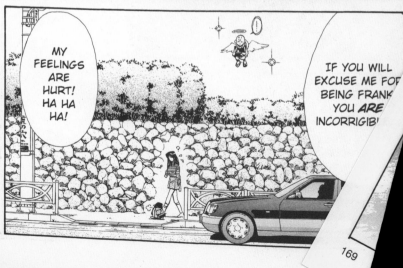

CHAPTER 7
MINAKO, WHERE ARE YOU!?

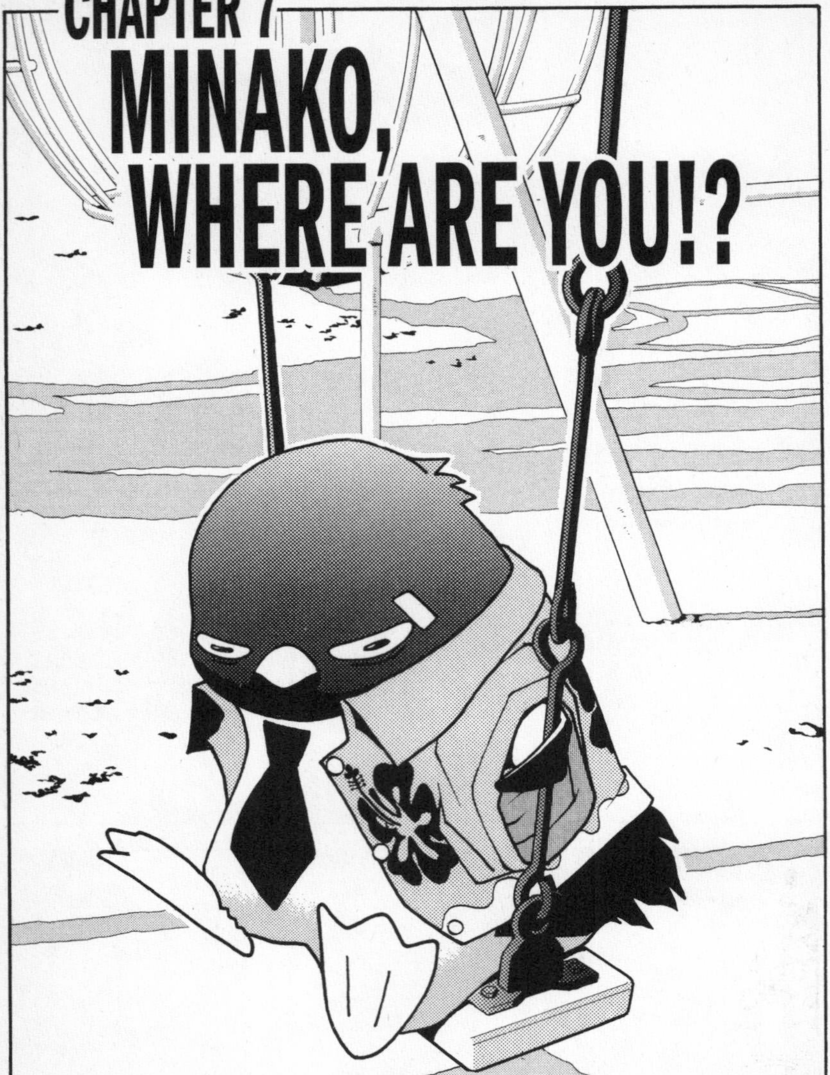

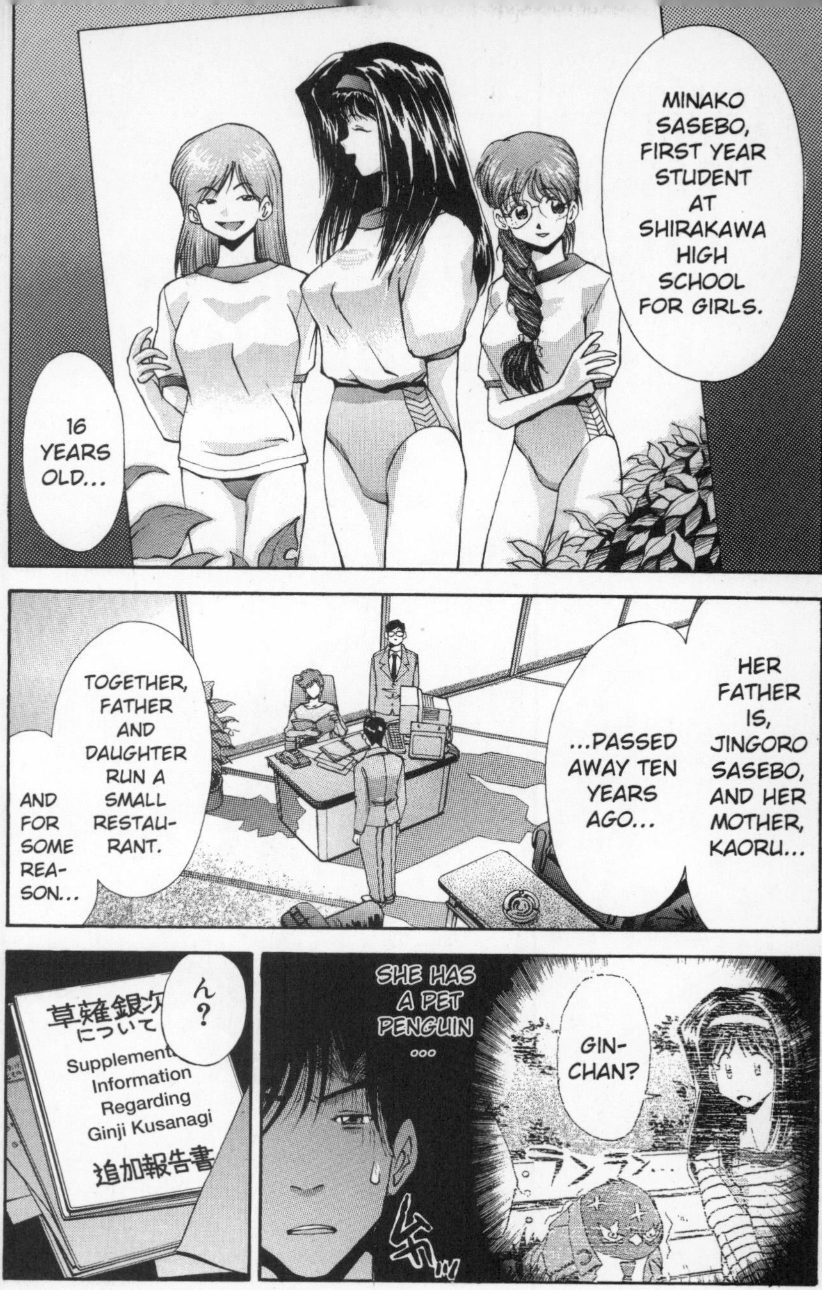
MINAKO SASEBO, FIRST YEAR STUDENT AT SHIRAKAWA HIGH SCHOOL FOR GIRLS.
16 YEARS OLD...
HER FATHER IS, JINGORO SASEBO, AND HER MOTHER, KAORU...
...PASSED AWAY TEN YEARS AGO...
TOGETHER, FATHER AND DAUGHTER RUN A SMALL RESTAURANT.
AND FOR SOME REASON...
SHE HAS A PET PENGUIN...
GIN-CHAN?
ラン ラン...
ん？
草薙銀次
について
Supplement
Information
Regarding
Ginji Kusanagi
追加報告書

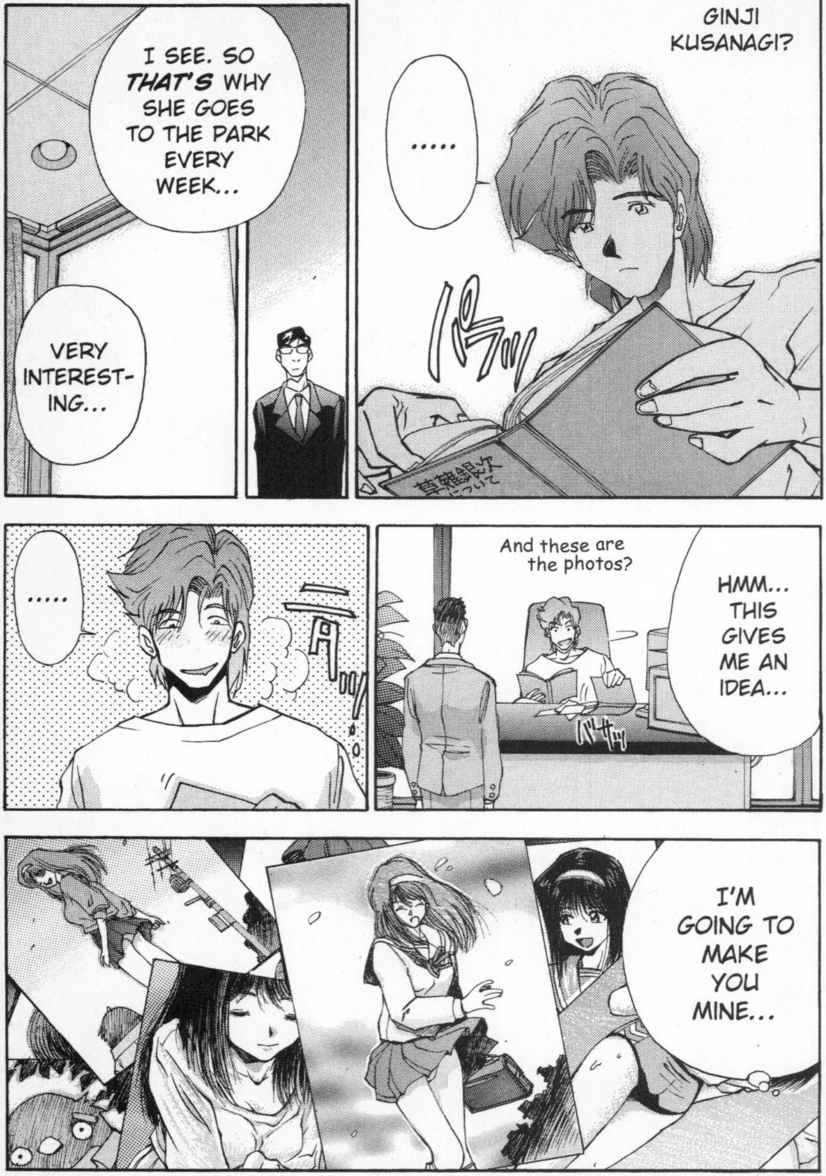
GINJI KUSANAGI?
.....
I SEE. SO *THAT'S* WHY SHE GOES TO THE PARK EVERY WEEK...
VERY INTEREST-ING...
And these are the photos?
HMM... THIS GIVES ME AN IDEA...
.....
I'M GOING TO MAKE YOU MINE...

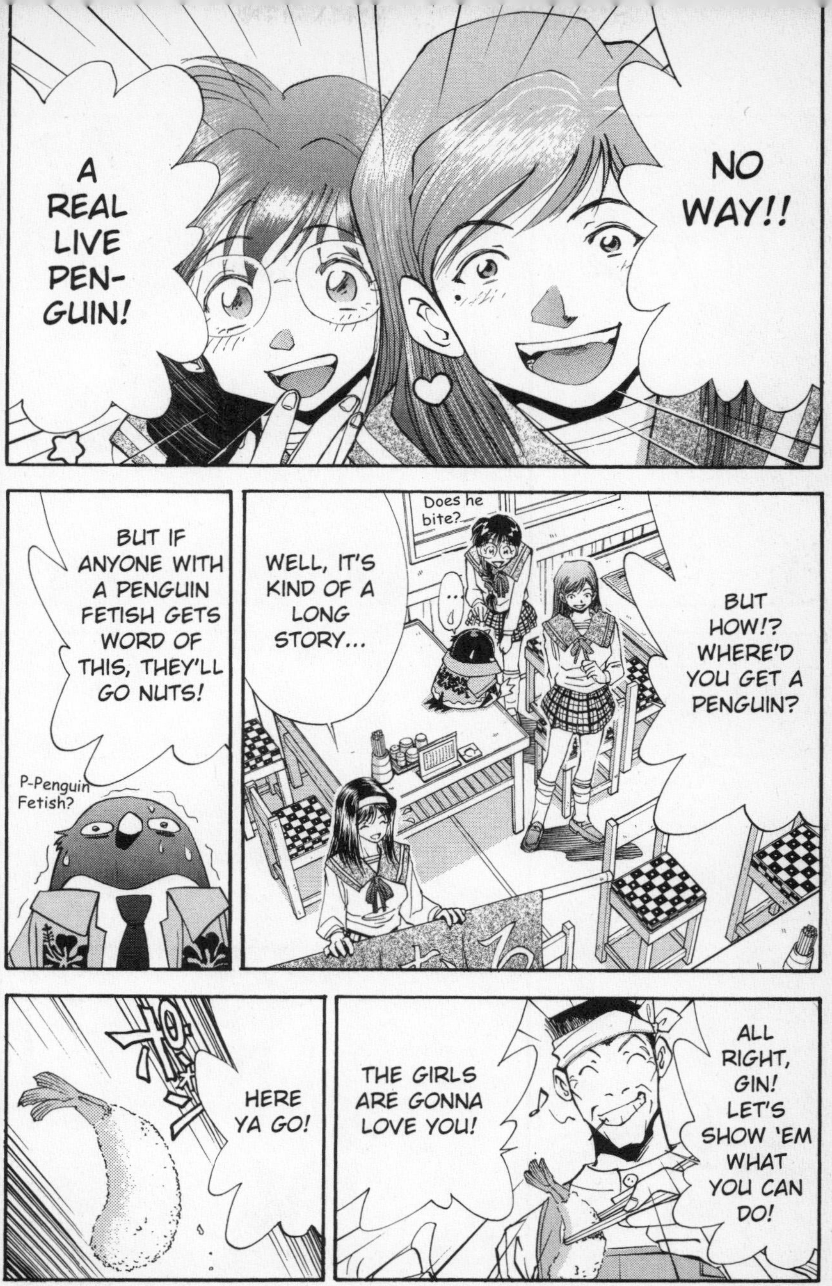

NO WAY!!
A REAL LIVE PEN-GUIN!
BUT HOW!? WHERE'D YOU GET A PENGUIN?
Does he bite?
WELL, IT'S KIND OF A LONG STORY...
...
BUT IF ANYONE WITH A PENGUIN FETISH GETS WORD OF THIS, THEY'LL GO NUTS!
P-Penguin Fetish?
ALL RIGHT, GIN! LET'S SHOW 'EM WHAT YOU CAN DO!
THE GIRLS ARE GONNA LOVE YOU!
HERE YA GO!

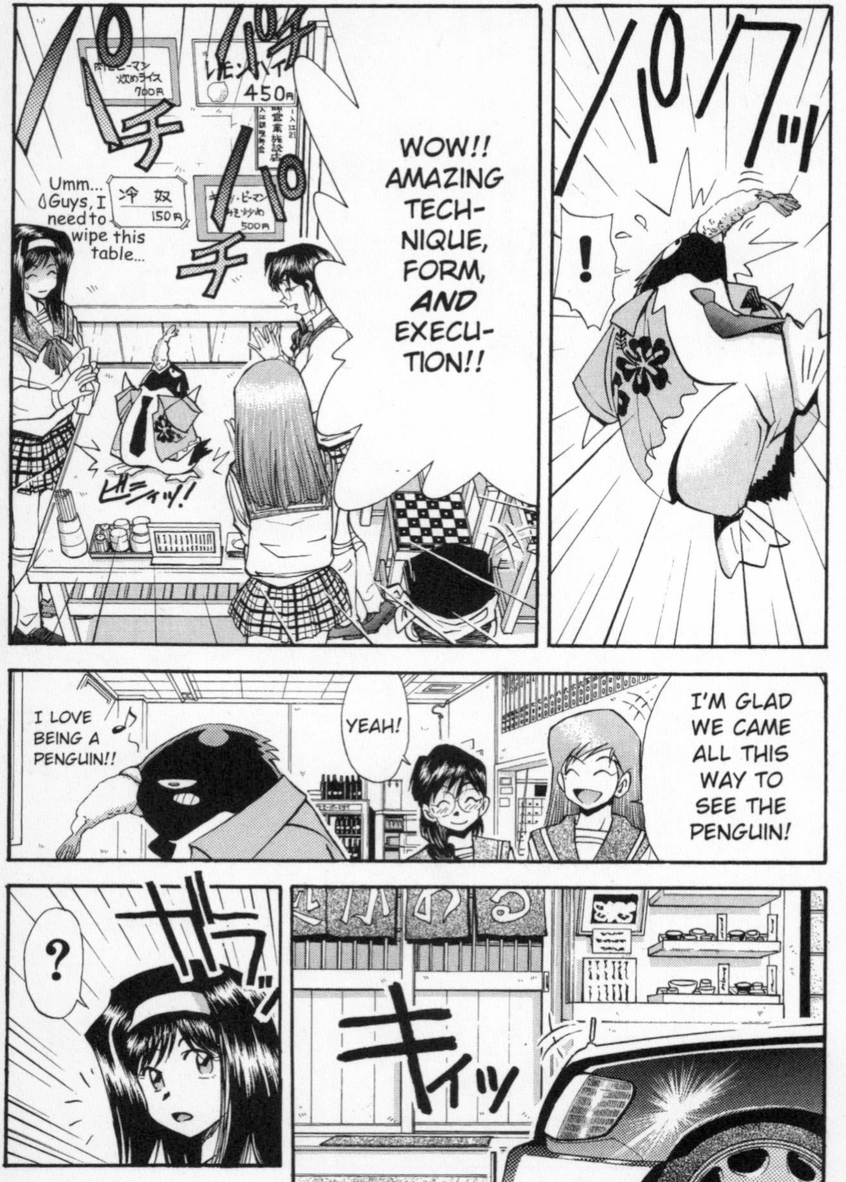
パクッ
!
WOW!! AMAZING TECH-NIQUE, FORM, AND EXECU-TION!!
Umm... Guys, I need to wipe this table...
レモンハイ 450円
冷奴 150円
I'M GLAD WE CAME ALL THIS WAY TO SEE THE PENGUIN!
YEAH!
I LOVE BEING A PENGUIN!!
キイッ
?

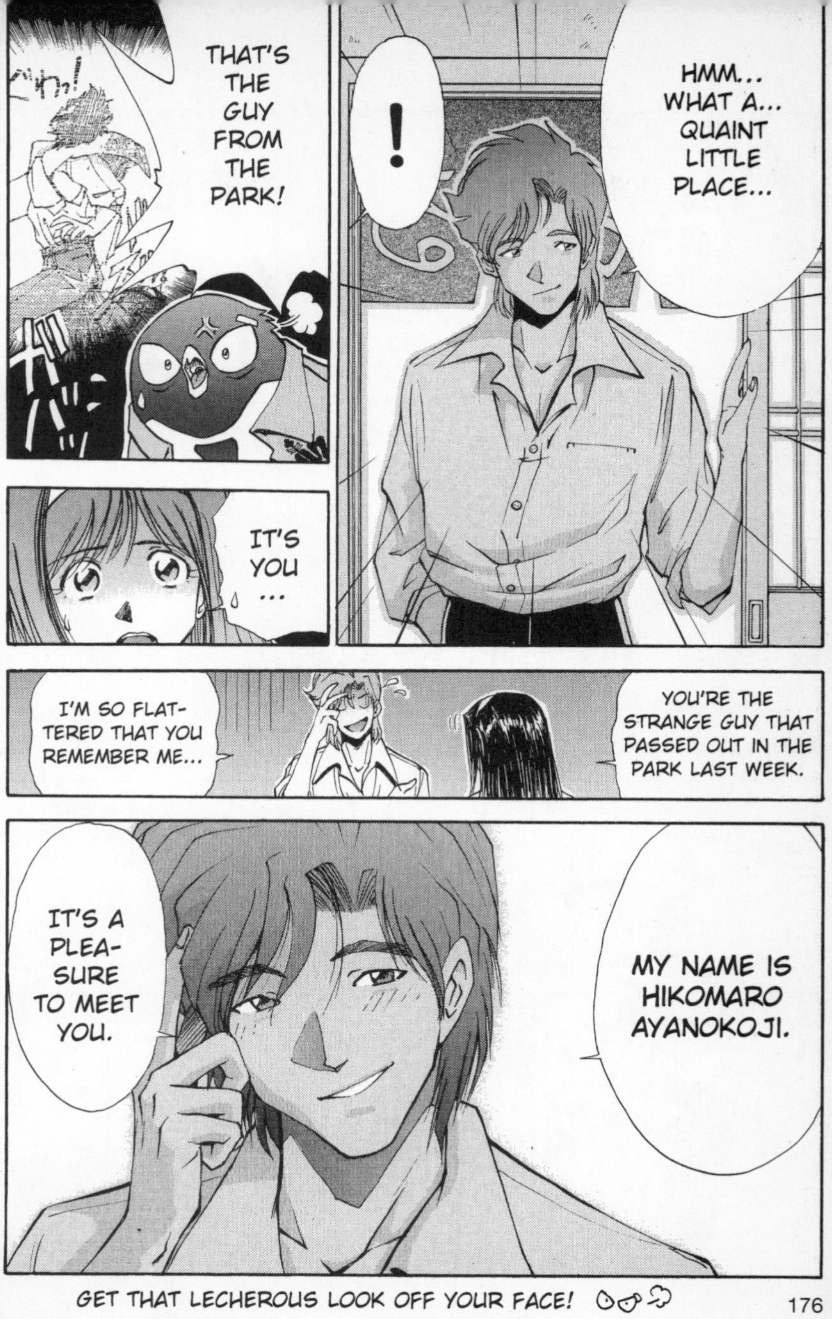
HMM... WHAT A... QUAINT LITTLE PLACE...
!
THAT'S THE GUY FROM THE PARK!
IT'S YOU ...
YOU'RE THE STRANGE GUY THAT PASSED OUT IN THE PARK LAST WEEK.
I'M SO FLAT-TERED THAT YOU REMEMBER ME...
MY NAME IS HIKOMARO AYANOKOJI.
IT'S A PLEA-SURE TO MEET YOU.

GET THAT LECHEROUS LOOK OFF YOUR FACE!

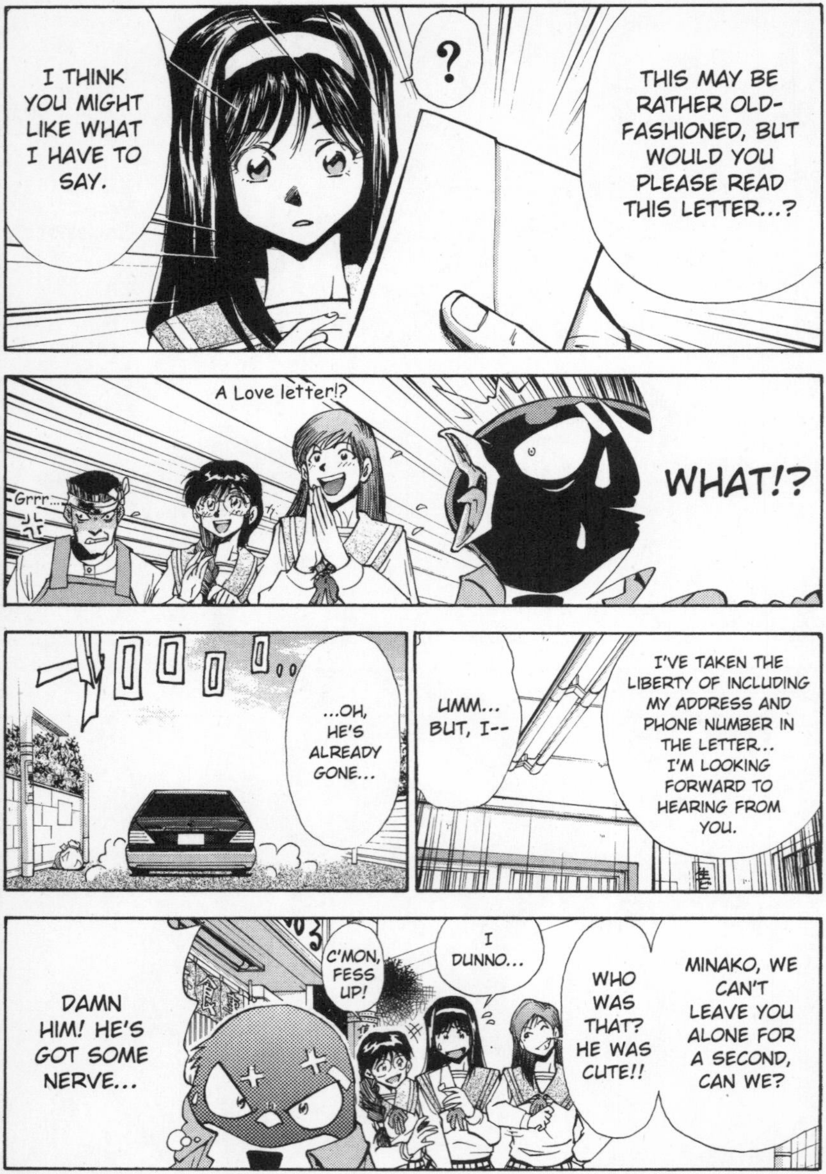
THIS MAY BE RATHER OLD-FASHIONED, BUT WOULD YOU PLEASE READ THIS LETTER...?
?
I THINK YOU MIGHT LIKE WHAT I HAVE TO SAY.
WHAT!?
A Love letter!?
Grrr...
I'VE TAKEN THE LIBERTY OF INCLUDING MY ADDRESS AND PHONE NUMBER IN THE LETTER.. I'M LOOKING FORWARD TO HEARING FROM YOU.
UMM... BUT, I--
...OH, HE'S ALREADY GONE...
MINAKO, WE CAN'T LEAVE YOU ALONE FOR A SECOND, CAN WE?
WHO WAS THAT? HE WAS CUTE!!
I DUNNO...
C'MON, FESS UP!
DAMN HIM! HE'S GOT SOME NERVE...

I GAVE HIM A TASTE OF MY "HIGH VOLTAGE FURY JAB FROM HELL" BUT I GUESS IT WASN'T ENOUGH...
HUH!?
LOOKS LIKE HE'S NOT GONNA GIVE UP ON MINAKO SO EASILY...
BUT HE DOESN'T HAVE A CHANCE! MINAKO'S NOT GONNA GIVE HIM THE TIME OF DAY...
THERE'S JUST NO WAY!
MINAKO AND I...
OUR LOVE IS AS STRONG AS A BATTLESHIP!!
MINAKO!
WHY DO YOU LOOK SO HAPPY!?
GASP!

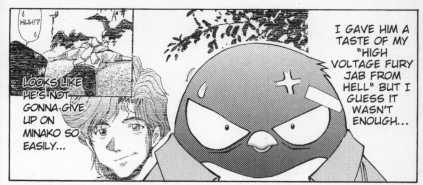

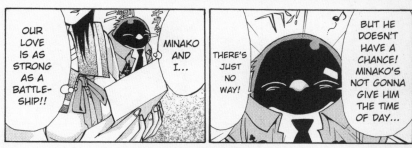

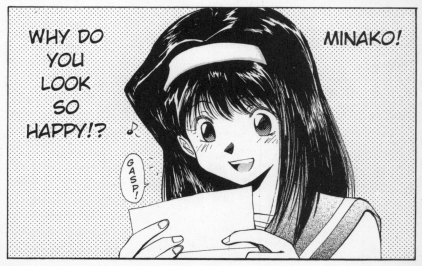

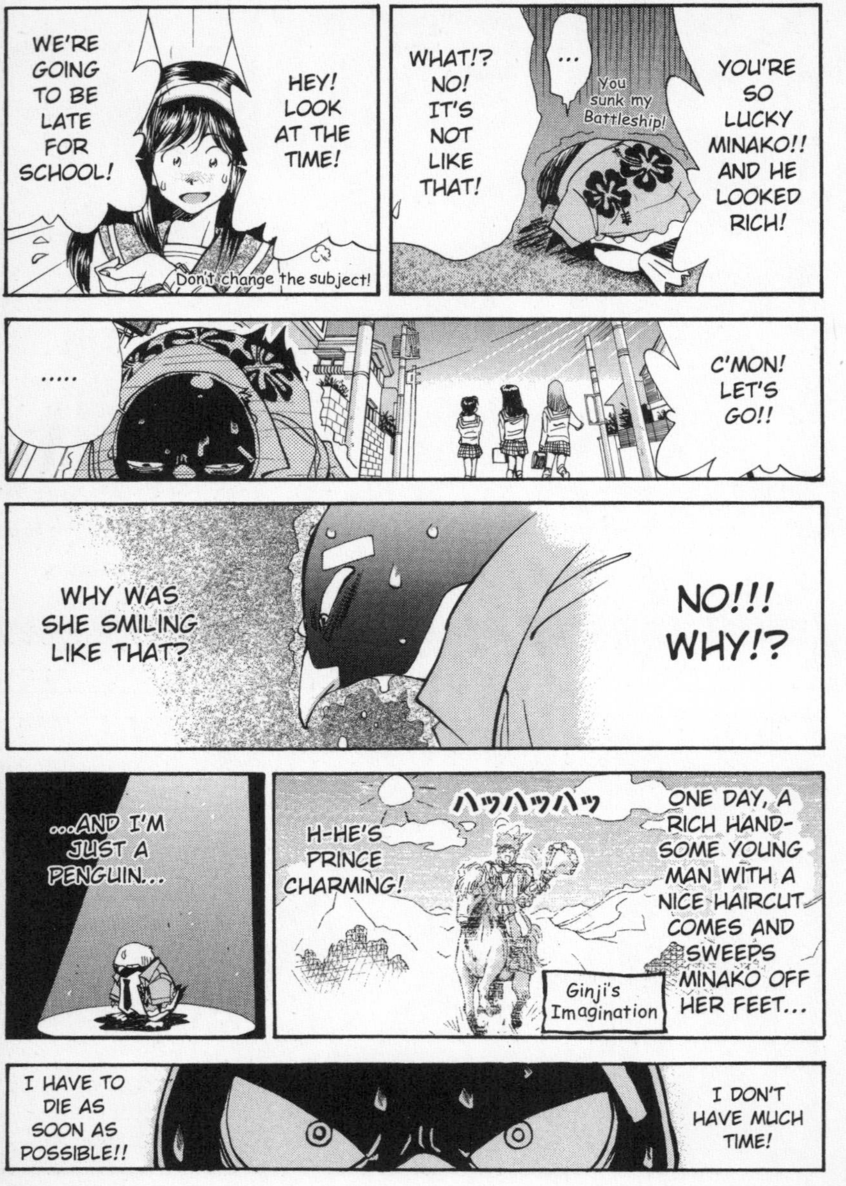

YOU'RE SO LUCKY MINAKO!! AND HE LOOKED RICH!
...
You sunk my Battleship!
WHAT!? NO! IT'S NOT LIKE THAT!
HEY! LOOK AT THE TIME!
WE'RE GOING TO BE LATE FOR SCHOOL!
Don't change the subject!
C'MON! LET'S GO!!
.....
NO!!! WHY!?
WHY WAS SHE SMILING LIKE THAT?
ONE DAY, A RICH HAND-SOME YOUNG MAN WITH A NICE HAIRCUT COMES AND SWEEPS MINAKO OFF HER FEET...
ハッハッハッ
H-HE'S PRINCE CHARMING!
Ginji's Imagination
...AND I'M JUST A PENGUIN...
I DON'T HAVE MUCH TIME!
I HAVE TO DIE AS SOON AS POSSIBLE!!

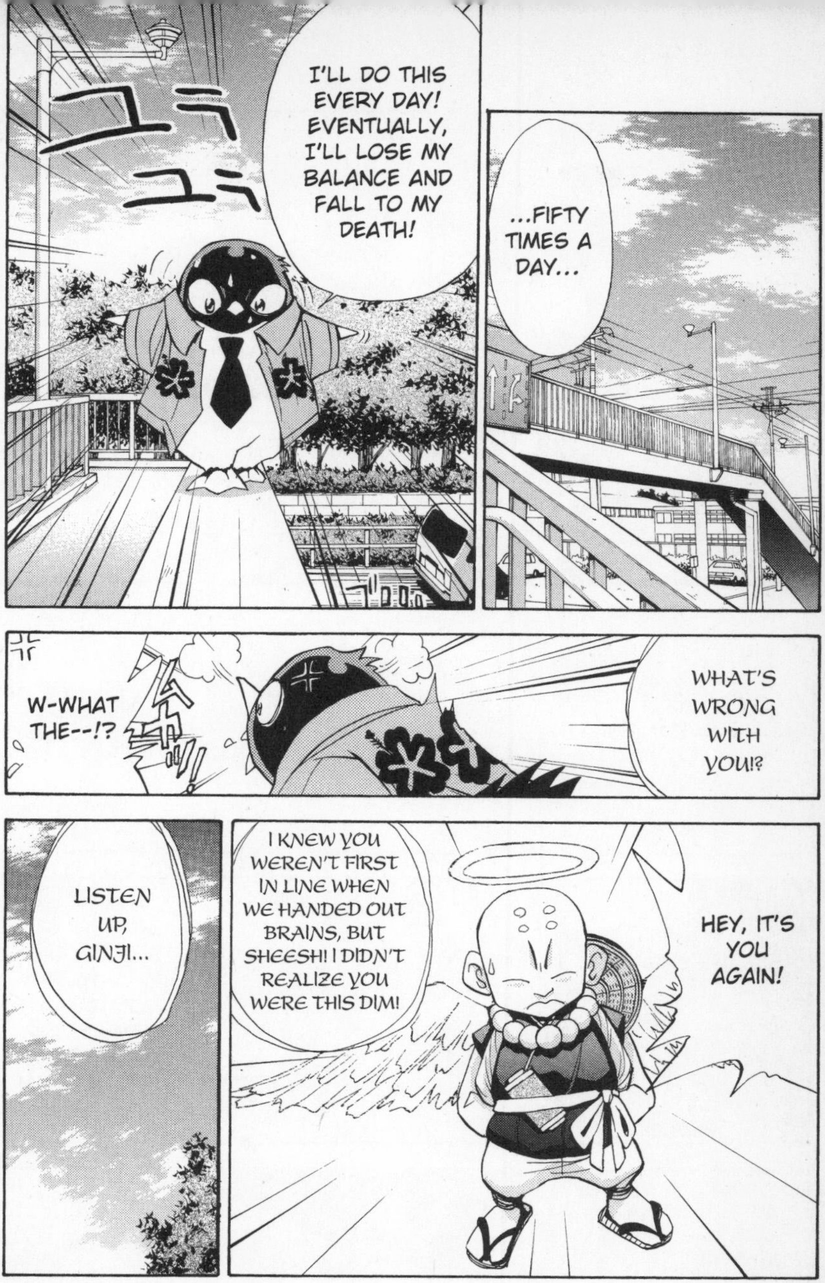
...FIFTY TIMES A DAY...
I'LL DO THIS EVERY DAY! EVENTUALLY, I'LL LOSE MY BALANCE AND FALL TO MY DEATH!
WHAT'S WRONG WITH YOU!?
W-WHAT THE--!?
HEY, IT'S YOU AGAIN!
I KNEW YOU WEREN'T FIRST IN LINE WHEN WE HANDED OUT BRAINS, BUT SHEESH! I DIDN'T REALIZE YOU WERE THIS DIM!
LISTEN UP, GINJI...

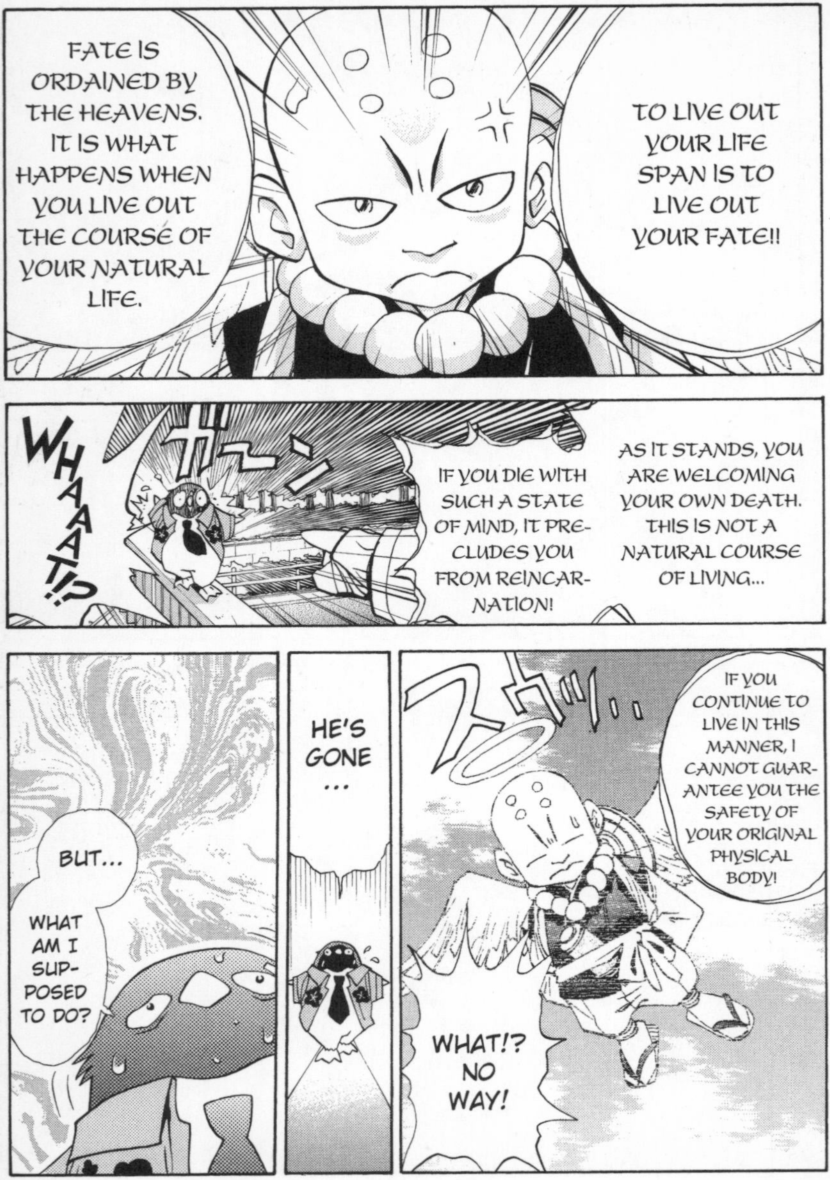

FATE IS ORDAINED BY THE HEAVENS. IT IS WHAT HAPPENS WHEN YOU LIVE OUT THE COURSE OF YOUR NATURAL LIFE.
TO LIVE OUT YOUR LIFE SPAN IS TO LIVE OUT YOUR FATE!!
AS IT STANDS, YOU ARE WELCOMING YOUR OWN DEATH. THIS IS NOT A NATURAL COURSE OF LIVING...
IF YOU DIE WITH SUCH A STATE OF MIND, IT PRE-CLUDES YOU FROM REINCAR-NATION!
WHAAAT!?
IF YOU CONTINUE TO LIVE IN THIS MANNER, I CANNOT GUAR-ANTEE YOU THE SAFETY OF YOUR ORIGINAL PHYSICAL BODY!
WHAT!? NO WAY!
HE'S GONE ...
BUT...
WHAT AM I SUP-POSED TO DO?

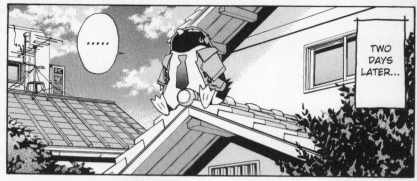

TWO DAYS LATER...
.....
WHAT SHOULD I DO...?
PHEW...
I can't even sleep...
MINAKO'S LATE... WHERE COULD SHE BE...?
くるっ
WHAT!?
Oh Nooo!
Thank you!

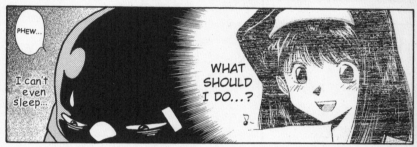

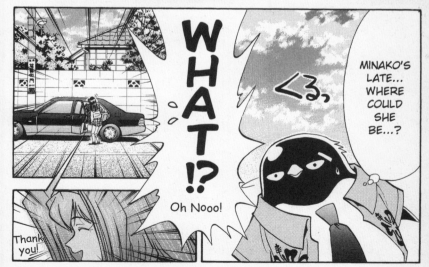

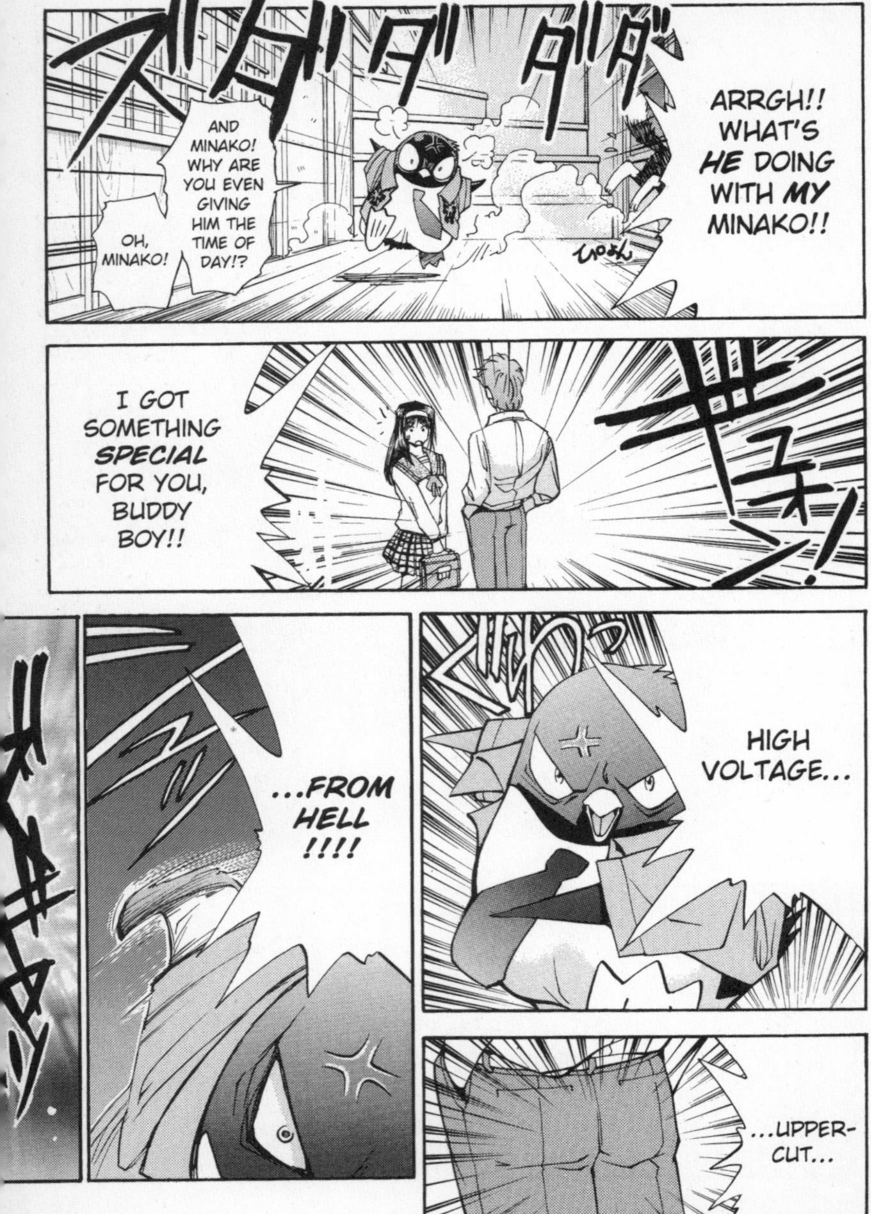
ARRGH!! WHAT'S HE DOING WITH MY MINAKO!!
AND MINAKO! WHY ARE YOU EVEN GIVING HIM THE TIME OF DAY!?
OH, MINAKO!
I GOT SOMETHING SPECIAL FOR YOU, BUDDY BOY!!
HIGH VOLTAGE...
...UPPER-CUT...
...FROM HELL !!!!

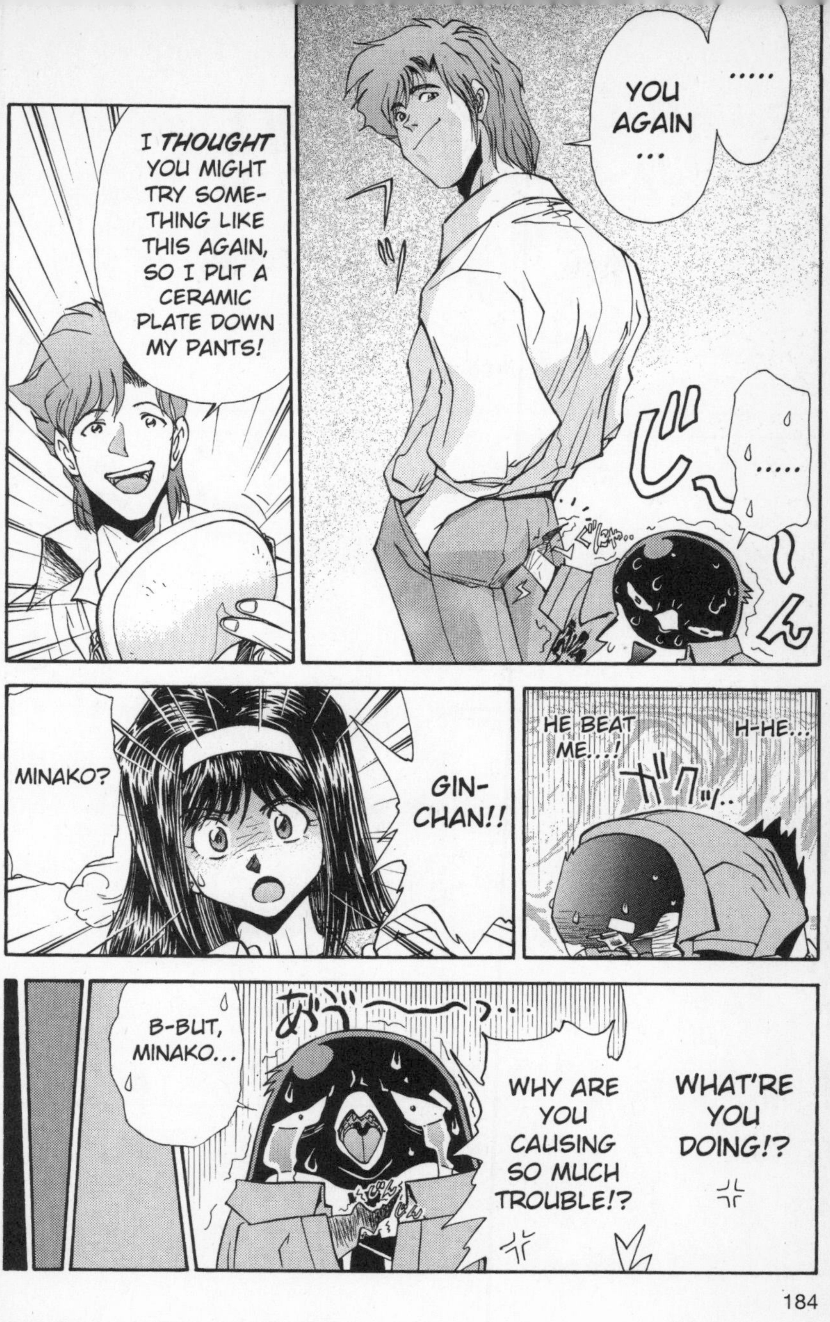
..... YOU AGAIN ...
.....
I *THOUGHT* YOU MIGHT TRY SOME-THING LIKE THIS AGAIN, SO I PUT A CERAMIC PLATE DOWN MY PANTS!
H-HE...
HE BEAT ME...!
GIN-CHAN!!
MINAKO?
WHAT'RE YOU DOING!?
WHY ARE YOU CAUSING SO MUCH TROUBLE!?
B-BUT, MINAKO...

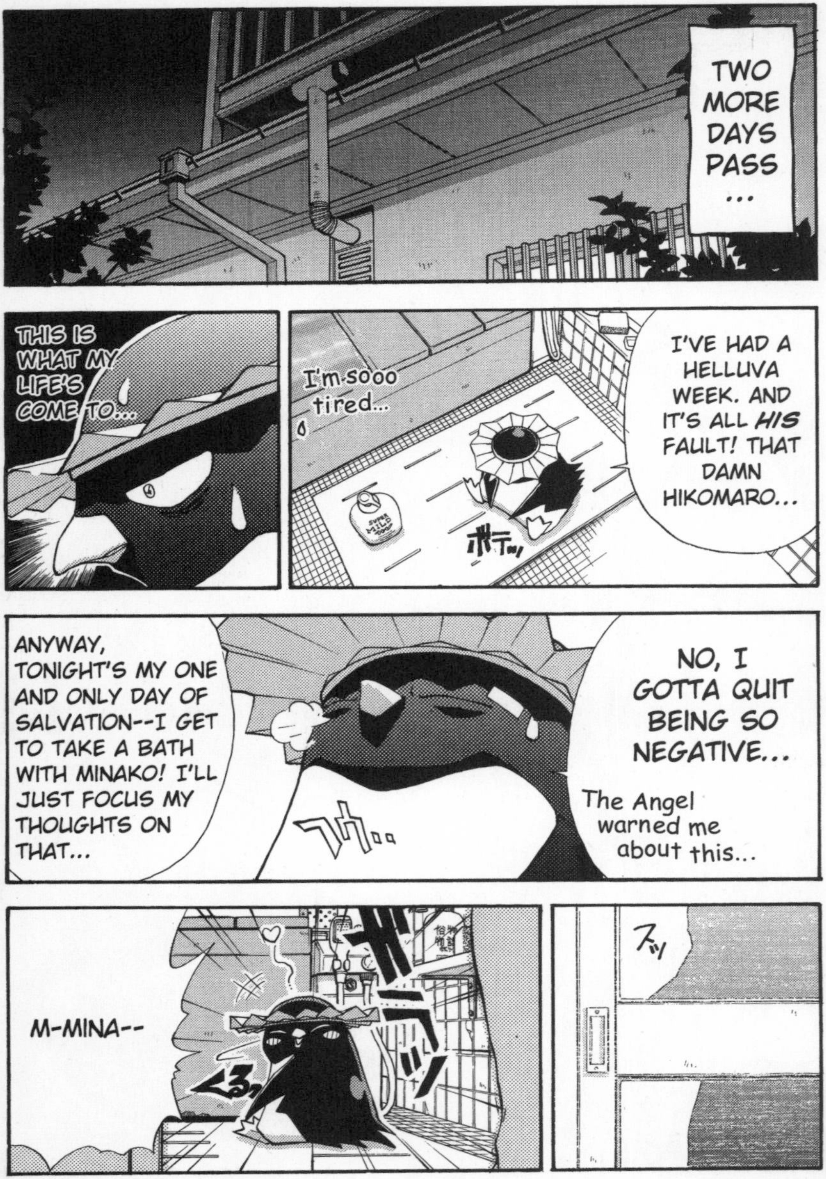
TWO MORE DAYS PASS ...
I'VE HAD A HELLUVA WEEK. AND IT'S ALL *HIS* FAULT! THAT DAMN HIKOMARO...
I'm sooo tired...
THIS IS WHAT MY LIFE'S COME TO...
NO, I GOTTA QUIT BEING SO NEGATIVE...
The Angel warned me about this...
ANYWAY, TONIGHT'S MY ONE AND ONLY DAY OF SALVATION--I GET TO TAKE A BATH WITH MINAKO! I'LL JUST FOCUS MY THOUGHTS ON THAT...
M-MINA--

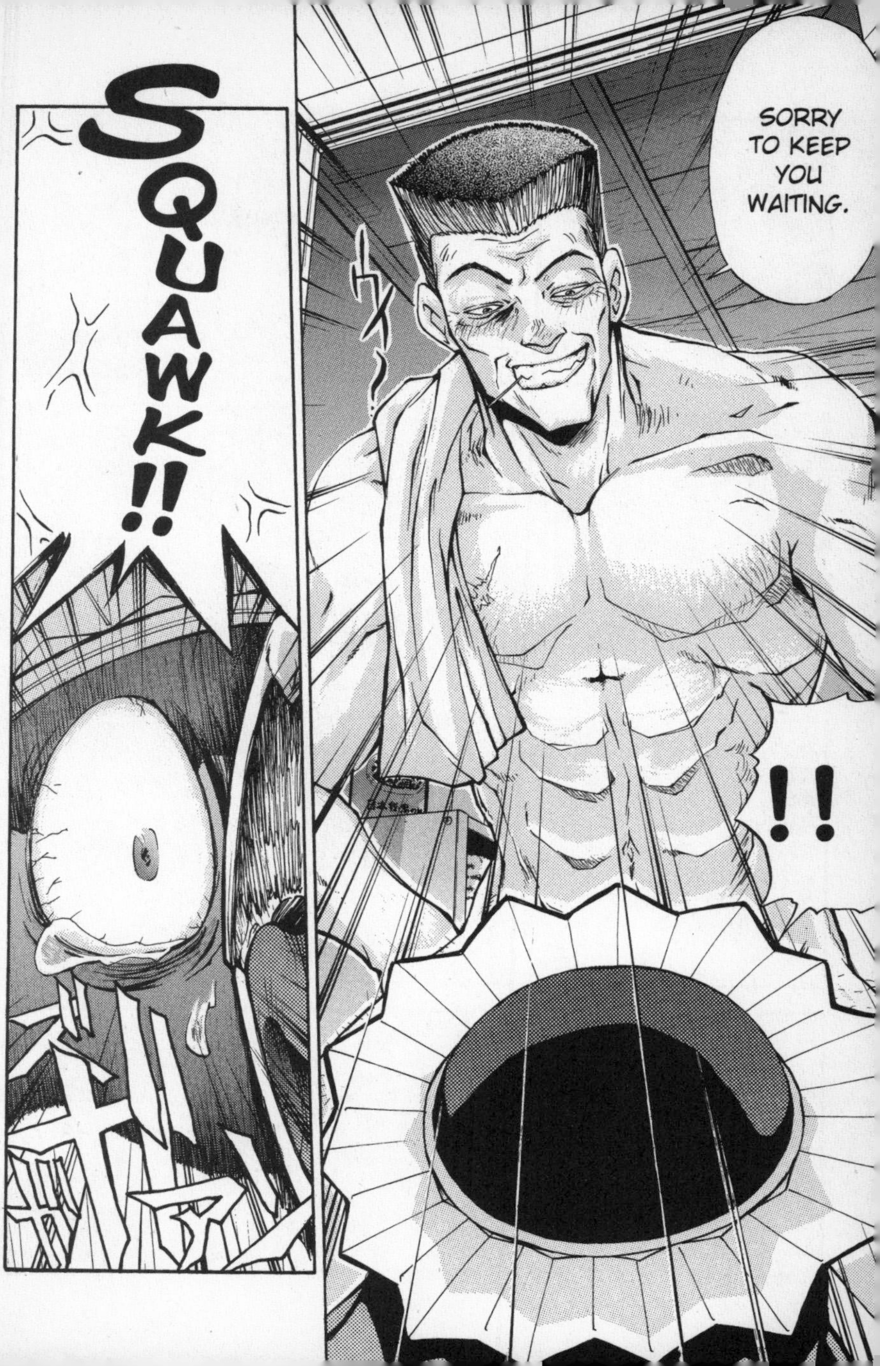
SORRY TO KEEP YOU WAITING.
!!
SQUAWK!!

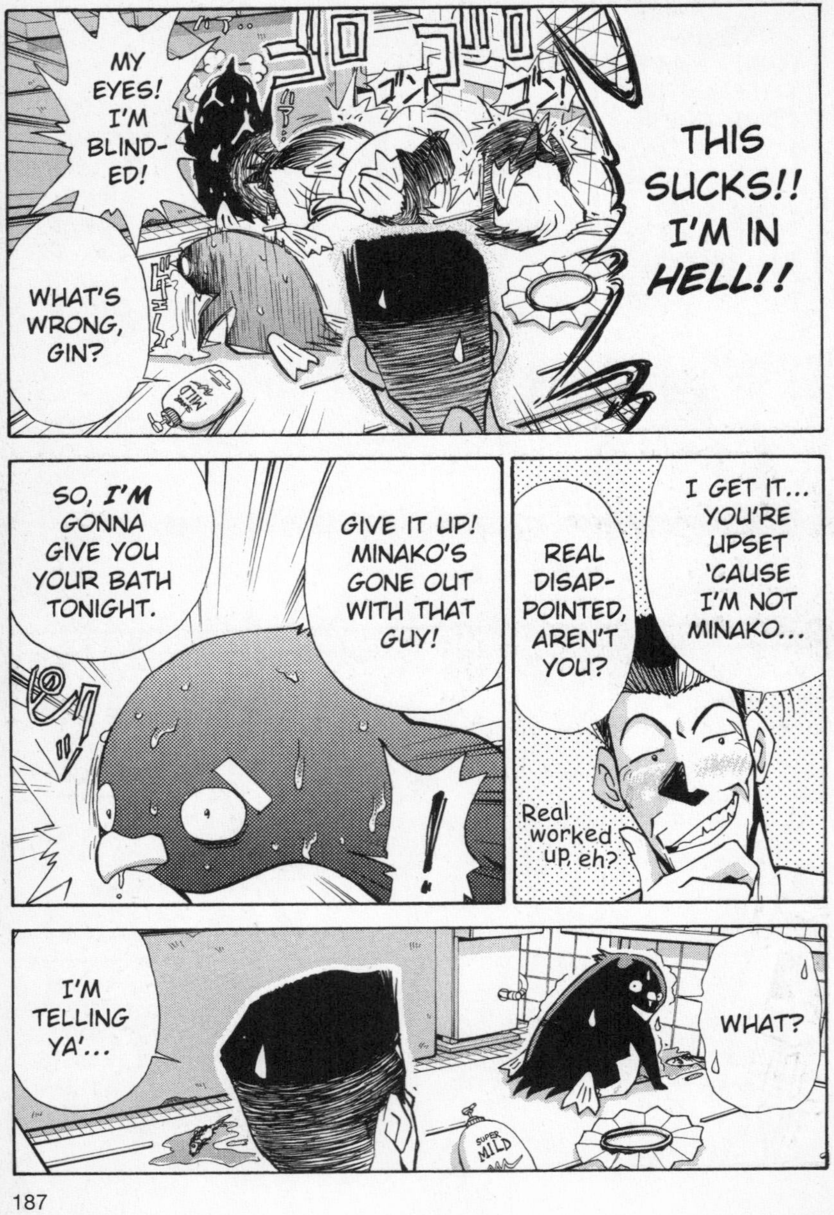
THIS SUCKS!! I'M IN *HELL!!*
MY EYES! I'M BLIND-ED!
WHAT'S WRONG, GIN?
I GET IT... YOU'RE UPSET 'CAUSE I'M NOT MINAKO...
REAL DISAP-POINTED, AREN'T YOU?
Real worked up, eh?
GIVE IT UP! MINAKO'S GONE OUT WITH THAT GUY!
SO, ***I'M*** GONNA GIVE YOU YOUR BATH TONIGHT.
!
WHAT?
I'M TELLING YA'...
SUPER MILD

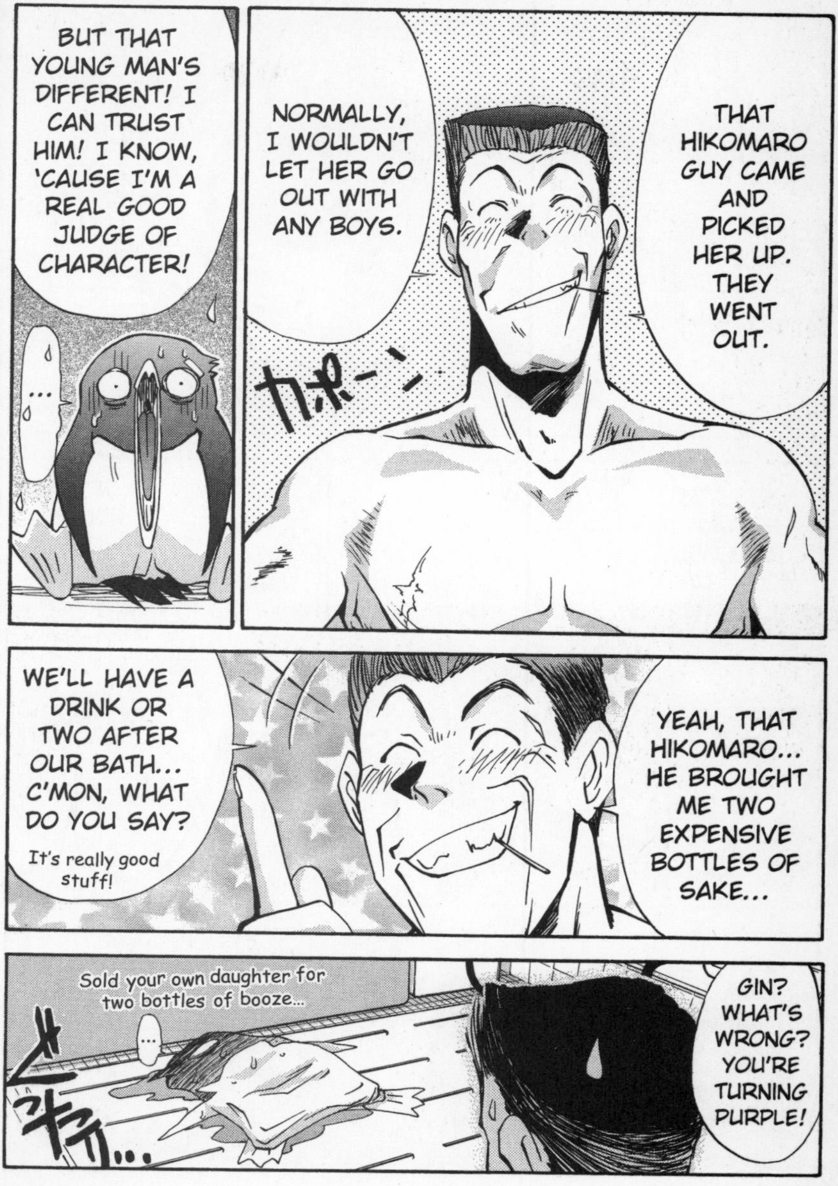
THAT HIKOMARO GUY CAME AND PICKED HER UP. THEY WENT OUT.
NORMALLY, I WOULDN'T LET HER GO OUT WITH ANY BOYS.
カポーン
BUT THAT YOUNG MAN'S DIFFERENT! I CAN TRUST HIM! I KNOW, 'CAUSE I'M A REAL GOOD JUDGE OF CHARACTER!
...
YEAH, THAT HIKOMARO... HE BROUGHT ME TWO EXPENSIVE BOTTLES OF SAKE...
WE'LL HAVE A DRINK OR TWO AFTER OUR BATH... C'MON, WHAT DO YOU SAY?
It's really good stuff!
GIN? WHAT'S WRONG? YOU'RE TURNING PURPLE!
Sold your own daughter for two bottles of booze...
...

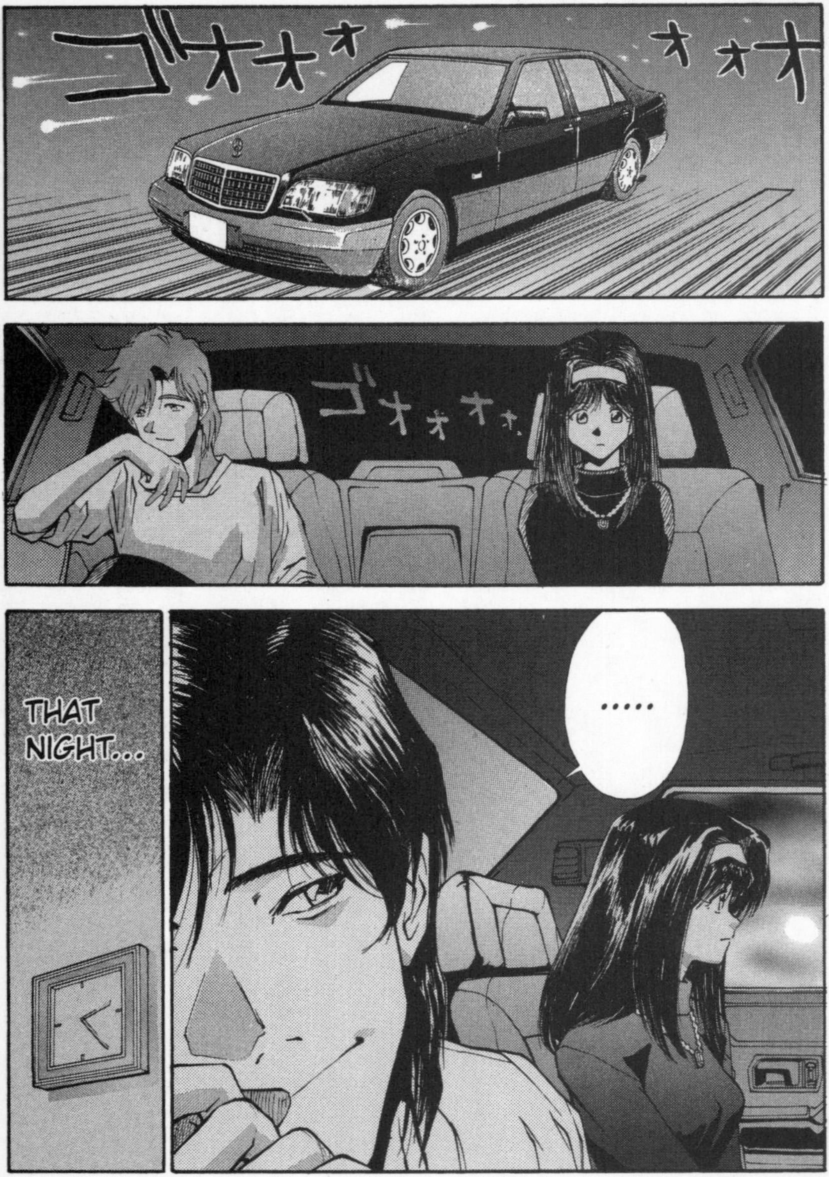
ゴオオオ
オオオ
ゴオォオォ
.....
THAT NIGHT...

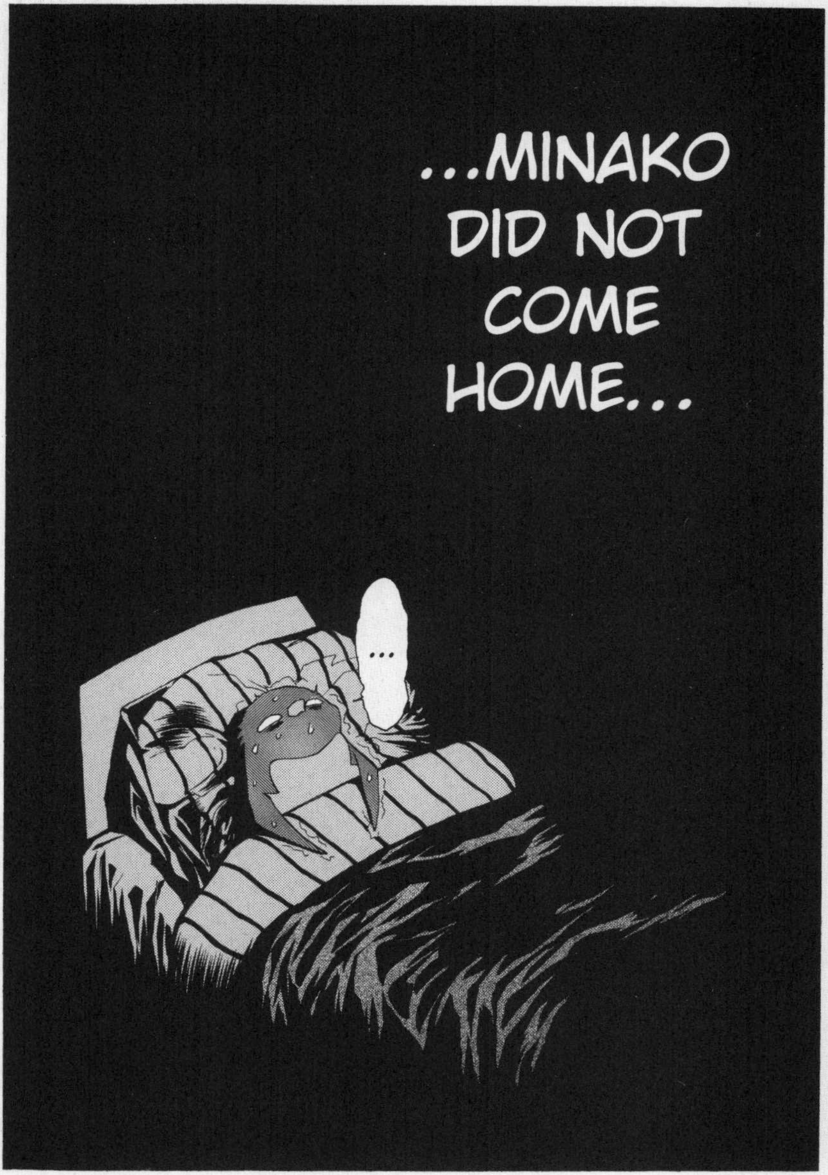
...MINAKO DID NOT COME HOME...
...

There's just got to be something to all these penguins in manga. In addition to *Tuxedo Gin*, there's also: Misato's pet penguin, Pen Pen, from *Neon Genesis Evangelion*; and there's a porn manga short story by Naoki Yamamoto called "Fancy." It's about a penguin poet and his human wife's affair with the postman. This story is included in Yamamoto's short story anthology, *Gakkō* ("School"). In addition, there's some *shōjo* manga such as *Penguin Brothers* by Shiina Ayumi and *Sora Tobu Penguin* ("Penguins that Fly the Skies") by Akisato Wakuni. These last two manga aren't specifically about penguins, but they still use the word "penguin" in the title. What is it about penguins? They're cute and they're certainly one of the easiest animals to anthropomorphize, but there's got to be something more...

More Manga!
More Manga!

If you like *Tuxedo Gin* here are some other manga you might be interested in:

© 1989 Naoki Yamamoto/Shogakukan

• Dance Till Tomorrow

Romantic comedy for mature readers. Naoki Yamamoto presents a mixed-up wishy-washy main character, crazy relationships, and titillating sex. What more could a young man who's about to inherit a million dollars want?

©1996 Masahito Soda/Shogakukan

• Firefighter!
Daigo of Company M

Story-driven manga about ordinary people doing extraordinary things. Meet Asahina Daigo—straight out of firefighting school, he's cocky and over-confident...until he goes out on his first call. He's got a lot to learn before he can call himself a true firefighter.

©1989 by Masakazu Katsura/Shueisha Inc.

• Video Girl Ai

A romantic love-comedy about a boy and a girl, and another girl who shows up to complicate things. The strange thing is that the second girl materialized from a video tape—and she says that her sole purpose is to improve the boy's lovelife!

Glossary of SOUND EFFECTS, SIGNS, and other Miscellaneous Notes

Each entry includes: the location, indicated by page number and panel number (so 3.1 means page 3, panel number 1); the phonetic romanization of the original Japanese; and our English "translation" – we offer as close an English equivalent as we can.

3.1	*VUOOON:* motorcycle engine
3.2	*VOOOO:* motorcycle engine
	PYON!: cat jumping
3.3	*DA!:* dash
3.4	*GUWA:* surprise
	GYAA!!: screaming
5.2	*GAAAN:* shocked
5.3	*GURA:* motorcycle shaking
5.4	*DOGASHA:* crash
6.1	*SHUUU:* steam escaping
6.2	*DOKI DOKI:* heart pounding
	CHIRIIN: cat's bell
6.3	*MUKKA!:* getting angry
	GABA: suddenly getting up
	HAOAA!: big gasp
	FUWA: floating
7.4	*JIIII:* cat staring
8.3	*HA:* sighing
9.1	*GYU:* tying firmly
10.1	1D Sasebo, Minako
	[name written on handkerchief]
10.4	*GE!:* exaggerated surprise
11.2	*DO DO DO:* Bike engine
11.4	*DOKO DOKO DOKO:* engine noise
	DO DO DO: engine noise
13.1	*OSHOKUJI DOKORO KAORU:* Restaurant Kaoru
13.2	*UTSURA UTSURA:* drowsy
13.3	*VUUU:* sleepy
13.5	*GARA:* opening sliding door
15.1	*KAAA:* blushing
	Ginji: Ha Ha ha ha…
	DOKI DOKI: heart pounding
15.2	*HYUUUUU:* wind of awkwardness
	TEKUTEKU TEKU TEKUTEKU: awkwardly walking
15.5	*KACHI KOCHI KACHI:* nervousness
16.3	*TEKUTEKUTEKUTEKUTEKUTEKU:* awkwardly walking
16.4	*TEKU TEKU TEKU TEKU TEKU TEKU:* awkwardly walking
16.5	*DO DO DO DO DO DO DO:* heart pumping
18.1	*HIKU:* nervous facial expression
	GOKURI: swallowing
18.3	*GATAN GOTON GATAN:* train passing by
	KURA: dizzy from nervousness
18.4	*SAAAAA:* panicking
19.1	*KAAAA:* getting embarrassed
20.1	*DOGO:* "kapow"
20.2	*KUAA:* shining display
21.2	*BOOOOO:* spaced out
21.4	*DO DO:* motorcycle engine
22.1	*VUOOOOON:* motorcycle engine
	DODOUU!!: motorcycle engine
	UOOON: motorcycle engine
23.2	*GU:* clenching fist
23.3	*GA:* clenching other fist
23.4	*GUBAA!:* letting go
24.1	*BIKU:* surprised
24.2	*BA:* grab
24.5	*OOOOO:* traffic
25.2	*KA:* bright light
25.3	*OOON:* motorcycle engine
26.2	*BA:* lifting bag
27.1	*BA:* balls fly out of bag

27.2 *GYOWAWAWA*: bike skidding
ZAAAA: screech
28.1 *DON*: crash
29.2 *GYA GYA GYA GYA*: screeching to a stop
30.2 *GABA*: suddenly getting up
31.1 *ZAZAN ZAZAN*: splash splash
31.4 *SU*: wing appearing
32.1 *GAAAAN*: extreme shock
32.2 *ZAZAZA*: splash splash
33.1 *BIKU*: spooked
33.2 *SAFUA*: holy light fx
BIBIKUN: even more spooked
34.6 *SURA*: unrolling scroll fx
37.4 *BO*: flame on
39.1 *IRIE EKI*: Irie Train Station
41.4 *CHIRIIN*: cat bell
42.1 *CHIRIIN*: cat bell
43.3 *CHIRIIN*: cat bell
45.2 *TRUSH*: [misspelling in the original art]
48.1 *BAKIIIIN!*: big cracking sound
48.3 *HYOKO HYOKO HYOKO*: waddle waddle
49.1 *ZUN*: fwump
51.1 *BISHI*: standing up straight
53.1 IRIE SUIZOKKAN PENGUIN HIROBA: Irie City Aquarium Penguins
53.2 *DOKI DOKI DOKI DOKI*: heart pumping
53.3 *HAA HAA HAA DOKI DOKI*: panting and heart pumping
54.1 *DOKI DOKI*: heart beat
54.2 *ZAZAZA*: water noise
PUKAH: floating
54.4 *KI*: sharp glare
DOOOON: melodramatic sudden appearance
54.5 *JIWA*: tears flowing
U: snif
55.1 IRIE SUIZOKKAN PENGUIN HIROBA: Irie City Aquarium Penguins
55.2 *OI OI OI OI*: hey hey hey!
55.4 *ZUKI*: knife in heart type of fx
56.1 *SAFAA*: holy light fx
ASERI: feeling anxious
56.2 *YOISHO YOISHO*: effort to move
56.4 *KOO*: cry of victory
57.1 *GOOOOO*: jet engine
57.3 *PERA*: flips memo book
57.4 In his notebook, Mike has written a barely legible "shio" meaning "salt."
58.1 *PETA PETA PETA*: webbed feet walking
58.2 *GAPO*: opens lid
58.3 *WANA WANA WANA*: Ginji trembling
58.4 *GU*: clenches fins
59.1 *ZAPAAAN*: wave hitting rocks.
59.2 *ZAZAAN*: waves
59.3 *DON*: push
59.4 *DOPAAN*: splash
59.5 *SHIIIIN*: dead silence
ZAPAAN: wave
BUKU BUKU: air bubbles
59.7 *GUWA GUWA*: penguins crying
60.2 *ZAZAAAN*: waves
UUUN... UUN...: groaning]
60.3 *ZURI ZURI ZURI*: body being pushed up against dock
ZAZAZAZAZA: waves
60.4 *GON*: head being banged on dock
ZAPAAAN: huge wave
61.1 *BIKU*: surprise
ZAZAZAZA: wave
UUUN: Ohhh...
61.2 *UUUN ITE ITE...*: ohhh...ouch ouch...
62.1 *SU*: suddenly wakes up
62.2 *MUKU*: getting up
62.3 *ZUKIIN*: pain in head
62.4 *CHIRIN*: cat bell ringing
63.1 *BARI BARI BARI*: scratching/chewing, being mauled
63.2 *GARA*: opens door
PIKU PIKU: trembling
65.1 DON – penguin hitting her
65.2 *MUGYUU*: Minako prying Ginji off
65.3 *HAA HAA HAA HAA ZE ZE*: panting wheezing
65.4 *ZUUUUN*: feeling depressed
66.1 *KAPOOON*: water drops echoing in bathroom
66.2 *CHAPOON*: splash
66.3 *GYU*: squeeze
66.4 *PUKAA*: floating
67.1 *NYU*: looking at Gin
DOKI: surprise
GATA: tub shakes
67.4 *ZUUUUUUN*: extreme depression
67.5 *UUUN*: thinking
UUU: crying
68.1 *HAAU!*: shock
DAKI: hug
68.3 *HA!*: gasp!
68.4 *UU!*: surprise
69.1 *ANCHOKU*: "Too Easy" - meaning Minako didn't put too much thought into the name.
SUTEEEN: slipping and falling from disappointment
69.2 *PURU PURU*: trembling
69.4 *DARA DARA*: crying eyes out
69.5 In Japan, people typically wash themselves before getting in the tub to relax and soak.
KYU: getting up
KURU: Ginji turning around
70.1 *SHUBI*: Ginji freaking out
71.1 *GAAAAA*: hair dryer
BOOOOO: spaced out
71.2 *CHIRIIN*: cat bell
71.3 *JIIIIII*: glare
71.5 *KURU*: turning around
71.6 *TOKO TOKO TOKO*: walking
72.1 OSHOKUJIDOKORO KAORU: Restaurant Kaoru

Glossary of SOUND EFFECTS, SIGNS, and other Miscellaneous Notes

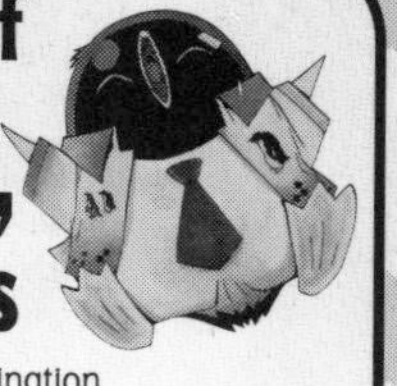

72.2 *MUNI*: pushed up against breasts
AAU: Uh… [happy/nervous]
72.3 *YORO*: wobble
KIIKO KIIKO: pedals squeaking
ZUSHI: a feeling of heaviness being conveyed
73.1 *IRIE EKI*: Irie Train Station
73.3 *BIKU*: surprised
74.3 *GUWAAAN GUWAAN GUWAAN*: panic anxiety
74.5 *KUWA*: glare
75.1 *BAKOOOON*: smack
75.2 *KUWAAAAA*: squawk
CHIKU x 7: punching with fin
Musashi: DAAA!? (Arrgh!)
75.3 *KUEEEEE*: squawk
BATA BATA BATA: flap
75.4 *HAA HAA HAA*: panting
76.1 *HAA HAA*: heavy breathing
DOOOON: Ginji in bag
76.2 *HAAA*: breathing hard
77.2 *PURU PURU*: trembling
78.3 *GANGARA GASSHAN*: loud commotion
78.4 *PURU PURU*: trembling
79.1 *UOOOOOM*: howling
GABA: getting up
79.3 *UUU*: crying
GON GON: clang clang
80.2 *TOBO TOBO* : walking away
80.4 *TORO TORO TORO*: engine running slow
80.5 *GAOON*: sudden acceleration
81.1 *VUOOON!*: engine
GA: grab
81.3 *GASU*: fwump
82.1 *GORON*: rolling over
83.4 *NYA*: smirk
GI: clenching teeth
88.1 *WANA WANA*: trembling in anger
88.2 *FU*: acting stiff
88.4 *BOOOO*: acting spaced out
89.1 *DOGA*: kaboot
89.3 *TOKO TOKO*: walking
89.4 *KURU*: turning around
GIRO: glare
89.5 *BACHICON*: kapow
90.1 *MUFUU*: anger
90.2 *VUON*: bike engine
90.3 *KYORO KYORO*: looking around
90.4 *SOOOOO*: being sneaky
91.1 *HYUUUU*: wind
95.3 *GUWA!*: determination
95.4 *YOKKORASE*: lifting
96.1 *BYUOOOON*: swinging
96.2 *GYUN*: swinging
96.3 *ZU*: sliding off
96.4 *DOKA*: fwump
97.1 *BACHIIN*: fwak
97.2 *BOOO*: regaining consciousness
97.3 *KUNE KUNE KUNE*: feeling woozy
97.4 *GABA*: dash
97.6 *GYUN*: crane swinging
98.1 *GO*: bonk
98.3 *KUAAAA!*: Squawk
GASHI GASHI GASHI: stomping
98.4 *SHUN*: swing
98.5 *GO*: bonk
ZUZUZU: skid
98.6 *DARARI DARARI*: drip
99.4 *GON*: bonk
99.5 *MERA MERA MERA MERA MERA*: flames
100.1 *DON*: kaboom
100.3 *GOOOO*: roar
100.4 *BA!*: dash
100.5 *GA*: headbutting Kurosaki
101.1 *BA*: getting up
101.2 *GASU!*: thwak
101.3 *DOSA*: fwump
102.1 *DAAA!*: dash
102.2 *UOOOOO!*: expending great effort
103.3 *UU*: thinking
103.4 *ZA*: stepping forward
103.5 *ZABO ZABO ZABO*: splash splash
104~105.1 *ZUBABABABABA*: splash splash
DOGO: bam
104~105.2 *GYUN*: fwoosh
106.1 *DOKA DOKA DOKA*: bonk bonk
106.4 *ZORO ZORO*: penguin crowd noise
108.2 *HAA HAA HAA*: panting
VUOOON!: engine noise [partially obscured]
GA: grab [partially obscured]
109.1 *ZA*: step
109.3 *BABABABABA*: penguins flying through air
109.4 *DOKA DOKA DOKA*: bwap bwap bwap
110.4 *ZA*: penguins advancing
110.5 *BUWAA*: overflowing penguins
110.6 *KEEE!!*: crying out in panic
KUWA!: squawk
UJA UJA: swarming

111.2 *UJA UJA UJA*: swarm
UZAZAZAZAZA: stampede
111.3 *WARA WARA*: waddling swarm
112.1 *ZA*: grab
112.2 *ZUZUZU*: leaning/sliding on wall
113.1 *GAROROROROROROROR*: van engine
113.2 *GAKU*: knees buckling
DADADA: sprinting
115.1 *BA*: jumping
115.2 *ZUZUZU*: leaning/sliding on wall
115.2 *ZABO*: splash
115.4 *GOBO*: glug
116.1 *ZUGOGOGOGOGOGOGO*: current in water
116.2 *KUWA*: squawk
117.1 *GABO*: glug
117.3 *BOOO*: losing consciousness
117.4 *GOBOBOBOBOBO*: glug glug
118.1 *TOSU*: gently hitting bottom
118.5 *YURA*: something emerging from water
119.1 *ZUBAAAN*: splash
119.2 *ZAPAAAN*: splash
119.3 *GOBOBOBO*: shooting through water
120.1 *GOOOOOO*: shooting through water
120.3 *GYUN*: dock approaching
120.4 *KUWA*: eye wide open
120.5 *ZUBAA!*: splash
121.3 *GUWA*: suddenly appearing
122.1 *DOKA*: bwam
123.1 *BASU*: hitting ground
GASHAAAN: glass breaking
124.1 *DOKU DOKU DOKU*: throbbing in pain
GUTTARI: limp body
124.2 *PIKU PIKU PIKU*: twitching
124.3 *DOGA*: car hitting wall
124.4 *YURA*: Minako falling
124.5 *GOOO*: wind noise
125.1 *PITA*: falling momentum suddenly stops
125.2 *PURU PURU*: twitching
125.2 *GOOO*: wind
125.4 *GARI GARI*: body skidding on ground
VUON: car driving off dock
GA: cement block being hit and chipping
126.2 *HAA HAA HAA*: panting
127.6 *MU... MUKU*: dread realization
128.3 *PURU PURU*: twitching from anger
128.4 *DOOOON*: dramatic expulsion of emotion
130.3 *PURU PURU*: twitching from anger
131.1 *YORO YORO*: wobbling over
131.4 *ZUI*: sudden stern look
134.3 *YUOOO*: cold lonely wind
134.4 *FUWOOON*: rising determination
ZUOOO: standing up tall
135.2 Ginji: *SA-SAMI NEMI...*
(It's freezing... I'm sleepy...)
GATA GATA GATA: shivering
135.3 *SA SA*: patting off snow
135.4 *KURA*: losing consciousness
GATA GATA GATA GATA: shivering
136.1 *GATA GATA GATA GATA*: shivering
136.2 *AU*: suffering
GATA GATA: shivering
137.1 *SU*: laying cloth on Ginji
137.4 *ZURA*: penguins gathering around
139.3 *SU*: a glimmer of consciousness
139.4 *GATA GATA GATA GATA*: shivering
140.3 *POTO*: wing listlessly falling to ground
142.1 *CHUN CHUN*: bird chirping
143.1 *HAA HAA*: breathing
143.2 *GORON*: something rolling off of Minako
143.3 *CHUN CHUN*: birds chirping
144.3 *PEEPOO PEEPOO PEEPOO*:
ambulance siren
CHICHICHI: chirping
146.1 *OSHOKUJIDOKORO KAORU*:
Restaurant Kaoru
146.2 *GARA*: sliding door
147.4 *MUSU*: dissatisfied expression
148.2 *DEPPURI*: sound of something chubby sitting
JIIIII: Shinnosuke staring
GOKURI: gulp...
148.3 GUWA: squawking
150.1 OSHOKUJIDOKORO KAORU:
Restaurant Kaoru
CHYUN CHYUN: chirping of birds
150.2 *PON*: toss
150.3 *PAKU*: snatching with mouth
150.4 *KA KA*: chomping
151.2 *HYOI*: lifting up shrimp
151.3 *ZUI*: getting in front of Ginji's face
MOGU MOGU MOGU: chewing
151.4 *PO*: blushing
MOGU: chewing
151.5 *AHAHAHAHAHAHA*: laughing
Daruma Doll: a bright red doll modeled after the Zen Master Boddhidharma. The doll is usually made with two blank eyes. When a new venture is started, one of the eyes is painted in. When the goal is met, the other eye is painted in.
152.3 *PAN*: snapping out wet clothing
152.4 *BOOO*: spacing out
152.5 *GATA*: something landing on wood floor
153.1 *GORO GORO GORO*: rolling around
153.2 *HAA HAA HAA*: panting
154.2 *DOKI DOKI*: heart beating
154.4 *KURU*: turn around
155.1 *BWASA BWASA*: flapping wings
155.2 *HA HA*: panting
GA GA: scratching at bags
155.3 *JIIIIII*: staring
156.1 *KAAA KAAA*: kaww kaww
156.3 *HA HA HA*: laughing
156.4 *UROCHYORO UROCHYORO*: pacing
SOWA SOWA: nervous
156.5 *KURU*: turning around
DOKI: scared
157.1 *WUI*: drunk
157.2 *PATA PATA*: waving wings

Glossary of SOUND EFFECTS, SIGNS, and other Miscellaneous Notes

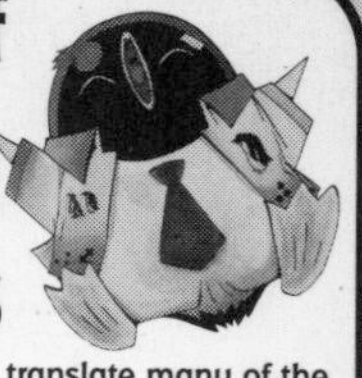

In order to leave the artwork as close to the original as possible, we didn't retouch and translate many of the sound effects and signs contained within this manga. However, we wouldn't want you to miss anything, so we've included a glossary of sound effects and other things not translated or retouched.

The Glossary begins on page 192.

157.3	*NOKOTTA NOKOTTA NOKOTTA*: a phrase that a referee calls out during a sumo match.
157.6	*HIKKU!*: hic!
	SHIMI JIMI: reminiscing
157.7	*ZUI*: offering up a glass
	PATA PATA: flapping wing
158.1	*DOKI*: heart leaps
	GATA: clatter
158.3	*GOGOGOGO*: rising anger
158.4	*GA GA GA*: punching fx
158.5	*KAPOON*: splash echo in bathroom
159.1	*GOSHI GOSHI*: scrubbing
159.2	*ZABAA*: pouring water
159.3	*MUKAKA*: rising anger
160.2	*HISHI*: hug
161.2	*SUU SUU*: breathing
161.3	*SUUU SUUU*: breathing
161.4	*BOOO*: spacing out
162.1	*PURU PURU*: shaking
162.2	*KUWAAAA*: squawk
	JITA BATA: squirming
162.3	*HAA HAA HAA*: heavy breathing
163.3	*SUU*: fading
164.1	*IRIE EKI*: Irie Station
164.2	*HYOKKO HYOKKO*: waddling around
164.3	*KURU*: turning around
166.1	*RAN RAN*: fierce stare
167.1	*GABA*: getting up
167.3	*BWASSA BASSA*: flapping wings
	VAAA: kaww
167.4	*YUSSA YUSSA*: shaking
167.5	*GUWA*: shouting in pain
	BASU: jab
	Ginji: URYAA! (Umf!)
168.2	*PURU PURU*: shaking
168.3	*KURU*: turning around
169.1	*KA*: determination
169.3	*KUWAAA*: squawk!
172.3	*RAN RAN*: fierce stare
	MUKA: getting irritated
173.1	*PARA*: flipping through pages
173.4	*BASA*: photos falling out
173.5	*NITA*: smirk
174.5	*PON*: toss
175.1	*PAKU*: snatching up in mouth
175.2	*PACHI PACHI PACHI*: clapping
	BISHI!: feet landing on table
175.4	*KIII*: screech
175.5	*GARA*: sliding door opening
176.2	*GUWA!*: grunting in pain
	BASU: jab
	GABA: Ginji getting up
177.4	*BURORORORO*: car zooming away
178.2	*FUFUN*: hmph!
178.3	*CHIRA*: peeking
	NIKKORI: smiling
179.4	*HA HA HA HA*: laughing
180.2	*YURA YURA*: balancing
180.3	*MUKA*: surprised
181.2	*GAAAAAN*: shock
181.3	*SUUU*: fading away
182.3	*KURU*: turning around
183.1	*ZUDADADADA*: sprinting
	PYON: hop
183.2	*GYUON*: quickly approaching
183.3	*GUWA*: squawk
183.5	*SHU*: winding up
183.6	*ZUGYA*: punch hitting target
184.1	*FU*: hmph
	JIIIIIN: trembling in pain
	GUNYA: bent flipper
184.3	*GAKU*: fwump
184.5	*VAVUUUUU*: crying
	JIN JIN: flipper throbbing in pain
185.2	*BOTE*: plopping down
185.4	*FUU*: sighing
185.5	*SU*: someone approaching
185.6	*GARA*: sliding door opening
	KURU: turning around
186.1	*UIII*: drunkenly walking in
186.2	*ZUGAGAAN*: experiencing extreme shock
187.1	*GORO GORO*: rolling around
	GON GON: bumping into things
	HAA HAA: panting
	GEEE: puking
187.3	*PIKU*: feeling startled
188.1	*KAPOON*: splashy echo in bathroom
188.4	*GUTTARI*: going completely limp
189.1	*GOOOOOO*: car engine noise
	GOOOOOO: car engine noise

How many anime and/or manga titles have you purchased in the last year? How many were VIZ titles? (please check one from each column)

ANIME
- ☐ None
- ☐ 1-4
- ☐ 5-10
- ☐ 11+

MANGA
- ☐ None
- ☐ 1-4
- ☐ 5-10
- ☐ 11+

VIZ
- ☐ None
- ☐ 1-4
- ☐ 5-10
- ☐ 11+

I find the pricing of VIZ products to be: (please check one)
- ☐ Cheap
- ☐ Reasonable
- ☐ Expensive

What genre of manga and anime would you like to see from VIZ? (please check two)
- ☐ Adventure
- ☐ Comic Strip
- ☐ Detective
- ☐ Fighting
- ☐ Horror
- ☐ Romance
- ☐ Sci-Fi/Fantasy
- ☐ Sports

What do you think of VIZ's new look?
- ☐ Love It
- ☐ It's OK
- ☐ Hate It
- ☐ Didn't Notice
- ☐ No Opinion

THANK YOU! Please send the completed form to:

NJW Research
42 Catharine St.
Poughkeepsie, NY 1...

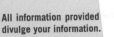

All information provided ~~~~~~~~~~~~~~~~~~~ omise not to sell or otherwise divulge your information.